THE ORGANIZATIONAL FRONTIERS SERIES

The Organizational Frontiers Series is sponsored by the Society for Industrial and Organizational Psychology (SIOP). Launched in 1983 to make scientific contributions to the field, the series has attempted to publish books that are on the cutting edge of theory, research, and theory-driven practice in industrial/organizational psychology and related organizational science disciplines.

Our overall objective is to inform and to stimulate research for SIOP members (students, practitioners, and researchers) and people in related disciplines, including the other subdisciplines of psychology, organizational behavior, human resource management, and labor and industrial relations. The volumes in the Organizational Frontiers Series have the following goals:

1. Focus on research and theory in organizational science, and the implications for practice
2. Inform readers of significant advances in theory and research in psychology and related disciplines that are relevant to our research and practice
3. Challenge the research and practice community to develop and adapt new ideas and to conduct research on these developments
4. Promote the use of scientific knowledge in the solution of public policy issues and increased organizational effectiveness

The volumes originated in the hope that they would facilitate continuous learning and a continuing research curiosity about organizational phenomena on the part of both scientists and practitioners.

Previous Frontiers Series volumes, all published by Jossey-Bass, include:

Emotions in the Workplace
Robert G. Lord, Richard J. Klimoski, Ruth Kanfer, Editors

Measuring and Analyzing Behavior in Organizations
Fritz Drasgow, Neal Schmitt, Editors

The Nature of Organizational Leadership
Stephen J. Zaccaro, Richard J. Klimoski, Editors

Compensation in Organizations
Sara L. Rynes, Barry Gerhart, Editors

Multilevel Theory, Research, and Methods in Organizations
Katherine J. Klein, Steve W. J. Kozlowski, Editors

The Changing Nature of Performance
Daniel R. Ilgen, Elaine D. Pulakos, Editors

New Perspectives on International Industrial/Organizational Psychology
P. Christopher Earley and Miriam Erez, Editors

Individual Differences and Behavior in Organizations
Kevin R. Murphy, Editor

The Changing Nature of Work
Ann Howard, Editor

Team Effectiveness and Decision Making in Organizations
Richard A. Guzzo, Eduardo Salas, and Associates

Personnel Selection in Organizations
Neal Schmitt, Walter C. Borman, and Associates

Work, Families, and Organizations
Sheldon Zedeck, Editor

Organizational Climate and Culture
Benjamin Schneider, Editor

Training and Development in Organizations
Irwin L. Goldstein and Associates

Productivity in Organizations
John P. Campbell, Richard J. Campbell, and Associates

Career Development in Organizations
Douglas T. Hall and Associates

Work Careers

A Developmental Perspective

Daniel C. Feldman
Editor

Foreword by Neal Schmitt

JOSSEY-BASS
A Wiley Imprint
www.josseybass.com

Published by Jossey-Bass
A Wiley Imprint
989 Market Street, San Francisco, CA 94103-1741   www.josseybass.com

Jossey-Bass books and products are available through most bookstores. To contact Jossey-
Bass directly, call our Customer Care Department within the U.S. at 800-956-7739, outside
the U.S. at 317-572-3993 or fax 317-572-4002.

Jossey-Bass also publishes its books in a variety of electronic formats. Some content that
appears in print may not be available in electronic books.

Library of Congress Cataloging-in-Publication Data

Work careers : a developmental perspective / [edited by] Daniel C. Feldman.
p. cm.—(The organizational frontiers series)
Includes bibliographical references and index.
ISBN 0-7879-5916-2
1. Career development.   2. Vocational guidance.   I. Feldman, Daniel C.
II. Series.
HF5381 .W67   2002
331.7'02—dc21
2002008557

FIRST EDITION
HB Printing   10 9 8 7 6 5 4 3 2 1

The Jossey-Bass
Business & Management Series

The Organizational Frontiers Series

SERIES EDITOR

Neal Schmitt
Michigan State University

111002

Contents

Foreword   xi
Neal Schmitt

Preface   xv

The Contributors   xix

Part One: Foundations of Career Development

1   **Stability in the Midst of Change: A Developmental Perspective on the Study of Careers**   3
Daniel C. Feldman

2   **More Than the Big Five: Personality and Careers**   27
Jill C. Bradley, Arthur P. Brief, Jennifer M. George

3   **Skill Acquisition and Person-Environment Fit**   63
Cheri Ostroff, Yuhyung Shin, Barbara Feinberg

Part Two: Career Development Across the Life Span

4   **When You Come to a Fork in the Road, Take It: Career Indecision and Vocational Choices of Teenagers and Young Adults**   93
Daniel C. Feldman

5   **The School-to-Work Transition**   126
Elizabeth Wolfe Morrison

6   **The Establishment Years: A Dependence Perspective**   159
Terri A. Scandura

7   **Career Development in Midcareer**   186
     Harvey L. Sterns, Linda M. Subich

8   **Career Issues Facing Older Workers**   214
     Terry A. Beehr, Nathan A. Bowling

Part Three: The Changing Context of Career Development

9   **Public Policy and the Changing Legal Context
     of Career Development**   245
     Jon M. Werner

10   **The Changing Organizational Context of Careers**   274
     Carrie R. Leana

11   **International Careers as Repositories of Knowledge:
     A New Look at Expatriation**   294
     Gregory K. Stephens, Allan Bird, Mark E. Mendenhall

Part Four: Directions for Industrial/Organizational Practice and Research

12   **Organizational Assistance in Career Development**   323
     Manuel London

13   **Advancing Research on Work Careers:
     A Developmental Perspective on Theory
     Building and Empirical Research**   346
     Daniel C. Feldman

     Name Index   373

     Subject Index   385

Foreword

This is the seventeenth book in a series published by Jossey-Bass and initiated by the Society for Industrial and Organizational Psychology in 1983. Originally published as the Frontiers Series, the SIOP Executive Committee voted in 2000 to change the name of the series to Organizational Frontiers Series in an attempt to enhance the identity and visibility of the series. The purpose of the publication of series volumes in a general sense was to promote the scientific status of the field. Ray Katzell first edited the series. He was followed by Irwin Goldstein and Sheldon Zedeck.

The topics of the volumes and the volume editors are chosen by the editorial board. The series editor and the editorial board then work with the volume editor in planning the volume and, occasionally, in suggesting and selecting chapter authors and content. During the writing of the volume, the series editor often works with the editor and the publisher to bring the manuscript to completion.

The success of the series is evident in the high number of sales (now over forty thousand). Volumes have also received excellent reviews, and individual chapters as well as volumes are cited frequently. A recent symposium at the SIOP annual meeting examined the impact of the series on research and theory in industrial and organizational psychology. Although such influence is difficult to track and volumes varied in intent and perceived centrality to the discipline, the conclusion of most participants was that the volumes have exerted a significant impact on research and theory in the field and are regarded as being representative of the best the field has to offer.

The first volume was *Career Development in Organizations*, edited by Tim Hall (1986), which has been the most successful volume in terms of sales to date. *Work Careers: A Developmental Perspective* reflects new thinking and research on careers since that time. We hope this volume will redirect and reenergize researchers in this important area of our discipline and stimulate new ways to develop career program by practitioners.

This book, edited by Daniel Feldman, represents a significant and successful effort to compile in one volume various psychological theories and research about how careers develop at different times or stages in one's work life. The chapter authors include individuals who have done research and theoretical work on the nature of careers and career decisions, as well as those who have investigated the applied and theoretical implications of individual changes in a work setting. Bringing the best of psychological science to bear on work-related problems and to the attention of organizational researchers has been the major goal of the Organizational Frontiers series, and I believe this volume will have a major impact on those concerned with the manner in which work careers develop.

The developmental perspective adapted here seeks to consider how early childhood and adolescent experiences shape work values and preferences for work activities, how those experiences influence the development of skill sets and career identities, how personal life issues interact with work demands to affect important career decisions, and how careers change as a function of various environmental demands.

The book is organized in four parts. Part One describes the basic elements of a developmental perspective on careers (personality, vocational interests, and skills) and reviews the literature on career and life-stage models. Part Two examines career development issues at different phases of the life cycle: childhood and adolescence, school-to-work transitions, early adult, midcareer, and late-career issues. Part Three addresses issues related to the context in which careers develop, with specific attention to legal, organizational, and cross-cultural effects. Part Four seeks to identify theoretical and research issues that are common across the developmental spectrum, areas in which additional scientific work is needed, and methods concerns that must be resolved or addressed in future work. It also addresses some innovative approaches to career development in organizations today.

The target audience for this book includes faculty and graduate students in industrial, organizational, social, developmental, and counseling psychology; faculty and graduate students in organizational behavior and human resource management in business schools; faculty and graduate students in vocational and educational psychology in education schools; and researchers and practitioners in organizational settings who want to gain knowledge on the most up-to-date data and theory regarding career issues.

I believe that this book will make recent literature on careers and behavior accessible to professionals who do not often read the basic literature in this area. It should also facilitate an interchange among those who have directed their attention to different developmental time frames. By doing so, it advances the primary goal of the Organizational Frontiers series. I also believe that this book will stimulate and promote more intelligent reading of the basic research literature on careers and foster a greater understanding of developmental issues in the workplace, as well as promote investigation of a wide array of interesting and important questions. Finally, I think it will be of interest to all of us as individuals as we make our career decisions.

The chapter authors deserve our gratitude for pursuing the goal of clearly communicating the nature, application, and implications of career theory and research described in this book. Production of a book such as this involves the hard work and cooperative effort of many individuals. The chapter authors, the editor, and the editorial board all played important roles in this endeavor. Because all royalties from the series volumes are used to help support SIOP financially, none of the authors received any remuneration. They deserve our appreciation for engaging in a difficult task for the sole purpose of furthering our understanding of organizational science. We also express our sincere gratitude to Cedric Crocker, Julianna Gustafson, and the entire staff at Jossey-Bass. Over many years and several volumes, they have provided support during the planning, development, and production of the series.

JULY 2002

Neal Schmitt
MICHIGAN STATE UNIVERSITY
SERIES EDITOR, 1998–2003

Preface

This book is about careers: the sequences of occupations and jobs we hold over a forty- or fifty-year period of work. Most of us will spend eight or ten hours a day—over ten thousand days of our lives—at work and much of our time not at work thinking about it, worrying about it, reveling in it, or recouping from it. How successful we are in our careers and how positively we feel about them has a tremendous impact on the quality of our lives (Feldman, 1988).

Work Careers: A Developmental Perspective takes a chronological approach to the study of careers. First, we examine the basic building blocks of careers: personality traits, vocational interests, skills, and abilities. Then we examine how individuals choose careers, make the transition from school to work, expand their career interests and work skills in early career, shift career paths and readjust to new life demands in midcareer, and ultimately withdraw from the workforce, fully or partially, in retirement. Finally, we explore how the altered landscape of careers—the major changes in the nature of organizations, public policy, global business, and our ideas about what constitutes a successful career—influences how individuals manage their own career development.

The chapter authors, individually and collectively, have balanced a wide variety of perspectives in examining career development. They examine how earlier career decisions open up, as well as constrain, subsequent career paths that employees and managers can take. Although the primary focus of the book is on work careers, the authors also address the interplay of family issues and career issues, illustrating how major changes in one arena create forces for change in the other. Similarly, the chapter authors balance treatment of what Hall (1976) calls objective and subjective careers. At one level, we are concerned about the observable choices individuals make about their careers: what fields they pursue, what jobs they accept, and what career changes they make. At the same time, however, we also need to be concerned with how individuals perceive their careers and feel about their current job situations. For some, making vice president is a level of achievement far beyond their wildest career aspirations; for others, "only" making vice president is a deep failure. To understand career development, then, we need to understand not only the observable choices individuals make about their careers but also why they make them and how they experience their jobs.

Perhaps most critical, the chapter authors approach career development from the perspective of both the individual and the organization. For organizations where we work, the management of careers is equally important. How organizations approach career development influences whether the best job candidates are retained, how effectively employees are utilized on their jobs, and how much loyalty and commitment individuals have to their employers (Arthur, Hall, & Lawrence, 1989).

Over the past fifty years, careers scholars have taken widely divergent approaches to the interaction of individuals' developmental needs and organizations' demands of employees. In 1957, William Whyte argued in *The Organization Man* that organizations were domineering in their approach to career development and demanded overconformity to their every whim. In the 1960s and 1970s, Chris Argyris argued that the needs of individuals and organizations could be genuinely and fully integrated. If organizations provided jobs that were challenging and allowed employees to participate in decisions at work, the needs of the employees and the demands of organizations could be brought into congruence (Argyris, 1964). Recently, career scholars have focused more on the limited relationships between individuals and organizations; this research suggests that individuals' and organizations' "psychological contracts" are only partial and temporary in nature and are more easily abrogated by either party (Turnley & Feldman, 1999). No matter which theoretical perspective ultimately prevails, though, we need to discover how the friction and misutilization that occur in career development in organizations can be minimized with better planning on both sides.

We hope that this book not only provides a useful source of information about what we know about career development, but also energizes and guides further theoretical work and innovative management practice in the area. The chapter authors have drawn extensively from a broad array of literatures on career development, so we hope that academics and practitioners from organizational behavior, human resource management, industrial and organizational psychology, vocational and counseling psychology, educational administration, and nonprofit administration will find the chapters directly relevant to their needs.

I especially want to express my appreciation to Neal Schmitt, Rick Klimoski, the Society for Industrial and Organizational Psychology Board of Directors, and the staff at Jossey-Bass for their unflagging encouragement and support of this project. Most of all, I want to thank the chapter authors for their tremendous contributions, not only to this book but to our understanding of career development more broadly. *Work Careers: A Developmental Perspective* reflects both the diversity of interests of careers scholars as well as our shared commitment to advancing theory and improving practice in managing careers.

COLUMBIA, SOUTH CAROLINA   Daniel C. Feldman
JULY 2002

References

Argyris, C. (1964). *Integrating the individual and the organization.* New York: Wiley.

Arthur, M., Hall, D. T., & Lawrence, B. S. (1989). *Handbook of career theory.* Cambridge: Cambridge University Press.

Feldman, D. C. (1988). *Managing careers in organizations.* Glenview, IL: Scott Foresman.

Hall, D. T. (1976). *Careers in organizations.* Pacific Palisades, CA: Goodyear Publishing.

Turnley, W. H., & Feldman, D. C. (1999). The impact of psychological contract violations on exit, voice, loyalty, and neglect behaviors. *Human Relations, 52,* 895–922.

Whyte, W. H., Jr. (1957). *The organization man.* Garden City, NY: Anchor Books.

The Contributors

Daniel C. Feldman is the James Bradley Distinguished Foundation Fellow at the University of South Carolina (USC) Moore School of Business. He received his Ph.D. in organizational behavior from Yale. Before joining the faculty at USC, he served on the faculties of Yale College, the University of Minnesota Industrial Relations Center, Northwestern's Kellogg Graduate School of Management, the University of Florida, and as a Visiting Sloan Scholar at Massachusetts Institute of Technology. He is the editor-in-chief of the *Journal of Management,* the associate editor of *Human Resource Management,* and the consulting editor for the *Journal of Organizational Behavior,* and he has served as chair of the Careers Division of the Academy of Management. He has published widely on such career issues as socialization, career indecision, expatriation, job loss, underemployment, part-time work, and early retirement.

Terry A. Beehr is professor of psychology and director of the Ph.D. program in industrial/organizational psychology at Central Michigan University. He received his Ph.D. in psychology from the University of Michigan. Beehr has also served as a research investigator at the Survey Research Center of the Institute for Social Research and an assistant professor of psychology at Illinois State University. He is the coauthor of *Human Stress and Cognition in Organizations* (1985) and the author of *Psychological Stress in the Workplace* (1995) and *Basic Organizational Psychology* (1996). His main research interests are job stress, retirement, and careers.

Allan Bird is the Eiichi Shibusawa-Seigo Professor of Japanese Studies at the University of Missouri at St. Louis. His research interests focus on the cross-cultural aspects of career development.

Nathan A. Bowling is a doctoral student in industrial/organizational psychology at Central Michigan University. His research interests include job satisfaction, occupational stress, the role of physical attractiveness in the workplace, and aging.

Jill C. Bradley is a doctoral student in industrial/organizational psychology at Tulane University. Her research interests include career choice, race discrimination, sex discrimination, group processes, and health and safety training.

Arthur P. Brief is the Lawrence Martin Chair of Business at Tulane's A. B. Freeman School of Business and the director of its William B. and Evelyn Burkenroad Institute for the Study of Ethics and Leadership in Management. He received his Ph.D. from the University of Wisconsin at Madison. He is a recipient of the Academic Leadership Award from the Aspen Institute's Initiative for Social Innovation through Business and the World Resources Institute for integrating social and environmental concerns into business education. His most recent book is *Attitudes In and Around Organizations* (1998).

Barbara Feinberg is a doctoral candidate in the social/organizational psychology program at Teachers College, Columbia University. Her research interests include leadership, multisource feedback, person-environment fit, and group dynamics.

Jennifer M. George is the Mary Gibbs Jones Professor of Management in the Jesse H. Jones Graduate School of Management at Rice University and holds a joint appointment in psychology. She received her Ph.D. in management and organizational behavior from New York University. Her research interests include affect, mood, and emotion in the workplace; personality, prosocial behavior, and customer service; and stress and well-being. A prolific author, she has served as associate editor of *Journal of Applied Psychology*, consulting editor for the *Journal of Organizational Behavior*, and is on the editorial board of the Society for Industrial and Organizational Psychology's Organizational Frontiers Series.

Carrie R. Leana is professor of business administration and public and international affairs at the University of Pittsburgh. She received her Ph.D. from the University of Houston and has previously served on the faculty of the University of Florida and as a Fulbright scholar in Italy. She has published widely and is coeditor (with Denise Rousseau) of *Relational Wealth: The Advantages of Stability in a Changing Economy* (2000) and coauthor (with Daniel Feldman) of *Coping with Job Loss: How Individuals, Organizations, and Communities Respond to Layoffs* (1992). She has served on the editorial boards of *Academy of Management Review* and the *Journal of Organizational Behavior.*

Manuel London is professor and director of the Center for Human Resource Management in the Harriman School for Management at the State University of New York at Stony Brook. He is also associate provost for enrollment at Stony Brook. He received his Ph.D. in industrial/organizational psychology from Ohio State University. He has served as a professor at the University of Illinois and as a human resource manager at AT&T. He has authored numerous books and articles on upward feedback, 360-degree feedback, management development, and career motivation. He is a consultant to major organizations in the areas of career development and continuous learning.

Mark E. Mendenhall holds the J. Burton Frierson Chair of Excellence in Business Leadership in the College of Business Administration at the University of Tennessee at Chattanooga. He received his Ph.D. from Brigham Young University. He has authored numerous research articles on international human resource management issues, and his most recent book is *Developing Global Business Leaders: Policies, Processes, and Innovations,* coauthored with Torsten Kuhlmann and Gunter Stahl (2001).

Elizabeth Wolfe Morrison is professor of management and organizational behavior, the Peter Drucker Faculty Fellow, and the chair of the Department of Management at New York University Stern School of Business. She received her Ph.D. in organization behavior from Northwestern University. In 1999, she received the Cummings

Scholar Award from the Organizational Behavior Division of the Academy of Management. Her research focuses on ways in which newcomers are proactive at work, different forms of employee initiative, and systematic barriers to employee voice within organizations.

Cheri Ostroff is associate professor of psychology and education at Teachers College, Columbia University. She received her Ph.D. in industrial/organizational psychology from Michigan State University. She received the Ernest J. McCormick Award for Early Career Contributions from the Society for Industrial and Organizational Psychology and the Distinguished Scientific Award for Early Career Contributions in Applied Research from the American Psychological Association. Her research interests include person-environment fit and socialization. She serves on the editorial boards of the *Journal of Applied Psychology, Personnel Psychology,* and *Human Resource Management.*

Terri A. Scandura is professor of management and psychology at the University of Miami. She received her Ph.D. in organizational behavior from the University of Cincinnati. Her research interests include mentorship, leadership, and careers, and her articles have been published in numerous major journals. She has been a visiting scholar in Japan, the United Kingdom, Australia, Hong Kong, and China and is the president-elect of the Southern Management Association.

Yuhyung Shin is a doctoral candidate in the social/organizational psychology program at Teachers College, Columbia University. Her research interests include person-environment fit, organizational culture, and human resource issues in virtual organizations.

Gregory K. Stephens is chair of the Department of Management at the M. J. Neeley School of Business at Texas Christian University. He earned his Ph.D. from the University of California at Irvine. His current research addresses Mexican-U.S. cross-cultural management challenges and dispute resolution through mediation. Bilingual in English and Spanish, he is a Texas court qualified mediator and serves on the board of directors of Settlement Solutions.

Harvey L. Sterns is professor of psychology and director of the Institute for Life-Span Development and Gerontology at the University of Akron. He is also a research professor of gerontology and codirector of the Western Reserve Geriatric Education Center at the Northeastern Ohio Universities College of Medicine. He received his Ph.D. from West Virginia University. He has published extensively in the areas of work and retirement and career development in middle age. He is president-elect of Division 20, Adult Development and Aging, of the American Psychological Association.

Linda M. Subich is chair of the Department of Psychology at the University of Akron and teaches in its collaborative program in counseling psychology. Her professional interests focus on vocational psychology theory and research, particularly on issues relevant to women and minorities. In 2000, she won the Holland Award for outstanding achievement in career or personality research from Division 17 (Counseling Psychology) of the American Psychological Association and is a fellow of that division. She has served as associate editor of the *Journal of Vocational Behavior* and the *Career Development Quarterly*.

Jon M. Werner is associate professor of management at the University of Wisconsin at Whitewater. He received his Ph.D. in organizational behavior from Michigan State University. His research has covered such topics as organizational citizenship behavior, legal issues in human resource management, use of the Family and Medical Leave Act, team effectiveness, and trust. He is the coauthor with Randy DeSimone and David Harris of *Human Resource Development* (2002) and serves on the editorial board of the *Journal of Management*.

PART 1

Foundations of Career Development

Stability in the Midst of Change

A Developmental Perspective on the Study of Careers

Daniel C. Feldman

For the past twenty years, the changing organizational context of careers has received an enormous amount of attention. The widespread use of computers, the emergence of the Internet, and improvements in telecommunications technology have allowed workers unparalleled flexibility in where and when they work (Arthur & Rousseau, 1996). Periodic recessions, rapidly escalating fringe benefits costs, and high litigation costs associated with terminations have all contributed to organizations' willingness to experiment with contingent forms of employment relations—outsourcing, part-time and temporary employment, subcontracting, and limited partnerships. At the same time, increases in the number of dual-career couples and single-parent households, greater numbers of college students and retirees who want to work part time, and higher wages for contingent employment have generated greater enthusiasm about nontraditional career paths on the part of individuals, too (Feldman, 1995, 1996).

Not surprisingly, a growing number of researchers have been examining how the nature of organizational career management practices, individual career planning strategies, and the shape of traditional career paths have changed in the face of increasing environmental complexity (Brousseau, Driver, Eneroth, & Larsson,

1996; London & Stumpf, 1986). Moreover, flexibility has replaced stability as the major lodestone and benchmark of practitioners involved in career planning and career counseling (Bolles, 2001; Sharf, 1997).

Beneath the surface of these dramatic environmental changes, though, the amount of stability within individuals' careers over time is impressive, too. Early life experiences are critical in shaping individuals' lifelong career interests, and those interests are remarkably stable over the life span (Betz & Voyten, 1997; Caspi, Bem, & Elder, 1989; Holland, 1985). Moreover, individuals' first few jobs are pivotal in shaping their work skills and personal values for years to come (Greenberger & Steinberg, 1986; Habermas & Bluck, 2000). Furthermore, as Schein (1990) suggests, work skills and personal values developed in one's twenties play a major role in anchoring subsequent career decisions. Schein's notion of a career anchor does not imply that individuals stop growing professionally as their careers unfold. Rather, career anchors imply movement—but movement that is not random and that occurs within some circumscribed area (Feldman & Bolino, 1997).

If insufficient attention was paid to organizational contexts in the era of "dustbowl empiricism" and its emphasis on individual differences, perhaps today the pendulum has swung too much in the opposite direction. With our current focus on boundaryless careers and boundaryless organizations, perhaps we have failed to consider the role of individual differences and intraindividual development in sufficient detail. Indeed, if careers and organizations are truly boundaryless, it suggests that career trajectories are largely determined by within-individual factors or, at the minimum, interactions of individual and contextual factors.

Individuals' careers are not simply blowing in the wind in a world without boundaries. Although they may seem random on the surface, individuals' career decisions are often shaped by, and are best understood in terms of, personal history. In the midst of all the environmental change occurring today, there is still a great deal of intraindividual stability of career interests, skills, and values over time. Certainly, strong situations can overpower individual differences; most people, no matter how psychologically hardy, feel depressed when they are suddenly fired (Leana & Feldman, 1992). Nonetheless, many of the visible changes we see in how individuals pursue careers are recurring variations on underlying themes rather than totally new compositions.

This volume of the Organizational Frontier Series takes a developmental perspective to the study of work careers. It investigates the influence of intraindividual factors and person-environment interactions in shaping the trajectories of careers. The book examines not only the forces for change in career development but also the forces for stability; it explores not only changes in environments but also changes within people over time. This chapter identifies the major recurring themes in the literature on managing careers, examines the specific tenets of a developmental approach to the study of work careers, and provides a brief overview of this book in terms of overall structure and the contents of specific chapters.

Recurring Themes in the Research on Careers

In the social sciences, research relevant to understanding careers has been ongoing since the nineteenth century. In the latter half of the 1800s, organization theorists like Max Weber (1947) started to examine the structure of promotional ladders in bureaucracies, and early psychologists like Binet, Galton, and Ebbinghaus looked at individual differences in order to predict school and work achievement (Dunnette, 1976). However, the study of careers as a separate and distinct field of research in the organizational sciences can be traced more directly to the 1950s. At that time, educational and counseling psychologists (Holland, 1959; Roe, 1956; Super, 1957) brought widespread attention to the existence of vocational preferences, the benefits of matching individual preferences to occupational demands, and the utility of interest testing and career counseling to achieve person-organization fit. Since that time, both scholarly interest in the study of careers and popular interest in managing careers have grown dramatically.

By the term *careers,* I mean the sequence of a person's work experiences from initial formation of career interests through retirement (Feldman, 1988). Over the past fifty years, careers have been studied extensively in a wide range of disciplines, including sociology, various subfields of psychology (industrial, organizational, developmental, and social), gender and race studies, vocational and educational counseling, organization theory, and organizational behavior (Arthur, Hall, & Lawrence, 1989). Despite the diversity of perspectives taken to the study of careers, though, several important themes consistently recur throughout the literature. The following basic assumptions and tenets inform much of the ongoing research on career development today:

1. *Careers can be defined both objectively and subjectively.* On one end of the continuum, industrial psychologists are mainly concerned with objective, measurable, and observable differences across individuals that predict career achievement. For example, in his review chapter on individuals' aptitudes, abilities, and skills, Dunnette (1976) writes, "We are concerned here with those human attributes which may affect work performance *directly* without the mediating influence of perceptions based on social interaction" (p. 474). On the other end of the spectrum, some social psychologists define careers as "individually *mediated responses* to outside role messages" (Schneider & Hall, 1972, p. 448). For these researchers, subjective perceptions play as important a role, if not a more important role, in understanding career dynamics.

By and large, though, most careers researchers (including those cited above) agree that we need to explore both the verifiable, measurable attributes of individuals, jobs, and organizations and perceptual data. For example, to understand the role of gender in career development, we need to examine objective group differences between males and females, as well as gender differences in perceptions of career opportunities, career barriers, and career strategies.

2. *Work skills, career interests, and personal values all play major roles in career development.* Although researchers vary in terms of which components of careers they study in depth, most scholars agree that the three basic building blocks of careers are work skills, career interests, and personal values. Entry into occupations, successful job performance, stability within organizations, and advancement opportunities all rely to some extent on individuals' work abilities, their interests in various occupational opportunities, and the consistency of their values with the values of their employers (Crites, 1969; Dunnette, 1976; Holland, 1985).

Moreover, these three components of careers may not be fully substitutable for each other. That is, having very strong interests in a career may not compensate for a palpable lack of skill. The world is full of teenagers who dream of being professional basketball players but who lack the physical attributes and raw talent to achieve their goal. Drive and determination will not make them grow six inches taller; practice alone will not improve eye-hand-foot coordination.

3. *Careers need to be examined as they unfold over time.* Most researchers agree that career dynamics can be understood only by examining individuals' experiences over time. Individuals' decisions about their career moves are not solely determined by current skills and interests. Instead, career plans are shaped by previous work histories and long-term plans for the future as well. Careers, then, are neither static nor self-encapsulating in nature. Rather, they evolve over time and are influenced by both past events and future aspirations.

In addition, the evolution of careers over time needs to be considered in terms of both career stages and life stages. Whether researchers agree on the existence of separate and distinct stages of careers, most researchers agree that organizations' work demands on individuals change over time (Dalton, Thompson, & Price, 1977), particularly as employees gain more years of experience or advance higher in the organization. Furthermore, what individuals find fulfilling changes dramatically over the forty or more years they work (Gould, 1978; Valliant, 1977). Where twenty-five year olds may be excited by being connected to work "24/7," sixty-five year olds may prefer having to work only twenty-four hours per week, seven months a year. Consequently, important career decisions have to be understood in the context of changes in both career stages and life stages.

4. *Individuals' career development is inextricably linked with their family networks.* Certainly, the major focus of careers researchers has been individuals' experiences at work. Nonetheless, researchers are becoming increasingly aware of the impact of individuals' experiences outside the workplace on their career trajectories. Individuals' commitments to their spouses, children, and parents shape how many hours they work each week, what they value in their

jobs, what types of work situations they find most attractive, the level of their career aspirations, and even when they decide to retire (Hochschild, 1997; Kim & Feldman, 2000).

Moreover, spouses' career opportunities, the availability of child care support, joint custody agreements, elder care responsibilities, and demands of second families all have an impact on an individual's range of vocational choices and rate of job mobility. While ignoring stability in the midst of change is an error to be avoided, investigating individual career decisions without considering family context is misguided as well. Individuals' career decisions do not take place in a vacuum.

5. *A broad array of macro level forces (such as the health of the economy or the demographic diversity of the workforce) influence individuals' career opportunities and organizations' career development needs.* It is not only the immediate nuclear family that affects how individuals' careers unfold; broad forces in society at large have an impact on career behaviors, too. For example, overall economic conditions and the health of particular sectors of the economy influence individuals' career opportunities and career constraints. A robust economy allows parents to spend more on their children's higher education, and hence improve their children's access to higher-paying professions (Harper, 1998; Shea, 2000). Similarly, the decline or emergence of various industries influences the availability of different employment opportunities. The deindustrialization of the steel industry and the rise of e-commerce have certainly influenced young adults' preferences for careers in those sectors.

In fact, the effects of macro-level forces may be even greater on individuals' perceptions of the desirability of various career options. The value that society at large places on various vocations influences the perceptions of occupations' desirability and individuals' rates of occupational entry. In a recent article, Goldin (2001) notes that enrollment in electrical engineering programs declined by 19 percent between 1983 and 1997. During the same period, the number of students earning degrees in parks, recreation, and leisure increased 400 percent. Each year now, thousands more students are earning degrees in parks, recreation, and leisure than in engineering. Surely these shifts are not caused by rapid changes in the underlying distribution of individuals' skills and abilities, but rather by broader shifts in social values and individuals' perceptions of occupations.

Changes in the demographic composition of the workforce can also influence how both individuals and organizations perceive career development. For example, tremendous growth in the numbers of females in medicine, law, and business increases the likelihood that young women will view these professions as desirable and realistic career paths. At the same time, increases in the number of women employees force organizations to design career development programs that are more flexible and less lockstep in nature (Feldman, 1995; Hochschild, 1997).

6. *Organizations no longer have unilateral control over how individuals' careers unfold.* Individuals have increasingly become free agents in the labor market and have thus begun to reshape the nature of organizations themselves. There has been a major shift in the power balance between individuals and organizations. Fifty years ago, the majority of employees in the United States worked in large, bureaucratic organizations that had enormous control over individuals' wages, working conditions, and advancement opportunities (Whyte, 1957). In contrast, increasingly large numbers of employees today are self-employed, work on a contingent basis for a variety of firms, change organizations frequently during their careers, and actively negotiate their own salaries, working hours, and place of employment (Arthur & Rousseau, 1996).

As a result of these changes, the influence of organizations on individuals' careers is no longer unidirectional. As more and more individuals become free agents, how organizations manage careers has changed, too. Increasingly, organizations are using nonmonetary incentives such as offering overseas travel opportunities to get employees to join their firms, providing continuous learning and training opportunities to retain their employees, and helping employees balance work and family demands through flextime and telecommuting. Thus, changes in organizations do more than affect how individuals' careers unfold; changes in individuals' expectations have an impact on how organizations design and implement career development programs as well.

7. *Career paths are not necessarily linear; many career transitions are horizontal, radial, downward, or seemingly discontinuous in nature.* As

Dalton (1989) points out, the original use of the term *career* had connotations of speed, direction, and advancement; it originally derives from the French word *carrière,* meaning a race course, and for many years, careers were studied in terms of these three criteria. Indeed, the term *fast-track career* still refers to careers where individuals are "groomed" early for a rapid "run" up the hierarchy (Thompson, Kirkham, & Dixon, 1985).

However, as the result of major changes in family dynamics and social forces, careers can no longer be studied only as continuous, linear, and upward movement. For a variety of reasons, individuals are taking lateral transfers, changing occupations and starting all over again at the bottom, or taking time out from the workforce altogether (Arthur et al., 1996; Brousseau et al., 1996). Thus, the key challenge facing career researchers is not just predicting how far and how fast individual employees will rise. Career researchers now have to be as attentive to workforce withdrawal as to entry and as attentive to decisions declining advancement as to accepting promotions.

The Developmental Approach to Careers

Researchers who take a developmental perspective to the study of careers share many, if not all, of the tenets described above. Within the careers literature, though, researchers with a developmental perspective are guided by an additional set of assumptions as well. These principles revolve around when and how career identity is formed, the impact of early career experiences on subsequent career trajectories, the role of aging as a force in career development, and the importance of person-occupation fit. Next, we consider these assumptions in some more detail.

1. *Career identity begins to form in early childhood and is strongly influenced by early experiences within the family.* One of the distinctive features of a developmental perspective on work careers is its attention to career attitudes and behaviors prior to individuals' entering the workforce itself. It assumes that important elements of career identity—skills, career interests, and work values—begin forming at an early age and are shaped by experiences with members of the nuclear and extended family (Schmitt, Sacco, Ramey, Ramey, & Chan,1999).

Research suggests that from as young as five years of age, children understand such concepts as unemployment and welfare; beginning around age ten, children become knowledgeable about such concepts as pay, working conditions, and work conflict (Barling, 1990; Pautler & Lewko, 1985; Piotrowski & Stark, 1987). By the time they hit adolescence, many teenagers are role modeling their parents' level of work involvement and work habits (Brooks, 2001; Shellenbarger, 1998). In addition, parents' wealth influences how much education students can obtain and their levels of career aspiration (Shea, 2000), and how much time parents spend in career planning with their children influences their levels of career salience and career motivation (Kush & Cochran, 1993). Perhaps most critical, parents reinforce (or extinguish) children's participation in activities that heighten various career-related skills and interests (O'Brien & Fassinger, 1993; Salamone & Slaney, 1978). If parents encourage children to work on math puzzles and participate in science fairs, those students are more likely to develop both greater skill and greater interest in scientific activities. Conversely, if parents discourage children from participating in art classes, theater groups, and band, children will be less likely to develop either talent or interest in creative pursuits.

2. *Early interactions within school settings and work settings play a major role in shaping an individual's long-term career interests, personal values, and work skills and abilities.* The developmental perspective on work careers also pays particular attention to how early experiences in educational settings and part-time jobs influence subsequent career interests and work involvement. For example, independent of the level of education that individuals attain, where individuals attend school is important to the quantity and quality of career resources they receive. Research suggests that the expertise of teachers and the backgrounds of other students in the school are significant predictors of teenagers' academic achievement, even after controlling for the students' own socioeconomic status (Griffith, 1995). Moreover, there is a significant association between school climate and levels of student psychopathology (Kasen, Johnson, & Cohen, 1990). School settings can buffer teenagers from or heighten their exposure to deviant peer groups and subcultures as well (Fuligni, Eccles, Barber, & Clements, 2001).

Both the amount and type of early experiences in the work-force also have an impact on the formation of career identity. Although the evidence is mixed, the bulk of the research suggests that amount of part-time work experience in high school is negatively correlated with school attendance, grades received, and likelihood of going to college (Greenberger & Steinberg, 1986; Stern, Stone, Hopkins, & McMillion, 1990). Nevertheless, these adverse effects appear to be significantly mitigated by the quality of early workforce experiences (Barling, Rogers, & Kelloway, 1995). The effects of early work experiences on subsequent career trajectories tend to be most positive when students work fewer than twenty hours per week, are given challenging assignments, and receive mentoring from adult supervisors rather than from teenaged peers (Barling et al., 1995; Feldman, Folks, & Turnley, 1998). At their best, structured part-time work experiences can help students crystallize their vocational interests, lessen the entry shock of moving from school to work, increase students' relevant work experience, and improve their chances of getting hired after graduation, too (Taylor, 1988).

3. *Personality traits and personal styles are developed early in life and have long-term consequences for how individuals perceive themselves, their environments, and their careers.* Careers researchers who take a developmental perspective on the study of careers are similarly interested in how personality traits, personal styles, and personal values formed early in life continue to shape career decisions for years to come. For example, research on the Big Five personality traits suggests that important components of adult personality (neuroticism, extraversion, openness to experience, agreeableness, and conscientiousness) are formed during childhood and adolescence (Digman, 1990; Hogan, Hogan, & Roberts, 1996). Furthermore, these personality traits influence the degree of effort put into, and the degree of success in making, subsequent career moves.

For instance, individuals who have high self-esteem and high self-efficacy have higher aspiration levels, are less easily discouraged by initial setbacks, and are more confident in their abilities to achieve their career goals (Albert & Luzzo, 1999; Betz & Voyten, 1997; Lent, Brown, & Hackett, 2000). Extraversion, openness to experience, and conscientiousness are significant predictors of how well individuals do in preparing for interviews, performing in interviews, and getting recommended for hiring (Caldwell & Burger, 1998). The Big Five influence individuals' work performance on a wide variety of dimensions once they have entered the workforce, too (Barrick & Mount, 1991); for example, personality traits have been linked to performance in training programs, ratings in job proficiency, and supervisory ratings. Kanfer, Wanberg, and Kantrowitz (2001) found that the Big Five significantly affect not only individuals' intensity of job search behavior after leaving school, but also their job search intensity after layoffs later in their careers.

Furthermore, personality influences how individuals perceive their careers and their environments over time. For example, the work of Staw and Barsade (1993) suggests that individuals' enduring predispositions to be basically happy or unhappy with their lives are stronger predictors of reactions to work situations than the specific working conditions themselves. Similarly, Holland's research (1985) suggests that individuals' preferences for different kinds of work environments form relatively early in life and remain fairly stable across subsequent career stages. Thus, personality traits formed early in life cast a long shadow over the course of individuals' careers across time (Tett, Jackson, & Rothstein, 1991).

4. *There are some stable patterns of work skills, career interests, and personal values that remain fairly constant throughout the adult life span.* Although work skills, career interests, and personal values evolve as people age, there is evidence that certain core competencies and preferences remain remarkably stable across time. Research using specialized aptitude batteries has found that work-relevant abilities, developed in childhood and adolescence, are significantly related to multiple indicators of subsequent job performance across time (Kanfer & Kantrowitz, 2002). Similarly, general intelligence, general cognitive ability, and information processing ability appear to be relatively stable over time and are significantly related to job performance. Ackerman (1996) suggests that these individual differences are especially critical when individuals are faced with novel tasks and novel settings, where picking things up quickly is central to work effectiveness. However, these enduring attributes may become less important after individuals have learned their jobs and fully adjusted to new work situations.

There is substantial stability of work interests and personal values over time, too. Fuligni and his colleagues (2001) have found that adolescents' orientation toward peers is stable over time and has major consequences for subsequent school achievement. Specifically, they found that seventh graders who were willing to sacrifice school performance to obtain peer approval still had significantly lower academic achievement and more behavioral problems five years later. In a study of adolescent women, O'Brien and Fassinger (1993) found that women's gender identification is formed early in life through interactions with parents (especially the mother) and has lasting consequences for women's career motivation, career choices, and attitudes toward work. For instance, they found that young women who are socialized toward work accomplishment early in life subsequently tend to select nontraditional careers; in contrast, young women who do not receive such socialization subsequently cluster into gender-stereotypical occupations like teaching and nursing.

These studies and others like them suggest that patterns of skills and career interests form early in life and have long-term consequences for career behaviors. Major changes, while more newsworthy, may be less important than intraindividual stability in understanding career development.

5. *The aging process itself creates incentives for individuals to modify their career interests, values, and skills across the life span.* Much of the recent research on careers has focused on how changing organizational contexts (such as downsizing, redefinition of the psychological contract, increased technology, and globalization) have altered the ways that individuals think about themselves, their careers, and their definitions of career success. As important as these external forces may be, there is another equally important—but internal—force operating at the same time: the process of aging itself creates conditions that energize individuals to reconsider and modify their career paths across the course of their lives.

Aging changes physical and physiological reactions to work tasks and job environments. For instance, Avolio and Waldman (1994) found that age was inversely related to general intelligence, verbal skills, and numerical skills, with correlations ranging from $-.10$ to $-.20$. The negative relationships between age and scores on form perception, motor coordination, finger dexterity, and manual dexterity tests were even stronger in magnitude ($r = -.28$ to $r = -.39$). Certainly, experience helps compensate for loss of skills as one ages (Marrow, Leirer, Altieri, & Fitzsimmons, 1994); moreover, the effects of aging are less prominent for professionals than for nonprofessional workers (McEvoy & Cascio, 1989). Nonetheless, decreases in information-processing capabilities (Schacter, 2001) and physical capabilities (Rhodes, 1983) appear to motivate individuals to acquire different skills or to seek out new work environments over time.

Perhaps more important, aging may affect individuals' career interests and career values. For example, as young adults move from their twenties into their thirties, they become much more interested in finding jobs where they can work independently and produce significant results (Dalton, 1989); the jobs that at age twenty-one appeared so challenging seem boring and micromanaged at age thirty-one. Similarly, as individuals hit their forties and fifties, they become much more interested in mentoring others and planning for the overall direction of the organization. In these life stages, individuals are more motivated to achieve a sense of generativity, that is, the feeling that they have worthwhile knowledge and skills to pass on to the next generation (Kram, 1985; Levinson, 1978).

Aging also intersects with family dynamics in stimulating career redirection. Marriage and child rearing may energize individuals to reconsider how invested in their careers they want to be, how many hours they wish to work, and how much responsibility for others they wish to take on. Similarly, health problems with spouses or parents may force individuals to rethink their level of work involvement, their levels of aspiration, and their long-term career plans (Stephens & Feldman, 1997). Thus, while external changes in organizational contexts clearly influence individuals' interests, values, and skills, the maturation process itself stimulates many of the changes in careers we see in individuals across the life span.

6. *Attaining fit between individuals' skills, interests, and values and organizational demands is critical in ensuring both individual psychological well-being and organizational effectiveness.* Finally, a major thrust of the developmental approach to studying careers has been its

attention to models of person-environment fit (Tinsley, 2000). The basic premise of this research stream is that when individuals' work skills, career interests, and personal values match the demands of jobs, occupations, and organizations, there will be positive benefits for individuals and institutions alike. Individuals will experience greater job satisfaction, work motivation, organizational commitment, and job involvement. At the same time, institutions will benefit from enhanced work performance, greater group cohesiveness, and lower levels of turnover (Edwards, 1991; Kristof, 1996).

The need to achieve fit between individuals and institutions is important not only in terms of career interests, but also in terms of work skills. Without question, the bulk of the research in this area has examined the relationships between individuals' career interests and the occupations, organizations, and jobs they choose (Hogan & Blake, 1996; Holland, 1985). However, the importance of achieving fit in terms of skills is being increasingly illustrated as well. For example, Wilk, Desmarais, and Sackett (1995) demonstrated that young adults gravitate to occupations commensurate with their abilities over time and progress in occupational hierarchies as a function of skill fit. In general, it appears that interest fit is a better predictor of occupational choice, while skill fit is a better predictor of long-term occupational membership (Austin & Hanish, 1990).

Moreover, different types of fit tend to reinforce each other over time. For instance, employed adults who are in occupations congruent with their interests are more likely to exert effort to increase their skill levels over time, either by increasing observational learning or participating in structured school programs (Blustein, Phillips, Jobin-Davis, Finkelberg, & Roarke, 1997). To the extent that there is an asymmetry of influence, it appears that congruence of skills may be more powerful than congruence of interests in driving career decisions. For example, when individuals have career aspirations that are inconsistent with their work skills, they are more likely to change their aspirations than their occupations (Gottfredson & Becker, 1981). That is, once skill acquisition and the achievement of skill congruence have taken place, it is easier to change career goals and interests than it is to acquire a whole new set of skills (Wilk et al., 1995).

Structure of the Book

Each of the chapter authors takes a developmental perspective in studying careers. Each chapter considers career development from the viewpoint of both the individual and the organization, and each addresses both theories of career development and implications for management practice.

Besides this introductory chapter, Part One contains two chapters on the basic building blocks of careers from a developmental perspective: the role of personality development in shaping career interests and vocational choices and the role of skill acquisition in achieving person-occupation fit.

Part Two examines the various stages of career development in chronological order. It begins with initial occupational choices (Chapter Four) and the school-to-work transition (Chapter Five), continues through the establishment years (Chapter Six) and mid-career issues (Chapter Seven), and concludes with retirement planning, workforce withdrawal, and postretirement employment (Chapter Eight).

Part Three examines the changing context in which individuals' careers unfold. In this part, the authors explore public policy issues and the changing legal context of career development (Chapter Nine), the changing organizational context of careers (Chapter Ten), and cross-cultural influences on career development (Chapter Eleven).

Part Four explores overall directions for industrial/organizational research and practice in the area of career development. Chapters Twelve and Thirteen examine avenues for future theory building, suggestions for modifications and innovations in methodology, and ideas for improving the quality of career planning and career management in organizational settings. Each of the chapters is described in more detail below.

Part One: Foundations of Career Development

The treatment of the basic building blocks of career development begins with Jill Bradley, Art Brief, and Jennifer George's chapter, "More Than the Big Five: Personality and Careers." This chapter examines the relationship between early personality development and the formation of career interests and preferences in childhood and adolescence. It helps us understand which personality traits are both most stable and most influential in determining career preferences across the life span. The chapter also explores the interplay of changes in personality and changes in vocational interests over time and how personality traits developed early in life can affect subsequent career paths.

In Chapter Three, "Skill Acquisition and Person-Environment Fit," Cheri Ostroff, Yuhyung Shin, and Barbara Feinberg explore how individuals gravitate into various occupations based on their perceptions of congruence. In particular, they highlight how critical it is to think about fit not only in terms of career interests but also in terms of work skills. The authors suggest how universities and employers can help individuals more accurately identify their areas of talent and obtain additional training and education to develop their skills.

Part Two: Career Development Across the Life Span

The treatment of career development across the spectrum of career stages and life stages begins with Daniel Feldman's "When You Come to a Fork in the Road, Take It: Career Indecision and Vocational Choices of Teenagers and Young Adults." Chapter Four first examines stage models of how adolescents and college students choose their initial vocations and the factors that are most critical in determining those initial choices. It then investigates the obverse problem: why so many teenagers and young adults have difficulty forming even tentative career plans. The chapter concludes with observations on individual career planning strategies and the design of institutional support systems for this population.

In Chapter Five, "The School-to-Work Transition," Elizabeth Wolfe Morrison provides an in-depth examination of how individuals making the transition from school to work acquire new task knowledge, build interpersonal relationships with supervisors and peers, and redefine or clarify their career identities. She uses a wide variety of social science perspectives (among them, uncertainty reduction theory, self-regulation theory, network theory, and socialization theory) to explain how this major career transition unfolds. The chapter also highlights both the individual-level and organizational-level factors that facilitate the school-to-work transition.

Chapter Six, "The Establishment Years," by Terri Scandura, discusses the impact of early career success and failure on subsequent career achievements and identifies the major developmental tasks that individuals face as they settle into their careers. The chapter also examines the important roles that developmental relationships with supervisors and mentors play in the socialization of individuals to their immediate work groups and their occupations more broadly. In addition, Scandura explores the critical intersection of work and nonwork demands for those in their twenties and thirties, when many adults are establishing families at the same time they are trying to establish their careers.

In Chapter Seven, "Career Development in Midcareer," Harvey Sterns and Linda Subich explore the ways in which an initial fit between individual needs and organizational demands can diminish by midcareer; they also examine how both intraindividual changes and environmental changes generate the need for redirecting career paths in midlife. In addition, Sterns and Subich explore how the challenges of dealing with teenaged children, often coupled with increased responsibilities for parents, create pressures on middle-aged workers to find new ways of integrating their careers with their personal lives. The chapter concludes with a discussion of individual and organizational strategies for dealing effectively with midcareer and midlife issues.

In "Career Issues Facing Older Workers" (Chapter Eight), Terry Beehr and Nathan Bowling first discuss age-related changes in abilities and interests and how those changes can affect late-career aspirations, work performance, retirement intentions, and involvement in postretirement employment. They also investigate both individual-level and environmental factors that affect older workers' opportunities for advancement into senior leadership positions. The chapter concludes with a discussion of how older workers can continue to grow and learn in their careers and how organizations can better accommodate the career interests and talents of older workers.

Part Three: The Changing Context of Career Development

The developmental perspective on work careers suggests that there are some relatively stable skills and interests that guide career development across the life span. At the same time, major changes in institutional contexts frequently prompt individuals to change directions or change strategies for managing their careers. The three chapters in this part address how major changes in institutional contexts also spur changes in individuals' career paths and career decisions.

In Chapter Nine, "Public Policy and the Changing Legal Context of Career Development," Jon Werner examines not only the ways governments attempt to eliminate barriers to career advancement (through affirmative action and the Family Leave Act, for example), but also how governments try to enhance existing career opportunities, too (such as through college loan programs and retraining initiatives). In addition, Werner addresses the tension between government interventions to aid career development and the role of free markets in shaping employment relationships. The chapter examines a wide array of public policy initiatives and labor laws geared to individuals at all stages of their careers, ranging from the School-to-Work Opportunities Act to legislation governing retirement age and pension benefits.

In Chapter Ten, "The Changing Organizational Context of Careers," Carrie Leana examines how major changes in organizational life have fueled changes in the ways individuals view their careers. She considers how the growth of information technology, the increased prevalence of downsizing, and the expansion of outsourcing have moved us from the 1950s model of "the organization man" to the 2000 model of "free agents." Leana examines both the opportunities and the challenges presented by this shift in organizational life and which new models of employment relations and career development are likely to emerge.

Chapter Eleven, "International Careers as Repositories of Knowledge: A New Look at Expatriation," examines the issues raised by the globalization of business and the international aspects of managing careers. Gregory Stephens, Alan Bird, and Mark Mendenhall highlight how conceptions of careers and career success vary across national and cultural borders. They also explore in detail the opportunities and challenges created by expatriate assignments in terms of developing individuals' own knowledge bases as well as transferring organizational knowledge more broadly. In addition, the authors explore the individual-level and organizational-level factors that facilitate transitions into and out of overseas assignments. Moreover, they examine how individuals' skills, values, and career interests may be shaped by living and working in another country.

Part Four: Directions for Industrial/Organizational Practice and Research

This final part of the book examines the implications of the ideas presented in the previous chapters for management practice and future research. In Chapter Twelve, "Organizational Assistance in Career Development," Manuel London looks at the ways in which organizations can foster continuous learning. He identifies both intraindividual and institutional factors that influence the effectiveness of various organizational career development programs, including competency identification and assessment, training, succession planning, Internet-based delivery of self-managed career resources, career coaching, and 360-degree feedback.

In the last chapter, "Advancing Research on Work Careers: A Developmental Perspective on Theory Building and Empirical Research," Daniel Feldman highlights a number of theoretical dimensions along which scholars in career development vary: for example, focusing on within-person changes versus changes in career paths themselves, examining internal versus external forces for change, and developing theories generalizable across populations versus developing theories geared to specific populations or specific contexts. Among the methodology issues highlighted here are the increased need for testability (and empirical tests) of career development theories, the importance of moving away from reliance on M.B.A. student and M.B.A. alumni samples, the lack of attention given to so-called blue-collar and pink-collar careers, and increased attention to generational differences in career development.

Conclusion

Some chapters in this book place more emphasis on intraindividual development, while others place more emphasis on the contexts in which career development takes place. Some of the chapters here are more focused on early-career issues, and others are focused on midcareer and late-career phenomena. All of the authors, though, examine the interplay of changes within individuals and across contexts over time. Perhaps most critical, each chapter advances career theory and provides implications for management practice. We hope this book will be of broad interest to scholars and practitioners in a wide variety of social science disciplines, educational institutions, and organizational settings.

References

Ackerman, P. L. (1996). A theory of adult intellectual development: Process, personality, interests, and knowledge. *Intelligence, 22,* 229–259.

Albert, K. A., & Luzzo, D. A. (1999). The role of perceived barriers in career development: A social cognitive perspective. *Journal of Counseling and Development, 77,* 423–430.

Arthur, M. B., Hall, D. T., & Lawrence, B. S. (Eds.). (1989). *Handbook of career theory.* Cambridge: Cambridge University Press.

Arthur, M. B., & Rousseau, D. M. (1996). *The boundaryless career: A new employment principle for a new organizational era.* New York: Oxford University Press.

Austin, J. T., & Hanish, K. A. (1990). Occupational attainment as a function of abilities and interests: A longitudinal analysis using Project Talent data. *Journal of Applied Psychology, 75,* 77–86.

Avolio, B. J., & Waldman, D. A. (1994). Variations in cognitive, perceptual, and psychomotor abilities across the working life span: Examining the effects of race, sex, experience, education, and occupational type. *Psychology and Aging, 9,* 430–442.

Barling, J. (1990). *Employment, stress, and family functioning.* New York: Wiley.

Barling, J., Rogers, K. A., & Kelloway, E. K. (1995). Some effects of teenagers' part-time employment: The quantity and quality of work make the difference. *Journal of Organizational Behavior, 16,* 143–154.

Barrick, M. R., & Mount, M. K. (1991). The Big Five personality dimensions and job performance. *Personnel Psychology, 44,* 1–26.

Betz, N. E., & Voyten, K. K. (1997). Efficacy and outcome expectations influence career exploration and decidedness. *Career Development Quarterly, 46,* 179–189.

Blustein, D. L., Phillips, S. D., Jobin-Davis, K., Finkelberg, S. L., & Roarke, A. E. (1997). A theory-building investigation of the school-to-work transition. *Counseling Psychology, 25,* 364–402.

Bolles, R. N. (2001). *What color is your parachute?* Berkeley, CA: Ten Speed Press.

Brooks, D. (2001). The organization kid. *Atlantic Monthly, 287,* 40–55.

Brousseau, K. R., Driver, M. J., Eneroth, K., & Larsson, R. (1996). Career pandemonium: Realigning organizations and individuals. *Academy of Management Executive, 10,* 52–66.

Caldwell, D. F., & Burger, J. M. (1998). Personality characteristics of job applicants and success in screening interviews. *Personnel Psychology, 51,* 119–136.

Caspi, A., Bem, D. J., & Elder, G. H. (1989). Continuities and consequences of interactional styles across the life course. *Journal of Personality, 57,* 375–406.

Crites, J. O. (1969). *Vocational psychology.* New York: McGraw-Hill.

Dalton, G. W. (1989). Developmental views of careers in organizations. In M. B. Arthur, D. T. Hall, & B. S. Lawrence (Eds.), *Handbook of career theory* (pp. 89–109). Cambridge: Cambridge University Press.

Dalton, G. W., Thompson, P. H., & Price, K. L. (1977). The four stages of professional careers: A new look at performance by professionals. *Organizational Dynamics, 6,* 19–42.

Digman, J. M. (1990). Personality structure: Emergence of the five-factor model. *Annual Review of Psychology, 41,* 417–440.

Dunnette, M. D. (1976). Aptitudes, abilities, and skills. In M. D. Dunnette (Ed.), *Handbook of industrial and organizational psychology* (pp. 473–520). Skokie, IL: Rand McNally.

Edwards, J. R. (1991). Person-job fit: A conceptual integration, literature review, and methodological critique. *International Review of Industrial and Organizational Psychology, 6,* 283–357.

Feldman, D. C. (1988). *Managing careers in organizations.* Glenview, IL: Scott, Foresman.

Feldman, D. C. (1995). Part-time and temporary employment relationships: Achieving fit between individual needs and organizational demands. In M. London (Ed.), *Employees, careers, and job creation* (pp. 121–141). San Francisco: Jossey-Bass.

Feldman, D. C. (1996). Managing careers in downsizing firms. *Human Resource Management, 35,* 145–163.

Feldman, D. C., & Bolino, M. C. (1997). Careers within careers: Reconceptualizing the nature of career anchors and their consequences. *Human Resource Management Review, 6,* 89–112.

Feldman, D. C., Folks, W. R., & Turnley, W. H. (1998). The socialization of expatriate interns. *Journal of Managerial Issues, 10,* 403–418.

Fuligni, A. J., Eccles, J. S., Barber, B. L., & Clements, P. (2001). Early adolescent peer orientation and adjustment during high school. *Developmental Psychology, 37,* 28–36.

Goldin, D. (2001). Help wanted: The head of NASA forecasts a bleak future for American science. *Atlantic Monthly, 288,* 28.

Gottfredson, L. S., & Becker, H. J. (1981). A challenge to vocational psychology: How important are aspirations in determining male career development? *Journal of Vocational Behavior, 18,* 121–127.

Gould, R. (1978). *Transformations: Growth and change in adult life.* New York: Simon & Schuster.

Greenberger, E., & Steinberg, L. (1986). *When teenagers work.* New York: Basic Books.

Griffith, J. (1995). An empirical examination of a model of social climate in elementary schools. *Basic and Applied Social Psychology, 17,* 97–117.

Habermas, T., & Bluck, S. (2000). Getting a life: The emergence of the life story in adolescence. *Psychological Bulletin, 126,* 748–769.

Harper, L. (1998, June 10). Hot job market may melt teens' plans for college. *Wall Street Journal,* A2–A3.

Hochschild, A. R. (1997). *The time bind.* New York: Holt.

Hogan, R., & Blake, R. J. (1996). Vocational interests: Matching self-concept with the work environment. In K. Murphy (Ed.), *Individual differences and behavior in organizations* (pp. 89–144). San Francisco: Jossey-Bass.

Hogan, R., Hogan, J., & Roberts, B. W. (1996). Personality measurement and employment decisions: Questions and answers. *American Psychologist, 51,* 469–477.

Holland, J. L. (1959). A theory of vocational choice. *Journal of Counseling Psychology, 6,* 35–44.

Holland, J. L. (1985). *Making vocational choices: A theory of careers* (2nd ed.). Upper Saddle River, NJ: Prentice Hall.

Kanfer, R., & Kantrowitz, T. M. (2002). Ability and non-ability predictors of performance. In S. Sonnentag (Ed.), *Psychological management of individual performance: A handbook in the psychology of management in organizations.* New York: Wiley.

Kanfer, R., Wanberg, C. R., & Kantrowitz, T. M. (2001). Job search and employment: A personality-motivational analysis and meta-analytic review. *Journal of Applied Psychology, 86,* 837–855.

Kasen, S., Johnson, J., & Cohen, P. (1990). The impact of school emotional climate on student psychopathology. *Journal of Abnormal Child Psychology, 18,* 165–177.

Kim, S., & Feldman, D.C. (2000). Working in retirement: The antecedents and consequences of bridge employment and its consequences for quality of life in retirement. *Academy of Management Journal, 43,* 195–210.

Kram, K. E. (1985). *Mentoring at work.* Glenview, IL: Scott, Foresman.

Kristof, A. L. (1996). Person-organization fit: An integrative review of its conceptualizations, measurements, and implications. *Personnel Psychology, 49,* 1–49.

Kush, K., & Cochran, L. (1993). Enhancing a sense of agency through career planning. *Journal of Counselling Psychology, 40,* 434–439.

Leana, C. R., & Feldman, D. C. (1992). *Coping with job loss: How individuals, organizations, and communities respond to layoffs.* Oldwick, NJ: Macmillan.

Lent, R. W., Brown, S. D., & Hackett, G. (2000). Contextual supports and barriers to career choice. *Journal of Counseling Psychology, 47,* 36–49.

Levinson, D. J. (1978). *The seasons of a man's life.* New York: Knopf.

London, M., & Stumpf, S. A. (1986). Individual and organizational career development in changing times. In D. T. Hall (Ed.), *Career development in organizations* (pp. 21–49). San Francisco: Jossey-Bass.

Marrow, D., Leirer, V., Altieri, P., & Fitzsimmons, C. (1994). When expertise reduces age and differences in performance. *Psychology and Aging, 9,* 134–148.

McEvoy, G. M., & Cascio, W. F. (1989). Cumulative evidence of the relationship between employee age and job performance. *Journal of Applied Psychology, 74,* 11–17.

O'Brien, K. M., & Fassinger, R. E. (1993). A causal model of the career orientation and career choice of adolescent women. *Journal of Counseling Psychology, 40,* 456–469.

Pautler, K. J., & Lewko, J. H. (1985). Student opinion of work in positive and negative economic climates. *Alberta Journal of Economic Research, 31,* 201–208.

Piotrowski, C. S., & Stark, E. (1987). Children and adolescents look at their parents' jobs. In J. H. Lewko (Ed.), *How children and adolescents view the world of work* (pp. 3–19). San Francisco: Jossey-Bass.

Rhodes, S. R. (1983). Age-related differences in work attitudes and behavior: A review and conceptual analysis. *Psychological Bulletin, 93,* 328–367.

Roe, A. (1956). *The psychology of occupations.* New York: Wiley.

Salamone, P. R., & Slaney, R. B. (1978). The applicability of Holland's theory to nonprofessional workers. *Journal of Vocational Behavior, 13,* 63–74.

Schacter, D. L. (2001). *The seven sins of memory.* Boston: Houghton Mifflin.

Schein, E. A. (1990). *Career anchors: Discovering your real values.* San Diego, CA: Pfeiffer.

Schmitt, N., Sacco, J. M., Ramey, S., Ramey, C., & Chan, D. (1999). Parental employment, school climate, and children's academic and social development. *Journal of Applied Psychology, 84,* 737–753.

Schneider, B., & Hall, D. T. (1972). Toward specifying the concept of work climate: A study of Roman Catholic diocese priests. *Journal of Applied Psychology, 56,* 447–455.

Sharf, R. (1997). *Applying career development theory to counseling.* Pacific Grove, CA: Brooks/Cole.

Shea, J. (2000). Does parents' money matter? *Journal of Public Economics, 77,* 155–184.

Shellenbarger, S. (1998, June 3). Teens are inheriting parents' tendencies toward work overload. *Wall Street Journal,* B1–B2.

Staw, B. M., & Barsade, S. G. (1993). Affect and managerial performance: A test of the sadder-but-wiser vs. happier-and-smarter hypothesis. *Administrative Science Quarterly, 38,* 304–331.

Stephens, G. K., & Feldman, D.C. (1997). A motivational approach for understanding work versus personal life investments. In G. R. Ferris (Ed.), *Research in Personnel and Human Resources Management, 15,* 333–378.

Stern, D., Stone, J. R., Hopkins, C., & McMillion, M. (1990). Quality of students' work experience and orientation toward work. *Youth and Society, 22,* 263–282.

Super, D. E. (1957). *The psychology of careers.* New York: HarperCollins.

Taylor, M. S. (1988). The effects of college internships on individual participants. *Journal of Applied Psychology, 73,* 393–401.

Tett, R. P., Jackson, D. N., & Rothstein, M. (1991). Personality measures as predictors of job performance: A meta-analytic review. *Personnel Psychology, 44,* 703–742.

Thompson, P. H., Kirkham, K. L., & Dixon, J. (1985). Warning: The fast track may be hazardous to organizational health. *Organizational Dynamics, 13,* 21–33.

Tinsley, H.E.A. (2000). The congruence myth: An analysis of the efficacy of the person-environment fit model. *Journal of Vocational Behavior, 56,* 147–179.

Valliant, G. (1977). *Adaptation to life.* New York: Little, Brown.

Weber, M. (Trans.). (1947). *The theory of social and economic organization.* New York: Oxford University Press.

Whyte, W. H., Jr. (1957). *The organization man.* New York: Anchor Books.

Wilk, S. L., Desmarais, L. B., & Sackett, P. R. (1995). Gravitation to jobs commensurate with ability: Longitudinal and cross-sectional tests. *Journal of Applied Psychology, 80,* 79–85.

CHAPTER 2

More Than the Big Five
Personality and Careers

Jill C. Bradley, Arthur P. Brief,
Jennifer M. George

In 1976, Holland criticized vocational interest research for being unorganized and poorly integrated with the fields of psychology and sociology. He was right, and based on our readings of the organizational psychology literature concerned with careers, he still is right. Although Holland (1966, 1985, 1999) repeatedly has asserted that vocational interests *are* personality, the careers literature remains largely unaffected by eighty years of research on personality by vocational psychologists.

Here, we aspire to correct this oversight. More generally, we intend to provide an overview of the ways in which personality may be entwined in the "unfolding sequence of a person's work experience over time [that is, career]" (Arthur, Hall, & Lawrence, 1989). In doing so, we will be inclusive in looking back at the vocational psychology literature on personality and forward toward the ways in which the current popularity of the Big Five model (Costa & McCrae, 1985; Goldberg, 1990; Tupes & Christal, 1992) might be limiting. By providing such an overview, we hope to stimulate more varied research on the relationships between personality and careers.

We thank Kristin Smith-Crowe for her insightful comments and suggestions on a draft of this chapter.

Necessary to understanding the relationships between personality and careers are working definitions of the constructs of career and personality. Traditionally, careers were thought of as high-status professions that offered vertical mobility within an organizational hierarchy (Hall, 1976). In addition, career development was assumed to be a largely irreversible process completed in early adulthood (Ginzberg, Ginsburg, Axelrad, & Herma, 1951). Today, however, careers increasingly are viewed as flexible in terms of the kinds of jobs that would be included in a career and the pattern of career development (Arthur & Rousseau, 1996). Feldman (1988) defined careers simply as "the sequence of jobs individuals hold over their work lives" (p. 1). This definition includes both traditional career paths and nontraditional career paths in which people move between organizations and occupations throughout their work lives. This definition does not restrict the term *career* to high-status jobs as past definitions have done.

Although this definition is an improvement over traditional approaches emphasizing vertical advancement, it nonetheless constrains notions of careers in ways that may limit understanding. More specifically, the term *job* generally connotes paid employment in an organizational context. However, there are other forms of work that meaningfully contribute to people's careers and are not generally thought of as being subsumed under the job construct. People who work at home taking care of children and performing household tasks and people who volunteer in hospitals, social service agencies, and schools all do work, and from a societal perspective, the work they do may be just as important as (or even more important than) work performed as part of paid employment in organizational contexts. Yet we implicitly or explicitly consider these activities as outside the career domain.

For example, the single inner-city mother struggling to provide her children with the necessities of life in a loving home is "working" very hard as a mother. Indeed, her "job" is a crucial one with real human consequences, and her resourcefulness and resilience as a single mother speak to a different kind of career that has its own challenges and rewards. Similarly, volunteers who build houses as part of programs such as the Habitat for Humanity also are working, and their volunteer work can be seen as contributing to their careers.

Hence, we favor a definition of careers that encompasses the sequence of work activities that individuals engage in over the course of their lifetimes. Work activities can be broadly defined as "any activity we need or want to do in order to achieve the basic requirements of life or to maintain a certain life style" (Gini, 2001, p. 14).

We also are concerned that organizational scholars have become too restrictive in their views of personality. In particular, the Big Five, despite its popularity, is only one of several ways to understand personality. By relying predominantly on one approach to personality, such as the Big Five, our understanding of the ways in which personality influences careers will be limited. In this chapter, we take a more catholic approach in defining personality as "regularities and consistencies in the behavior of individuals in their lives" (Snyder & Ickes, 1985, p. 883). This definition does not favor a particular theory of personality nor does it insist that the concept of a trait is necessary to an understanding of personality.

The remainder of the chapter progresses according to the following plan. First, we provide a brief review of the history of personality research in this area, emphasizing Holland's interest inventories. We propose alternatives to the Big Five and Holland's interest inventories such as the theory of work adjustment (Dawis, England, & Lofquist, 1964) and Cantor's (1990) life task approach to personality. Finally, we then discuss the substantive and methodological challenges that career researchers face in broadening and enriching the way in which we view both careers and personality.

Personality Research in Vocational Psychology: A Historical Perspective

Career theory can be traced to the early twentieth century when Frank Parsons established the Vocation Bureau in 1908 to help people identify their strengths and the jobs in which these strengths could be applied best (Brown, Brooks, & Associates, 1984). Parsons (1909) articulated the first conceptual framework for career decision making and asserted that both employees and employers would benefit from careful vocational choices as opposed to more haphazard job searches and drifting into jobs. He believed that knowledge of the self, knowledge of the job, and a method of matching the two were crucial to the selection of an ideal job. Although Parsons's approach encouraged self and career exploration, it lacked a systematic method of assessing and classifying people based on their interests and abilities. The development of systematic interest inventories was stimulated by the introduction of psychometric tests used to place soldiers during World War I and II and to help the unemployed find work during the Great Depression (Betz, Fitzgerald, & Hill, 1989).

Strong's Vocational Interest Inventory, introduced in 1927, marked the first interest inventory in the area of vocational guidance. The inventory was aimed at assessing the interests of the individual in comparison to the interests of people already in an occupation. In contrast, inventories like the Kuder Preference Record (Kuder, 1946) were developed to evaluate the likes and dislikes of an individual in relation to the job content, tasks, and working conditions of different occupations.

Despite the different approaches to creating their interest inventories, Kuder and Strong both subscribed to a trait-factor career theory positing that a match between individual traits and occupational factors was desirable. Similarly, theorists such as Roe (1956), Dawis et al. (1964), and Holland (1959, 1973) asserted that people are attracted to, and are more likely to be satisfied and successful performers in, jobs that match their personality. Trait-factor career theorists principally focus on an optimal person-occupation match at the time of career choice. In contrast, career process theorists like Ginzberg et al. (1951) and Super (1957) have attempted to understand the entire career in terms of career choices people make over time and the stages through which they progress during their work lives (Patton & McMahon, 1999).

Although trait-factor theorists and career process theorists are somewhat different in their focus, both recognize personality as an important influence on careers. For example, Super (1957) asserted that the career process is unique for each individual, such that people progress through career stages in differing sequences and frequencies. He attributed these differences to the individual's personality, as well as parental socioeconomic level, mental ability, and opportunities presented in the environment. Similarly, Holland (1985) asserted that an individual's personality type and the environment in which he or she lives relates to outcomes such as career choice, competence and achievement, and job changes.

Holland has written extensively about personality and careers, continually refining the theory that he first articulated in 1959. In spite of various criticisms (Schwartz, 1992; Tinsley, 2000), Holland's theory is the most popular perspective on personality within vocational psychology and has dominated this body of literature for the past forty years (Furnham, 2001). Rayman and Atanasoff (1999) attribute the popularity of the theory to its conceptually straightforward organization, face validity, and practical applications. Because of the significant impact Holland's theory has had on vocational psychology and its links to personality, we explore it as the bridge between past and current career research.

Holland's Theory of Careers

In 1959, Holland proposed a theory of vocational choice based on the concept of congruence between the individual and the occupational environment. Holland deemed previous theories either too broad to generate testable hypotheses or too narrow in their consideration of the range of factors that influence career choice. Based in part on factor-analytic research conducted by Strong (1943) and Guilford, Christensen, Bond, and Sutton (1954), Holland described a classification system of people and jobs comprising six categories, which he subsequently labeled realistic, intellectual (later renamed investigative), artistic, social, enterprising, and conventional (RIASEC).

According to Holland (1997), the realistic type is most related to careers of the manual, mechanical, agricultural, or technical nature. Investigative individuals tend to pursue scientific and mathematical careers that enable them to use observational and analytical skills. The artistic type is drawn to jobs related to language, drama, music, or other areas within the fine arts. Individuals classified by Holland's social type prefer activities in which they can interact with others to educate, understand, or assist. The enterprising individual also tends to enjoy social interactions, but this type of person is prone to take the role of leader, organizer, or persuader in exchanges with others. Finally, the conventional type prefers activities that involve the systematic manipulation of data such as found in clerical and computational jobs.

Interest inventories can be used to determine an individual's RIASEC classification (Holland, 1959), and environments can be defined in terms of the distribution of types present in them (Astin & Holland, 1961). Holland (1966) asserted that personality-type classifications vary in differentiation and consistency. That is, some people and environments have a differentiated, or well-defined, profile that clearly resembles one personality type; other people and environments are less differentiated and may be defined better in terms of two or more of the six types. Because many people and environments are not simply defined by one of the six types, the issue of consistency arises. Consistency can be thought of as the compatibility of types that are found within one person or environment. For example, it would be more consistent for someone to have both social and enterprising tendencies as opposed to conventional and artistic tendencies (Holland, 1976).

In addition to classifying people and environments into the six types, Holland, Whitney, Cole, and Richards (1969) showed that the personality types could be arranged in a hexagonal structure (see Figure 2.1) such that types next to each other in the hexagon are most closely related or consistent, and those opposite each other in the arrangement are least related. Once an individual and environment have been classified according to the six types, Holland posited that congruency between the individual and the environment is related to the distance between personality types as they are arranged in the hexagonal structure. For example, artistic and conventional types are opposite each other in the hexagon; therefore, artistic people are expected to be least satisfied and successful in conventional environments. Individuals are more likely to thrive in environments congruent with their personality types because such environments provide rewards that are valued by that type of person (Holland, 1973, 1985, 1997).

A number of studies have tested Holland's congruency hypothesis. In a recent review of the literature, Spokane, Meir, and Catalano (2000) reported mixed findings about the relations between congruence and various career outcomes. Two separate meta-analyses conducted by Assouline and Meir (1987) and Tranberg, Slane, and Ekeberg (1993) revealed mean congruence-job satisfaction correlations (uncorrected) of .21 and .20, respectively. Modest congruence-achievement and congruence-job stability correlations also were observed (Assouline & Meir, 1987).

Both groups of authors noted that the magnitudes of the correlations varied depending on the way congruence was measured,

Figure 2.1. Holland's Hexagonal Arrangement
of the Personality Types.

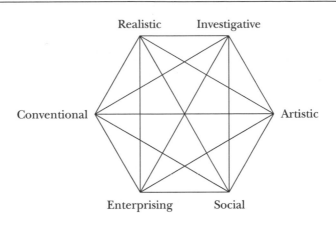

which is a concern we will address later in the chapter. In addition, Tranberg et al. (1993) found that the congruence-satisfaction relationship was strongest for the Holland social type and weakest for the realistic type. Similarly, a more recent meta-analysis conducted by Young, Tokar, and Subich (1998) indicated that the congruence-satisfaction relationship varied as a function of Holland personality type rather than the method of calculating congruence. In reaction to the meta-analytic results, Holland (1997) noted that despite the relatively weak magnitude of the correlations, the relations were almost entirely positive, indicating that the pattern of results supported the congruence hypothesis.

Beyond offering a classification system for personality and work environments, Holland has attempted to explain how interests develop. He posited that people learn to prefer certain activities over others and that such learning is influenced by forces including heredity, family and friends, social class, culture, and the physical environment (Holland, 1959). Over time, these preferred activities are thought to become strong interests, which, along with one's abilities, create a particular disposition or tendency to behave in a consistent manner. Based on this rationale, Holland, like his graduate school adviser, John Darley (1941), asserted that vocational choice is an expression of personality.

This view of vocational interests differs markedly from those that narrowly defined vocational interests as the likes and dislikes related to one's vocation (Lent, Brown, & Hackett, 1994; Strong, 1943). Savickas (1999), in agreement with Holland, argued that needs, values, and interests all represent personality, with interests comprising the means by which people fulfill their needs and values. Thus, interest inventories can be thought of as one way to assess personality.

Two issues with regard to vocational interest psychology are worth noting here. First, as is true of many other literatures, this approach has tended to downplay or ignore work that is performed in the home, such as the raising of children. Second, although time is intimately connected to certain theoretical arguments, it has been largely neglected in empirical work, which may influence obtained results in unexpected ways (George & Jones, 2000). For example, Holland suggests that people learn to prefer certain activities over time due to a variety of factors, and such preferences serve to form their vocational interests. This suggests that a person's work experience to date will influence his or her expression of careers interests (as well as measures of congruence). Hence, to the extent that research studies include participants with varying amounts of tenure in the workforce (defined broadly), their work histories may have varying effects on their expression of interests (and congruence).

For example, a high school graduate looking for employment and a mechanic with twenty years of work experience in machine shops may initially have had similar interests at the time of graduation from high school. However, the work history of the mechanic may serve to guide his interests over time such that he reports interests and capabilities that are congruent with the kind of work he has performed over the past two decades. Thus, while the new high school graduate may report interests that reflect his personality, the mechanic reports interests that reflect his ongoing work experiences; these experiences color the mechanic's views about what work can and should be like and the areas in which he excels. Two such individuals therefore may report similar vocational interests, but the underlying construct being assessed might differ between the two.

In any case, vocational interest psychology, and Holland's work in particular, has played an important role in both the history of vocational psychology and recent research. Following the lead of Holland, we will consider interests and interest inventories as reflections of personality.

Current Career Research: RIASEC and the Big Five

Scholars testing Holland's assertion that interests are reflective of personality have explored the relationship between interest inventories and personality inventories (see reviews by Ackerman & Heggestad, 1997; Furnham, 2001; Tokar, Fischer, & Subich, 1998). Early attempts in this vein were largely unsuccessful (Super, 1957). However, as Costa, McCrae, and Holland (1984) noted, many of these early studies relied on dated measures that lacked adequate coverage of the range of personality. Subsequent investigations (Costa et al., 1984; Darley & Hagenah, 1955; Goh & Leong, 1993; Holland, 1968; Seiss & Jackson, 1970) revealed significant relationships between a variety of personality and interest inventories.

Perhaps because of its current popularity, many recent studies have focused on comparing the Big Five traits to Holland's RIASEC variables. The Big Five taxonomy evolved out of a series of factor-analytic studies. According to Costa and McCrae (1985), the Big Five factors are extraversion (sociability, activity, and positive emotions), neuroticism (emotional adjustment), openness to experience (imagination, creativity, and desire to explore the unknown), agreeableness (altruistic, trusting, and good-natured), and conscientiousness (discipline, organization, and dependability).

In one of the earliest studies comparing the Big Five to Holland's RIASEC theory, Costa et al. (1984) correlated scores from Holland's Self-Directed Search with the Big Five traits of neuroticism, extraversion, and openness to experience (NEO). Strong positive relationships were found between openness to experience and Holland's investigative and artistic types. Extraversion also was related strongly to social and enterprising types, and the authors noted that almost all of Holland's types were positively related to extraversion and openness to experience. Costa et al. reasoned that the confidence and excitement of extraverts and the curiosity of open individuals lead them to contemplate many vocational options; thus, personality seems to influence not only the specific types of work that individuals consider, but also the extent to which they are interested in a wide versus a narrow range of possibilities. Alternatively, these findings may indicate that although personality is related to the expression of vocational interests, measures of the two constructs are tapping into distinct domains.

Costa et al. (1984) empirically observed that the realistic and conventional types did not clearly map onto any of the NEO factors, although openness was negatively related to the conventional type. Neuroticism did not correlate with any of the Holland types in this investigation, although other scholars (Holland, Johnston, & Asama, 1994) have reported negative relationships between neuroticism and the Holland types. If individuals high in neuroticism tend to be disinterested in all six of the Holland types, they might be expected to have difficulties in choosing a career path and may be dissatisfied with their choices. Consistent with this reasoning, studies have shown that neuroticism is related to career indecision (Chartrand, Rose, Elliott, Marmarosh, & Caldwell, 1993) and low levels of job satisfaction (Costa, McCrae, & Zonderman, 1987; Perone, DeWaard, & Baron, 1979). It appears that neuroticism may be indicative of global disinterest and dissatisfaction, which could potentially extend to multiple occupations (Watson & Clark, 1984).

More recent studies have considered conscientiousness and agreeableness in addition to the NEO factors, thus comparing all five factors to Holland's typology. These studies tend to replicate the findings of Costa et al., as well as suggest new relations involving conscientiousness and agreeableness (Tokar & Swanson, 1995). Overall, research suggests that neuroticism, agreeableness, and conscientiousness are not adequately represented by the Holland types (Costa, McCrae, & Kay, 1995), nor are Holland's conventional and realistic types captured consistently by the Big Five dimensions (Schinka, Dye, & Curtis, 1997).

The sum of the evidence suggests some overlap between subsets of Holland's RIASEC types and subsets of the Big Five. However, as Tokar and Swanson (1995) aptly noted, "RIASEC does not appear to be subsumed by the Big Five" (p. 103). Similarly, Holland's typology does not seem to provide full coverage of the Big

Five. Commenting on the empirical research relating RIASEC to the Big Five, Holland (1999) concluded, "It seems reasonable to believe that personality can be assessed by inventories, scales, or ratings that use vocational *or* nonvocational content. Or people express their personality in multiple activities and situations, not just in a particular inventory" (p. 98).

Because interest inventories and more traditional personality inventories offer somewhat unique information, many authors (Costa et al., 1995) recommend the use of both approaches for vocational counseling. Empirically, RIASEC and the Big Five have been shown to be at least partially distinct. Conceptually, the two approaches also offer unique perspectives. Holland's approach is a typology, while the Big Five is a trait perspective. Typologies like RIASEC serve to classify people into more or less distinct categories, while trait approaches like the Big Five assume that people can be described in degree, or the extent to which they are high or low on a given set of traits. Typological approaches to personality have been relatively neglected in the applied literature, which, some researchers maintain, has hindered progress in this area. For example, Schneider and Hough (1995) posit that people might "differ in kind rather than in degree on some (though certainly not all) personality characteristics. To assume that all personality variables are dimensional at this point seems premature" (p. 84). Consistent with this view, Magnusson and Toerestad (1993) supported the use of typological approaches as a complement to more popular trait approaches, suggesting that type classifications may explain variance beyond that explained by traits like the Big Five.

Clearly, trait-related behavior and goals may distinguish different personality types. Because personality types may offer unique information in addition to personality traits, we support Schneider and Hough's push (1995) for more rigorous theoretical and empirical research on personality types, including further research on Holland's typology. The empirical research surveyed here shows that Holland's typology may offer unique insights into the career process that the Big Five trait approach might fail to capture. However, the Big Five has explained career outcomes that the RIASEC typology has not. Thus, researchers should consider both the Big Five and RIASEC when exploring the ways in which personality relates to careers.

Current Career Research: The Big Five and Career Outcomes

Contemporary research has focused on correlations between Big Five traits and career outcomes, consistent with the current popularity of the Big Five. Unfortunately, all too often in this and other areas, empirical research has tended simply to correlate a host of predictor and criterion variables, without any theory guiding the relations explored.

Unlike studies of Holland's theory, which typically correlate congruence scores with career outcomes, research using the Big Five approach usually involves correlating personality traits directly with career outcomes. Research exploring the relationship between the Big Five and performance, for example, has suggested that only conscientiousness is consistently and positively related to job performance across a variety of job types (Barrick & Mount, 1991, 1993; but see Schneider & Hough, 1995). Nonetheless, other research suggests that even relations between conscientiousness and performance may be more complicated than previously thought, depending on the nature of performance and the work context. For example, George and Zhou (2001) found that conscientiousness was negatively related to creative behavior when supervisors engaged in close monitoring and coworkers were unsupportive. Extraversion also has been linked to performance (but principally for jobs that require extensive interpersonal interactions), frequent and high-quality job searches, and number of job changes (Tokar et al., 1998).

With regard to affective career outcomes, research has found that neuroticism is negatively related to job satisfaction (Brief, 1998) and positively associated with occupational stress (see a review by Tokar et al., 1998; but also see Burke, Brief, & George, 1993). On the other hand, extraversion is positively related to job satisfaction (Tokar & Subich, 1997), and conscientiousness has been linked to increased job-seeking activities as well as a positive sense of self-worth despite being unemployed (Wanberg, Watt, & Rumsey, 1996).

A recent study by Judge, Higgins, Thoresen, and Barrick (1999) investigated the relationships between Big Five personality traits and intrinsic career success (for example, job satisfaction) and extrinsic career success (such as salary and ascendancy). This unique investigation used longitudinal data on individuals' personality, general mental ability, and career success. Results indicated that personality, especially as measured during adulthood, was related to career success even when controlling for general mental ability. Specific findings included a positive relationship between conscientiousness and both intrinsic and extrinsic career success and a negative relationship between neuroticism and extrinsic career success. In a similar investigation, Seibert and Kraimer (2001) found that agreeableness and neuroticism were negatively related to career satisfaction. Openness was related to lower salary levels, and extraversion corresponded with higher salary levels.

Despite the presence of correlations between Big Five dimensions and career behaviors and outcomes, findings often are not coupled with an underlying theoretical rationale. In fact, Block (1995) criticized the very use of the term *model* in reference to the Big Five itself: "As the term 'model' is used in conventional parlance among psychologists, it means a theoretically based, logically coherent, working representation or simulation that, in operation, attempts to generate psychological phenomena of interest. However, no identifiable hypotheses, theories, or models guided the emergence of or decision on this five-fold space (although some have been offered post hoc)" (p. 188).

An additional problem with the Big Five is that it may not be as inclusive as some would believe. Studies comparing the Big Five to alternative personality taxonomies (McCrae, Costa, & Piedmont, 1993) have created doubt about the comprehensiveness of the Big Five (Block, 1995). Hogan (1982), for example, suggested a six-factor taxonomy based on the Big Five, with extraversion separated into two factors labeled sociability and assertiveness (subsequently relabeled ambition). His proposal was based on the premise that sociability and assertiveness are conceptually distinct and are correlated only moderately. Hogan asserted that sociability is more related to needs and goals associated with affiliation, whereas ambition represents status and power goals.

Aside from criticisms concerning its atheoretical nature and questionable comprehensiveness, the Big Five does have some important advantages. Perhaps the biggest appeal of the Big Five is that the same five factors have emerged consistently across a variety of samples (Digman & Takemoto-Chock, 1981; Goldberg, 1990; John, Angleitner, & Ostendorf, 1988), even cross-cultural ones (McCrae & Costa, 1997). In addition, the Big Five traits appear to have a genetic basis (Digman, 1989) and remain fairly stable over time (Costa & McCrae, 1992; but see Caspi & Roberts, 2001). Finally, the Big Five provides researchers with a quantifiable approach that is arguably a more parsimonious method of assessing personality than more qualitative personality views.

However, we suggest that researchers broaden their conceptualizations of personality and careers as well as consider career outcomes from a whole life perspective. Traditionally, the careers literature considers career outcomes from the perspective of organizational and work-related perceptions, reactions, and behaviors such as job satisfaction, job stress, job performance, salary level, and advancement or ascendancy. However, given our broad conceptualization of careers and work, in conjunction with the fact that work and other parts of life are intimately entwined, perhaps we should consider career outcomes that manifest themselves outside the workplace, such as well-adjusted and happy children, healthy familial and marital relations, and continued individual growth and development. Ironically, when family members work in the home to perform one of the most important functions in a family and society, the raising of children, their careers are seen as brought to a halt or nonexistent altogether (Crittenden, 2001) rather than as a part of a lifelong sequence of work.

Moreover, in gauging extrinsic success by such indicators as ascendancy and salary, perhaps we need to consider the costs that might accompany certain kinds of careers typically viewed as successful and whether these costs are differentially borne by certain segments of society. For example, research suggests that it is much more difficult for women to achieve extrinsic career success, as gauged by ascendancy and salary, while simultaneously raising a family than it is for men (Crittenden, 2001). Numerous statistics point to the fact that men who rise to the top of their occupations and professions are much more likely to have children than women who are similarly extrinsically successful (Catalyst, 2000, cited in Crittenden, 2001) Interestingly enough, perhaps personality also plays a role in determining how people are able to balance the different aspects of their lives and achieve some degree of career success (however defined) while simultaneously not making undue sacrifices in other parts of their lives.

Careers and Personality: Alternative Approaches

Throughout the chapter, we have suggested that researchers need to move beyond popular approaches such as Holland's model and the Big Five. Here, in an exemplary fashion, we consider alternatives to these dominant perspectives and the additional insights they might yield. Although there are many personality theories and conceptualizations, we have selected the alternatives that appear to be particularly relevant to the study of careers yet have been recently neglected: the theory of work adjustment (Dawis & Lofquist, 1984), Cantor's life task approach to personality (Cantor, 1990), and other trait approaches aside from the Big Five.

Theory of Work Adjustment

The theory of work adjustment (TWA), like Holland's theory, relies on a congruence, or fit, notion to tackle the problem of vocational adjustment. Like Holland's theory, TWA began in the vocational psychology literature; however, its influence in that literature appears to have waned considerably. TWA focuses on the concept of correspondence between the individual and the environment. Specifically, the theory emphasizes the process through which individuals attempt to obtain and maintain correspondence with their environments, because correspondence fluctuates over time due to changes in the individual and the environment (Dawis, Lofquist, & Weiss, 1968). Individuals may change themselves or their environments to achieve fit, and environments or jobs may change over time, resulting in increased or decreased correspondence between the individual and the environment.

Two different types of correspondence are identified within TWA. The first type, labeled satisfactoriness, results from a match between the individual's abilities and the duties and requirements of the job. The second type, satisfaction, refers to a match between the individual's needs and desires and the rewards offered by the job. TWA predicts that both satisfactoriness and satisfaction will increase as a function of tenure. The process of change over time toward increased satisfactoriness and satisfaction is thought to depend on both environmental and individual factors.

TWA identifies, among other factors, four personality styles, which describe an individual's typical manner of interacting with the environment. *Celerity,* for example, refers to the speed with which the individual typically initiates interactions with the work environment. Celerity is thought to relate to the individual's tolerance for a lack of correspondence. Individuals who are bothered greatly by a lack of correspondence are likely to be high in celerity. These individuals might engage in frequent job changes or be more likely to initiate self or environment change within their current job than people low in celerity.

The other three personality styles relate to the way in which the individual initiates change. *Pace* refers to the level of effort exerted in interactions. Some individuals are thought to devote more effort than others in obtaining correspondence. One person may be willing, for example, to undergo extensive training in order to meet the demands of the job better, while another person may struggle through the same tasks and settle with a low level of correspondence. Individuals also are posited to differ in *rhythm,* or the pattern (say, steady or erratic) of effort expended. Some people consistently strive for correspondence with their environment, while others tend to go through cyclical periods of effort aimed at increasing correspondence. Finally, *endurance* denotes the length of time the individual commits to the interaction. TWA assumes that these four personality styles are relatively stable, representing an individual's tendency to interact with the environment in a relatively consistent way over time (Dawis & Lofquist, 1984).

The TWA has the potential to enrich our understanding of personality and careers as it focuses on the ongoing process of career adjustment. Careers, by definition, unfold over time, and this approach is unique in terms of trying to gain a handle on the unfolding nature of careers and individual differences that might influence basic processes of career adjustment. The TWA personality styles are different from the Big Five traits and Holland's RIASEC typology in that they focus on the style or typical way in which individuals interact with the environment. While Dawis (1996) has claimed that both Big Five personality traits and vocational interests are higher-order variables comprising the lower-order TWA variables, how the TWA personality styles relate to these and other conceptualizations of personality is a theoretical and empirical question in need of attention.

Although proposed over three decades ago, the TWA has not received adequate research attention despite the fact that it might offer unique and important benefits as a dynamic model of fit or correspondence (Tinsley, 2000). For example, because of its focus on the process of achieving correspondence rather than on career selection, TWA might enrich our understanding of career processes and outcomes after an occupation has been chosen. Holland's theory, in contrast, focuses less on change in fit over time and more on optimizing congruence between the person and environment at the time of career choice. Due to its unique focus on process and continued interaction between the person and environment, we encourage career researchers to add the TWA to their repertoire of personality approaches.

Personal Strivings, Personal Projects, and Life Tasks

Differing from both the trait and typological conceptualizations, some personality psychologists emphasize the importance of life goals in the structure of personality. Despite different names for these goals, such as *personal strivings* (Emmons, 1997) and *personal projects* (Little, 1989), the theories commonly focus on the idiographic nature of goals and the strategies used to obtain goals. In the interest of length and parsimony, we have chosen to focus on Cantor's life tasks as representative of these personality theories. We believe that the goal-focus of her approach is particularly relevant to the study of careers because many people choose and frame their careers in terms of their goals and values.

Cantor (1990) has suggested that a cognitive approach to personality can supplement trait perspectives by showing how different individuals interpret life situations, envision their future selves, and formulate plans to adapt and cope with life's demands. Cantor (Harlow & Cantor, 1994) asserted that trait approaches such as the Big Five often have failed to consider how traits may be manifested differently across contexts; thus, individuals are portrayed as static and passive. A cognitive personality approach, in contrast, explores the ways in which individuals actively perceive themselves and the world around them and how these perceptions influence behavior and subsequent outcomes. In addition, Cantor's perspective acknowledges individual differences in life tasks (that is, goals) as well as individual differences in strategies employed to obtain these life tasks. Such tasks or goals are thought to be "the primary force behind personality coherence over time" (Sanderson & Cantor, 1999, p. 382).

In Cantor's view, individuals are, for the most part, assumed to be consciously aware of their life tasks; therefore, researchers using this personality approach typically rely on self-report strategies to assess life tasks. Life task assessments usually require individuals to list, rank, and rate their life tasks on dimensions such as importance, enjoyment, difficulty, and control. Because individuals are usually working on several life tasks at one time, the pursuit of one task may facilitate or hinder other life tasks.

For example, in a longitudinal study of students making the transition from high school to college, Cantor and Langston (1989) found that academic-related life tasks often conflicted with social-related life tasks. Undoubtedly, studying and getting good grades can detract from spending time with friends or engaging in extracurricular activities. The students were found not only to have different goals and life tasks but also employed different strategies to achieve those goals. The Cantor and Langston study demonstrated the complex interaction between goals and strategies in relation to student performance; however, the results may be somewhat different in the world of work.

Clearly, assessments of life tasks and strategies are likely to provide important information relevant to the study of careers. If the majority of an individual's life tasks are related to career goals, such as receiving promotions, finishing a work project, or being recognized as the best in one's field, one might expect very different types of behaviors and outcomes than if an individual reports many life tasks related to having and raising children and devoting time to leisure and hobbies. Life tasks clearly provide another way to understand individual differences in career choice and outcomes and ought to be given more serious consideration by careers researchers. The unique emphasis on the idiographic nature of goals and means to achieve those goals has the potential to add a dimension to the careers literature not now evident.

Traits Beyond the Big Five

Researchers have postulated and identified a number of personality variables outside the scope of the Big Five, although they have not articulated or organized them into a theory of careers or personality. What follows is an overview of research suggesting the existence of traits beyond the Big Five and various proposals for how these traits might be integrated into career research.

In an article aptly titled "What Is Beyond the Big Five?" Saucier and Goldberg (1998) evaluated fifty-three person-descriptive word clusters that they believed could be beyond the scope of the Big Five. The word clusters represented a wide variety of individual differences related to personality, demographic characteristics, and physical attributes. Although clusters related to demographics and physical attributes such as height, girth, and employment status were clearly independent of the Big Five, the authors concluded that the Big Five are relatively comprehensive in terms of the word clusters related to personality.

Saucier and Goldberg considered the cluster of religiousness to be the clearest outlier to the Big Five. Clusters relating to fashionableness, sensuality and seductiveness, beauty, masculinity, frugality, humor, wealth, prejudice, folksiness, cunning, and luck were considered to be "*potentially* beyond the Big Five" (p. 495), although Saucier and Goldberg argued that these clusters had Big Five multiple correlations between .30 and .45 and therefore are not completely distinct. Paunonen and Jackson (2000) reanalyzed the same data using a somewhat more relaxed criterion for deciding whether a word cluster fell within the Big Five domain (.20 communality versus .09 communality) and alternatively concluded that the Big Five is not comprehensive in its coverage of personality.

Paunonen and Jackson (2000) posited that many Big Five studies have not revealed the nine missing dimensions because previous studies often were based on the lexical hypothesis: societies invent words to describe the things of significance in life, so the more important something is, the more words are created to describe it. Paunonen and Jackson challenged the lexical hypothesis: "But just because the words describing a domain of behavior are relatively few in number, does that mean that the domain is any less important than is some bigger one?" (p. 832). The lexical hypothesis, although useful in some instances, perhaps should be considered more a rule of thumb than a definitive justification for the relative importance of personality traits.

Challenges in the Study of Personality and Careers

We turn now to some of the substantive and methodological challenges that personality and careers researchers face. In particular, we focus on the conceptual and methodological issues surrounding personality-career fit and the role of racial and gender diversity.

The Ambiguous Status of Fit as a Psychological Construct

Congruence or *correspondence* are the terms used in Holland's theory and the TWA (Dawis et al., 1964), respectively, to describe the fit between an individual and the environment. The notion of positive outcomes resulting from a match between the worker and the job is appealing intuitively and has received some empirical support. Person-environment fit research is quite popular and almost paradigmatic in nature (Muchinsky, 1999; Walsh, Craik, & Price, 2000). However, the notion of fit is open to criticism (Tinsley, 2000; Weiss & Brief, in press) on the grounds of being an ambiguous theoretical construct that means different things to different sets of researchers.

A major issue for fit research, which is central to correcting the confusion in this area, is conceptual consensus on the definition of this somewhat elusive construct. Researchers studying fit often do not articulate their notion of the construct and then proceed to measure it without explaining why such measurements were made and assumed to be of importance. For example, some researchers have focused on fit between the individual and the occupation (for example, congruence research on Holland's theory), while others view the fit between the individual's values and organizational values as paramount (Cable & Judge, 1997). Complicating the matter, as Furnham (2001) notes, is the fact that fit researchers have described the environment in a variety of ways, including physical, social, and cultural attributes (Meir, Hadas, & Noyfeld, 1997).

Clearly, researchers do not agree on the aspects of the individual and the aspects of the environment that are important with regard to fit. Many do not have a theory to guide them in choosing the aspects of fit on which to focus. Furthermore, although most fit research assumes that an individual is best suited for environments that are most similar to his or her personality and needs, perhaps fit could occur if an individual is dissimilar to the environment but fulfills some missing aspect of that environment.

In the former conceptualization of fit, each person in the environment is like a link in a chain. The chain and each individual link are strongest when each link is like every other link. The latter conceptualization of fit, in contrast, is like a puzzle with pieces that are unique but fit together to form the overall picture. Muchinsky and Monahan (1987), George (1992) and Kristof (1996) refer to these very different views of fit as supplementary fit, in which the individual matches the characteristics of the people already in the job, and complementary fit, in which the individual contributes characteristics that are missing from the work environment.

Holland's theory seems to imply a supplementary fit view, particularly when focusing on individuals' affective reactions to their jobs and careers. However, from a performance or productivity perspective, complementary fit might actually lead to more positive outcomes. George (1992), Schneider (1987a, 1987b), and others have noted that while there might be powerful forces resulting in similarity across individuals occupying the same work setting, this similarity can lead to performance problems, particularly in the long term or when change is rapid. In fact, even in the short term and under stable conditions, complementary fit might have performance advantages.

For example, artistic individuals may offer unique viewpoints and creative solutions to a work group that is predominantly conventional. However, in order for such a beneficial outcome to be obtained, the work environment must not be overly rule-oriented or controlling, since such an environment might result in artistic individuals' failing to express their artistic nature in the workplace. Empirical research supports this line of reasoning. For example, George and Zhou (2001) reasoned that openness to experience would be associated with creative performance in the workplace to the extent that the work context supports, and allows for the manifestation of, creative inclinations. Consistent with their reasoning, they found that individuals who were high on openness to experience were the most creative when they were performing heuristic tasks and received positive feedback.

More generally, research is needed that addresses the question of whether "complementary fit and supplementary fit [are] compatible with each other or are . . . always going to be incompatible" (George, 1992, p. 197). This unanswered research question is particularly troubling for fit research. More specifically, fit research seems to assume that fit results in positive outcomes and that these positive outcomes cluster together. Clearly, this may not be so, and in the case of an artistic individual in a supportive yet conventional environment, productivity could improve at the loss of job satisfaction.

Conceptually, fit is a thorny matter. Even if researchers could agree on a conceptual definition of fit, Weiss and Brief (in press) question the usefulness of fit in explaining the process by which people generate judgments like satisfaction. Arguing that people probably do not make conscious or unconscious comparisons between their own goals, values, and needs and the offerings of the environment, Weiss and Brief conclude that the fit concept "appears not to deserve its explanatory monopoly" (p. 52). They encourage research that would aid in the explanation of fit processes rather than mere prediction of outcomes related to fit.

Tinsley (2000), taking a more extreme position, asserted that most fit research suffers from a confirmatory bias; therefore, research should be conducted to "actively investigate possibilities that would disconfirm the P-E [person-environment] fit model" (p. 153). For example, Tinsley encouraged further investigation of the "present status model," which posits that vocational outcomes are only a product of the supplies and demands of the job. This model assumes that individual differences in values and abilities are relatively unimportant in outcomes like satisfaction compared to the rewards (supplies) and requirements (demands) of the job.

Beyond the conceptual challenges of fit research are important measurement issues in need of resolution. Correlations between congruence, in terms of the RIASEC personality types, and job satisfaction vary depending on the method of measuring congruence (Assouline & Meir, 1987). For example, congruence can be defined in terms of the individual's and environment's predominant Holland type, such as in the case of a realistic person in a realistic environment. Alternatively, the individual and environment might be described in terms of their highest (predominant), second highest, and third highest Holland scores, creating a profile like realistic-investigative-conventional. Operational problems for approaches to fit other than Holland's also are evident. For example, the TWA (Dawis et al., 1964) recognizes that fit is a dynamic process; therefore, researchers must decide the timing and frequency with which they assess both the individual and the environment. As of now, though, such process issues are ignored in large part.

Depending on the method employed, congruence may appear to be more or less related to outcomes like satisfaction. An additional consideration, recognized by Tranberg et al. (1993) and Young et al. (1998), is the variation of the congruence-satisfaction correlation between different Holland types. It appears that fit may be more important for some people than others, which may cause different individuals to display different types of reactions when faced with a poor match to the environment. Clearly, fit research will be further complicated if personality is considered not only as an aspect of the person or environment, but also as an important moderator of the relationship between fit and outcomes like satisfaction. Most fit researchers operate under the assumption that fit is equally important across people and situations. However, observations like those of Tranberg et al. and Young et al. should perhaps prompt researchers to explore cases in which fit is *not* important.

In sum, fit is not a unitary construct, particularly because of the dynamic nature of fit. The TWA, for example, asserts that correspondence or fit should be viewed as a process rather than a static entity. Because most fit research is cross-sectional, little is known about how individuals and environments change over time to achieve, or not achieve, fit (Furnham, 2001). Fit may increase or decrease over time, and only through longitudinal research can such patterns be revealed.

Cross-sectional research can not explain whether individuals themselves become more similar to their work environment or whether people alter their work environments. Dissimilar individuals might simply exit the environment in search of a more suitable environment. Another possibility is that fit may not matter in some cases, or change may not be feasible for certain people in certain situations. A single mother with little education, for example, likely will not achieve fit (fulfilling her need for a living wage) by moving from one low-paying, low-status job to another, with more rewarding jobs likely beyond her reach. Thus, questions of when and for whom fit matters remain.

The fit concept is more ambiguous than perhaps many researchers have acknowledged. Schneider (2001), addressing the state of fit research, concluded, "There is considerable ambiguity over what is appropriate research from a person-environment perspective; there are fits over fit" (p. 150). Schneider argued that although a broad definition of fit results in ambiguity, such an encompassing view allows scholars to answer many different types of questions from many different perspectives. We are less enthusiastic and optimistic than Schneider. More specifically, we believe that the meaningful accumulation of knowledge is dependent on a consistent and coherent conceptual definition of fit. If fit researchers are not willing to articulate and evaluate their conceptualizations of fit, the rest of us can only be left to guess at just what fit means and why it is so important. (For more on the general issue of fit, see, for example, Edwards, 1994.)

Personality and Occupations at Lower Levels of Specificity

While the use of higher-order personality traits and types to study personality-outcome relationships certainly has been productive, we argue that research likely will benefit from employing more specific trait descriptors. Guion (1991), for example, has advocated the use of more specific personality predictors, arguing that they are more directly work related and face valid than Big Five traits. Consistent with this advocacy, Moon (2001) found that two facets of conscientiousness, duty and achievement striving, affect decision making in escalation situations in an opposite manner. In his study, while conscientiousness per se was not significantly associated with escalation of commitment, achievement striving was positively associated, and duty was negatively associated, with escalation of commitment. These results suggest that looking at the overall correlations between Big Five traits and career outcomes might be misleading to the extent that facets of the Big Five have differential relations with the outcomes that offset each other when overall measures are used.

More generally, Paunonen and Ashton (2001) found that facets of the Big Five had stronger associations with criterion variables than the Big Five traits themselves. Consistently, Saucier and Ostendorf (1999) have asserted, "A broad factor is not so much one thing as a collection of many things that have something in common. It is easy to be overly schematic, ignoring the diverse character of the variables contained within a broad factor. A better way to understand each factor might be to characterize its crucial subcomponents, which, although correlated, are conceptually distinct" (p. 613).

Some Big Five facet researchers (Costa & McCrae, 1985; Goldberg, 1990), working from a hierarchical perspective, have viewed each facet as a lower-order subcomponent of only one of the Big Five factors. In contrast, the Abridged Big Five Dimensional Circumplex taxonomy of personality traits depicts facets as blends of the two Big Five factors on which they load the highest (Hofstee, de Raad, & Goldberg, 1992). For example, the subcomponent domineering primarily loads positively on extraversion but has a secondary negative loading on agreeableness. It appears that some subcomponents (but not most) are truly hierarchical in nature, loading on only one factor, while other subcomponents tend to load on two or more factors. Regardless of whether a facet falls beneath single or multiple factors, it may relate to outcomes like career choice and job satisfaction in different ways than the five broad-based factor (or factors) to which it belongs.

Competitiveness, for example, which falls within the extraversion-conscientiousness sector (with positive loadings on both), might be related to choice of a career or organization in which individual efforts and success are rewarded. Competitive individuals likely need to feel they are getting ahead, so this personality trait might also predict the number of promotions or salary increases an individual receives over time. In contrast, boisterousness, which also fits in the extraversion-conscientiousness sector (with a positive loading on extraversion and a negative loading on conscientiousness), might also be related to a desire to succeed and get ahead of one's peers. However, boisterous individuals, unlike competitive individuals, may be more prone to irritate their coworkers and supervisors. Thus, they may be less likely than competitive individuals to receive promotions and salary increases. Despite similarly high extraversion scores, the competitive individual and the boisterous individual could plausibly have very different career outcomes.

Just as personality may be broadly or narrowly conceptualized, so, too, may occupations. For example, the broad occupational title "lawyer" includes courtroom defense lawyers, prosecuting attorneys, tax lawyers, environmental lawyers, and lawyers who specialize in divorce or family law. These specialties of law certainly share some common aspects; however, the daily tasks and work environments differ in important ways between some of these areas. The trial lawyer, for example, may be better described by Holland's enterprising type and be higher in extraversion than the tax lawyer, who may be closer to Holland's conventional or realistic type and display high conscientiousness. Consequently, researchers who explore only generic career categories like "lawyer," "teacher," or "nurse" might misinterpret the extent to which people in career specialties (kindergarten teacher versus college professor) have similar personalities.

In addition to the influence that personality may have on choice of specialty within a career, personality also has been shown to be related to the organizations that individuals join. In fact, Schneider's (1987a) attraction-selection-attrition model asserts that organizations are relatively homogeneous in terms of personality and demographic variables because people are differentially attracted to, selected by, and retained by the organization. This theory has received support in several investigations (Schneider, Goldstein, & Smith, 1995; Schneider, Smith, Taylor, & Fleenor, 1998), indicating that organizations can be defined by the characteristics of people in them.

Researchers generally have not considered how personality and occupational and organizational memberships might interact to affect an individual's career outcomes. For example, a personality trait or type that typically is not suitable for a particular sort of organization might be especially suitable for a particular type of occupation, and it may be that ideal occupational characteristics compensate for less than desirable organizational attributes (and vice versa).

Limitations to Free Choice

The focus of this chapter has been to address the role of personality in careers, particularly career choice. In some cases, however, personality may have very little to do with the choices people make about jobs and the decisions they make once in a job. Factors such as race, gender, nationality, parental socioeconomic status, physical and cognitive abilities, and the physical environment may preclude any possible effects that personality has on careers. Scholars such as Hotchkiss and Borow (1996) and Gottfredson (1996) have considered such limiting factors in their studies of careers.

Gottfredson's theory of circumscription and compromise (1996), for example, views vocational choice "largely as a process of eliminating options and narrowing one's choices" (p. 182) and explores "how individuals compromise their goals, wisely or not, in coming to terms with reality as they try to implement their aspirations" (p. 182). The theory considers, among other factors, the importance of aspects of a career such as prestige, field of interest, and gender type (that some careers are thought to be "masculine" while others are perceived as "feminine"). Depending on the attractiveness of alternatives that individuals have available to them when choosing a career, individuals will have to make small, moderate, or great compromises. When a number of attractive alternatives exist and compromise is low, the individual's interests and personality are thought to be of prime importance. In contrast, when attractive options are few to none, individuals are believed to forgo their interests and select a career that fits their gender type. Men especially appear to be averse to engaging in "feminine" work, while women are more open to cross-gender occupations (Betz, Heesacker, & Shuttleworth, 1990).

Despite evidence that occupations in industrialized societies are less sex segregated today than in the past, Reskin (1993) argued that the majority of workers do not pursue cross-gender occupations and that women, in particular, face barriers to entering, remaining, and succeeding in certain types of jobs. For example,

Crittenden (2001, p. 36) reports that "a 206-page guidebook put out by the Harvard Women's Law Association in 1995 . . . advised . . . 'Act like a man and time your pregnancies appropriately.'" Moreover, some women in careers such as law perceive that they cannot have children and be successful in a sizable organization such as a large law firm (Crittenden, 2001).

Race also limits access to certain occupational pursuits. Although race-segregated work, like sex-segregated work, appears to be on the decline, racial minorities remain overly represented in low-status, low-income occupations (Saunders, 1995). Clearly, this sad state of affairs is attributable at least in part to racial discrimination (Brief, 1998; Brief & Hayes, 1997).

Arguably, personality will have a lesser effect on career choice for low-income individuals than for middle- and upper-class individuals. For example, parents in low-paying service careers might not introduce their children to the possibility of a career that requires extensive training or education because they cannot afford to provide their children with such opportunities.

In sum, despite the many potential influences personality may have on careers, under certain conditions the effects of personality may be negligible due to constraints (real or imagined) on individuals' freedom of choice. We have touched on only a few of the many real factors such as gender, race, socioeconomic status, education, and the physical and economic environment that may limit the free choice people have in relation to their careers.

Conclusion

Although we have argued that researchers should move beyond the Big Five in their studies of careers, we have not directed them to or proposed a "better" approach. Rather, we have urged researchers to expand their views of personality and careers from multiple vantage points. Personality has the potential to play multiple roles in occupational and organizational choice, number of career moves, psychological adjustment to work, job performance, and extrinsic and intrinsic career success. Understanding of these multiple roles will be enhanced to the extent that we can enrich and expand our current conceptualizations of personality, work, careers, and career success.

Moreover, career research is likely to advance to the extent that we are able to address certain ongoing challenges and potential areas of concern for career researchers. Clearly, given the status and popularity of the fit construct in this literature, theorists and researchers must strive to develop conceptual and empirical clarity and consensus on the types, nature, causes, consequences, and measurement of fit.

In addition, there are level-of-analysis issues on both the personality and career sides of the equation that need to be addressed both theoretically and empirically. Moreover, an implicit and often explicit assumption in this literature is freedom of choice and individual potency in all aspects of work and career choice. However, ample statistics and evidence point to the real obstacles portions of the working population face that serve to limit their work and career choices. Rather than continuing to ignore or neglect consideration of these constraints, we urge researchers to consider limits to free choice in their studies of personality and careers and ways to overcome such limits.

The study of personality in the careers literature, with few exceptions (Judge et al., 1999), appears to have gone adrift. This need not be the case. The study of personality and careers can become interesting and exciting once again if we enrich and broaden our perspectives while constructively challenging the status quo.

References

Ackerman, P. L., & Heggestad, E. D. (1997). Intelligence, personality, and interests: Evidence for overlapping traits. *Psychological Bulletin, 121,* 219–245.

Arthur, M. B., Hall, D. T., & Lawrence, B. S. (1989). *Handbook of career theory.* Cambridge: Cambridge University Press.

Arthur, M. B., & Rousseau, D. M. (1996). *The boundaryless career: A new employment principle for a new organizational era.* New York: Oxford University Press.

Assouline, M., & Meir, E. (1987). Meta-analysis of the relationship between congruence and well-being measures. *Journal of Vocational Behavior, 28,* 319–332.

Astin, A. W., & Holland, J. L. (1961). The environmental assessment technique: A way to measure college environments. *Journal of Educational Psychology, 52,* 308–316.

Barrick, M. R., & Mount, M. K. (1991). The Big Five personality dimensions and job performance: A meta-analysis. *Personnel Psychology, 44,* 1–26.

Barrick, M. R., & Mount, M. K. (1993). Autonomy as a moderator of the relationships between the Big Five personality dimensions and job performance. *Journal of Applied Psychology, 78,* 111–118.

Betz, N. E., Fitzgerald, L. F., & Hill, R. E. (1989). Trait-factor theories: Traditional cornerstone of career theory. In M. B. Arthur, D. T. Hall, & B. S. Lawrence (Eds.), *Handbook of career theory* (pp. 26–40). Cambridge: Cambridge University Press.

Betz, N. E., Heesacker, R. S., & Shuttleworth, C. (1990). Moderators of the congruence and realism of major and occupations plans of college students: A replication and extension. *Journal of Counseling Psychology, 37,* 269–276.

Block, J. (1995). A contrarian view of the five-factor approach to personality description. *Psychological Bulletin, 117,* 187–215.

Brief, A. P. (1998). *Attitudes in and around organizations.* Thousand Oaks, CA: Sage.

Brief, A. P., & Hayes, E. L. (1997). The continuing "American dilemma": Studying racism in organizations. In C. L. Cooper and D. M. Rousseau (Eds.), *Trends in organizational behavior.* New York: Wiley.

Brown, D., Brooks, L., and Associates. (1984). *Career choice and development.* San Francisco: Jossey-Bass.

Burke, M. J., Brief, A. P., & George, J. M. (1993). The role of negative affectivity in understanding relations between self-reports of stressors and strains: A comment on the applied psychology literature. *Journal of Applied Psychology, 78,* 402–412.

Cable, D., & Judge, T. (1997). Interviewers' perception of person-organization fit and organizational selection decisions. *Journal of Applied Psychology, 82,* 546–561.

Cantor, N. (1990). From thought to behavior: "Having" and "doing" in the study of personality and cognition. *American Psychologist, 45,* 735–750.

Cantor, N., & Langston, C. A. (1989). "Ups and downs" of life tasks in a life transition. In L. A. Pervin (Ed.), *Goal concepts in personality and social psychology* (pp. 127–167). Mahwah, NJ: Erlbaum.

Caspi, A., & Roberts, B. W. (2001). Personality development across the life course: The argument for change and continuity. *Psychological Inquiry, 12,* 49–66.

Chartrand, J. M., Rose, M. L., Elliott, T. R., Marmarosh, C., & Caldwell, S. (1993). Peeling back the onion: Personality, problem-solving, and career decision making style correlates of career indecision. *Journal of Career Assessment, 1,* 66–82.

Costa, P. T., Jr., & McCrae, R. R. (1985). *The NEO Personality Inventory manual*. Odessa, FL: Psychological Assessment Resources.

Costa, P. T., Jr., & McCrae, R. R. (1992). Four ways five factors are basic. *Personality and Individual Differences, 13*, 653–665.

Costa, P. T., Jr., McCrae, R. R., & Holland, J. L. (1984). Personality and vocational interests in an adult sample. *Journal of Applied Psychology, 69*, 390–400.

Costa, P. T., Jr., McCrae, R. R., & Kay, G. G. (1995). Persons, places and personality: Career assessment using the Revised NEO Personality Inventory. *Journal of Career Assessment, 3*, 123–139.

Costa, P. T., Jr., McCrae, R. R., & Zonderman, A. B. (1987). Environmental and dispositional influences on well-being: Longitudinal follow-up of an American national sample. *British Journal of Psychology, 78*, 299–306.

Crittenden, A. (2001). *The price of motherhood*. New York: Metropolitan Books.

Darley, J. G. (1941). *Clinical aspects and interpretation of the Strong Vocational Interest Blank*. New York: Psychological Corporation.

Darley, J. G., & Hagenah, T. (1955). *Vocational interest measurement: Theory and practice*. Minneapolis: University of Minnesota Press.

Dawis, R. V. (1996). The theory of work adjustment and person-environment correspondence counseling. In D. Brown, L. Brooks, and Associates, *Career choice and development* (pp. 75–120). San Francisco: Jossey-Bass.

Dawis, R. V., England, G. W., & Lofquist, L. H. (1964). A theory of work adjustment. *Minnesota Studies in Vocational Rehabilitation*, no. 15, 1–27.

Dawis, R. V., & Lofquist, L. H. (1984). *A psychological theory of work adjustment*. Minneapolis: University of Minnesota Press.

Dawis, R. V., Lofquist, L. H., & Weiss, D. J. (1968). A theory of work adjustment: A revision. *Minnesota Studies in Vocational Rehabilitation*, no. 23, 1–14.

Digman, J. M. (1989). Five robust trait dimensions: Development, stability, and utility. *Journal of Personality, 57*, 195–214.

Digman, J. M., & Takemoto-Chock, N. K. (1981). Factors in the natural language of personality: Re-analysis, comparison, and interpretation of six major studies. *Multivariate Behavioral Research, 16*, 149–170.

Edwards, J. R. (1994). The study of congruence in organizational behavior research: Critique and a proposed alternative. *Organizational Behavior and Human Decision Processes, 58*, 51–100 (erratum, *58*, 323–325).

Emmons, R. A. (1997). Motives and goals. In R. Hogan & J. Johnson (Eds.), *Handbook of personality psychology* (pp. 485–512). Orlando, FL: Academic Press.

Feldman, D. C. (1988). *Managing careers in organizations*. Glenview, IL: Scott, Foresman.

Furnham, A. (2001). Vocational preference and P-O fit: Reflections on Holland's theory of vocational choice. *Applied Psychology: An International Review, 50*, 5–29.

George, J. M. (1992). The role of personality in organizational life: Issues and evidence. *Journal of Management, 18*, 185–213.

George, J. M., & Jones, G. R. (2000). The role of time in theory and theory building. *Journal of Management, 26*, 657–684.

George, J. M., & Zhou, J. (2001). When openness to experience and conscientiousness are related to creative behavior: An interactional approach. *Journal of Applied Psychology, 86*, 513–524.

Gini, A. (2001). *My job, my self*. New York: Routledge.

Ginzberg, E., Ginsburg, S. W., Axelrad, S., & Herma, J. L. (1951). *Occupational choice: An approach to a general theory*. New York: Columbia University Press.

Goh, D. S., & Leong, F. T. (1993). The relationship between Holland's theory of vocational interest and Eysenck's model of personality. *Personality and Individual Differences, 15*, 555–562.

Goldberg, L. R. (1990). An alternative "description of personality": The Big-Five factor structure. *Journal of Personality and Social Psychology, 59*, 1216–1229.

Gottfredson, L. S. (1996). Gottfredson's theory of circumscription and compromise. In D. Brown, L. Brooks, & Associates, *Career choice and development* (pp. 179–232). San Francisco: Jossey-Bass.

Guilford, J. P., Christensen, P. R., Bond, N. A., Jr., & Sutton, M. S. (1954). A factor analysis study of human interests. *Psychological Monographs, 68*, no. 375.

Guion, R. M. (1991). Personnel assessment, selection, and placement. In M. D. Dunnette & L. M. Hough (Eds.), *Handbook of industrial and organizational psychology* (2nd ed., Vol. 2, pp. 327–397). Palo Alto, CA: Consulting Psychologists Press.

Hall, D. T. (1976). *Careers in organizations*. Pacific Palisades, CA: Goodyear Publishing.

Harlow, R. E., & Cantor, N. (1994). A functional agenda for trait psychology. *Psychological Inquiry, 5*, 130–134.

Hofstee, W.K.B., de Raad, B., & Goldberg, L. R. (1992). Integration of the Big Five and circumplex approaches to trait structure. *Journal of Personality and Social Psychology, 63*, 146–163.

Hogan, R. T. (1982). Socioanalytic theory of personality. In M. M. Page (Ed.), *Nebraska Symposium on Motivation: Personality-current theory and research* (pp. 55–89). Lincoln: University of Nebraska Press.

Holland, J. L. (1959). A theory of vocational choice. *Journal of Counseling Psychology, 6,* 35–45.

Holland, J. L. (1966). A psychological classification scheme for vocations and major fields. *Journal of Counseling Psychology, 13,* 278–288.

Holland, J. L. (1968). Explorations of a theory of vocational choice: IV. A longitudinal study using a sample of typical college students. *Journal of Applied Psychology, 52,* 1–37.

Holland, J. L. (1973). *Making vocational choices: A theory of careers.* Upper Saddle River, NJ: Prentice Hall.

Holland, J. L. (1976). Vocational preferences. In M. D. Dunnette (Ed.), *Handbook of industrial and organizational psychology* (pp. 521–571). Skokie, IL: Rand McNally.

Holland, J. L. (1985). *Making vocational choices.* Upper Saddle River, NJ: Prentice Hall.

Holland, J. L. (1997). *Making vocational choices: A theory of vocational personalities and work environments* (3rd ed.). Odessa, FL: Psychological Assessment Resources.

Holland, J. L. (1999). Why interest inventories are also personality inventories. In M. L Savickas & A. R. Spokane (Eds.), *Vocational interests: Meaning measurement, and counseling use* (pp. 87–101). Palo Alto, CA: Davies-Black Publishing/Consulting Psychologists Press.

Holland, J. L., Johnston, J. A., & Asama, N. F. (1994). More evidence for the relationship between Holland's personality types and personality variables. *Journal of Career Assessment, 2,* 331–340.

Holland, J. L, Whitney, D. R., Cole, N. S., & Richards, J. M., Jr. (1969). *An empirical occupational classification derived from a theory of personality and intended for practice and research* (ACT Research Report No. 29). Iowa City: American College Testing Program.

Hotchkiss, L., & Borow, H. (1996). Sociological perspective on work and career development. In D. Brown, L. Brooks, and Associates, *Career choice and development* (pp. 281–334). San Francisco: Jossey-Bass.

John, O. P., Angleitner, A., & Ostendorf, F. (1988). The lexical approach to personality: A historical review of trait taxonomic research. *European Journal of Personality, 2,* 171–205.

Judge, T. A., Higgins, C. A., Thoresen, C. J., & Barrick, M.R. (1999). The Big Five personality traits, general mental ability, and career success across the life span. *Personnel Psychology, 52,* 621–652.

Kristof, A. (1996). Person-organization fit: An integrative review of its conceptualization, measurement, and implications. *Personnel Psychology, 49,* 1–49.

Kuder, G. F. (1946). *Manual, Kuder preference record, vocational.* Chicago: Science Research Associates.

Lent, R. W., Brown, S. D., & Hackett, G. (1994). Toward a unifying social cognitive theory of career and academic interest, choice, and performance. *Journal of Vocational Behavior, 45,* 79–122.

Little, B. R. (1989). Personal projects analysis: Trivial pursuits, magnificent obsessions, and the search for coherence. In D. M. Buss & N. Cantor (Eds.), *Personality psychology: Recent trends and emerging directions* (pp. 15–31). New York: Springer-Verlag.

Magnusson, D., & Toerestad, B. (1993). A holistic view of personality: A model revisited. In M. R. Rosenzweig & L. W. Porter (Eds.), *Annual review of psychology* (Vol. 44, pp. 427–452). Palo Alto, CA: Annual Reviews.

McCrae, R. R., & Costa, P. T., Jr. (1997). Personality trait structure as a human universal. *American Psychologist, 52,* 509–516.

McCrae, R. R., Costa, P. T., Jr., & Piedmont, R. L. (1993). Fold concepts, natural language, and psychological constructs: The California Psychological Inventory and the five-factor model. *Journal of Personality, 61,* 1–26.

Meir, E., Hadas, C., & Noyfeld, M. (1997). Person-environment fit in small army units. *Journal of Career Assessment, 5,* 21–29.

Moon, H. (2001). The two faces of conscientiousness: Duty and achievement striving in escalation of commitment dilemmas. *Journal of Applied Psychology, 86,* 533–540.

Muchinsky, P. M. (1999). Applications of Holland's theory in industrial and organizational settings. *Journal of Vocational Behavior, 55,* 127–135.

Muchinsky, P. M., & Monahan, C. J. (1987). What is person-environment congruence? Supplementary versus complementary models of fit. *Journal of Vocational Behavior, 31,* 268–277.

Parsons, F. (1909). *Choosing a vocation.* Boston: Houghton Mifflin.

Patton, W., & McMahon, M. (1999). *Career development and systems theory: A new relationship.* Pacific Grove, CA: Brooks/Cole.

Paunonen, S. V., & Ashton, M. C. (2001). Big Five factors and facets and the prediction of behavior. *Journal of Personality and Social Psychology, 81,* 524–539.

Paunonen, S. V., & Jackson, D. N. (2000). What is beyond the Big Five? Plenty! *Journal of Personality, 68,* 821–835.

Perone, M., DeWaard, R. J., & Baron, A. (1979). Satisfaction with real and simulated jobs in relation to personality variables and drug use. *Journal of Applied Psychology, 64,* 660–668.

Rayman, J., & Atanasoff, L. (1999). Holland's theory of career intervention: The power of the hexagon. *Journal of Vocational Behavior, 55,* 114–126.

Reskin, B. (1993). Sex segregation in the workplace. *Annual Review of Sociology, 19,* 241–270.

Roe, A. (1956). *The psychology of occupations.* New York: Wiley.

Sanderson, C. A., & Cantor, N. (1999). A life task perspective on personality coherence: Stability versus change in tasks, goals, strategies, and outcomes. In D. Cervone & Y. Shoda (Eds.), *The coherence of personality* (pp. 372–392). New York: Guilford Press.

Saucier, G., & Goldberg, L. R. (1998). What is beyond the Big Five? *Journal of Personality, 66,* 495–524.

Saucier, G., & Ostendorf, F. (1999). Hierarchical subcomponents of the Big Five personality factors: A cross-language replication. *Journal of Personality and Social Psychology, 76,* 613–627.

Saunders, L. (1995). Relative earnings of black men to white men by region, industry. *Monthly Labor Review, 118,* 68–73.

Savickas, M. L. (1999). The psychology of interests. In M. L Savickas & A. R. Spokane (Eds.), *Vocational interests: Meaning measurement, and counseling use* (pp. 87–101). Palo Alto, CA: Davies-Black Publishing/Consulting Psychologists Press.

Schinka, J. A., Dye, D. A., & Curtis, G. (1997). Correspondence between five-factor and RIASEC models of personality. *Journal of Personality Assessment, 68,* 355–368.

Schneider, B. (1987a). The people make the place. *Personnel Psychology, 40,* 437–453.

Schneider, B. (1987b). $E = f(P,B)$: The road to a radical approach to person-environment fit. *Journal of Vocational Behavior, 31,* 353–361.

Schneider, B. (2001). Fits about fit. *Applied Psychology: An International Review, 50,* 141–152.

Schneider, B., Goldstein, H. W., & Smith, D. B. (1995). The ASA framework: An update. *Personnel Psychology, 48,* 747–773.

Schneider, B., Smith, D. B., Taylor, S., & Fleenor, J. (1998). Personality and organizations: A test of the homogeneity of personality hypothesis. *Journal of Applied Psychology, 83,* 462–470.

Schneider, R. J., & Hough, L. M. (1995). Personality and industrial/organizational psychology. *International Review of Industrial and Organizational Psychology, 10,* 75–121.

Schwartz, R. H. (1992). Is Holland's theory worthy of so much attention, or should vocational psychology move on? *Journal of Vocational Behavior, 40,* 179–187.

Seibert, S. E., & Kraimer, M. L. (2001). The five-factor model of personality and career success. *Journal of Vocational Behavior, 58,* 1–21.

Seiss, T. F., & Jackson, D. N. (1970). Vocational interests and personality. *Journal of Counseling Psychology, 17,* 27–35.

Snyder, M., & Ickes, W. (1985). Personality and social behavior. In G. Lindzey & E. Aronson (Eds.), *Handbook of social psychology: Vol. 2.*

Special fields and applications (3rd ed., pp. 883–947). New York: Random House.

Spokane, A. R., Meir, E. I., & Catalano, M. (2000). Person-environment congruence and Holland's theory: A review and reconsideration. *Journal of Vocational Behavior, 57,* 137–187.

Strong, E. K., Jr. (1943). *Vocational interests of men and women.* Stanford, CA: Stanford University Press.

Super, D. E. (1957). *The psychology of careers: An introduction to vocational development.* New York: HarperCollins.

Tinsley, H.E.A. (2000). The congruence myth: An analysis of the efficacy of the person-environment fit model. *Journal of Vocational Behavior, 56,* 147–179.

Tokar, D. M., Fischer, A. R., & Subich, L. M. (1998). Personality and vocational behavior: A selective review of the literature, 1993–1997. *Journal of Vocational Behavior, 53,* 115–153.

Tokar, D. M., & Subich, L. M. (1997). Relative contributions of congruence and personality dimensions to job satisfaction. *Journal of Vocational Behavior, 50,* 482–491.

Tokar, D. M., & Swanson, J. L. (1995). Evaluation of the correspondence between Holland's vocational personality typology and the five-factor model of personality. *Journal of Vocational Behavior, 46,* 89–108.

Tranberg, M., Slane, S., & Ekeberg, S. (1993). The relation between interest congruence and satisfaction: A meta analysis. *Journal of Vocational Behavior, 42,* 253–264.

Tupes, E. C., & Christal, R. E. (1992). Recurrent personality factors based on trait ratings. *Journal of Personality, 60,* 225–251.

Walsh, W. B., Craik, K. H., & Price, R. H. (Eds.). (2000). *Person-environment psychology: New directions and perspectives* (2nd ed.). Mahwah, NJ: Erlbaum.

Wanberg, C. R., Watt, J. D., & Rumsey, D. J. (1996). Individuals without jobs: An empirical study of job-seeking behavior and reemployment. *Journal of Applied Psychology, 81,* 76–87.

Watson, D., & Clark, L. A. (1984). Negative affectivity: The disposition to experience aversive emotional states. *Psychological Bulletin, 96,* 465–490.

Weiss, H., & Brief, A. P. (in press). Affect at work: An historical perspective. In R. L. Payne & C. L. Cooper (Eds.), *Emotions at work: Theory, research, and application in management.* New York: Wiley.

Young, G., Tokar, D. M., & Subich, L. M. (1998). Congruence revisited: Do 11 indices differentially predict job satisfaction and is the relation moderated by person and situation variables? *Journal of Vocational Behavior, 52,* 208–223.

CHAPTER 3

Skill Acquisition and Person-Environment Fit

Cheri Ostroff, Yuhyung Shin,
Barbara Feinberg

Since the 1900s, the notion of person-environment (P-E) fit or congruence has pervaded theory and research across many domains (Tinsley, 2000) and has been used to examine relationships between individuals and the environments in which they find themselves (Ostroff, 1993). The basic premise of the fit literature is that alignment between characteristics of people and their environments results in positive outcomes for individuals and organizations alike (Schneider, Smith, & Goldstein, 2000). Fit between person and environment has been related to greater satisfaction, commitment, performance, adjustment, job involvement, and longer tenure at the individual level and to greater productivity, effectiveness, cohesiveness, and reduced turnover at the group and organizational level (Kristof, 1996; Spokane, 1985).

The alignment between person and environment can be supplementary, in that the characteristics of people are similar to those of others in their environment, or complementary, whereby deficiencies in the environment are made up for by individual strengths (Muchinsky & Monahan, 1987). Supplementary fit is often deemed more important for individual outcomes and complementary fit for organizational outcomes (Schneider et al., 2000).

Person-occupation (P-OC) fit is a form of P-E fit that generally refers to supplementary fit between characteristics of individuals and those of their occupation. The focus here has largely been on congruence between individuals' interests and occupational types or congruence between individuals' preferences (for autonomy or challenge, for example) and the reinforcements offered by the job. Individuals are continuously trying to find occupations, organizations, and jobs that best suit their interests, needs, values, goals, aptitudes, skills, and abilities. In other words, individuals try to achieve fit with their work environment across a number of dimensions. Of these various types of fit, how individuals achieve skill-based fit, or fit between their proficiencies and skills and those required by their occupations, has received the least attention (Tinsley, 2000).

This chapter addresses the role of skill acquisition in achieving person-occupation fit within a broader P-E fit framework. We provide an overview of relevant P-E fit concepts, develop a general model that serves as a heuristic for examining linkages between skill acquisition and fit, provide an overview of some of the factors that drive the decision process for determining which occupations fit one's talents and abilities, and address the extent to which traditional means for skill acquisition (such as education, training, work experience, and internships) have an impact on person-occupation fit.

Theories of Person-Environment Fit

Three broad-based distinctions among P-E fit constructs can be delineated. The first addresses individual desires and environmental supplies (Edwards, 1991; Tinsley, 2000). Desires reflect personal needs, goals, values, interests, and preferences; they essentially pertain to the attractiveness of various job attributes to employees. Environmental supplies refer to the reinforcers, benefits, and payoffs provided by the work environment and include characteristics such as pay, role clarity, autonomy, participation in decision making, and challenge.

The second class of P-E fit constructs pertains to abilities and demands (Edwards, 1991). Abilities pertain to individuals' education, experience, aptitudes, abilities, and intelligence, while environmental demands reflect work environment characteristics such as workload, task requirements, and ability requirements. Fit between desires and supplies and between abilities and demands is believed to be important for improving individuals' attitudes, decreasing their stress, stabilizing their tenure in vocations, and enhancing their job performance and occupational success.

A third distinction can be made among these classes of P-E fit theories by focusing on different levels of analysis: occupations, organizations, jobs, and groups (Kristof, 1996). That is, fit can be examined between individual characteristics and characteristics of (1) broad-based industry or occupational categories that encompass different organizations and jobs; (2) entire organizations in terms of cultures, values, and goals; (3) specific jobs within an organization and job attributes; and (4) work group characteristics and functions.

Occupational Level

At the occupational level, the assumption is that matching employees to occupations using aptitude tests, interviews, and information about occupational ability patterns leads to a more effective and stable labor force (Tinsley, 2000). By far, the best-known theories of person-occupation fit are Holland's theory of vocational choice (Holland, 1973, 1985) and the theory of work adjustment (Dawis & Lofquist, 1984; Lofquist & Dawis, 1991).

The preponderance of empirical studies have been directed at testing Holland's model (Tinsley, 2000). In Holland's theory, the primary focus has been on interests. Both individuals and the occupational environment are characterized by the RIASEC typology (realistic, investigative, artistic, social, enterprising, and conventional). Holland's original work suggests that the environment is a function of the career interests and nature of its members; thus, the environment is typically described in terms of the characteristics of people employed there. Individuals seek out vocations that have a career environment that matches their own interests. Congruence is posited to result in satisfaction, vocational stability, and achievement, whereas poor fit is likely to result in dissatisfaction and ultimately leaving that occupation to join an occupational environment that provides a better fit.

The theory of work adjustment (Lofquist & Dawis, 1991) was also originally developed as a model of vocational choice. Here, too, the focus is on a match between individuals' preferences or needs (for autonomy or challenge, for example) and the extent to which those attributes are reinforced by characteristics of the job. Although most often classified as a model of person-occupation fit, the theory of work adjustment has also been used to examine fit between people and specific jobs, as well as between characteristics of people and their organizations. It is also important to note that both Holland's theory and the theory of work adjustment have addressed ability-demand fit (Holland, 1985; Gottfredson & Holland, 1991; Lofquist & Dawis, 1991); however, the preponderance of the empirical work in P-OC fit testing these and related theories has been directed at the desire-supply aspect of fit.

Research has consistently demonstrated congruence between interests and occupations based on Holland's framework and between preferences or needs and environmental reinforcers based on the theory of work adjustment; congruence has been consistently related to academic achievement, academic persistence, vocational stability, satisfaction with career choice, and job satisfaction (Spokane, 1985; Rounds, Dawis, & Lofquist, 1987). Reviews and meta-analyses also consistently indicate that the relationship between congruence and outcomes is weak to moderate (Spokane, Meir, & Catalano, 2000; Tranberg, Slane, & Exberg, 1993). Many have argued that the weak findings for P-OC fit are due to measurement and methodological problems (Spokane et al., 2000). However, because P-E fit is a complex phenomenon, the weak findings could be due to failure to consider fit along a number of dimensions and levels simultaneously.

Organizational Level

In recent years, there has been burgeoning interest in person-organization (P-O) fit. The assumption is that positive outcomes for individuals are largely driven by fit to the organization, not simply fit to one's chosen occupation. That is, a person may achieve fit to his or her chosen occupation but not to the particular organization in which he or she carries out work since the cultures, climates, and values of individual organizations vary widely. P-O fit focuses on congruence between the values, needs, personality, or goals of individuals and the value systems, culture, climate, rewards, or goals of the organization. A greater degree of P-O fit has been related to a variety of individual outcomes, including increased satisfaction, commitment, adjustment, performance, and reduced turn-over (see Kristof, 1996, for a review).

Job Level

Specific jobs within occupations vary, and jobs with the same title often vary across organizations. Person-job (P-J) fit addresses fit between abilities and demands at the level of the specific job. Fit occurs when employees' proficiencies, skills, and abilities are congruent with job requirements (Werbel & Gilliland, 1999). P-J fit is the primary goal in selection. Jobs are first analyzed to determine the required knowledge, skills, and abilities for completing tasks, and then selection strategies are devised to assess applicants' skills and proficiencies to match them to job requirements (Brousseau, 1984). Actual P-J fit in terms of a profile comparison between individuals' competencies and job requirements has also been shown to relate to performance and job attitudes across a variety of jobs (Caldwell & O'Reilly, 1990).

Group Level

In recent years, the notion of person-group (P-G) fit has been proposed. It refers to a match between the individual and the immediate work group or work unit (Kristof, 1996). Models of P-G fit have included similarity between demographic characteristics of an individual and those of their work group (Jackson et al., 1991); similarity of personality, values, and goals (Klimoski & Jones, 1995); and possession of the necessary interpersonal skills for effective cooperation and communication with other group members (Werbel & Gilliland, 1999). Another type of P-G fit is complementary. Different group members may need to have unique characteristics or skills that complement, rather than replicate, one another (Werbel & Gilliland, 1999).

Statis Versus Dynamic Fit

Most P-E fit treatments employ a static model, focusing on relatively stable aspects of the person and the environment. Moreover, most empirical tests have examined congruence at a fixed, single point in time (Spokane et al., 2000). However, P-E fit is both a developmental and dynamic process (Tinsley, 2000). The dynamic nature of the fit process is explicitly addressed in Holland's theory, the theory of work adjustment, and some models of P-O fit (Schneider et al., 2000); in these models, both the individual and the environment affect and cause change in each other.

The developmental nature of fit has also been addressed in the gravitational hypothesis (McCormick, DeNisi, & Staw, 1979); over the course of their labor market experiences, individuals are posited to gravitate to or sort themselves into jobs that are compatible with their interests, values, and abilities. According to this hypothesis, it is assumed that a lack of fit will prompt a change in career, organization, or job in the hope of achieving greater fit. However, this theory and subsequent tests of it focus primarily on ability-demand fit rather than desire-supply fit.

Taken together, the research on fit suggests that people who better fit their occupation, organization, job, and group will have more positive career outcomes. While determining which occupation fits their interests best is an important challenge for individuals, they must also be able to develop skills and abilities that fit their occupations, and find work in groups and organizations that value and use those goals. Thus, our primary focus in this chapter is on skill acquisition and its role in achieving fit.

A General Framework

Career success has been defined as the real or perceived achievements individuals have accumulated as a result of their work experiences; it comprises both extrinsic and intrinsic components (Judge, Higgins, Thoresen, & Barrick, 1999). Extrinsic components consist of visible outcomes, such as pay, advancement, and occupational status, while intrinsic components include an individual's subjective reactions to his or her own career and job attitudes.

Figure 3.1 presents a general model for achieving fit during young adulthood and indicates that the skill acquisition process is ultimately related to fit along a number of dimensions. Our general framework is informed by Pervin's goal model of P-E fit (1983, 1989). Individuals are assumed to be goal directed and their behavior motivated by the consideration of multiple goals.

Goals have a cognitive component (a picture of the desired end point and construction of plans or paths to achieve that end), an affective component (the affect associated with goals), and a behavioral component (the behaviors associated with plans or paths to goal achievement). This conceptualization is useful because occupational choice among young adults essentially involves determining an occupational goal or aspiration, developing a plan for achieving that goal (including development of skills and abilities necessary for occupational attainment), and considering the affective responses to those goals and choices (Lent, Brown, & Hackett, 1994).

An individual's background and social demographic status (for example, family characteristics, socioeconomic status, gender, race), personal characteristics (for example, self-esteem, self-awareness, decision-making ability), experiences (for example, work, academic experiences, hobbies), and initial skill levels (for example, cognitive abilities, technical skills, interpersonal skills) are important factors in determining one's occupational interests and aptitudes. These interests and perceived talents help the individual to make an initial occupational choice and formulate career goals. This implies that (1) information pertaining to one's occupational goal must be gathered through self-assessment of one's interests and talents, inquiries about different careers, experiences, counseling and vocational services, mentors, internships, and so forth; and (2) appropriate skills must be acquired to meet one's career initial aspiration, through formal or informal training and education, and work experiences.

Individuals' reactions to reaching, or failing to reach, goals are also important considerations (Pervin, 1983). Individuals are likely to reassess and reevaluate their career goals continuously as they learn more and acquire more skills. Positive responses from the environment tend to result in greater goal persistence, persistence in career choice, and relevant skill acquisition, whereas negative reactions will likely entail a reassessment and potential shifting of goals and career choices (Lent et al., 1994). This suggests that initial assessment of P-OC fit will be based largely on one's experiences during the skill acquisition process. However, since congruence rarely involves a relationship between a single attribute or personality characteristic and a single dimension of the environment

Figure 3.1. A Model for Achieving Fit During Early Career.

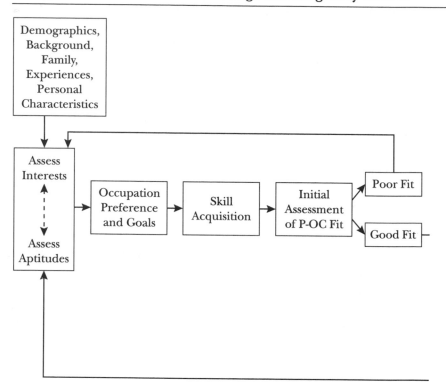

(Pervin, 1989), fit in terms of desire-supply, ability-demand, and different levels (occupation, organization, group, and job) must also be considered.

Our model suggests that if the initial assessment of fit is poor in terms of either desire-supply or ability-demand, reevaluation is likely, and choosing another occupation is warranted. If the initial assessment of fit is positive during skill acquisition, individuals eventually will seek out jobs that also fit their personalities, values, and specific sets of competencies. In contrast, poor P-OC fit in terms of desire-supply is likely to prompt starting over with the assessment of vocational interests and aptitudes.

Other types of poor fit may also motivate different kinds of career transitions. For example, if P-O fit is poor, individuals are likely to attempt to change organizations. If P-G fit is poor, individuals

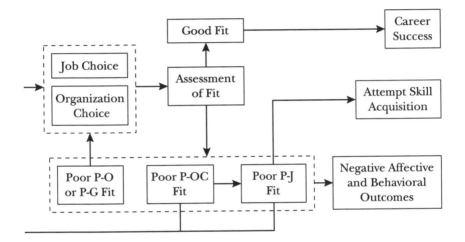

may be motivated to seek transfers or relocations. If P-J fit is poor, several different scenarios are possible. If both P-OC fit and P-J fit are low, individuals may be prompted to begin the process of occupational choice again. If P-OC fit remains high but P-J fit is poor, individuals may attempt to change to a job better suited to their skills but within the same career category. They may also attempt to acquire additional training or skills to enhance P-J fit. If P-J fit still continues to be poor, this may prompt starting over with more general assessment of interests and aptitudes. If poor fit persists on any major dimension, negative outcomes are more likely to result.

Given that our primary focus is on the skill acquisition process in the young adult years, we direct our attention in the remainder of this chapter to the means of acquiring skills and assessing outcomes of ability-demand fit for occupations (the bold linkages in

Figure 3.1). However, given that multiple types of fit are critical in understanding this process fully, we address skill acquisition within the broader P-E fit domain.

Antecedents of Fit

A large number of antecedent variables have been studied in relation to occupational choice in early career development. It is beyond the scope of this chapter to review antecedent factors (see Chapters Two and Four in this volume), but we touch on a few of the factors that may be particularly relevant to fit and skill acquisition.

Gender differences in vocational interests, for example, tend to be much larger than ethnic differences (Arbona, 2000). When individuals' gender is consistent with sex concentration of the job (for example, males in male-dominated occupations), satisfaction tends to increase as congruence between interest and occupation increases. However, little impact of congruence on satisfaction is observed when gender is inconsistent with sex concentration of the occupation (Fricko & Beehr, 1992). Interactions among gender, socioeconomic, race, and achievement perceptions have also been related to choice of college major characterized by Holland interest types (Trusty & Ng, 2000).

Empirical work has consistently shown that different personality characteristics (the Big Five traits, for example) are differentially related to occupational types, particularly Holland's types (Hogan & Blake, 1996). In a comparison of vocational interests and personality characteristics, vocational interests (Holland RIASEC types) were found to be more predictive of the type of employment an individual entered (occupational group), whereas personality traits were more predictive of whether an individual was employed and in what organization (De Fruyt & Mervielde, 1999). In general, interests appear to be more directly related to P-OC fit, while personality may be more relevant for P-O, P-J, or P-G group after congruence is achieved at the occupational level.

Relative Role of Interests-Desires and Aptitudes-Abilities

The preponderance of empirical work in P-OC fit has addressed the importance of interests in relation to occupations. The most commonly used vocational interest inventories focus largely on preferences for behaviors, situations, reinforcer systems, roles, activities, and types of people (Hogan & Blake, 1996). Thus, based on the nature of these measures, studies testing P-OC fit models typically assess desire-supply fit. From a practical standpoint, interest inventories have been heavily used to guide young adults into careers. However, vocational and career counselors often acknowledge that the work world is too complex to predict behavior based on an interest inventory (Spokane, 1985). Therefore, the focus on desire-supply congruence as operationalized in terms of interests does not appear to be sufficient. Indeed, previous research suggests that work experiences, school studies, institutional pressures, and pressures from parents or others may be stronger influences on occupational choices than interests (Borow, 1966).

Ability-demand congruence is also embedded in theories of P-OC fit (Tracey & Hopkins, 2001). In fact, there is some evidence that young adults gravitate to occupations commensurate with their abilities over time. In a series of studies (Wilk, Desmarais, & Sackett, 1995; Wilk & Sackett, 1996), cognitive ability predicted movement in an occupational hierarchy (based on occupation and job complexity within occupation) over five- to fourteen-year periods. Individuals in jobs that required higher cognitive ability than what they possessed tended to move to lower-level occupational jobs over time; individuals in jobs with more cognitive ability than demanded by their jobs tended to move toward higher occupational jobs over time. Moreover, the extent of ability-demand incongruence was greater in earlier time periods. This suggests that individuals gravitate to occupations commensurate with their abilities and then stay in those occupations.

Recently, typologies of occupations based on duties and skill requirements have been developed in an effort to move beyond classifying occupations based on the personal characteristics of incumbents within them (Gottfredson & Holland, 1991; Gottfredson & Richards, 1999). Similar structures between abilities and interests have been found along Holland types (Prediger, 1999). Aptitude-based work categories that overlap with interest characteristics of jobs along Holland's model have also been delineated (Gottfredson, 1986). Thus, aptitude and ability demands are related to interest-based models, but the relationship occurs largely through the activity demands that different occupations make. For example, realistic occupations involve the extensive use of hands, tools, and machines but require little involvement with people, whereas the reverse is true of social occupations (Gottfredson & Richards, 1999).

Given the importance of both abilities and interests in P-OC fit, it is surprising that little research has examined their relative and combined effects. Research has shown that interests and abilities have a high level of correspondence with occupational choice, but their relative importance has not been consistently demonstrated. For example, interests appeared to be more predictive of occupational choice than self-rated abilities in a sample of high school seniors (Tracey & Hopkins, 2001), while abilities appeared to be more predictive of long-term occupational membership than interests (Austin & Hanish, 1990).

Studies examining both interest-supply and ability-demand congruence as they relate to outcomes are rare. However, a series of studies by Meir and Melamed (for example, Meir & Melamed, 1986; Meir, Melamed, & Dinur, 1995) illustrates that when fit is assessed by aggregating across multiple aspects of congruence, it is consistently related to greater well-being, such as job satisfaction and reduced stress, than when fit is assessed by only a single aspect of congruence. In a related study, Fricko and Beehr (1992) found that congruence between college major and occupation was related to subsequent career satisfaction, but congruence between interests and occupation choice was not. Fricko and Beehr note that while students may choose majors on the basis of interests, they also presumably acquire some skills and expertise in their major areas as well. Thus, one reason for the stronger findings of college major as opposed to career interests is that college major reflects fit in terms of both interests and abilities.

Taken together, it is clear that abilities are as important as interests in understanding P-E and P-OC fit. However, the role of abilities has often been underplayed by vocational counselors (Austin & Hanish, 1990) and has been underresearched. Furthermore, the inconsistent findings on the role of abilities relative to interests may be due in part to when interests and abilities are measured. Occupational interests and abilities crystallize at different points in individuals' development (Snell, Stokes, Sands, & McBride, 1994), often well into their twenties (Gottfredson, 1979; Worthington & Juntunen, 1997). Thus, early measures of interests may not be strongly predictive of later vocational outcomes. In addition, there is likely to be a reciprocal and dynamic relationship between interests and abilities in achieving P-OC fit.

Dynamics Among Interests, Abilities, Skill Acquisition, and Fit

If individuals are successful in matching their interests to occupations and developing appropriate skills, few people would change jobs or occupations in their first few years on the job. Yet initial choices do not always result in good occupation, organization, or job fit, prompting a change (Gottfredson, 1977; Wilk & Sackett, 1996). In a sample of young adults in their first career experiences who made a job change, McCall (1990) found that 41 percent changed occupations when they changed jobs and 59 percent stayed in the same occupation but changed employers. There was also considerable variation across occupations in the percentage of individuals switching—for example, 62 percent in sales versus 31 percent in professional occupations. Similarly, in a study of newly hired bank tellers, 45 percent left their initial organization within four months, but two-thirds of those who left became reemployed in the same occupational category (Gottfredson & Holland, 1990). Taken together, these studies imply that job change (that is, change to another employer) without occupation change may be a search for better P-O fit, while job change with occupation change indicates that people are continuing to search for an occupation that results in a better fit on any number of dimensions.

To understand early career turnover better, the dynamic relationship between vocational interests and work skills needs to be more fully explored. Few studies have specifically addressed such issues, particularly empirical and longitudinal studies. Nevertheless, a few insights can be gleaned from the available theory and research.

Dynamic Relationships

Interests help youth identify career goals in terms of liked or disliked activities, while abilities determine the range of available means for reaching those goals (Strong, 1955). An individual may be able to state an initial interest or preference for an occupation.

However, interest in that occupation may flag after exploring and beginning a path of acquiring skills if ability is weak or performance on work tasks is poor. Conversely, an individual may express little initial interest in a vocation but after exposure through learning, activities, or experiences, interest may rise. Thus, interest can prompt skill acquisition, and the skill acquisition process and experience can prompt rethinking of interests.

The social-cognitive career process theory (SSCT; Lent et al., 1994) proposes dynamic and reciprocal relationships among interests, abilities, career goals, career choice, and skill acquisition. At early ages, children do not typically have a good grasp of their capabilities or various career paths and hence are likely to have fluid career interests and goals. As adolescents gain more experience and skills with a variety of performance tasks through formal educational experiences, hobbies, and activities and the outcomes associated with these tasks, they begin to develop differentiated notions of their self-efficacy (beliefs about their ability to perform certain types of tasks). Moreover, as their interests become more defined and stable, teenagers revise their career goals. Thus, perceptions of competence based on learning and task experience nurture interest, which in turn motivates intentions to continue engaging in the task or acquiring relevant skills.

In contrast, negative task experiences and self-efficacy beliefs about the ability to perform well in activities provoke dislike and avoidance, thereby reducing interest in the career goals of vocations related to those tasks. Thus, performance experiences in young adulthood continually provide opportunities for revising one's perceived talents and abilities and interests and altering career goals. Empirical studies offer some support for SSCT (Betz, Harmon, & Borgen, 1996; Chartrand, Camp, & McFadden, 1992; Feehan & Johnston, 1999; Gottfredson, 1979, 1994; Swaney & Prediger, 1985).

Furthermore, it is important to point out that self-perceptions about ability and talents play a critical role in achieving fit, independent of actual ability. Although some have argued that self-assessments are generally accurate reflections of ability (Prediger, 1999), attributions and perceptions play important roles, too. For example, after controlling for ability, women in engineering majors were more likely to persist in this major when they attributed success in their courses to their own efforts, whereas those changing majors attributed their departure to lack of ability (Nauta, Epperson, & Waggoner, 1999). Indeed, self-estimates of ability are often better predictors of career choice than measured abilities (Prediger, 1999).

Therefore, initial assessment of P-OC fit is likely to be an iterative and dynamic process. Early notions of one's interests and perceived talents are likely to drive formation of an initial career goal and plans for developing skills to achieve that goal. As more information is obtained through experience and skill development, interests and goals may change to achieve a better fit. A reassessment of interests and new occupational goals may be prompted when one dislikes the work engaged in during skill acquisition or when poor performance results. In such cases, new goals and new strategies for reaching these goals will result. Alternatively, during skill acquisition, interests may change to match one's chosen field (for example, college major or vocational training field), thereby increasing P-OC fit in a different way.

Skill Development and Fit

The skill acquisition process plays a critical role in occupational goal attainment. Here, we address the different types of skills that individuals need and the mechanisms young adults can use to acquire these skills.

Universal-Generalizable Skills Versus Specific-Technical Skills

Due to the rapid changes in today's workplace (Cappelli et al., 1997), generalizable, universal skills may help an employee attain higher wages and be more valued by employers over a longer period of time than narrow, specific technical skills (U.S. Department of Labor, 1992). In a large-scale longitudinal study from childhood through age twenty-one, poor basic skills (literacy and math) led to problems acquiring broader work-related personal skills, such as interpersonal skills, flexibility, adaptability, and ability to work in a team. Furthermore, basic skills were found to be critical factors for gaining employment after leaving school, but personal skills were more important to successful functioning on the job itself (Bynner, 1997).

Therefore, both specific proficiency and more universal generalizable skills are necessary for career success, as well as to meet the needs of today's employers (Ryan, 2000). The relative importance of these different skill sets, though, is likely to depend on the occupation and job. For jobs that have major technical requirements, such as engineering, computer programming, and nursing, developing technical skills for P-J fit is critical. In contrast, in semiskilled labor occupations, technical skills may be learned on the job and broader-based skills may be more important (Werbel & Gilliland, 1999). Similarly, the changing work environment creates more transitory requirements for jobs and increases the need for greater adaptability and flexibility. Hence, the ability to work with others and update training may be more important than specific job skills in occupations operating in rapidly changing markets (Werbel & Gilliland, 1999).

Worthington and Juntunen (1997) propose that to reduce unemployment, changing jobs, and employment in low-skill jobs with little opportunity for advancement, young adults will need to learn both general skills (for example, dependability and punctuality) and industry-specific skills. A variety of formal and informal mechanisms, such as testing, counseling, internships, and mentoring, can aid young adults in the development of appropriate plans and skill acquisition.

Education and Training

Education and training programs purportedly provide young adults with skills that will enable them to enter some occupation. Much more work on fit has been conducted using samples of college students than high school graduates or those obtaining vocational credentials (Spokane et al., 2000). In particular, the focus has largely been on interests or relationships between college major and occupational choice. A 1991 review conducted by Pascarella and Terenzini concluded that academic major has a trivial impact on general intelligence and cognitive outcomes. However, once interests become more defined through exposure to different courses and information from placement offices, for example, college courses in one's major presumably allow one to focus on acquiring skills for that occupation. Some evidence suggests that students in majors congruent with their interests had higher grade point averages than incongruent students (Henry, 1989), providing indirect support that congruence between interests and abilities can result in better skill acquisition.

The importance of fit in acquiring skills during college was examined in a recent study by Feldman, Smart, and Ethington (1999). They found that students whose interests were congruent with their choice of major and students who switched to majors more consistent with their interests showed greater increases in relevant abilities for their occupations than did students with incongruent majors. This suggests that whether one's interests remain stable and congruent with academic field or whether one experiments and then achieves congruence, interest-based congruence is important for developing appropriate skills.

A college degree is not the only viable route to skill development. Vocational training through non-degree-granting institutions and apprenticeships may be more valuable than a four-year college degree, especially if the degree is unrelated to the occupational job (Kerckhoff & Bell, 1998). The importance of providing opportunities for all youths, not just the college bound, to gain technical skills, training, and education has been widely recognized in the school-to-work (STW) movement.

Although there are various kinds of STW programs, their contents converge on four domains: self-knowledge, occupational knowledge, technical skills, and general skills (Helwig, 1987; Swanson & Fouad, 1999). That is, students need to know their own skills, interests, and values, as well as the characteristics of the occupations of interest, in order to maximize P-E fit and P-OC fit. Thus, STW programs should provide sufficient time for students' self-exploration and teach the basic elements underlying P-E fit and P-OC fit.

Most STW programs—tech-prep programs, industry-specific training, cooperative education, and apprenticeships—focus on providing technical training (Worthington & Juntunen, 1997). Such programs aim to teach high school students the connections between school and work and help them complete their education with an industry-recognized skill certificate or a high school diploma, or both (Krumboltz & Worthington, 1999). Along with the concern for technical skills, general employability skills are becoming increasingly stressed in STW programs due to the growing awareness that young adults need to prepare for several different types of jobs rather than a single job (Krumboltz & Worthington, 1999).

Savickas (1999) proposed career management techniques and role rehearsal as mechanisms to aid in the development of general skills. Career management techniques encourage youth to improve teamwork skills and personal credibility to enable them to adapt to a wide variety of work environments. Role rehearsal prepares adolescents and young adults to solve problems that may occur at work and often includes role playing and case studies. To the extent that STW programs provide exposure to a variety of occupations and skills, they can help foster students' self and occupational knowledge (desire-supply fit), in addition to providing them with the tools for acquiring technical and general skills (ability-demand).

Work Experience and Internships

Students who work during high school or college are likely to acquire broad-based employability skills, such as punctuality and personal responsibility. However, most students work part time in occupations unrelated to their career aspirations, educational studies, or interests, which may contribute to their floundering among jobs and occupations once they are in the full-time labor market (Stone & Mortimer, 1998). That is, although the attainment of broad-based skills and work experience may increase employability and earnings, work experiences that do not help youth explore different occupational activities and crystallize their interests are unlikely to contribute to fit, persistence in the occupation, and satisfaction.

Work experience through targeted internships, however, has been shown to help youth crystallize their vocational interests, gain a better understanding of their abilities, acquire both general and job-related skills, and obtain better employment (Brooks, Cornelius, Greenfield, & Joseph, 1995; Eyler, 1995; Taylor, 1988). Most graduate and postgraduate students plan to seek or already occupy jobs in the same areas as their internships or practicum experience (Richmond & Sherman, 1991), supporting the notion that internships play an important role in helping young adults choose a career that fits their interests and abilities. Although research has generally shown positive effects for internships on career outcomes, most of this research has depended on self-report measures, and the responses may have been positively biased by the employment edge provided by an internship. In general, there has been not much research on how internships aid young adults in achieving desire-supply fit and ability-demand fit.

Career Counseling and Interventions

Career counselors have a variety of assessment tools available to them to help young adults resolve indecision about their careers. For example, in addition to interest measures, assessment tools are available that focus on gathering information; generating, evaluating, and selecting alternatives; formulating plans for implementing decisions; and identifying self-efficacy beliefs pertaining to abilities. Such tools can help counselors focus interventions on an individual's unique and specific problems and help him or her acquire skills needed to make career decisions (Osipow, 1999).

Few rigorous studies have investigated the impact of these interventions, and results to date have been inconsistent. One reason for the weak findings may be that counseling has been dominated by interest assessments; only recently have decision making, ability-demand fit, and skill acquisition processes been explicitly addressed. The potential contribution of skill-based counseling was demonstrated by Luzzo and his colleagues (1999), who found that videos of successful students in math-related majors and performance accomplishments on math-related tasks increased students' beliefs about their abilities to perform as well in math- and science-related courses. In addition, job club programs, study materials, and simulations not only acquaint adolescents with various occupations and provide and help them learn about the world of work (Krumboltz & Worthington, 1999), but also help them crystallize their career interests (Swanson & Fouad, 1999) and develop greater self-efficacy beliefs (Lent et al., 1999).

Perhaps a useful model to guide career counselors is one evidenced in the mentoring literature (Kram, 1985). Eby (1997) distinguished between two mentoring functions: job-related skill development and career-related skill development. Job-related skill development functions help protégés achieve ability-demand fit by aiding them in the acquisition of technical skills required for a specific job. Career-related skill development functions help achieve desire-supply fit by not only aiding long-term career planning but also by assisting protégés to find alternative careers that fit their interests. Although little work has examined the impact of mentoring on helping individuals achieve person-occupation fit, career counselors may be able to provide both types of mentoring functions.

Conclusion

The role of skill acquisition in achieving fit is a complex one. Given that P-E fit is a reciprocal and developmental process, a number of factors must be considered simultaneously and longitudinally. Unfortunately, very little work has considered the skill acquisition process along with other types of fit processes; longitudinal studies are even rarer.

To date, the preponderance of work on person-occupation fit has addressed congruence between interests and occupations, with the assumption that people seek and choose careers where their interests fit their career environments (Holland, 1985). It is clear that this perspective on person-occupation congruence is viable since research has consistently shown that interests and occupational environments are consistent among employed adults. However, relationships between this desire-supply type of person-occupation fit and the primary outcomes investigated in the fit literature— turnover or stability, academic performance, job performance, reduced stress, and satisfaction—have been weak. Although many have proposed that the generally weak findings are due to methodological problems (Spokane et al., 2000; Tinsley, 2000), we argue that the weak findings are also largely due to failure to consider multiple dimensions of fit, multiple levels of fit, and the effects of fit over time.

Several types and levels of congruence may exist and may differentially affect outcome measures (Spokane et al., 2000). Examinations of the impact of P-OC fit on job satisfaction, adjustment, and turnover may show weak results because P-OC fit effects may be confounded with P-O, P-J, or P-G fit. For example, change to a different job could be due to poor P-OC, P-O fit, P-G fit, P-J fit, or some combination of these. Moreover, within these types of fit, lack of congruence could be due to poor desire-supply fit, poor ability-demand fit, or some combination of the two.

Few studies have attempted to disentangle job changes to other careers from those of movement to other organizations (McCall, 1990, is an exception), career changes due to poor desire-supply fit versus poor ability-demand fit, and whether change is due to poor P-O or P-G fit. Some evidence of the importance of these considerations can be gleaned from the work of Meir and his colleagues (Meir, Keinan, & Segal 1986; Meir, Tziner, & Glazner, 1997). These researchers examined the importance of an individual's work group as a moderator of the relationship between person-occupation interest fit and satisfaction. These studies show that the more individuals' immediate work group environments are important to them, the stronger is the relationship between congruence and satisfaction.

In a related vein, the importance of different types of congruence may vary for different people (Spokane et al., 2000). For example, if P-OC fit is poor but P-O and P-G fit are high, an individual who values occupational fit to a greater extent than fit to the work environment or coworkers may change careers. In contrast, a person who places more value on P-O than P-OC fit will likely remain in the organization and attempt to acquire more skills or otherwise adjust better to his or her occupation.

In general, skill acquisition is most directly related to P-OC and P-J fit. At the occupational level, different sets of aptitudes and abilities are required (Holland, 1985) and vary by job level or job complexity within an occupation (Gottfredson, 1986). At the job level, P-J fit occurs when employees' proficiencies, skills, and abilities are congruent with the job requirements (Werbel & Gilliland, 1999). Consequently, it could be argued that P-J fit is necessary, but not sufficient, for career success and positive affective responses to job. With poor P-J fit, an individual will likely quit, receive low performance ratings, be counseled to another job or career, be fired, or require additional training; P-OC, P-O, and P-G fit would be irrelevant here.

The concern, then, is how appropriate skill acquisition for achieving ability-demand fit can be fostered. As we have highlighted, the role of the skill acquisition process cannot be viewed in isolation of the dynamic and interrelated issues of determining initial vocational preference and interests. Studies that simultaneously examine both desire-supply and ability-demand fit in person-occupation congruence, though, are relatively rare. The little work that has been done in this regard has tended to focus on self-perceptions of ability or has examined fit only in academic environments (Feldman et al., 1999; Meir et al., 1995).

Thus, not only is more rigorous research needed that considers the relative roles of both ability-demand and desire-supply fit in examining the impact of person-occupation fit on outcomes, but substantially more research is needed to address the dynamic relationships of fit over time. Path-analytic studies such as those of Gottfredson (1994) point to the success of such an approach. Studies examining how interests and beliefs about abilities interact and become mutually reinforcing are sorely needed, with explicit attention given to the role of skill acquisition in this process.

Because interactions between congruence and background characteristics, particularly sex and race, have been documented (Elton & Smart, 1988; Fricko & Beehr, 1992; Swaney & Prediger, 1985), complex nonlinear relationships between congruence and outcomes across occupational types may exist. The underlying reasons for these are not well known. More studies are needed to determine the impact of these background characteristics on the initial process of fitting interests and abilities and the dynamics of gaining skills to help achieve later fit. Similarly, more research is needed to address the relative importance of universal versus specific skills by occupation. Depending on the occupation and job level, ability-demand fit is likely to be more important in terms of universal skills than specific skills (Stone & Mortimer, 1998; Werbel & Gilliland, 1999).

From a practical standpoint, career counselors might be wise to focus young adults' attention more carefully on the importance of congruence, and particularly skill congruence, in defining career choices (Fricko & Beehr, 1992). Gottfredson (1981) suggests that over time, adolescents and young adults move away from an exclusive focus on interests to examine realistic choices within their zone of acceptable choices. Part of this process of making realistic choices includes greater attention to one's own skills and the demand for those skills in the labor market (Armstrong & Crombie, 2000). A great deal more research is needed on the impact of counseling, internships, information sources, and other interventions to help young adults determine their talents and make appropriate choices for acquiring more skills in those areas.

References

Arbona, C. (2000). Practice and research in career counseling and development—1999. *Career Development Quarterly, 49,* 98–134.

Armstrong, P. I., & Crombie, G. (2000). Compromises in adolescents' occupational aspirations and expectations from grades 8 to 10. *Journal of Vocational Behavior, 56,* 82–98.

Austin, J. T., & Hanish, K. A. (1990). Occupational attainment as a function of abilities and interests: A longitudinal analysis using Project TALENT data. *Journal of Applied Psychology, 75,* 77–86.

Betz, N. E., Harmon, L. W., & Borgen, F. H. (1996). The relationships of self-efficacy for the Holland themes to gender, occupational group membership and vocational interests. *Journal of Counseling Psychology, 43,* 90–98.

Borow, H. (1966). Development of occupational motives and roles. In L. W. Hoffman & M. L. Hoffman (Eds.), *Review of child development research* (pp. 373–422). New York: Russell Sage Foundation.

Brooks, L., Cornelius, A., Greenfield, E., & Joseph, R. (1995). The relation of career-related work or internship experiences to the career development of college seniors. *Journal of Vocational Behavior, 46,* 332–349.

Brousseau, K. R. (1984). Job-person dynamics and career development. *Research in Personnel and Human Resource Management, 2,* 125–154.

Bynner, J. (1997). Basic skills in adolescents' occupational preparation. *Career Development Quarterly, 45,* 305–321.

Caldwell, D. F., & O'Reilly, C. A., III (1990). Measuring person-job fit with a profile-comparison process. *Journal of Applied Psychology, 75,* 648–657.

Cappelli, P., Bassi, L., Katz, H., Knoke, D., Osterman, P., & Useem, M. (1997). *Change at work.* New York: Oxford University Press.

Chartrand, J. M., Camp, C. C., & McFadden, K. L. (1992). Predicting academic adjustment and career indecision: A comparison of self-efficacy, interest congruence and commitment. *Journal of College Student Development, 33,* 293–300.

Dawis, R. V., & Lofquist, L. H. (1984). *A psychological theory of work adjustment.* Minneapolis: University of Minnesota Press.

De Fruyt, F., & Mervielde, I. (1999). RIASEC types and Big Five traits as predictors of employment status and nature of employment. *Personnel Psychology, 52,* 701–727.

Eby, L. T. (1997). Alternative forms of mentoring in changing organizational environments: A conceptual extension of the mentoring literature. *Journal of Vocational Behavior, 51,* 125–144.

Edwards, J. R. (1991). Person-job fit: A conceptual integration, literature review, and methodological critique. *International Review of Industrial and Organizational Psychology, 6,* 283–357.

Elton, C. F., & Smart, J. C. (1988). Extrinsic job satisfaction and person-environment congruence. *Journal of Vocational Behavior, 32,* 226–238.

Eyler, J. (1995). Graduates' assessment of the impact of a full-time college internship on their personal and professional lives. *College Student Journal, 29,* 186–194.

Feehan, P. F., & Johnston, J. A. (1999). The self-directed search and career self-efficacy. *Journal of Career Assessment, 7,* 145–149.

Feldman, K. A., Smart, J. C., & Ethington, C. A. (1999). Major field and person-environment fit. *Journal of Higher Education, 70,* 642–669.

Fricko, M.A.M., & Beehr, T. A. (1992). A longitudinal investigation of interest congruence and gender concentration as predictors of job satisfaction. *Personnel Psychology, 45,* 99–117.

Gottfredson, G. D. (1977). Career stability and redirection in adulthood. *Journal of Applied Psychology, 62,* 436–445.

Gottfredson, L. S. (1979). Aspiration-job match: Age trends in a large nationally representative sample of young white men. *Journal of Counseling Psychology, 26,* 319–328.

Gottfredson, L. S. (1981). Circumscription and compromise: A developmental theory of occupational aspirations. *Journal of Counseling Psychology, 28,* 545–579.

Gottfredson, L. S. (1986). Occupational aptitude patterns map: Development and implication for a theory of job aptitude requirements. *Journal of Vocational Behavior, 18,* 127–137.

Gottfredson, L. S. (1994). *The person in person-environment interactions.* Paper presented at the annual meeting of the American Psychological Association, Los Angeles.

Gottfredson, G. D., & Holland, J. L. (1990). A longitudinal test of the influence of congruence: Job satisfaction, competency utilization, and counterproductive behavior. *Journal of Counseling Psychology, 37,* 389–398.

Gottfredson, G. D., & Holland, J. L. (1991). *The Position Classification Inventory.* Odessa, FL: Psychological Assessment Resources.

Gottfredson, L. S., & Richards, J. M., Jr. (1999). The meaning and measurement of environments in Holland's theory. *Journal of Vocational Behavior, 55,* 57–73.

Helwig, A. A. (1987). Information required for job hunting: 1,121 counselors respond. *Journal of Employment Counseling, 24,* 184–190.

Henry, P. (1989). Relationship between academic achievement and measured career interest: Examination of Holland's theory. *Psychological Reports, 64,* 35–40.

Hogan, R., & Blake, R. J. (1996). Vocational interests: Matching self-concept with the work environment. In K. Murphy (Ed.), *Individ-*

ual differences and behavior in organizations (pp. 89–144). San Francisco: Jossey-Bass.

Holland, J. L. (1973). *Making vocational choices.* Upper Saddle River, NJ: Prentice Hall.

Holland, J. L. (1985). *Making vocational choices: A theory of vocational personalities and work environments* (2nd ed.). Upper Saddle River, NJ: Prentice Hall.

Jackson, S. E., Brett, J. F., Sessa, V. I., Cooper, D. M., Julin, J. A., & Peyronnin, K. (1991). Some differences make a difference: Individual dissimilarity and group homogeneity as correlates of recruitment, promotions and turnover. *Journal of Applied Psychology, 76,* 675–689.

Judge, T. A., Higgins, C. A., Thoresen, C. J., & Barrick, J. R. (1999). The Big Five personality traits, general mental ability, and career success across the life span. *Personnel Psychology, 52,* 621–652.

Kerckhoff, A. C., & Bell, L. (1998). Hidden capital: Vocational credentials and attainment in the United States. *Sociology of Education, 71,* 152–174.

Klimoski, R., & Jones, R. G. (1995). Staffing for effective group decision making: Key issues in matching people and teams. In R. Guzzo, Eduardo Salas, and Associates (Eds.), *Team effectiveness and decision making in organizations* (pp. 291–332). San Francisco: Jossey-Bass.

Kram, K. E. (1985). *Mentoring at work: Developmental relationships in organizational life.* Glenview, IL: Scott, Foresman.

Kristof, A. L. (1996). Person-organization fit: An integrative review of its conceptualizations, measurements, and implications. *Personnel Psychology, 49,* 1–49.

Krumboltz, J. D., & Worthington, R. L. (1999). The school-to-work transition from a learning theory perspective. *Career Development Quarterly, 47,* 312–325.

Lent, R. W., Brown, S. D., & Hackett, G. (1994). Toward a unifying social cognitive theory of career and academic interest, choice and performance. *Journal of Vocational Behavior, 45,* 79–122.

Lofquist, L. H., & Dawis, R. V. (1991). *Essentials of person-environment-correspondence counseling.* Minneapolis: University of Minnesota Press.

Luzzo, D. A., Hasper, P., Albert, K. I., Bibby, M. A., & Martinelli, E. A., Jr. (1999). Effects of self-efficacy-enhancing interventions on the math/science self-efficacy and career interests, goals, and actions of career undecided college students. *Journal of Counseling Psychology, 46,* 233–243.

McCall, B. P. (1990). Occupational matching: A test of sorts. *Journal of Political Economy, 98,* 45–69.

McCormick, E., DeNisi, A., & Staw, J. (1979). Use of the Positional Analysis

Questionnaire for establishing the job component validity of tests. *Journal of Occupational Psychology, 56,* 347–368.

Meir, E. I., Keinan, G., & Segal, Z. (1986). Group importance as a mediator between personal-environment congruence and satisfaction. *Journal of Vocational Behavior, 28,* 60–69.

Meir, E. I., Melamed, S., & Dinur, C. (1995). The benefits of congruence. *Career Development Quarterly, 43,* 257–266.

Meir, E. I., Tziner, A., & Glazner, Y. (1997). Environmental congruence, group importance and job satisfaction. *Journal of Career Assessment, 5,* 343–353.

Muchinsky, P. M., & Monahan, C. J. (1987). What is person-environment congruence? Supplementary versus complementary fit. *Journal of Vocational Behavior, 31,* 268–277.

Nauta, M., Epperson, D., & Waggoner, K. M. (1999). Perceived causes of success and failure: Are women's attributions related to persistence in engineering majors? *Journal of Research in Science and Teaching, 36,* 663–676.

Osipow, S. H. (1999). Assessing career indecision. *Journal of Vocational Behavior, 55,* 147–154.

Ostroff, C. (1993). The effects of climate and personal influences on individual behavior and attitudes in organizations. *Organizational Behavior and Human Decision Processes, 56,* 56–90.

Pascarella, E. G., & Terenzini, P. T. (1991). *How college affects students: Findings and insights from twenty years of research.* San Francisco: Jossey-Bass.

Pervin, L. A. (1983). The stasis and flow of behavior: Toward a theory of goals. In M. Page (Ed.), *Personality: Current theory and research* (pp. 1–53). Lincoln: University of Nebraska Press.

Pervin, L. A. (1989). Persons, situations, interactions: A history of controversy and a discussion of theoretical models. *Academy of Management Review, 14,* 350–360.

Prediger, D. J. (1999). Basic structure of work-relevant abilities. *Journal of Counseling Psychology, 46,* 173–184.

Richmond, J., & Sherman, K. J. (1991). Student-development preparation and placement: A longitudinal study of graduate students' and new professionals' experiences. *Journal of College Student Development, 32,* 8–16.

Rounds, J. B., Dawis, R. V., & Lofquist, L. H. (1987). Measurement of person-environment fit and prediction of satisfaction in the theory of work adjustment. *Journal of Vocational Behavior, 31,* 297–318.

Ryan, E. S. (2000). Comparing 21st century job-skill acquisition with self-fulfillment for college students. *Education, 119,* 529–536.

Savickas, M. L. (1999). The transition from school to work: A developmental perspective. *Career Development Quarterly, 47,* 326–336.

Schneider, B., Smith, D. B., & Goldstein, H. W. (2000). Attraction-selection-attrition: Toward a person-environment psychology of organizations. In W. B. Walsh, K. H. Craik, & R. H. Price (Eds.), *Person-environment psychology* (pp. 61–86). Mahwah, NJ: Erlbaum.

Snell, A. F., Stokes, G. S., Sands, M. M., & McBride, J. R. (1994). Adolescent life experiences as predictors of occupational attainment. *Journal of Applied Psychology, 79,* 131–141.

Spokane, A. R. (1985). A review of research on person-environment congruence in Holland's theory of careers. *Journal of Vocational Behavior, 26,* 306–343.

Spokane, A. R., Meir, E., & Catalano, M. (2000). Person-environment congruence and Holland's theory: A review and reconsideration. *Journal of Vocational Behavior, 57,* 137–187.

Stone, J. R., III, & Mortimer, J. T. (1998). The effect of adolescent employment on vocational development: Public and educational policy implications. *Journal of Vocational Behavior, 53,* 184–214.

Strong, E. K., Jr. (1955). *Vocational interests 18 years after college.* Minneapolis: University of Minnesota Press.

Swaney, K., & Prediger, D. (1985). The relationship between interest-occupation congruence and job satisfaction. *Journal of Vocational Behavior, 46,* 292–309.

Swanson, J. L., & Fouad, N. A. (1999). Applying theories of person-environment fit to the transition from school to work. *Career Development Quarterly, 47,* 337–347.

Taylor, M. S. (1988). Effects of college internships on individual participants. *Journal of Applied Psychology, 73,* 393–401.

Tinsley, H.E.A. (2000). The congruence myth: An analysis of the efficacy of the person-environment fit model. *Journal of Vocational Behavior, 56,* 147–179.

Tracey, T.J.G., & Hopkins, N. (2001). Correspondence of interests and abilities with occupational choice. *Journal of Counseling Psychology, 48,* 178–189.

Tranberg, M., Slane, S., & Exberg, S. E. (1993). The relation between interest congruence and satisfaction: A meta-analysis. *Journal of Vocational Behavior, 42,* 253–264.

Trusty, J., & Ng, K. (2000). Longitudinal effects of achievement perceptions on choice of postsecondary major. *Journal of Vocational Behavior, 57,* 123–135.

U.S. Department of Labor. (1992). *Learning for a living: A blueprint for high performance.* Washington, DC: U.S. Government Printing Office.

Werbel, J. D., & Gilliland, S. W. (1999). Person-environment fit in the selection process. *Research in Personnel and Human Resource Management, 17,* 209–243.

Wilk, S. L., Desmarais, L. B., & Sackett, P. R. (1995). Gravitation to jobs commensurate with ability: Longitudinal and cross-sectional tests. *Journal of Applied Psychology, 80,* 79–85.

Wilk, S. L., & Sackett, P. R. (1996). Longitudinal analysis of ability-job complexity fit and job change. *Personnel Psychology, 49,* 937–967.

Worthington, R. L., & Juntunen, C. L. (1997). The vocational development of non–college bound youth: Counseling psychology and the school-to-work transition movement. *Counseling Psychologist, 25,* 323–363.

PART 2

Career Development Across the Life Span

When You Come to a Fork in the Road, Take It

Career Indecision and Vocational Choices of Teenagers and Young Adults

Daniel C. Feldman

Yogi Berra's infamous line, "When you come to a fork in the road, take it," nicely captures the quandary of adolescents and young adults in choosing vocations and launching their careers. Most teenagers in industrialized societies have unparalleled independence to pursue whatever vocations they choose, freer than ever before from family pressures or government dictates. However, having the freedom to be anything at all, many young adults see no reason to be anything in particular (Bloom, 1987). Encouraged to keep their options open, many young adults now approach vocational choice with increased dread—not only that their choices might be wrong but that they might irrevocably close some future options as well (Feldman, 1988). This abundance of choices, coupled with a desire to keep options open, can trap young adults in a self-perpetuating state of hesitancy and confusion about beginning their careers.

In the first section of this chapter, we examine how adolescents and young adults formulate their initial vocational choices. This section focuses on two issues, in particular: stage models and content models of vocational choice (Roe, 1956; Sharf, 1997; Super,

1957). The next section of the chapter examines the converse question: Why do so many teenagers and young adults have such trouble coming to any vocational decision at all? Here, we examine the key components of this career indecision: procrastination in seeking career information and making college and job applications, frequent switching of educational programs or jobs, and inability to formulate early-career goals (Betz & Voyten, 1997; Griliches, 1980; Habermas & Bluck, 2000). In the last section of the chapter, we examine the potential consequences of career indecision. The chapter concludes with some implications for the design and implementation of early-career counseling programs, both to assist young adults in making appropriate vocational choices and in breaking out of the cycles of indecision.

Stage Models of Early-Career Development

For the past fifty years, almost all models of vocational choice have explicitly posited some typology of developmental stages among adolescents and young adults (Roe, 1956). These models generally suggest that the vocational decision-making process goes through several phases, beginning with adolescents' general fantasies about work and culminating in young adults' realistic choices of vocations appropriate to their skills and interests. These stage models, and the developmental processes they suggest, are described in more detail next.

Phases of Early-Career Development

Seminal works by Super (1957) and Ginzberg, Ginzberg, Axelrod, and Herna (1951) suggest that individuals go through three stages as they choose their initial careers. In the first stage, the exploratory period, teenagers begin to consider what their interests and values are and where their talents lie. In the second stage, the crystallization period, individuals begin to think more specifically about which career options they could realistically pursue and what the advantages and disadvantages of different careers might be. In the third stage, the specification period, individuals make concrete decisions about the career they will enter and commit themselves to pursuing.

The work of London and Mone (1987) and London and Stumpf (1986) also implicitly suggests that the formation of career identity is a three-pronged process. As individuals pass through childhood and adolescence, they develop some level of career resilience, that is, self-confidence in their skills and some persistence in the face of obstacles. As they enter late adolescence and their twenties, they subsequently begin to develop greater career insight. Here, individuals receive feedback from the environment on how well they are performing and begin formulating realistic career goals. Ultimately, individuals develop a career identity. At this point, they become more involved in their jobs, feel more committed to their professions, and have a greater sense of direction for the years ahead (Osipow, 1990).

Empirical research that tests stage models of early- career development has substantially lagged theoretical exposition of such frameworks. However, previous research generally does suggest that the major stumbling blocks for adolescents and young adults are making the transition into the specification stage and formulating career identity. That is, adolescents appear to give considerable thought to career options and to have experimented with various courses of action, but many remain unable to make any commitments to a particular line of work (Bartley & Robitschek, 2000; Rysiew et al., 1999; Walls, 2000).

Psychological Processes Underlying Early-Career Development

Most developmental psychologists would agree that the main tasks of teenagers and young adults in terms of career development are discovering their skills and interests, gathering information about various career paths, and winnowing down the large number of potential choices to a more manageable and realistic set. Next, we consider the psychological processes that guide and influence the direction of early-career development.

Cumulative Continuity

Cumulative continuity refers to the processes by which individuals select environments that strengthen their initial predispositions to explore particular career paths (Caspi, Bem, & Elder, 1989; Kokko

& Pulkkinen, 2000). For example, Holland's work (1985) suggests that individuals with a nascent interest in a particular activity will gravitate to environments that reinforce that interest and build specific skills in that area. Thus, teenagers who are interested in theater may gravitate to summer jobs and extracurricular involvement in acting, where their initial interest will be legitimated and their talent for acting may be improved by practice. Much as in evolutionary theory, then, initial predispositions for careers may be selectively reinforced and sustained through teenagers' choices of receptive environments.

Interactional Continuity

Interactional continuity refers to the processes by which individuals' choices of careers are shaped by the feedback they receive from others (Caspi et al., 1989; Kokko & Pulkkinen, 2000). Individuals' self-perceptions of their own skills and abilities, as well as their assessments of succeeding in a field, are often formed by interactional continuity.

For example, many adolescents have high hopes of ultimately becoming professional athletes. As they face increasingly tough competition in high school and college, students' self-perceptions of their abilities are shaped by the feedback they receive from the environment. Those who receive highly positive feedback are invited to participate in elite teams and encouraged to get personal training; those who sit on the bench begin to turn away from athletics as a career goal and start exploring other potential career paths. Again, as in evolutionary theory, there is an implicit survival of the fittest that occurs through interactional continuity: the best are encouraged to continue, and the weakest get signals to drop out.

Personal and Contextual Buffering

There is a fine line in early-career development between realistic responses to honest feedback and overreacting to random signals from the environment. For example, there is a difference between ending premed studies because of failing grades in all science classes and dropping out of premed because the first quiz grade in calculus was a C.

Both intraindividual and situational factors can amplify—or suppress—reactions to early environmental feedback (Kokko & Pulkkinen, 2000; Masten & Coatsworth, 1998). For example, supportive parents appear to increase the aspiration levels of teen-agers, energize their children to engage in more search behavior, and buffer teenagers from overreacting to initial defeats (Kerr & Stattin, 2000; Kush & Cochran, 1993). In contrast, young adults with low self-esteem are more likely to view themselves as deserv-ing the negative feedback they receive and to withdraw more quickly in the face of initial disappointments (Betz & Voyten, 1997; Lent, Brown, & Hackett, 2000).

Dissonance Reduction and Memory Distortion

If one dysfunctional career behavior of adolescents is premature withdrawal from a potentially reasonable vocational choice, the converse problem is unreasonable perseverance in pursuit of an unrealistic career path. The major perceptual distortion that has been examined in this light is post-decision dissonance (Janis & Mann, 1977; Tiedeman & O'Hara, 1963). The research on this phenomenon suggests that after choosing a career, many young adults have lingering doubts about the alternatives they did not choose. As a way to reduce this dissonance (the feeling that they made the wrong choice), adolescents and young adults continue to seek out more positive information about the career path cho-sen and more negative information about the alternatives dis-carded (Roese, 1997; Wood, 2000).

Recent research on the human memory has helped illuminate some of the dynamics underlying this post-decision dissonance. As Schacter (2001) suggests, consistency biases often make it difficult for young adults to separate recall of "the way they were" from cur-rent appraisals of "the way they are." Because people change their perceptions of the choices they faced in the past, they have diffi-culty learning from failure and recognizing why they made a bad decision. Moreover, as a result of this hindsight bias, adolescents and young adults may block out disconfirming data about their fu-ture chances of success and continue to escalate commitment to a poor course of action.

Content Models of Vocational Choice

These stage models are largely descriptive in nature and address how the career identification process unfolds in early career. By and large, these models do not address how adolescents and young adults end up in one specific type of career or another. In contrast, content models of vocational choice more directly address how teenagers' initial inclinations to pursue a particular career are reinforced by—or extinguished by—contextual factors (Szymanski & Hanley-Maxwell, 1996; Vondracek & Schulenberg, 1992). The context factors that appear to play the greatest roles here are political and societal trends, macroeconomic conditions, educational experiences, parental attitudes and values, and adolescents' own initial work experiences.

Political and Societal Trends

Even without consciously seeking out information about careers, teenagers and young adults are exposed to a great deal of data about what careers are trendy and what are not. The most obvious manifestations of these influences are annual surveys in such periodicals as *Fortune* and *Wall Street Journal* on the fifty hottest careers of the future, the one hundred best organizations to work for, and so forth. Although it is difficult to estimate the exact degree of influence that political and societal trends have on young adults' career choices, some evidence of that influence is highly visible. For example, the space race of the 1950s encouraged pursuit of careers in engineering, just as the 1990s Internet boom has encouraged many adolescents to pursue careers in information technology.

Although being vigilant of the environment can be functional for young adults as they choose careers, there are considerable risks associated with picking (or avoiding) careers based on futurist thinking. Simply because a career is hot now does not mean it will be hot by the time an individual graduates from college or graduate school; many young adults ignore (or misestimate) the lags in information flow and staffing in the open labor market. Perhaps more important, young adults may be enticed by these trend analyses to enter occupations in which they have neither genuine interest nor ability. Entering accounting because there are labor shortages and high salaries does not make the field more personally interesting or compensate for a young adult's lack of math aptitude. Overreliance on political and societal trends, then, can result in either rejecting an appropriate vocation or entering an inappropriate one.

Macroeconomic Conditions

Macroeconomic conditions can influence the vocational choices of adolescents and young adults directly and indirectly. Robust economic conditions raise the average income levels of parents, who then have more money to spend on their children's education (Shea, 2000). In strong economies, teenagers and young adults can also earn higher wages themselves in part-time and summer jobs to pay for their own education (Harper, 1998).

Another, and perhaps more subtle, impact of macroeconomic conditions is raising the aspirations of adolescents and young adults for fulfilling work (Maslow, 1954; Veblen, 1934). When teenagers and young adults grow up in conditions of economic depression or recession, they have strong incentives to pursue careers perceived to have good employment prospects and high job security, such as accounting and nursing, independent of how much they find such careers exciting. In contrast, in strong economies, young adults may place a higher premium on entering careers that are truly self-actualizing for them (Brooks, 2001). Only in a powerful economy like that of the United States in 2000 could enrollments in medical school decline while enrollments in film studies skyrocket. Third, macroeconomic conditions can have an impact on the timing of education. While increasing the affordability of higher education, robust labor markets may also induce young adults to delay entering college or to take time out to accept high-paid employment (Albert & Luzzo, 1999).

Educational Experiences

Independent of the level of education that young adults attain, the environments in which they attend school may also have an impact on the quality of that education. The expertise of teachers and the backgrounds of other students in the school are significant predictors of teenagers' academic achievement, even after controlling for the students' own socioeconomic status (Griffith, 1995; Kasen, Johnson, & Cohen, 1990). School settings may also have a major impact on the quality of career advising. Perhaps somewhat cynically, Bloom (1987, p. 339) argues that too many faculty are "carnival barkers," trying to entice students into taking their classes.

However, his more general point—that students are not getting career advising of "the whole person"—may indeed be valid.

Although there has been little conclusive research on this issue, it could be hypothesized that students at small schools are likely to get better guidance in making career decisions. Faculty in small schools are more likely to know individual students, engage them in important discussions about career issues, and recognize individual students' strengths and weaknesses. Another difference between small and large schools may lie in the ways career services are delivered. Large schools may rely more heavily on library resources, databases, and self-diagnostic surveys, which allow interested students to search for relevant career information on their own. Faculty and counselors at smaller schools may initiate more contacts with students about career planning and provide more specific guidance about educational and employment opportunities.

Parental Attitudes and Values

Parents can reinforce or extinguish children's participation in activities that heighten various career-related skills and interests (O'Brien & Fassinger, 1993; Salamone & Slaney, 1978). Parents' wealth also influences how much education students can obtain and their levels of aspiration (Shea, 2000). Moreover, parents' attitudes and values can have an even broader influence on young adults' vocational choices (Piotrowski & Stark, 1987).

Parents influence their children's perceptions of the world of work through explicit verbal discussions about jobs, through changes in mood or behavior, and by providing role models (Harvey, 1999). From as young as five years of age, children understand such concepts as unemployment and welfare; between ages ten and seventeen, teenagers become knowledgeable about the concepts of pay, working conditions, and work conflict (Barling, 1990; Pautler & Lewko, 1985; Piotrowski & Stark, 1987). For example, recent research suggests that parents' job insecurity and unemployment have negative consequences for their children. Parents' employment problems distract children from their own learning; adolescents whose parents are experiencing job insecurity receive poorer school grades (Barling et al., 1998; Barling, Zacharatos, & Hepburn, 1999).

At the most direct level, parents can influence their children's self-efficacy in seeking out career-related information and pursuing employment opportunities. Teenagers who participated in structured career planning with their parents in grade 12 showed greater career certainty and less career indecision than those in control groups (Kush & Cochran, 1993; Palmer & Cochran, 1988). There is also considerable evidence that teenagers role-model their parents' level of work involvement and work habits (Brooks, 2001; Shellenbarger, 1998). Thus, although parents do not fully determine their children's career interests, they can shape the direction and speed of career identity formation.

Early Labor Market Experiences

Over the past ten years, increasing attention has been paid to teenagers' own experiences in the labor market and how they shape subsequent career trajectories. Today, 38 percent of college students in the Untied States are employed part time, and another 14 percent attend school full time and work full time (Lipke, 2000). Twenty-five percent of high school students also work on a part-time basis (Grensing-Pophal, 1999).

Perhaps the most influential research in this area was conducted by Greenberger and Steinberg (1986). Their research first attracted considerable attention because their results ran counter to much of the prevailing wisdom about teenagers' part-time work. They found that instead of building character and teaching discipline, part-time work often distracted teenagers from academic performance and taught adolescents antisocial behaviors, such as loafing on the job and taking company merchandise for personal consumption.

Other research has extended and refined these early findings about teenagers' work experiences. Gottfredson (1985) found that part-time work does decrease school attendance but does not translate into increases in delinquent behavior. Stern, Stone, Hopkins, and McMillion (1990) found that students who were employed longer hours did receive poorer school grades and were less likely to go on to college, but that the evidence was neither as strong nor as consistent as Greenberger and Steinberg (1986) suggested. However, Stern et al. (1990) did reinforce earlier findings about the "moral education" component of part-time employment. That is, they, too, found that working long hours can contribute to a wide range of "dysfunctional, unethical, and self-destructive behaviors among young high school students" (p. 278) and questioned the wisdom of federal policies encouraging even greater youth employment.

Barling and his colleagues have tried to untangle the effects of quantity of part-time work from quality of part-time work (Barling, Rogers, & Kelloway, 1995; Loughlin & Barling, 1998). In general, these research studies found that quantity of work did not have strong linear or nonlinear effects on work-related attitudes, aspirations, and career maturity but that quality of work assignments did. When students are learning new skills, working near older adults, and engaged in meaningful work, the negative effects of part-time employment are significantly lessened. In their research on young part-time and temporary workers, Feldman and his colleagues found similar results: negative attitudes toward work and careers in general are more prevalent among youth who are underemployed in jobs that do not require much education or training (Feldman & Doerpinghaus, 1992; Feldman, Doerpinghaus, & Turnley, 1995).

Researchers have also turned their attention to more structured part-time work experiences, such as internships and cooperative work programs. Where research on teenagers' part-time employment has largely examined jobs that adolescents obtain on their own, research on internships and co-op programs has examined part-time employment either chosen by school faculty and administrators or monitored closely by them. In general, that research has shown beneficial (although modest) effects of internship and co-op programs (Douglas & Brewer, 1999). For example, Taylor (1985, 1988) found support for three benefits of internship programs: they help students crystallize their vocational interests and values, help lessen the reality shock of moving from school to work, and increase students' chances of getting hired on graduation. The factors most likely to enhance the quality of internship experiences are job autonomy, task identity, congruence of internships with the tentative career plans of young adults, and the degree of mentoring from internship supervisors (Feldman & Weitz, 1990; Feldman, Folks, & Turnley, 1998).

Taken as a whole, these studies suggest three recurring themes. First, part-time employment in and of itself does not build either career identity or good work habits among teenagers. Second, particularly if students engage in extensive part-time employment, it may adversely affect the level of academic achievement, the speed of graduation, and the likelihood of going on to college (Ross & Marriner, 1985; Stern, 1997). Third, the quality of part-time work and the quality of supervision play significant moderating roles in determining whether adolescents reap positive or negative consequences from their employment (Feldman, 1999).

Career Indecision and Delays in the Formation of Early-Career Identity

Research on the career development of teenagers has largely focused on the vocational choice process, but recently there has been growing concern about the extent to which adolescents and young adults are having difficulties making any decision at all about their careers. Although many students are highly energized and focused on their careers goals, more and more are delaying their education or entry into the workforce because they feel burned out or want additional time to "find themselves."

The formation of an initial career identity does not imply that career identity will never subsequently change or evolve over the life span. As Arthur and Rousseau (1996) suggest, individuals' career needs and external circumstances change considerably over time, and consequently, individuals' career identities will change over time as well. Rather, the major focus here is on young adults' reluctance or inability even to begin their careers, not on their rigidity in hewing the path first chosen throughout their lives.

Delays in the Formation of Early-Career Identity

For our purposes, delays in the formation of early-career identity will be defined in terms of three behaviors: procrastination in making early-career decisions, frequent switching of career paths and programs of study, and inability to formulate early-career goals. Each of these variables has been central in previous research on early-career issues in the vocational counseling and organizational behavior literatures (Betz & Voyten, 1997; Lent et al., 2000; Luzzo et al., 1997). Moreover, these components have the added advantage of being observable behaviors on which non-self-report data can be, and have been, collected.

Procrastination

Undoubtedly, many individuals make important career decisions quickly and intuitively. For instance, Beach and Mitchell's (1990) image theory suggests that some individuals do not engage in much reflection or cognitive processing at all when making important career decisions. They simply choose (or eliminate) career options based on their consistency (or inconsistency) with overall self-images of the future. However, other research suggests that many individuals in early career do indeed procrastinate when faced with difficult choices.

Procrastination may occur when young adults delay decisions about picking undergraduate majors, finishing the requirements for graduation, attending graduate school, or picking a career path to pursue after formal schooling ends. This delaying may be the result of defensive avoidance; that is, young adults may put off important decisions because they believe the process (or the outcomes) of their decision making will be unpleasant (Janis & Mann, 1977). Because the costs of making a poor choice can be tremendous, high stress levels may slow the speed of decision making, too (Langer & Schank, 1994).

In fact, 33 percent of high school graduates in the United States delay beginning college after receiving their high school diplomas. The average number of years between high school graduation and completion of the bachelor's degree has also increased dramatically. Since 1977, the proportion of students receiving bachelor's degrees within four years of high school graduation has declined from 45 percent to 31 percent, while the proportion of students needing more than six years to complete their degrees has risen from 25 percent to 32 percent. More and more baccalaureate recipients are also delaying entry into graduate school, although delaying entry is directly related to never obtaining any graduate degree at all (National Center for Education Statistics, 1996a, 1996b, 1997, 1999).

Frequent Switching of Career Paths and Fields of Study

Some switching of career paths and fields of study is natural among young adults as they discover their strengths, weaknesses, and the realistic demands of various careers. As individuals begin to explore various career options available to them, they typically narrow their choices by first eliminating career paths that they intuitively or instinctively dislike (Moss & Frieze, 1993). As a result of this process, adolescents typically have much more certainty about which careers they want to avoid than they have about which careers they want to pursue (Reutefors, Schneider, & Overton, 1979).

Repeated and extended switching of career paths is becoming increasingly common among teenagers and young adults. For example, more and more students are transferring colleges, dropping out of college for extended periods of time, or graduating more slowly because they have changed majors and need more credit hours to complete their degrees. Forty-five percent of all U.S. college students attend at least two different universities while attaining their bachelor's degrees; 12 percent attend three or more colleges before ultimately graduating. Thirty-two percent of these students drop out of school for at least six months when they transfer; 19 percent of transfer students have enrollment gaps of two years or longer (National Center for Education Statistics, 1996b, 1999). This phenomenon is becoming even more salient at the graduate level: one-third of baccalaureate degree recipients leave graduate school without obtaining any degree at all.

Inability to Identify Early-Career Goals

The third component considered here is the inability to identify early-career goals. Some young adults get so caught up in obsessive information gathering, referred to as hypervigilance, that they have no psychological energy left to analyze their options in thoughtful ways (Janis & Mann, 1977; Schacter, 2001). Similarly, some young adults have so many criteria they want to maximize in a career— many of which are unlikely to co-occur—that no career option seems particularly attractive (Dunegan, 1993). It is difficult to imagine, for instance, a career that simultaneously pays a lot of money, allows a great deal of leisure time, is socially meaningful, and involves working outdoors. Rather than "satisfice" with an option that at least minimally meets all the relevant criteria (Simon, 1976), "the perfect" becomes the enemy of the "good enough" for many adolescents.

Some archival data support the notion that large numbers of adolescents and young adults are having trouble identifying early-career goals. One in three late-entering or nontraditional students in the United States drops out of college without any degree at all, and even one in five traditional students does so (National Center for Education Statistics, 1999, 1996b). Six percent of college graduates are neither enrolled in any type of graduate program nor participating in the workforce in any way six months after graduation, and another 5 percent are employed only in part-time jobs. During the 1990s, the percentage of young adults earning a master's or doctoral degree declined as well (National Center for Education Statistics, 1999, 1998), again reflecting a general lack of conviction or commitment to some particular vocation or career path.

Antecedents of Career Indecision

The stage models of early-career development (Ginzberg et al., 1951; Super, 1957) and subsequent research on these stage models (Bartley & Robitschek, 2000; Walls, 2000) highlight the four sets of factors that are most likely to contribute to delays in the formation of early-career identity.

In the *exploratory stage,* the two sets of factors that have been identified as contributing most heavily to delays in the formation of early-career identity are demographic differences (for example, gender) and personality (for example, self-esteem). These variables have been studied as important influences on individuals' aspiration levels (Trusty, Ng, & Plata, 2000), level of activity in seeking out career information (Luzzo, Hitchings, Retish, & Shoemaker, 1999), and accuracy of self-perceptions and perceptions of the environment (Betz & Voyten, 1997; Digman, 1990).

In the *crystallization stage,* researchers have focused on two additional sets of factors that influence career indecision: the normative pressures a teenager experiences and the number (and types) of vocational abilities an adolescent possesses. One set of researchers has examined how normative pressures—from peers, parents, and cultural values—shape and mold individuals' early-career choices (Bloom, 1987; Habermas & Bluck, 2000), while another set has examined how the number and types of vocational ability (for example, artistic versus investigative) affect occupational choice (Holland, 1985; Tinsley, 2000).

These four sets of factors have been identified as critical in determining whether individuals progress from the exploration and crystallization stages of career identity formation into the *specification stage,* where individuals are able to make specific choices and concrete commitments to their initial occupations.

Demographic Differences

The demographic variable given the most attention in the context of career indecision has been gender, particularly the ways in which women may be channeled into sex-stereotypical occupations when they are young (Hochschild, 1997). Although previous research has not explicitly investigated gender differences in career indecision, indirect evidence suggests that men are more likely to experience delays in the formation of early-career identity than women.

Women are more likely to attend college right after high school, and women receive the majority of college degrees (55 percent female versus 45 percent male). Young women also typically outperform young men in terms of college grades received; for instance, in the United States, women account for 64.8 percent of all students who receive grade point averages of 3.5 or higher. Even after controlling for men's greater propensity to enter science-related classes (for example, 86 percent of all engineering undergraduates are male), where grades are typically lower, females appear to be more goal oriented than males in college (National Center for Education Statistics, 1996a, 1996b).

A wide variety of potential explanations for this relationship might be offered. Young males may receive more peer pressure to compete in nonacademic arenas in high school, and hence be less motivated or adequately equipped to compete academically in college. Young women may also mature more quickly than men and consequently be better able to identify appropriate career goals for themselves at an earlier age (Post-Kammer & Smith, 1985). Young women may be more likely to self-select themselves into a highly identifiable subset of careers where work-family balance is seen as readily attainable. For instance, women comprise 79 percent of the

education majors and 75 percent of the nursing majors in the
United States (National Center for Education Statistics, 1996b,
1996c).

Disabilities may contribute to delays in the formation of early-
career identity as well. Individuals with physical or learning disabilities may have less self-confidence in their abilities to find
occupations appropriate to their conditions. Consequently, they
may be less active in looking for career information and less accurate in their perceptions of themselves and the external labor market (Luzzo, 1999). Moreover, there is some evidence that traditional
career assessment tools are not as reliable and valid when applied
to individuals with disabilities. These errors in testing may decrease
the opportunities of those with disabilities for accurate guidance
or for fairness in selection (Enright, Conyers, & Szymanski, 1996).
Also, despite legislative mandates, individuals with disabilities may
be subjected to various biases in selection from university admis-
sions offices and potential employers (Tagalakis, Amsel, & Fichten,
1988). Thus, access to some potentially appropriate vocations may
be much more difficult for those who are disabled.

Personality Traits

The evidence is certainly clear and consistent that individuals with
low self-esteem are more likely to experience delays in the formation of early-career identity. Young adults with low self-esteem are
often less accurate perceivers of themselves, frequently viewing
their own capabilities in an unnecessarily harsh light (Shamir,
1985). Consequently, they are more likely to perceive frustrations
in new endeavors as the result of their own ineptitude, prematurely
bail out of various career paths they enter, and otherwise experience more false starts in their early careers. Along similar lines,
previous research has shown that college students who have high
self-efficacy about their career search skills are less likely to experience delays in the formation of early-career identity (Albert &
Luzzo, 1999; Lent et al., 2000). For example, college students with
high self-efficacy are more likely to seek out their advisers to discuss career opportunities in their majors, obtain career information from multiple sources, and remain in school to complete their
degrees (Betz & Voyten, 1997; Luzzo et al., 1997).

Although they have not yet been studied extensively in the context of career-identity formation, the Big Five personality traits of neuroticism, extraversion, openness to experience, agreeableness, and conscientiousness (Digman, 1990) are also likely to have an impact on early-career indecision. One interesting study along these lines, conducted by Caldwell and Burger (1998), found that extraversion was particularly critical in early career, since it facilitated seeking out information about careers from faculty members and employees of various companies. Moreover, recruiters made more positive attributions about extraverted young adults, perceived they would display better social skills at work than their introverted peers, and gave them more favorable hiring recommendations.

Number and Types of Skills and Interests

In the vocational guidance literature, there is a long tradition of examining the role of vocational interests and abilities in young adults' choice of careers (Donnay & Borgen, 1999; Tinsley, 2000). In essence, this literature argues that when young adults choose careers that are consistent with their vocational interests, their long-term attachment to those careers will be greater.

Here, we suggest that the number of skills and interests can also play a role in generating career indecision. In their work on multipotentiality, Rysiew et al. (1999) make an interesting observation on the formation of early-career identity. Their research on gifted adolescents suggests that when teenagers possess many vocational interests and abilities, they have much more difficulty identifying any one career path to pursue with fervor and determination. Ironically, then, the greater the number of vocational interests and abilities an individual possesses, the more likely he or she is to experience a delay in the formation of early-career identity.

In addition, individuals with different types of skills and interests will have varying levels of success in finding careers that fit their profiles. In particular, we suggest that adolescents with social and artistic vocational interests (Holland, 1985) will be more likely to experience delays in the formation of early-career identity for four reasons.

First, the range of career options available to young adults with social and artistic interests may be less obvious and straightforward. For example, individuals with investigative career interests can readily identify appropriate career paths for themselves in engineering and physics. In contrast, individuals with high social interests have a potentially broader, but less easily identifiable, set of career choices to consider, ranging from talk show host to telemarketer to therapist.

Second, some of the career paths associated with social and artistic vocational interests (such as musician and actor) have very high rates of failure and often pay quite poorly. Thus, even if young adults with social or artistic interests can accurately identify the careers that best suit them, they may still be hesitant about building their lives around these vocations.

Third, college students pursuing undergraduate studies in these kinds of areas often see fewer connections between what they are learning in class and realistic career paths (Bloom, 1987). For instance, liberal arts students are encouraged to read the great Greek plays for learning's sake, not for their instrumentality in later life. In contrast, students in preprofessional programs (such as business) are regularly exposed to course material that closely mirrors specific career paths.

Fourth, it may be less clear to potential employers what tangible skills students with social and artistic interests possess and for which jobs they are best suited. For instance, 7.3 percent of male recipients of humanities degrees are unemployed six months after graduation, compared to only 3.8 percent of male recipients of bachelor's degrees in business (National Center for Education Statistics, 1998).

Normative Pressures

McHale, Updegraff, Helms-Erikson, and Crouter (2001) have conducted some interesting research on the influences of siblings on adolescents' attitudes, personalities, and leisure pursuits. They found that firstborn siblings' attributes (attitudes, personalities, and leisure pursuits) predicted second-born children's qualities three years later, even when controlling for baseline data at time 1. Adolescents tend to look upward toward higher-status role models. Thus, younger siblings are more influenced by older siblings than vice versa, and first-borns are more strongly influenced by parents than their younger siblings are.

Peers can also influence the career behaviors of adolescents, although the magnitude and direction of that influence is often hard to estimate (Griffith, 1995; Schmitt, Sacco, Ramey, Ramey, & Chan, 1999). The most consistent finding in this research area is that adolescents who become deeply involved in deviant peer groups in middle school and high school tend to have lower academic achievement and more behavioral problems with adults (Fuligni, Eccles, Barber, & Clements, 2001).

In general, the impact of peer influences on early-career decisions is infrequently studied and warrants much greater research attention. For instance, it is quite likely that peer influences are not equally strong across all areas of an adolescent's life. In a recent study of adolescent friendships, Hamm (2000) found that adolescents varied in the extent to which they used academic orientation, ethnic identity, and involvement in deviant activity as the bases for choosing friends.

Even broad cultural values can influence the speed with which adolescents choose vocations and the energy they invest in launching their careers (Hofstede, 1980). For example, young adults in individualistic cultures such as the United Kingdom are raised to be relatively autonomous and self-oriented, while young adults in collectivist cultures such as China are socialized to weigh group expectations heavily in making individual decisions. Consequently, we might predict that delays in the formation of early-career identity will be greater among young adults in individualistic cultures (or subcultures) than among young adults in collectivist cultures. Young adults in individualistic cultures may receive less pressure from their parents to pursue any one occupation in particular, whereas young adults in collectivist cultures may view their career options as much narrower in scope.

Consequences of Career Indecision

Many academics and popular business writers are highly positive about the prospects for "boundaryless" careers that cross multiple functions and multiple firms (Arthur & Rousseau, 1996). For these scholars, delays in the formation of early-career identity may be desirable because they facilitate young adults' discovering their true vocational interests and abilities. Nevertheless, many employers still question the motivation and commitment of applicants with noticeable delays in college graduation, numerous gaps in their employment history, and frequent changes in jobs. Indeed, many of the most popular career advice books focus on helping job applicants construct a linear "story" in their resumés that makes sense of their (seemingly random) sets of experiences (Bolles, 2001). In the following section, we identify the personal consequences that may be associated with delays in the formation of early-career identity.

Loss of Earnings and Underemployment

The two outcomes that have been most frequently examined in this literature—and the two outcomes that are typically most negative for individuals—are potential losses of earnings and underemployment. Education is a major predictor of earnings potential; thus, noncompletion of college is directly related to loss of earnings early in one's career (Fain, 1999). For instance, over the past several years, only 4 percent of bachelor's degree recipients aged twenty to twenty-four had no jobs; the unemployment rate for college dropouts was double that (U.S. Bureau of Labor Statistics, 1998; National Center for Education Statistics, 1997, 1996b).

The term *underemployment* refers to jobs that do not fully use individuals' previous education and training, are not in individuals' fields of expertise, or do not provide as many work hours as desired (Feldman, 1996). Young adults who take leaves from school often accept a series of part-time or temporary jobs to hold them over financially until they come to firmer decisions about their career goals (National Center for Education Statistics, 1996c).

These delays can sometimes lead to destructive cycles of career failure (Feldman & Turnley, 1995). Young adults may drop out of school (or delay going to school) to discover their true calling. Unfortunately, they may not get jobs that teach them high-level skills because they have insufficient education. The cycle perpetuates itself because young adults are reluctant to go back to school without more certainty and goal direction, but they cannot get more certainty and goal direction until they try out higher-skilled jobs. Moreover, the longer young adults are undecided about their career goals, the longer they may remain underemployed; the longer they stay underemployed, the less desirable they become as candidates for better jobs or graduate programs.

Person-Occupation Fit and Psychological Well-Being

Two potential positive outcomes of delays in the formation of early-career identity are improved person-occupation fit and greater psychological well-being. If adolescents and young adults take more time to consider various career options and obtain more accurate information about themselves and the job market, they may ultimately choose career paths for which they are better suited (Holland, 1985).

The achievement of this congruence has been particularly linked with an increased sense of psychological well-being (Tinsley, 2000). For example, the achievement of person-occupation fit may result in employees' being better performers in their chosen occupations and more satisfied with those occupations. As Smith (1968) suggests, if individuals ultimately start their careers in occupations that suit their needs, benign cycles of growth and development are likely to follow. Some delays in the formation of early-career identity—if they lead to greater person-occupation fit—may result in longer-term satisfaction with work, careers, and life in general.

Moderator Variables

What determines whether career indecision and delays in the formation of early-career identity result in positive or negative consequences for adolescents and young adults? We identify four moderator variables of potential interest here.

First, it is reasonable to propose that the overall demand for labor will moderate the relationships of career indecision with loss of earnings and underemployment. When overall demand for labor in the economy is high, the quality of jobs young adults can obtain and the amount of money that individuals taking breaks from school can earn are relatively high (Fallick, 1999; Lent et al., 2000; Mickelwright, Rajah, & Smith, 1995). A robust economy, then, creates conditions where delays in the formation of early-career identity will be less strongly related to negative financial consequences.

The second moderator variable important to consider here is the quality of gap time—that is, the extent to which breaks from school and employment facilitate individual development and growth. All other factors being equal, the relationships between delays in early-career identity formation and negative individual outcomes will be weaker when quality of gap time is high.

Dustmann, Mickelwright, Rajah, and Smith (1996) present some interesting data on the effects of paid employment on the subsequent educational achievement of young adults. Their results suggest that while working extensively may negatively affect young adults' ultimate level of educational attainment, working does help young adults become better at organizational ability and managing time. Thus, improvements in work motivation and work habits may partially compensate for fewer years of formal schooling. This finding is also consistent with the work of Greenberger and Steinberg (1986) on the quality of students' part-time work experiences while still in school. If students are segregated into "teenage ghettos" (Greenberger & Steinberg, 1986), they are much more likely to learn antiorganizational behaviors like loafing and the use of equipment and supplies for personal benefit. In contrast, when young adults are integrated with older adults into meaningful work activities, they are much more likely to develop career resilience and career insight (Barling et al., 1995; Griliches, 1980).

Rigidity of occupational career paths, the third moderator variable, may also temper or exacerbate the effects of career indecision. Some occupations are less receptive to delays in career entry than others. For example, most medical schools still have a decided preference for new entrants under age thirty because of the lengthy training period required for physicians. Extended delays in the formation of early-career identity may present significant barriers to entry for those who decide to become doctors later in life and for hospitals and health centers that want to hire these latecomers. Early-career demands of long night and weekend shifts are geared toward young adults in their twenties with few, if any, children—not to middle-aged adults with heavy family responsibilities.

Finally, rigidity in organizational career paths may also play an important moderating role in the effects of career indecision. As Van Maanen and Schein (1979) suggest, organizations vary in the extent to which they have implicit (or explicit) guidelines for career progression. With some exceptions, most major public accounting firms tend to have very structured internal career ladders with little leeway for delays or time-outs. In contrast, career paths in media companies like newspapers tend to be much more fluid, with individuals of all ages entering and exiting over time. Thus, the more boundaryless the organization is where an individual begins his or her career, the more readily the firm may adjust to a young adult's idiosyncratic background.

Implications for Management Practice and Vocational Counseling

We conclude by examining the potential implications of delays in the formation of career identity for organizations that recruit, hire, and socialize young adults. In addition, we consider some potential implications for the delivery of vocational counseling to teenagers and young adults who are experiencing career indecision.

Implications for Management Practice

Career indecision can influence the human resource management of young adults in a variety of ways. Here, we focus on recruitment and selection, socialization, orientation and training, retention and turnover, and work attitudes.

Recruitment and Selection

In the short run, delays in the formation of early-career identity may be associated with organizational difficulties in recruiting and hiring new employees. A smaller percentage of college students are graduating from college within a four-year period. One of the problems facing hiring organizations, then, may be finding enough qualified new employees for entry-level positions. In addition, young adults who have not yet formed an early-career identity may be interested in only short-term gap employment between periods of enrollment in college or graduate school. As a result, some organizations may have more difficulty hiring and retaining people and accurately forecasting labor needs.

Socialization, Orientation, and Training

In the short run, delays in the formation of early-career identity may also have negative consequences for those in charge of managing organizational entry. It may not be easy to build enthusiasm, excitement, and conscientiousness among newly hired employees who view themselves as just passing through (Feldman, 1988).

Furthermore, delays in the formation of early-career identity may make organizational allocations of training resources more problematic. On one hand, young adults who have not yet firmed up their career plans may greatly desire extensive training as a way of discovering their vocational interests and abilities. On the other hand, training can be an expensive investment for organizations. If organizations invest heavily in training young adults who ultimately leave out of disinterest rather than dissatisfaction, the financial costs of training may be especially high.

Retention and Turnover

Delays in the formation of early-career identity may have more positive consequences for organizations in the long run than in the short run. It is reasonable to assume that individuals who are having trouble identifying early-career goals will have higher turnover and that their organizational employers will have more difficulties retaining them. However, if these delays ultimately result in better person-occupation fit, then organizations may actually benefit in the long run. Once having found their niches, young adults may be much more stable, in terms of organizational mobility, in subsequent years.

Work Attitudes

The consequences of delays in the formation of early-career identity are also likely to be mixed. In the short run, these delays are likely to be associated with poorer work attitudes. When young adults have trouble defining what types of jobs they want or procrastinate in job hunting, they are much more likely to end up with jobs that they find unchallenging and unrewarding; the jobs left at the end of the recruiting season also tend to be the least desirable ones (Feldman, 1996; Feldman & Turnley, 1995). Nevertheless, these delays may not necessarily have long-term negative consequences for employees' work attitudes. Once they find occupations that truly fit their interests and abilities, individuals may exhibit higher work motivation and commitment than their peers who settled too quickly for less (Arthur & Rousseau, 1996).

As this discussion suggests, it might be useful to frame the consequences of delays in the formation of early-career identity along three dimensions: individual-organizational, positive-negative, and short term–long term. To date, most of the research in this area has focused on short-term, negative consequences for teenagers and young adults themselves. More empirical research on the organizational consequences, the potential positive outcomes associated with delays, and the longer-term consequences of career indecision is clearly warranted.

Implications for Vocational Counseling

If the ideas presented here hold true, they suggest that the dominant advice given to teenagers and young adults about choosing careers—do more research and get more information—may be a double-edged sword. On one hand, it is certainly true that some young adults make decisions with inadequate information and unrealistic expectations. On the other hand, many young adults are so swamped by the number of career possibilities and the volume of data available to them that they experience information overload. The search for new information seems endless, while the attention given to the synthesis of that information seems inadequate. As Janis and Mann (1977) suggest, then, the hypervigilance of obsessive information search needs to be counterbalanced by increased attention to data analysis. Urging teenagers to engage in more and more information search in the absence of more and more analysis may in fact be counterproductive.

Another possible implication for vocational counseling is helping young adults increase the weight given to skills and abilities in important career decisions. Much of the current emphasis in the career counseling literature has been on the identification of vocational interests, since young adults who find careers that fit their interests are more likely to remain in the occupations they choose (Holland, 1985). However, there is a much more tenuous relationship between the strength of vocational interests and successful performance in those occupations; liking social activities does not necessarily translate into becoming a good marketer or thera-pist. Thus, while it may be highly constructive to encourage stu-dents to pursue careers in which they have great interest, it might be equally constructive to help them diagnose their skills and tal-ents in the same depth.

The discussion points to a third potential implication of the ideas presented here: that one-on-one counseling may not be eas-ily supplanted by generic, self-guided career discovery exercises. Although such exercises can provide a useful starting point for se-rious discussions about career issues, it is important to understand that such inventories are susceptible to fakability. That is, if a stu-dent wants the results to show he or she should be an engineer, it is quite clear the student should answer questions involving at-traction to math and science in the affirmative. Moreover, young adults may discount data that disconfirm their initial decision-making inclinations or turn a blind eye toward their weaknesses as job candidates. Focused one-on-one counseling may be very in-strumental in penetrating young adults' defenses and flaws in their decision making.

Fourth, the research on delays in enrollment and in getting de-grees is quite convincing that unstructured gaps in educational progress increase the likelihood of lower earning power and longer-term underemployment. Although this does not necessar-ily suggest that students should move in a lockstep manner from degree to degree, it does suggest that young adults should make more constructive use of their time away from school in structured internships, co-op positions, and other activities that help crystal-lize career interests and build career competencies. Young adults making decisions about taking time away from school need to con-sider not only what might be gained but also what might be lost by these periods of leave.

Finally, the ideas presented here suggest that young adults may be focusing too much attention on keeping their options open rather than on bringing some career decisions to closure. It is cer-tainly understandable, and even desirable, for adolescents to keep as many options open as they can, particularly when they are quite young and have amorphous ideas about their future lives. How-ever, as individuals pass into their twenties, the effort to keep fu-ture options open can impede career progress as much as facilitate it. Since every career decision can potentially close more doors than it opens new ones, young adults may become too reluctant to commit to any one course of action for fear that some future course of action may be more attractive. Thus, just as in the stock market, it is important to teach young adults as much about when to exercise their options as when to accumulate them.

References

Albert, K. A., & Luzzo, D. A. (1999). The role of perceived barriers in career development: A social cognitive perspective. *Journal of Counseling and Development, 77,* 423–430.

Arthur, M. B., & Rousseau, D. M. (1996). *The boundaryless career: A new employment principle for a new organizational area.* New York: Oxford University Press.

Barling, J. (1990). *Employment, stress, and family functioning.* New York: Wiley.

Barling, J., Dupre, K. E., & Hepburn, C. G. (1998). Effects of parents' job insecurity on children's work beliefs and attitudes. *Journal of Applied Psychology, 83,* 112–118.

Barling, J., Rogers, K. A., & Kelloway, E. K. (1995). Some effects of teenagers' part-time employment: The quantity and quality of work make the difference. *Journal of Organizational Behavior, 16,* 143–154.

Barling, J., Zacharatos, A., & Hepburn, C. G. (1999). Parents' job insecurity affects children's academic performance through cognitive difficulties. *Journal of Applied Psychology, 84,* 437–444.

Bartley, D. F., & Robitschek, C. (2000). Career exploration: A multivariate analysis of predictors. *Journal of Vocational Behavior, 56,* 63–81.

Beach, L. R., & Mitchell, T. R. (1990). Image theory: A behavioral theory of image making in organizations. In B. Staw & L. L. Cummings (Eds.), *Research in organizational behavior* (Vol. 12, 1–41). Stamford, CT: JAI Press.

Betz, N. E., & Voyten, K. K. (1997). Efficacy and outcome expectations influence career exploration and decidedness. *Career Development Quarterly, 46,* 179–189.

Bloom, A. (1987). *The closing of the American mind.* New York: Simon & Schuster.

Bolles, R. N. (2001). *What color is your parachute?* (25th ed.). Berkeley, CA: Ten Speed Press.

Brooks, D. (2001). The organization kid. *Atlantic Monthly, 287,* 40–55.

Caldwell, D. F., & Burger, J. M. (1998). Personality characteristics of job applicants and success in screening interviews. *Personnel Psychology, 51,* 119–136.

Caspi, A., Bem, D. J., & Elder, G. H. (1989). Continuities and consequences of interactional styles across the life course. *Journal of Personality, 57,* 375–406.

D'Amico, R. (1984). Does employment during high school impair academic progress? *Sociology of Education, 57,* 152–164.

Digman, J. M. (1990). Personality structure: Emergence of the five-factor model. *Annual Review of Psychology, 41,* 417–440.

Donnay, D.A.C., & Borgen, F. H. (1999). The incremental validity of vocational self-efficacy: An examination of interest, self-efficacy, and occupation. *Journal of Counseling Psychology, 46,* 432–447.

Douglas, J. W., & Brewer, G. A. (1999). Supervisors' perceptions of the performance of cooperative education employees working in federal agencies. *Review of Public Personnel Administration, 19,* 50–60.

Dunegan, K. J. (1993). Framing, cognitive modes, and image theory: Toward an understanding of a glass half full. *Journal of Applied Psychology, 78,* 491–503.

Dustmann, C., Mickelwright, J., Rajah, N., & Smith, S. (1996). Earning and learning: Educational policy and the growth of part-time work by full-time students. *Fiscal Studies, 17,* 79–94.

Enright, M. S., Conyers, L. M., & Szymanski, E. M. (1996). Career and career-related educational concerns of college students with disabilities. *Journal of Counseling and Development, 75,* 103–114.

Fain, J. R. (1999). Ranking the factors that affect occupational outcomes. *Industrial Relations, 38,* 92–104.

Fallick, B. C. (1999). Part-time work and industry growth. *Monthly Labor Review, 122*(3), 22–29.

Feldman, D. C. (1988). *Managing careers in organizations.* Glenview, IL: Scott, Foresman.

Feldman, D. C. (1996). The nature, antecedents, and consequences of underemployment. *Journal of Management, 22,* 385–409.

Feldman, D. C. (1999). Toxic mentors or toxic proteges? A critical reexamination of dysfunctional mentoring. *Human Resource Management Review, 9,* 247–278.

Feldman, D. C., & Doerpinghaus, H. I. (1992). Patterns of part-time employment. *Journal of Vocational Behavior, 41,* 282–294.

Feldman, D. C., Doerpinghaus, H. I., & Turnley, W. H. (1995). Employee reactions to temporary jobs. *Journal of Managerial Issues, 7,* 125–141.

Feldman, D. C., Folks, W. R., & Turnley, W. H. (1998). The socialization of expatriate interns. *Journal of Managerial Issues, 10,* 403–418.

Feldman, D. C., & Turnley, W. H. (1995). Underemployment among recent college graduates. *Journal of Organizational Behavior, 6,* 691–706.

Feldman, D. C., & Weitz, B. A. (1990). Summer interns: Factors contributing to positive developmental experiences. *Journal of Vocational Behavior, 37,* 267–284.

Fuligni, A. J., Eccles, J. S., Barber, B. L., & Clements, P. (2001). Early adolescent peer orientation and adjustment during high school. *Developmental Psychology, 37,* 28–36.

Ginzberg, E., Ginzberg, S. W., Axelrod, W., & Herna, J. L. (1951). *Occupational choice: An approach to a general theory.* New York: Columbia University Press.

Gottfredson, D. C. (1985). Youth employment, crime, and schooling: A longitudinal study of a national sample. *Developmental Psychology, 21,* 419–432.

Greenberger, E., & Steinberg, L. (1986). *When teenagers work.* New York: Basic Books.

Grensing-Pophal, L. (1999). Teens at work: Handle with care. *HRMagazine, 44,* 55–59.

Griffith, J. (1995). An empirical examination of a model of social climate in elementary schools. *Basic and Applied Social Psychology, 17,* 97–117.

Griliches, Z. (1980). Schooling interruption, work while in school, and returns from schooling. *Scandinavian Journal of Economics, 82,* 291–303.

Habermas, T., & Bluck, S. (2000). Getting a life: The emergence of the life story in adolescence. *Psychological Bulletin, 126,* 748–769.

Hamm, J. V. (2000). Do birds of a feather flock together? The variable bases for African American, Asian American, and European American adolescents' selection of similar friends. *Developmental Psychology, 36,* 209–219.

Harper, L. (1998, June 10). Hot job market may melt teens' plans for college. *Wall Street Journal,* A2–A3.

Harvey, E. (1999). Short-term and long-term effects of early parental employment on children of the National Longitudinal Survey of Youth. *Developmental Psychology, 35,* 445–459.

Hochschild, A. R. (1997). *The time bind.* New York: Holt.

Hofstede, G. (1980). *Culture's consequences: International differences in work-related values.* Thousand Oaks, CA: Sage.

Holland, J. L. (1985). *Making vocational choices: A theory of careers* (2nd ed.). Upper Saddle River, NJ: Prentice Hall.

Janis, I. L., & Mann, L. (1977). *Decision making.* New York: Free Press.

Kasen, S., Johnson, J., & Cohen, P. (1990). The impact of school emotional climate on student psychopathology. *Journal of Abnormal Child Psychology, 18,* 165–177.

Kerr, M., & Stattin, H. (2000). What parents know, how they know it, and several forms of adolescent adjustment: Further support for a reinterpretation of monitoring. *Developmental Psychology, 36,* 366–380.

Kokko, K., & Pulkkinen, L. (2000). Aggression in childhood and long-term unemployment in adulthood: A cycle of maladaptation and some protective factors. *Developmental Psychology, 36,* 463–472.

Kush, K., & Cochran, L. (1993). Enhancing a sense of agency through career planning. *Journal of Counselling Psychology, 40,* 434–439.

Langer, E., & Schank, R. C. (1994). *Belief, reasoning, and decision making.* Mahwah, NJ: Erlbaum.

Lent, R. W., Brown, S. D., & Hackett, G. (2000). Contextual supports and barriers to career choice. *Journal of Counseling Psychology, 47,* 36–49.

Lipke, D. J. (2000). Work study. *American Demographics, 22,* 9–14.

London, M., & Mone, E. M. (1987). *Career growth and survival in the workplace.* San Francisco: Jossey-Bass.

London, M., & Stumpf, S. A. (1986). Individual and organizational career development in changing times. In D. T. Hall (Ed.), *Career development in organizations* (pp. 21–49). San Francisco: Jossey-Bass.

Loughlin, C. A., & Barling, J. (1998). Teenagers' part-time employment and their work-related attitudes and aspirations. *Journal of Organizational Behavior, 19,* 197–207.

Luzzo, D. A. (1999). Identifying the career decision-making needs of non-traditional college students. *Journal of Counseling and Development, 77,* 135–140.

Luzzo, D. A., Hitchings, W. E., Retish, P., & Shoemaker, A. (1999). Evaluating differences in college students' career decision making on the basis of disability status. *Career Development Quarterly, 48,* 142–156.

Luzzo, D. A., McWhirter, E. H., & Hutcheson, K. G. (1997). Evaluating career decision-making factors associated with employment among first-year college students. *Journal of College Student Development, 38,* 166–172.

Maslow, A. H. (1954). *Motivation and personality.* New York: HarperCollins.

Masten, A. S., & Coatsworth, J. D. (1998). The development of competence in favorable and unfavorable environments: Lessons from research on successful children. *American Psychologist, 53,* 205–220.

McHale, S. M., Updegraff, K. A., Helms-Erikson, H., & Crouter, A. C. (2001). Sibling influences on gender development in middle childhood and early adolescence: A longitudinal study. *Developmental Psychology, 37,* 115–125.

Mickelwright, J., Rajah, N., & Smith, S. (1995). Labouring and learning: Part-time work and full-time education. *National Institute Labor Review, 148,* 73–87.

Moss, M. K., & Frieze, I. H. (1993). Job preferences in the anticipatory socialization phase: A comparison of two matching models. *Journal of Vocational Behavior, 42,* 282–297.

National Center for Education Statistics. (1996a, Aug.). *A descriptive summary of bachelor's degree recipients one year later.* Washington, DC: U.S. Department of Education.

National Center for Education Statistics. (1996b, Nov.). *Nontraditional undergraduates.* Washington, DC: U.S. Department of Education.

National Center for Education Statistics. (1996c, May). *Postsecondary persistence and attainment.* Washington, DC: U.S. Department of Education.

National Center for Education Statistics. (1997, June). *Transfer behavior among beginning postsecondary students.* Washington, DC: U.S. Department of Education.

National Center for Education Statistics. (1998, July). *Postsecondary financing strategies: How undergraduates combine work, borrowing, and attendance.* Washington, DC: U.S. Department of Education.

National Center for Education Statistics. (1999, June). *Life after college.* Washington, DC: U.S. Department of Education.

O'Brien, K. M., & Fassinger, R. E. (1993). A causal model of the career orientation and career choice of adolescent women. *Journal of Counseling Psychology, 40,* 456–469.

Osipow, S. H. (1990). Convergence in theories of career choice and development: Review and prospect. *Journal of Vocational Behavior, 36,* 122–131.

Palmer, S., & Cochran, L. (1988). Parents as agents of career development. *Journal of Counseling Psychology, 35,* 71–76.

Pautler, K. J., & Lewko, J. H. (1985). Student opinion of work in positive and negative economic climates. *Alberta Journal of Economic Research, 31,* 201–208.

Piotrowski, C. S., & Stark, E. (1987). Children and adolescents look at their parents' jobs. In J. H. Lewko (Ed.), *How children and adolescents view the world of work* (pp. 3–19). New directions for child development, no. 35. San Francisco: Jossey-Bass.

Post-Kammer, P., & Smith, P. L. (1985). Sex differences in career self-efficacy, consideration, and interests of eighth and ninth graders. *Journal of Counseling Psychology, 32,* 551–555.

Reutefors, D. L., Schneider, L. J., & Overton, T. D. (1979). Academic achievement: An examination of Holland's congruency, consistency, and differentiation predictions. *Journal of Vocational Behavior, 14,* 181–189.

Roe, A. (1956). *The psychology of occupations.* New York: Wiley.

Roese, N. J. (1997). Counterfactual thinking. *Psychological Bulletin, 121,* 133–148.

Ross, S., & Marriner, A. (1985). Cooperative education: Experience-based learning. *Nursing Outlook, 33,* 177–180.

Rysiew, K. J., Shore, B. M., & Leeb, R. T. (1999). Multipotentiality, giftedness, and career choice: A review. *Journal of Counseling and Development, 77,* 423–430.

Salamone, P. R., & Slaney, R. B. (1978). The applicability of Holland's theory to nonprofessional workers. *Journal of Vocational Behavior, 13,* 63–74.

Schacter, D. L. (2001). *The seven sins of memory: How the mind forgets and remembers.* Boston: Houghton Mifflin.

Schein, E. H. (1990). *Career anchors.* San Diego, CA: Pfeiffer.

Schmitt, N., Sacco, J. M., Ramey, S., Ramey, C., & Chan, D. (1999). Parental employment, school climate, and children's academic and social development. *Journal of Applied Psychology, 84,* 737–753.

Shamir, B. (1985). Self-esteem and the psychological impact of unemployment. *Social Psychology Quarterly, 49,* 61–72.

Sharf, R. (1997). *Applying career development theory to counseling.* Pacific Grove, CA: Brooks/Cole.

Shea, J. (2000). Does parents' money matter? *Journal of Public Economics, 77,* 155–184.

Shellenbarger, S. (1998, June 3). Teens are inheriting parents' tendencies toward work overload. *Wall Street Journal,* B1–B2.

Simon, H. A. (1976). *Administrative behavior* (3rd ed.). New York: Free Press.

Smith, M. B. (1968). Competence and socialization. In J. A. Clausen (Ed.), *Socialization and society* (pp. 270–320). New York: Little, Brown.

Stern, D. (1997). The continuing promise of work-based learning. *CenterFocus,* no. 18. Berkeley, CA: National Center for Research in Vocational Education.

Stern, D., Stone, J. R., Hopkins, C., & McMillion, M. (1990). Quality of students' work experience and orientation toward work. *Youth and Society, 22,* 263–282.

Super, D. E. (1957). *The psychology of careers.* New York: HarperCollins.

Szymanski, E. M., & Hanley-Maxwell, C. (1996). Career development of people with developmental disabilities: An ecological model. *Journal of Rehabilitation, 62,* 48–55.

Tagalakis, V., Amsel, R., & Fichten, C. S. (1988). Job interview strategies for people with a visible disability. *Journal of Applied Social Psychology, 18,* 520–532.

Taylor, M. S. (1985). The roles of occupational knowledge and crystallization of vocational self-concept in students' school to work transition. *Journal of Counseling Psychology, 32,* 539–550.

Taylor, M. S. (1988). The effects of college internships on individual participants. *Journal of Applied Psychology, 73,* 393–401.

Tiedeman, D. V., & O'Hara, R. P. (1963). *Career development: Choice and adjustment.* Princeton, NJ: College Entrance Examination Board.

Tinsley, H.E.A. (2000). The congruence myth: An analysis of the efficacy of the person-environment fit model. *Journal of Vocational Behavior, 56,* 147–179.

Trusty, J., Ng, K., & Plata, M. (2000). Interaction effects of gender, SES, and race-ethnicity on postsecondary educational choices of U.S. students. *Career Development Quarterly, 49,* 45–59.

U.S. Bureau of Labor Statistics. Office of Employment and Unemployment Statistics. (1998, Sept.). *The condition of education.* Washington, DC: U.S. Government Printing Office.

Van Maanen, J., & Schein, E. H. (1979). Toward a theory of organizational socialization. In L. L. Cummings & B. M. Staw (Eds.), *Research in organizational behavior* (Vol. 1, pp. 209–264). Stamford, CT: JAI Press.

Veblen, T. (1934). *Theory of the leisure class.* New York: Modern Library. (Original work published 1899)

Vondracek, F. W., & Schulenberg, J. (1992). Counseling for normative and nonnormative influences on career development. *Career Development Quarterly, 40,* 291–301.

Walls, R. T. (2000). Vocational cognition: Accuracy of 3rd, 6th, 9th, and 12th grade students. *Journal of Vocational Behavior, 56,* 137–144.

Wood, W. (2000). Attitude change: Persuasion and social influence. *Annual Review of Psychology, 51,* 539–570.

CHAPTER 5

The School-to-Work Transition

Elizabeth Wolfe Morrison

As young adults move from school to their first full-time jobs, several adjustment processes begin to unfold: a transition to an occupation or line of work, a transition to a particular organization, and a transition to the world of work in general. The success of these transition processes has implications not only for the young adults making this important move, but also for the organizations and occupations in which they work, the educational institutions that they are leaving, and the society that they are entering.

Over the years, a great deal has been written in the socialization literature about the transition into a new organization (see Bauer, Morrison, & Calister, 1998; Saks & Ashforth, 1997), but much less has been written about other aspects of the school-to-work transition. This chapter reviews, synthesizes, and extends our knowledge about this critical step in the career development process.

Research suggests that people typically face a wide range of challenges and tasks as they assume their first full-time jobs. Although scholars have categorized these challenges in a variety of different ways, an overarching theme has been one of adaptation, or efforts by individuals to achieve mastery and comfort within their new organizational context (Ashford & Taylor, 1990). Research suggests that to accomplish this objective, individuals must master three challenges: acquiring knowledge, building relationships, and redefining and clarifying their identity. Each of these challenges is addressed in this chapter. In particular, the chapter highlights the individual and contextual factors that determine how smoothly each of these three adaptation processes proceeds. The implications of the ideas presented here for future research and management practice are outlined as well.

Acquiring Knowledge

The transition into a new organization or job has generally been viewed as a process of learning, whereby the individual needs to acquire and integrate new knowledge and behavioral routines to be effective (Chao, O'Leary-Kelly, Wolf, & Klein, 1994; Fisher, 1986; Saks & Ashforth, 1997; Schein, 1978). This learning cuts across several domains.

The Challenge of Knowing What and How to Learn

Schein (1978) has talked about the importance of young adults' learning how to work, which entails such tasks as learning how to define problems, gain cooperation from others, judge one's own performance validly, and cope with too little (or too much) job definition. Fisher (1986) identified an even broader set of learning areas. She argued that socialization into an organization has the following components: learning to do the job (learning scripts, procedures, facts, and jargon), learning to function in the work group (how to deal with group norms, politics, resistance, and incompetence), and learning about the organization (its values, hierarchy, goals, and culture). Most of the empirical work building on this framework has focused on the means by which individuals learn about their job responsibilities, their work group, and the organization (Chao et al., 1994; Feldman, 1981; Ostroff & Kozlowski, 1992) and how new employees learn about role expectations and their own performance (Morrison, 1993b).

It is important to note, however, that the learning that occurs as one moves from school to work is broader than learning related just to one's particular job and organization. Fisher (1986) argued that socialization also includes personal learning, or learning about one's own values, capabilities, and needs. The individual who is starting work is learning about the new occupational role that he or she has assumed and the place in society implied by that role (status, obligations, and so forth).

Recent graduates beginning work may need to learn how to balance a new set of life demands. They may be struggling with such basic changes as needing to get up early every morning, no longer having a summer vacation, having less flexibility in terms of leisure time, and having to dress appropriately for work each day. In addition, the transition to work in some cases means relocation, and hence learning about and adapting to life in a new geographical area. For many recent graduates, the start of permanent work is also the first time that they have been financially independent. This independence may open up new opportunities but also implies new choices and new financial responsibilities. In sum, there are many areas that need to be mastered in the transition from school to work.

In addition to the challenge of knowing what to learn, the individual beginning work is faced with the challenge of knowing how to learn. Most recent graduates are accustomed to classroom and textbook learning, which is far more structured than on-the-job learning. In particular, students are accustomed to being told what it is that they must know and to being given most of the information that they need. This is generally not the case at work. Hence, a critical first task is identifying the relevant gaps in one's knowledge base and figuring out how to fill those gaps. The new worker may need to sift through the information acquired from school to determine which, if any, is relevant in the work setting. In some cases, very little school information is relevant, and formerly acquired knowledge schemes may need to be discarded. This process may be similar to what Lewin (1951) termed "unfreezing."

A major reason that this knowledge acquisition process is especially difficult is that organizations are often not very forthcoming with their newly hired employees. Although organizations use a variety of socialization mechanisms to provide newcomers with information (Jones, 1986), these mechanisms are often imperfect, incomplete, or ineffective. Several works have noted the limitations of organizational socialization processes for helping new employees learn about and assimilate into an organization (Jablin, 1984; Miller & Jablin, 1991; Morrison, 1993a, 1993b). For example, Jablin (1984) argued that newcomers often exist in an information void, not knowing many of the things that they need to know to function effectively. Morrison (1995), too, found that the types of information that newcomers reported receiving from their organization did not match the types of information that they viewed as most useful, suggesting that new employees cannot assume that the information they need will be conveyed to them.

The Role of Information Seeking

Given these constraints, an important way in which new employees can acquire knowledge is by actively seeking information. During the past decade, there has been increasing recognition that organizational newcomers are often proactive in adapting to a new workplace, and researchers have begun to study proactive information seeking more fully (Ashford & Black, 1996; Feldman & Brett, 1983; Major & Kozlowski, 1997; Morrison, 1993a, 1993b, 1995; Ostroff & Kozlowski, 1992). Information seeking is an important way for newcomers to acquire new knowledge and thereby adapt to a new set of work demands. It is particularly useful when the information they need or desire is not otherwise or freely provided (Miller & Jablin, 1991).

Studies have shown that organizational newcomers do in fact seek out a variety of different types of information: information about their job, their role in the organization, organizational norms and processes, their colleagues, and their own performance (Ashford & Black, 1996; Morrison, 1993a, 1993b; Ostroff & Kozlowski, 1992). Research has also shown that newcomers use different tactics and sources for information seeking, depending on the type of information that they are trying to gather. For example, a study of new accountants showed that they relied more heavily on indirect modes of information seeking than direct modes, except when seeking task-related information that may be difficult to obtain through indirect means (Morrison, 1993b). Moreover, newcomers were shown to rely more on their supervisors when seeking information about their job or performance, but were more likely to use peers for obtaining information about norms and work group dynamics. Newcomers, then, tailor their information seeking to different sources.

Whereas most research on information seeking has focused specifically on the transition into an organizational role (and hence the seeking of organizationally relevant information from supervisors and peers), new graduates may also seek information about the transition to work more broadly. Concerns may center on balancing work and nonwork demands and on future directions for one's career. There has been little research focused on whether and how individuals seek out information related to concerns such as these. A question that can be raised for future research is whether individuals are comfortable asking about career issues directly or whether they tend to use more subtle and unobtrusive forms of information seeking.

Another future research direction is addressing the sources that individuals rely on for answers to career-related questions. Because many career concerns are not specific to one's current place of employment, individuals may turn to friends, family members, and other contacts outside the organization. Little research has explored the seeking of information from sources outside one's organization, and hence we know relatively little about the role that this may play in the transition to work. However, one study found that early in the transition process, information seeking from friends and family had a positive relationship with adjustment levels (Settoon & Adkins, 1997).

Uncertainty Reduction as a Motive for Seeking Information

Although many motives may come into play in the decision of whether, and how, to seek out job- or career-related information, the motive that has been viewed as the driving force underlying this process is uncertainty reduction. Scholars have tended to describe career transitions in terms of uncertainty and have used uncertainty reduction theory as a basis for explaining why such transitions encourage information seeking (Feldman & Brett, 1983; Miller & Jablin, 1991). They argue that uncertainty is noxious and creates both anxiety and stress. The individual is motivated to resolve these states by seeking information. In the next section, propositions to guide future research on uncertainty reduction are introduced and explained.

Miller and Jablin (1991) have argued that uncertainty is "a basic catalyst for newcomers' information-seeking behaviors" (p. 95). In an extension of this idea, Ashford and Black (1996) noted that uncertainty implies a lack of predictive control or an inability to know what will happen. They proposed that entry into a new organizational environment can be thought of as a process of temporarily losing and then attempting to regain a sense of control. Miller and Jablin (1991) found some evidence for this perspective in their study. In short, as Proposition 1 suggests, information seeking can be driven by the desire to regain a sense of efficacy and predictability.

Proposition 1: Uncertainty, anxiety, and stress will increase the amount of information seeking during the school-to-work transition.

Anxiety, stress, and perceived lack of control may not always be the dominant responses to the transition to work, and uncertainty reduction may not always be the primary motive for seeking information during this transition. Nicholson and West (1988) found that managers settling into a new job did express feelings of stress but also feelings of challenge, freedom, satisfaction, and fulfillment. Furthermore, Brett (1982) did not find a negative relationship between job change and feelings of well-being. Other studies, too, suggest that at least for job changers, the experience is often perceived as one of excitement and opportunity rather than stress and anxiety (Feldman & Brett, 1983; Nicholson & West, 1988).

An exclusive focus on uncertainty reduction as a motive for information seeking may therefore be too narrow. Perhaps it is more useful to identify some of the individual and situational variables that will determine the degree to which the school-to-work transition is experienced as uncertain and stressful, and hence, the likelihood that information seeking will be driven by the desire to reduce these internal states. One variable that is likely to play a role is the degree of difference between the new and old settings. Louis (1980) argued that the more changes in the new situation from the previous situation, the more an individual has to actively cope with the new environment. For example, a student who has grown up and attended college in a rural environment and then assumes a job on Wall Street is likely to experience much more anxiety and stress than a native New Yorker moving into the same job because the two contexts differ on numerous dimensions. This greater anxiety and stress implies a stronger drive to seek out information.

Proposition 2: The amount of uncertainty, anxiety, and stress experienced during the school-to-work transition will be positively related to the degree of change inherent in the transition.

A variety of pretransition factors are also likely to affect the amount of anxiety and stress experienced during the school-to-work transition, as well as the need to seek information. For example, individuals will experience less uncertainty if they have received relevant job and professional training while in school because such training will reduce the number of unknowns about the job situation. In general, therefore, students moving from a vocational or professional school environment into the workforce should experience less uncertainty than those moving from a more general educational environment. Work experience in the form of an internship or a summer job, adequate career counseling while in school, and contact with role models within one's chosen profession are also experiences that may reduce uncertainty, stress, and anxiety in the transition to work. Each of these experiences can provide realistic information prior to the transition and will reduce the amount of uncertainty about the new job. Less uncertainty implies less need to seek information after the transition.

Proposition 3: The amount of professional training, prior work experience, career counseling, and role models is inversely related to the amount of uncertainty, anxiety, and stress experienced during the school-to-work transition.

Individual difference variables may also affect whether the school-to-work transition is experienced as uncertain and stressful. Jones (1983) proposed that self-efficacy will influence the reality shock of organizational entry by framing how the individual views the transition process. More specifically, individuals with low self-efficacy will be more likely to view the transition as threatening, whereas those with high self-efficacy will be more likely to view it as an opportunity.

Negative affectivity may also affect the experience of anxiety and stress during the transition to work. Negative affectivity refers to people's tendency to experience negative feelings and emotional states, view the world negatively, and experience stress (Watson & Clark, 1984). Hence, individuals high on negative affectivity will be more likely to experience the school-to-work transition as stressful and anxiety provoking than those low on negative affectivity.

Proposition 4: Self-efficacy will be negatively related to, and negative affectivity will be positively related to, the amount of uncertainty, anxiety, and stress experienced during the school-to-work transition.

Regulatory Focus Theory: An Alternative Motive for Information Seeking

The research suggests that one way to broaden the understanding of information seeking during the school-to-work transition is to explore some of the factors that increase or mitigate uncertainty. Yet another way to broaden our understanding of information seeking as it relates to the school-to-work transition is to consider motives other than uncertainty reduction. A framework that may be useful in this regard is regulatory focus theory (Higgins, 1997). Regulatory focus theory distinguishes between two categories of desired goals: those related to safety and security and those related to advancement and growth. This theory further proposes the existence of two distinct regulatory systems for the two different goals. When the goal is safety or security, the regulatory focus is prevention, or the avoidance of negative outcomes. When the goal is advancement and growth, the regulatory focus is promotion, or the attainment of positive outcomes (Higgins, 1997).

Uncertainty reduction theory is consistent with the notion of a prevention focus, since it assumes the individual is seeking information to mitigate uncertainty and the anxiety that this creates. However, in some cases, information seeking may be promotion driven; that is, the seeker is trying to take advantage of opportunities and achieve positive ends rather than trying to avoid or mitigate negative internal states.

For example, Ashford's (1986) work on feedback seeking highlighted the idea that individuals seek feedback information to help them reach a variety of personal goals. Researchers have also proposed that individuals may seek feedback as a way to create a positive impression of themselves (Morrison & Bies, 1991). Both of these ideas are consistent with the notion that information seeking is sometimes promotion driven and not just to prevent the discomfort of uncertainty. In the context of the school-to-work transition, such a focus might lead individuals to seek information to build knowledge or competencies beyond what is immediately required, to plan for future career moves better, to create positive impressions of themselves with senior managers, or to increase their own power and influence.

When information seeking is promotion focused, it is likely to be driven by different internal and external factors than when it is prevention focused. For example, whereas prevention-focused information seeking is likely to be highest among individuals with low tolerance for uncertainty (Ashford & Cummings, 1983), promotion-focused information seeking is unlikely to be related to uncertainty tolerance; instead, it may relate more strongly to such variables as the need for achievement and learning goal orientation.

Individuals with a high need for achievement aspire to succeed at work and set high goals for themselves (McClelland, 1961). Because information seeking can facilitate goal attainment (Ashford & Cummings, 1983), individuals with a high need for achievement may purposefully seek out information as a way to reach their personal goals. Similarly, individuals with a learning orientation are focused on developing competence by acquiring new skills and mastering new situations (Dweck & Leggett, 1988). Hence, new graduates with an orientation toward learning may see information seeking as providing an opportunity to reach these desired ends.

Proposition 5: Information seeking during the transition from school to work can be either prevention focused or promotion focused.

Proposition 6: Need for achievement and learning goal orientation will be positively related to promotion-focused information seeking during the transition from school to work.

Expanding the conceptualization of information seeking to include a promotion focus implies not only different antecedents to information seeking during the transition to work but also different dynamics. For example, Ashford (1986) suggested that information seeking following a change or transition will decrease over time. The logic is that as uncertainty is reduced, individuals have less need for information, and hence their information seeking becomes less frequent. The frequency of promotion-focused information seeking, on the other hand, may sustain itself, or even increase, over time.

As individuals become more comfortable in their new environment and roles and begin to focus on longer-term career goals, they may try to gain additional information that will facilitate the attainment of promotion-related goals. In addition, the modes for seeking information may shift over time when the seeker is promotion focused. With increasing experience and confidence, for example, people may be more comfortable using direct inquiry. It is interesting to note that research has not found much effect of tenure on information seeking (Bauer et al., 1998). A possible reason is that previous research has not distinguished between prevention- and promotion-focused information seeking, which may be moving in opposite directions.

Building a Network

Much of the literature on the transition into a new organization has emphasized the central role of social relationships. Relationships with other newcomers, more experienced peers, and supervisors can serve a variety of functions. Louis (1990) proposed that veteran coworkers are often day-to-day guides, providing information and assistance that facilitate sense making and acculturation. Feldman (1981) argued that one of the central components of the transition process is the internalization of group norms and values and integration into the work group. He noted that members of one's work group can provide emotional support, solutions to work problems, and a normative referent for appropriate behavior. These various discussions imply that relationships with peers and more experienced members of one's organization can play a critical role during the transition into a work organization. Furthermore, relationships with others within one's profession, as well as support and guidance from friends and family members, may aid in the transition to work more broadly.

Empirical research has highlighted the importance of relationships in the adaptation to work. Louis, Posner, and Powell (1983), for example, found that organizational newcomers regarded interactions with peers, supervisors, and senior coworkers as extremely helpful in learning the ropes and becoming effective organizational members. As noted, studies have also shown that newcomers obtain a variety of types of information from these sources and that this information helps them to learn about and adjust to their new surroundings (Morrison, 1993a; Ostroff & Kozlowski, 1992). In addition, research on mentoring highlights the important impact of developmental relationships and social support on career outcomes in general (Higgins & Kram, 2001).

A broad range of research therefore suggests that interpersonal relationships are instrumental in helping one to manage the transition to a new work setting successfully. Nevertheless, questions such as the following remain: Which types of relationships are most important? Are more relationships better than fewer? What should the overall constellation of relationships that one has formed look like? To answer these questions, we can look to both the literature on personal networks and recent research on developmental relationships.

Social Networks During the School-to-Work Transition

The literature on social networks conceives of organizations as clusters of people joined by a variety of links (Brass, 1995). An assumption behind network research is that structured social relationships are more powerful sources of explanation than personal attributes of system members. Social network scholars argue that one can understand organizational phenomena and outcomes by considering not only the presence of social relationships but the overall pattern of relationships between people, too (Brass, 1995).

While much of the social network literature focuses on the entire web of relationships within an organization or organizational unit, a few studies have looked specifically at personal networks—or individuals' unique sets of social contacts, the people whom they consider to be friends, the people to whom they turn for advice, and so forth (Burt, 1997; Ibarra, 1995; Morrison, in press; Podolny & Baron, 1997). These studies have focused on understanding the types of personal networks that are most instrumental for career success. For example, research has looked at the effects of variables such as the size, density, and range of an individual's personal network, where size reflects the number of persons in the network, density reflects whether those persons are themselves interconnected, and range reflects the diversity of contacts within the network.

Research has shown that the size, density, and range of informational and friendship networks are significantly related to career processes and outcomes such as promotions and mobility. Podolny and Baron (1997), for example, showed that mobility is enhanced by having a large and not very dense network of informational sources. However, when these authors looked at social support rather than informational networks, they found that smaller, denser networks were better predictors of mobility. These results suggest that different types of personal networks should be configured differently.

There is also evidence that the effect of network structure varies depending on race and gender. Ibarra (1995) showed that the value of network characteristics such as range and status differs for minority and nonminority managers. Furthermore, Burt (1997) found that whereas men reap promotional benefits from large, low-density networks, women do better with small networks of interconnected contacts.

A recent study that looked specifically at employees who had recently moved from school to work also showed that personal network characteristics matter (Morrison, in press). Individuals in that study felt the most knowledgeable when they had developed informational networks that were relatively large, dense, and made up of strong ties, although these effects varied for different types of learning. The amount of learning was also positively related to the diversity and hierarchical status of the persons within one's informational network, suggesting that it is helpful to have contacts from different areas in the organization and with people in higher positions. In addition, Morrison found that individuals felt the most socially integrated when they had developed a strong and relatively large friendship network.

Insight into the role of personal networks in the context of the school-to-work transition may also be gleaned from research on developmental relationships. In a conceptual article, Higgins and Kram (2001) highlighted the importance of the strength and diversity of the relationships within an individual's developmental network. Higgins and Thomas (2001) then empirically studied the effects of these developmental constellations: the sets of people who take an active interest in, and help to advance, an individual's career. This research found that both short-term and long-term career outcomes, such as satisfaction and intentions to remain, are related to the amount of psychosocial and career assistance provided by one's constellation of relationships. Career outcomes were also positively related to the number of people within one's constellation and to the organizational status of those relationships.

Together, these works support the idea that individuals moving from school to work should pay some attention to the webs of relationships that they are building. However, the best type of network to develop is likely to depend on the particular outcome of interest (whether it is learning or career advancement, for example).

Individual Variation in Network Building

The importance of networking has been highlighted in both the academic and practitioner-oriented literatures (Arthur & Rousseau, 1996; Kanter & Eccles, 1992). Business school students, in particular, are often told about the importance of building networks (Forret & Dougherty, in press). It is unlikely, however, that individuals moving from school to work are equally effective at following this advice. Some may lack the motivation to do so, and others may lack the capability or opportunity. This section identifies some variables that help explain individuals' effectiveness at building high-quality networks. As noted, such networks may be critical in promoting the informational, psychosocial, and career assistance that persons making the transition from school to work need.

Social proaction is one variable that is likely to explain variation in the effectiveness of network building during the school-to-work transition. Reichers (1987) introduced the term *proaction* to capture the extent to which a new employee seeks out social interaction opportunities. She proposed that proaction will have a positive effect on the speed of adaptation into a new job. Ashford and Black (1996) studied social proaction empirically. They found that M.B.A. students reentering the workforce socialized with others as a way to adapt to their new workplace and consciously worked on building relationships with colleagues and with their bosses.

Forret and Dougherty (in press) have also studied what they call networking behavior. Their work, like Ashford and Black's, suggests that new workers will vary in the extent to which they actively work on building relationships. Although greater proaction will not always guarantee effective network building, we might expect there to be a relationship between the frequency of social proaction and the likelihood of building personal networks that aid in the school-to-work transition. All else equal, individuals who are more active at initiating and taking advantage of opportunities for social interaction should be more effective network builders.

Proposition 7: Individuals who exhibit greater social proaction during the school-to-work transition will be more successful at developing high-quality social networks than individuals who are less socially proactive.

Individual differences are also likely to affect network development. Newcomers who are more relationship focused (with high extraversion and high needs for affiliation, for example), should be more effective at building supportive and instrumental networks than those who are less so. Newcomers who are more politically focused or politically savvy (for example, with a high need for power and high self-monitoring) may also be more likely to focus on network building as they make the transition into a work setting. Several studies have shown that network ties are a source of power and influence within organizations (Brass, 1984; Brass & Burkhardt, 1993). Thus, individuals more concerned with building and exercising power and influence are likely to be more focused on, and more skilled at, network building.

Proposition 8: Extraversion and need for affiliation will be positively related to success at developing high-quality social networks during the school-to-work transition.

Proposition 9: Need for power and self-monitoring will be positively related to success at developing high-quality social networks during the school-to-work transition.

Organizations use a variety of tactics to assimilate new members (Van Maanen & Schein, 1979). Research by Jones (1986) suggests that these tactics can be ordered along a continuum. At one end of this continuum is an institutionalized approach, in which individuals are separated from more experienced members of the organization, trained as a group, given structured information, and proceed on a fixed timetable. At the other end of the continuum is an individualized approach, which is highly unstructured, informal, and variable. These different approaches to socialization have been shown to lead to different outcomes. Whereas institutionalized socialization has been found to encourage newcomers to accept their roles as given, individualized socialization encourages newcomers to challenge the status quo and develop novel approaches to their roles (Jones, 1986).

Socialization tactics may also affect network development. For example, because institutionalized tactics entail the grouping of new entrants together, these tactics may enable individuals to form networks of peer relationships more easily and may receive valuable social support. The development of relationships with more experienced members of the organization, however, may be delayed when institutionalized tactics are used. Conversely, individualized socialization tactics may result in a smaller number of relationships with other newcomers but networks that contain a greater proportion of experienced members of the organization. This type of network may be useful not only for learning about the organization but also for career progression because it may provide both greater visibility and access to influential others.

Proposition 10: Individuals' success at developing high-quality social networks with peers will be greater when the organization uses institutionalized socialization tactics.

Proposition 11: Individuals' success at developing high-quality social networks with senior members of the organization will be greater when the organization uses individualized socialization tactics.

Mentoring may also help newcomers build network ties. Although there has been little research on the role of mentors during the school-to-work transition (Feldman, 1999), mentoring experiences have been linked to measures of career success in other contexts. One important career function that a mentor can play is to increase the visibility of his or her protégé within the organization (Kram, 1985). This typically entails introducing the protégé to important others or drawing others' attention to the protégé and his or her accomplishments. These activities may help newcomers to develop connections within the organization, particularly with more senior members. Hence, network development should also be positively related to both the amount and quality of mentoring that one receives.

Proposition 12: Individuals' success at developing high-quality social networks during the school-to-work transition will be positively related to the amount and quality of mentoring they receive.

Forging a New Identity: Struggles and Tensions

Individuals making the transition from school to work are not just learning and building relationships; they are redefining their sense of self as well(Fisher, 1986; Louis, 1980; Schein, 1971; Van Maanen, 1976). Schein (1971) argued that although basic personality structure is relatively stable, one's social self may change quite drastically during career transitions. Newcomers often develop new attitudes, values, self-images, and ways of conducting themselves in social situations. Those who are faced with new roles reconstruct themselves to meet new demands (Schein, 1971).

The process of identity change that accompanies the school-to-work transition may be particularly challenging because the individual is assuming not just an organizational role but also an occupational role and a new career stage. One is no longer an economics student at Penn or an M.B.A. student at the University of Chicago, but an account manager at Pfizer or a trader at Salomon Smith Barney. This shift can have tremendous implications for how one sees oneself in the world and for the attitudes and values that one holds.

Researchers who study social identification at work make a distinction between identification and internalization (Ashforth & Mael, 1989). Identification reflects how one defines oneself relative to one or more social groups (for example, "I am a banker"), whereas internalization refers to the incorporation of values espoused by a particular social group (for example, "Capitalism is good"). These processes, however, are related and sometimes hard to disentangle (Ashforth & Mael, 1989). When a person adopts a new social identity, there is often an accompanying shift in values, and vice versa. Therefore, identity and value change are treated as interrelated processes here.

The literature on organizational socialization suggests that individuals are generally quite malleable with respect to changing their values and sense of self when they begin work. Socialization scholars have argued that because organizations need to control the behavior of their members, they must shape the attitudes and values of new employees in organizationally consistent ways (Fisher, 1986; Schein, 1971; Van Maanen, 1976). Newcomers, in turn, are expected to adapt to fit the demands of their new context, changing not just their outward behavior but also some of their internal values and beliefs as the price of membership (Fisher, 1986; Schein, 1968; Van Maanen & Schein, 1979).

Consistent with this perspective, organizational newcomers are typically portrayed as willing and receptive participants of influence processes (Van Maanen, 1976). Scholars have argued that newcomers are strongly motivated to become accepted members of their organization; they do so by adapting their behaviors, attitudes, and beliefs and by identifying with the organization and its members (Ashford & Taylor, 1990; Fisher, 1986; Van Maanen & Schein, 1979). This argument is aligned with both the literature on organizational culture and the related literature on person-organization fit, which have highlighted the importance of congruence between the personal values of employees and the values of their organization. There is evidence that person-organization fit increases over time as individuals change to fit the demands of the organization better (Chatman, 1991). The portrayal of individuals as willing to change aspects of their selves is also consistent with research demonstrating that people are often highly malleable in the face of social influence. In fact, Asch (1956) takes as axiomatic the notion that social influence shapes people's practices, judgments, and beliefs.

One reason that values and identity often change when people move from school to work is that the social pressure is simultaneously strong and subtle. For example, organizations often require employees to expend considerable time, effort, and energy in activities that exemplify the organization's values and norms. As employees then try to rationalize their engagement in these activities, their values and beliefs evolve in organizationally consistent ways (O'Reilly, 1989; Wanous, 1980). Schein (1968) describes this process as getting the newcomer to "make a series of small behavioral commitments which can only be justified by him through the acceptance and incorporation of company values" (p. 232). Similarly, Ashforth (1998) argues that occupational socialization processes often require individuals to make a series of minor claims to a new sense of self, such that the individual gradually moves toward a new occupationally consistent identity. In other words, identity gradually alters as one enacts new roles.

These various arguments suggest strong internal and external pressures for individuals to adopt a new identity and set of values when they move from school to work. At the same time, however, there may be countervailing forces that create resistance to these pressures (Feldman, 1994). This has been acknowledged within the organizational socialization literature but not explored in any depth. Schein (1968), for example, noted that if a novice enters an organization with values or behavior patterns that are out of line with those expected by the organization, he or she must first "undo" or "unfreeze" these values and behaviors. He argued that this process is often unpleasant and therefore requires either strong motivation to endure it or strong organizational forces to make one endure it.

Schein (1971) also noted that newcomers in some cases reject their organization's central values. Although he regarded newcomers as malleable with respect to their more peripheral values and selves, he argued that there are certain core aspects of the self that individuals typically are unwilling to change. He used the term *rebellion* to describe people who refuse to change in organizationally or occupationally desired ways. In a similar vein, Van Maanen (1976, p. 68) noted that "at its worst, the process [of socialization] may lead to rejection by the individual of the expressed requirements of the organization."

There is also research emphasizing that in addition to organizational efforts to influence employees, entry is also characterized by employees' efforts to alter organizational and occupational demands as well (Feldman, 1994). This occurs through a process known as role negotiation (Ashford & Taylor, 1990). Individuals presumably engage in role negotiation because they wish to find a mutually acceptable role for themselves, yet at the same time, they view certain demands or expectations as unacceptable. There are limits, however, to what an individual can alter. Certain aspects of a role may be nonnegotiable, and it is unrealistic to expect that newcomers can alter demands stemming from core values and goals of the organization.

Barnard's work (1938) sheds further light on the tensions inherent in the process of defining a new role and identity. Barnard argued that for any given individual, there is a range of work demands that will be accepted without question. He referred to this as an employee's zone of indifference. As this term implies, an employee will be indifferent to meeting the demands within this zone because the costs of complying are less than or equivalent to the inducements being offered. However, any demands falling outside this zone will elicit resistance, because the employee perceives the potential costs of meeting the demand as exceeding the available inducements. Although Barnard's ideas focus on role demands, a similar process of accommodation and resistance is likely to occur as individuals are faced with pressures to alter their values and identities.

Support for the idea that identity and value change may entail tension and even resistance can also be found in the literature on reactance. There is evidence that when individuals feel deprived of personal control, they may engage in attempts to regain control, a process known as reactance (Brehm, 1972). A common form that reactance may take is rebellion, whereby the individual holds even more firmly to his or her prior behavioral or attitudinal preferences. O'Reilly and Chatman (1996) argue that "so strong is the desire to maintain personal control, and so objectionable are salient attempts to influence others, that individuals sometimes choose to adopt a position they do not really support, or behave in uncharacteristic (e.g. rebellious) ways to avoid accepting the one being urged on them" (p. 163).

There may be two sets of countervailing forces, then, that impinge on individuals moving from a school setting to a work setting: forces for altering their values and sense of self and forces to resist such change by retaining prior values and identities. These two sets of forces may play out in different ways, with the greatest potential for ambivalence and tension occurring when both sets of forces are very strong. Both dispositional and contextual variables may help to explain the extent to which tension around identity change will be experienced.

Dispositional Variables Affecting the Identity Change Process

Dawis and Lofquist (1984) proposed that individuals vary in their tolerance for discrepancies between themselves and the demands of their environment. They also proposed that individuals have different characteristic styles for dealing with such discrepancies and implied that these styles are a function of various personality traits (Ashford & Taylor, 1990). Some of the individual traits that are likely to be relevant for how people deal with identity change are self-esteem, self-monitoring, need for control, and individualism.

Self-esteem reflects the extent to which people have pride in themselves and their capabilities. Brockner (1988) proposed that one of the primary ways in which high- and low-self-esteem individuals differ is that the latter are more susceptible to external influence. One reason for this greater plasticity is that low-self-esteem individuals lack self-confidence and are therefore more prone to regard external cues as appropriate guides for their thoughts and behaviors. Another potential reason is that individuals with low self-esteem are especially dependent on approval from others, and one way to obtain this approval is to conform to social pressures. Brockner's findings (1988) suggest that relative to individuals with low self-esteem, individuals with high self-esteem will be less easily socialized into new organizational and occupational roles and will be more likely to experience tensions in the face of external pressures to adopt new values, attitudes, behaviors, or identities.

Proposition 13: The higher the individual's self-esteem is, the greater the likelihood of tension related to identity and value change will be.

Self-monitoring is another attribute that affects people's susceptibility to environmental pressures. Self-monitoring refers to an individual's ability to adjust his or her behavior to external, situational factors (Snyder, 1974). Whereas high self-monitors regulate their behavior to match situational contingencies, low self-monitors are more resistant to situational pressures and act in accordance with their own internal beliefs and preferences. This dynamic suggests that high self-monitors will be more comfortable assuming a new social identity than will low self-monitors. Conversely, low self-monitors will be more likely to resist pressures to alter their identity when those pressures conflict with their internal beliefs and preferences.

Proposition 14: Relative to high self-monitors, low self-monitors will be more likely to experience tension related to identity and value change.

People have a need to control their environment and their own behavior (Greenberger & Strasser, 1986; White, 1959), yet research has also shown that individuals differ in the strength of their need for control (Ashford & Black, 1996; Greenberger, Strasser, & Lee, 1988). Those with a high need for control are strongly driven to master their environment and determine their own behavior. Individuals with a high need for control should be more likely to resist pressures to alter their identity. This prediction is consistent with Black and Ashford's finding (1995) that individuals with a high need for control were less likely to submit to socialization pressures and more likely to try to change the demands of their environment to fit their own goals and preferences.

In contrast, those with a low need for control are more comfortable surrendering control to external forces. Such individuals should be more inclined to accept pressures for both organizational and occupational socialization.

Proposition 15: The stronger the need for control is, the greater the likelihood of tension related to identity and value change will be.

There is a large body of research on the cultural dimension of individualism (Hofstede, 1980). This attribute has been shown to vary not only across cultures but also between individuals within a culture (Triandis, 1995). Individuals who are individualistic in orientation value independence, autonomy, and being unique. This can be contrasted with individuals who are collectivistic in orientation and value interdependence, membership within a group, and harmonious relationships with others (Hofstede, 1980; Triandis, 1995).

It is likely that differences in this orientation will affect how the transition into a new organizational or occupational role will be experienced. Because people who are collectivistic in orientation place heavy emphasis on fitting in and being part of a social group, they should be more likely to accept and feel comfortable with pressures for identification and value change. In contrast, people who are individualistic in orientation should be more likely to resist changing their values or identities.

Proposition 16: The stronger is one's individualistic orientation, the greater is the likelihood of tension related to identity and value change.

Contextual Variables Affecting the Identity-Change Process

In addition to individual-level variables, contextual or situational factors are also likely to affect the extent to which identity change during the school-to-work transition entails tensions and internal conflicts. For example, there is evidence suggesting that the nature of the transition one is making and characteristics of the new organizational setting will affect the ease with which the transition process unfolds. In particular, the novelty of the new context, volition in joining the new organization, strength of the organization's culture, and the organization's selection and socialization processes are all likely to play critical roles.

Although all career and role transitions entail change, the magnitude of the change can vary substantially. Novelty refers to the extent to which a given role transition differs from prior role transitions that the individual has made (Nicholson, 1984). Nicholson proposed that when a newly assumed role is relatively novel, individuals will be more likely to change themselves to fit the demands of that role. Conversely, individuals will tend to feel less need to change themselves when they are entering a role that is more familiar. Instead, they will be inclined to exhibit "familiar styles and well-practiced routines" (Nicholson, 1984, p. 178).

This research implies that tensions surrounding identity change will be positively related to the level of novelty inherent in a given role transition, since novel situations entail both more uncertainty and greater pressure to change one's values and sense of self. For example, a business school graduate who has held a summer job in an accounting firm should more easily settle into a corporate job than a history major whose only work experience has been waiting tables.

Proposition 17: The greater the novelty of the role transition is, the greater is the likelihood of tension related to identity and value change.

Fisher (1986) suggested that the amount of choice individuals feel they had in deciding to join an organization will relate to their subsequent motivation toward fully adjusting to their new role. She argued that when one freely chooses a new role, it most likely means that one prefers that role to others, and hence, the motivation to succeed in that new role should be high. Fisher also suggested that individuals will rationalize their adjustment behavior more when the volition of their choice is high. When individuals believe that they freely chose one alternative over another, they may show a high level of post hoc commitment to that choice in order to appear self-consistent (Staw, 1981). Conversely, commitment may be low if a course of action was not freely chosen, such as when an individual lacked other job options.

Drawing on these ideas, we can predict that when the degree of volition is low, individuals may be more likely to experience tensions with respect to altering their identity. In other words, individuals entering the workforce will be more likely to accept fully the demands being placed on them when they perceive that they have freely chosen their new occupational and organizational role.

Proposition 18: The less choice that the individual had in assuming the new occupational and organizational role, the greater is the likelihood of tension related to identity and value change.

Tensions around identity change will also be affected by characteristics of the organization that the individual is entering. For example, some organizations have strong cultures, characterized by deeply held and widely shared values and norms (O'Reilly, 1989). Within such organizations, there are strong pressures for employees to change their behaviors, attitudes, values, and beliefs to fit those of the organization, because there is the expectation that all workers will adhere to the organization's core values and norms (O'Reilly & Chatman, 1996). Under such conditions, there is likely to be disapproval of new entrants who wish to retain an identity that significantly diverges from the values and norms of the organization. Moreover, there is not likely to be much room for role negotiation in which the individual can alter the demands on him or her (Ashford & Taylor, 1990). For those whose identities or values are discrepant from those of the organization, this implies tension. On the other hand, in organizations with relatively weak cultures, newcomers will be faced with less pressure to adopt organizationally defined values or identities, and hence are likely to experience an easier transition.

Proposition 19: The stronger the organization's culture is, the greater is the likelihood of tension related to identity and value change.

The nature of the organization's selection process may also affect whether one experiences tensions around identity change (Chatman, 1991; Schneider, 1987). Organizations that invest more in the process of selecting members can have greater assurance of hiring those who share the organization's values and are comfortable with the idea of adopting an organizationally appropriate identity (Chatman, 1991). Organizations that do not invest much in this process will be more likely to hire individuals who do not share the organization's values or hold fast to organizationally discrepant identities. This difference may have implications for how newcomers respond to demands for value and identity change. When there is low person-organization fit at the time of hire, there will be a greater likelihood of newcomers' resisting attempts to shape them in organizationally desired ways.

The use of realistic job previews during the selection process is also likely to affect whether there is discomfort around identity change. When organizations use realistic job previews, the emphasis is on conveying an accurate, rather than an overly positive, picture of the organization (Wanous, 1980). This practice not only minimizes reality shock after hire but also increases person-organization fit by dissuading potential misfits from accepting jobs.

Hence, organizations that use realistic job previews should be more likely to hire individuals who accurately understand, accept, or share the organization's dominant values and norms and who will therefore experience less tension in the face of pressures to adopt new values and norms.

Proposition 20: Tension related to identity and value change will be less likely when the organization uses an intensive selection process and realistic job previews.

Organizational socialization is another way that person-organization fit can be shaped. As noted, an institutionalized approach to socialization is when newcomers are isolated from experienced members of the organization, learn with other newcomers in a formal setting, and are given clear information about the sequence and timing of the socialization process (Jones, 1986). Conversely, an individualized approach to socialization is when newcomers learn informally and individually and are not given much explicit information.

Research has shown that an institutionalized approach is more likely to produce newcomers who unquestioningly accept the demands related to their new role, whereas an individualized approach is more likely to produce newcomers who attempt to change those demands (Ashforth & Saks, 1996; Baker & Feldman, 1990; Jones, 1986). In other words, institutionalized socialization puts greater pressure on newcomers to alter themselves to fit the organization (Schein, 1968), while individualized socialization enables newcomers to maintain many of their prior values and behavioral patterns or to alter work demands to fit their own goals and preferences. This suggests that when individuals are predisposed to resist changing their sense of self (for example, those with high self-esteem or high need for control), institutionalized socialization may make the process of identity change more stressful and difficult:

Proposition 21: Tension related to identity and value change will be more likely when the organizational socialization process is institutionalized rather than individualized.

Implications for Practice

The ideas presented in this chapter may have some important implications for practice. The failure of new graduates to move effectively from school to work can be detrimental not only for those graduates but also for the organizations and professions in which they work, for the educational institutions that they have just left, and for society overall. A better understanding of the challenges inherent in the transition to work may enable managers, human resource practitioners, career counselors, and educators to ensure that new graduates have sufficient support and learning opportunities so that the transition can proceed smoothly.

Some specific steps can be taken to this end. For example, organizations may want to spread out the training for novice newcomers rather than providing it all at the start. Although a front-loaded approach might be appropriate for more experienced job changers, who have a more fully developed mental model within which to place new information, individuals moving from school to work often do not even know what they need to know and have little basis for sifting through the information that they are receiving. They may not have a good sense of what questions to ask or how to organize the information that is being disseminated. It may therefore be very difficult for them to benefit fully from a structured training process. Perhaps a better approach would use training that is either delayed a bit or spread out over several months as newcomers gradually become grounded in their new context and begin the process of learning how to learn. Organizations should also make sure that there are persons to whom newcomers can go with questions that arise during and even after the transition process.

Another implication related to timing is that organizations might be advised to provide more orientation before newcomers even begin work. Such a change could be facilitated through electronic communication, whereby those who are newly hired could access orientation materials and other information by e-mail or the company's Web page. This could have several advantages. For example, the identity change process might begin earlier, so that the transition will not feel so abrupt. In addition, it may enable new entrants to come up to speed more quickly once they begin working.

The ideas in this chapter also highlight the interrelationship between organizational recruitment and socialization. In fact, it may be advantageous for organizations to create an even stronger linkage between the two processes. Van Maanen's discussion of chains of socialization (1984) suggests that organizations can lessen the need for extensive socialization by recruiting from undergraduate and graduate programs that instill values similar to their own and from which they have recruited in the past. The ideas in this chapter support that argument and also help to clarify why such an approach might be useful. One benefit of a close link between recruitment and socialization is that the process of value and identity change begins far before the actual transition to work. Another benefit is that individuals will begin work with some established network contacts, which can be valuable sources of social support and information.

Indeed, it may be useful for organizations to recognize that many of the network ties that newcomers rely on during the transition to work are ties that they developed prior to the start of that transition. In the light of this fact, organizations may want to create opportunities for members of entering cohorts to get to know one another between the time that they have accepted jobs and the time that they begin work. This can be done either through informal social events or by Internet chatrooms. Creating relationships with coworkers so early in the process will no doubt help to build a sense of identification with the organization, alleviate anxiety, and provide a vehicle for information exchange.

Universities can help in the process of network building by maintaining strong alumni connections that students can use to obtain information about different organizations and professions. Such networks can be a source of ongoing relationships even after students enter the workforce. Universities may also be able to ensure a smoother school-to-work transition by providing some form of career training for graduating seniors. Either a short course or a workshop series on the basics of job hunting, workplace etiquette, and career planning might play an important role in reducing uncertainty, increasing work-related knowledge, and helping graduating students to begin shifting their self-identity.

Such training occurs as a matter of course in certain professions, such as accounting and nursing, but is lacking for many liberal arts and basic science majors. Preparation for the transition to work could also focus on information-seeking and networking skills. As noted, individuals who are proactive in the process of adapting to a new job appear to fare better than those who are less proactive. Hence, it may be especially valuable to train students to be more proactive.

Peer support may be particularly important in the school-to-work transition. Peers have recently experienced this transition themselves and thus may be better able than supervisors or mentors to offer social support and understand the anxieties, concerns, and information gaps that newcomers typically confront. Indeed, the research evidence suggests that newcomers are more comfortable asking peers than supervisors for many types of information. It is also likely that they are more comfortable sharing their problems and concerns with peers. One suggestion for practice, therefore, is for organizations to offer social events without supervisors so that newcomers can build and solidify a peer network. This may be particularly valuable for those individuals who are not part of a cohort or who, for whatever reason, are at a risk of being disconnected.

Conclusion

Information acquisition, network building, and identity change are three key processes in the transition from school to work. None is free of tension, although there may be steps that educational institutions and organizations can take to alleviate some of the tension and thereby ensure a smoother transition process. For most individuals, the initial move to work is the first of many career transitions. The dynamics of this first transition may have effects that extend far beyond the initial job and lay a foundation for future career development.

References
Arthur, M. B., & Rousseau, D. M. (1996). The boundaryless career as a new employment principle. In M. B. Arthur & D. M. Rousseau (Eds.), *The boundaryless career* (pp. 3–20). New York: Oxford University Press.

Asch, S. E. (1956). Studies of independence and conformity. *Psychological Monographs, 416,* 1–70.

Ashford, S. J. (1986). The role of feedback seeking in individual adaptation: A resource perspective. *Academy of Management Journal, 29,* 465–487.

Ashford, S. J., & Black, J. S. (1996). Proactivity during organizational entry: A role of desire for control. *Journal of Applied Psychology, 81,* 199–214.

Ashford, S. J., & Cummings, L. L. (1983). Feedback as an individual resource: Personal strategies for creating information. *Organizational Behavior and Human Performance, 32,* 370–398.

Ashford, S. J., & Taylor, M. S. (1990). Adaptations to work transitions: An integrative approach. *Research in Personnel and Human Resources Management, 8,* 1–39.

Ashforth, B. E. (1998). Becoming: How does the process of identification unfold? In D. Whetten & P. Godfrey (Eds.), *Identity in organizations: Developing theory through conversations* (pp. 213–232). Thousand Oaks, CA: Sage.

Ashforth, B. E., & Mael, F. (1989). Social identity theory and the organization. *Academy of Management Review, 14,* 20–39.

Ashforth, B. E., & Saks, A. M. (1996). Socialization tactics: Longitudinal effects on newcomer adjustment. *Academy of Management Journal, 39,* 149–178.

Baker, H. E., & Feldman, D. C. (1990). Strategies of organizational socialization and their impact on newcomer adjustment. *Journal of Management Issues, 2,* 198–212.

Barnard, C. I. (1938). *The functions of the executive.* Cambridge, MA: Harvard University Press.

Bauer, T. N., Morrison, E. W., & Calister, R. R. (1998). Organizational socialization: A review and directions for future research. *Research in Personnel and Human Resources Management, 16,* 149–214.

Black, S. S., & Ashford, S. J. (1995). Fitting in versus making jobs fit: Factors affecting mode of adjustment for new hires. *Human Relations, 48,* 421–437.

Brass, D. J. (1984). Being in the right place: A structural analysis of individual influence in an organization. *Administrative Science Quarterly, 29,* 518–539.

Brass, D. J. (1995). A social network perspective on human resources management. *Research in Personnel and Human Resources Management, 13,* 39–79.

Brass, D. J., & Burkhardt, M. E. (1993). Potential power and power use: An investigation of structure and behavior. *Academy of Management Journal, 36,* 441–470.

Brehm, J. W. (1972). *Responses to loss of freedom: A theory of psychological re-actance.* Morristown, NJ: General Learning Press.

Brett, J. M. (1982). Job transfer and well-being. *Journal of Applied Psychology, 67,* 450–462.

Brockner, J. (1988). *Self-esteem at work: Research, theory and practice.* Lexington, MA: Heath.

Burt, R. S. (1997). Contingent value of social capital. *Administrative Science Quarterly, 42,* 339–365.

Chao, G., O'Leary-Kelly, A., Wolf, S., & Klein, H. (1994). Organizational socialization: Its content and consequences. *Journal of Applied Psychology, 79,* 730–743.

Chatman, J. A. (1991). Matching people and organizations: Selection and socialization in public accounting firms. *Administrative Science Quarterly, 36,* 459–484.

Dawis, R. V., & Lofquist, L. H. (1984). *A psychological theory of work adjustment.* Minneapolis: University of Minnesota Press.

Dweck, C. S., & Leggett, E. L. (1988). A social-cognitive approach to motivation and personality. *Psychological Review, 95,* 256–273.

Feldman, D. C. (1981). The multiple socialization of organization members. *Academy of Management Review, 6,* 309–318.

Feldman, D. C. (1994). Who's socializing whom? The impact of the socialization of newcomers on insiders, work groups, and organizations. *Human Resource Management Review, 4,* 213–233.

Feldman, D. C. (1999). Toxic mentors or toxic protégés? A critical reexamination of dysfunctional mentoring. *Human Resource Management Review, 9,* 247–278.

Feldman, D. C., & Brett, J. M. (1983). Coping with new jobs: A comparative study of new hires and job changers. *Academy of Management Journal, 26,* 258–272.

Fisher, C. D. (1986). Organizational socialization: An integrative review. *Research in Personnel and Human Resources Management, 4,* 101–145.

Forret, M. L., & Dougherty, T. W. (in press). Correlates of networking behavior for managerial and professional employees. *Group and Organization Management.*

Greenberger, D. B., & Strasser, S. (1986). Development and application of a model of personal control in organizations. *Academy of Management Review, 11,* 164–177.

Greenberger, D. B., Strasser, S., & Lee, S. (1988). Personal control as a mediator between perceptions of supervisory behaviors and employee reactions. *Academy of Management Journal, 31,* 405–417.

Higgins, E. T. (1997). Beyond pleasure and pain. *American Psychologist, 52,* 1280–1300.

Higgins, M. C., & Kram, K. E. (2001). Reconceptualizing mentoring at work: A developmental network perspective. *Academy of Management Review, 26,* 264–288.

Higgins, M. C., & Thomas, D. A. (2001). Constellations and careers: Toward an understanding of multiple developmental relationships. *Journal of Organizational Behavior, 22,* 223–248.

Hofstede, G. (1980). *Culture's consequences: International differences in work related values.* Thousand Oaks, CA: Sage.

Ibarra, H. (1995). Race, opportunity, and diversity of social circles in managerial networks. *Academy of Management Journal, 38,* 673–703.

Jablin, F. M. (1984). Assimilating new members into organizations. In R. N. Bostrom (Ed.), *Communication yearbook* (Vol. 8, pp. 594–626). Thousand Oaks, CA: Sage.

Jones, G. (1983). Psychological orientation and the process of organizational socialization: An interactionist perspective. *Academy of Management Review, 8,* 464–474.

Jones, G. (1986). Socialization tactics, self-efficacy, and newcomers' adjustments to organizations. *Academy of Management Journal, 29,* 262–279.

Kanter, R. M., & Eccles, R. G. (1992). Making network research relevant to practice. In N. Nohria & R. G. Eccles (Eds.), *Networks and organizations: Structure, form and action* (pp. 521–527). Boston: Harvard University Press.

Kram, K. E. (1985). *Mentoring at work: Developmental relationships in organizational life.* Glenview, IL: Scott, Foresman.

Lewin, K. (1951). *Field theory in social science.* New York: HarperCollins.

Louis, M. R. (1980). Surprise and sense making: What newcomers experience in entering unfamiliar organizational settings. *Administrative Science Quarterly, 25,* 226–251.

Louis, M. R. (1990). Acculturation in the workplace: Newcomers as lay ethnographers. In B. Schneider (Ed.), *Organizational climate and culture* (pp. 85–129). San Francisco: Jossey-Bass.

Louis, M. R., Posner, B. Z., & Powell, G. N. (1983). The availability and helpfulness of socialization practices. *Personnel Psychology, 36,* 857–866.

Major, D. A., & Kozlowski, S.W.J. (1997). Newcomer information seeking: Individual and contextual influences. *International Journal of Selection and Assessment, 4,* 16–28.

McClelland, D. C. (1961). *The achieving society.* New York: Van Nostrand Reinhold.

Miller, V. D., & Jablin, F. M. (1991). Information seeking during organizational entry: Influences, tactics, and a model of the process. *Academy of Management Review, 16,* 92–120.

Morrison, E. W. (1993a). Longitudinal study of the effects of information seeking on newcomer socialization. *Journal of Applied Psychology, 78,* 173–183.

Morrison, E. W. (1993b). Newcomer information seeking: Exploring types, modes, sources, and outcomes. *Academy of Management Journal, 36,* 557–589.

Morrison, E. W. (1995). Information usefulness and acquisition during organizational encounter. *Management Communication Quarterly, 9,* 131–155.

Morrison, E. W. (in press). Newcomers' relationships: The role of social networks during socialization. *Academy of Management Journal.*

Morrison, E. W., & Bies, R. J. (1991). Impression management in the feedback seeking process: A literature review and research agenda. *Academy of Management Review, 16,* 522–541.

Nicholson, N. (1984). A theory of work role transitions. *Administrative Science Quarterly, 29,* 172–191.

Nicholson, N., & West, M. A. (1988). *Managerial job change: Men and women in transition.* Cambridge: Cambridge University Press.

O'Reilly, C. (1989). Corporations, culture and commitment: Motivation and social control in organizations. *California Management Review, 31,* 9–25.

O'Reilly, C. A., & Chatman, J. A. (1996). Culture as social control: Corporations, cults, and commitment. *Research in Organizational Behavior, 18,* 157–200.

Ostroff, C., & Kozlowski, S.W.J. (1992). Organizational socialization as a learning process: The role of information acquisition. *Personnel Psychology, 45,* 849–874.

Podolny, J. M., & Baron, J. N. (1997). Resources and relationships: Social networks and mobility in the workplace. *American Sociological Review, 62,* 673–693.

Reichers, A. E. (1987). An interactionist perspective on newcomer socialization rates. *Academy of Management Review, 12,* 278–287.

Saks, A. M., & Ashforth, B. E. (1997). Organizational socialization: Making sense of the past and present as a prologue for the future. *Journal of Vocational Behavior, 51,* 234–279.

Schein, E. H. (1968). Organizational socialization and the profession of management. *Industrial Management Review, 9,* 1–16.

Schein, E. H. (1971). The individual, the organization, and the career: A conceptual scheme. *Journal of Applied Behavioral Science, 7,* 401–426.

Schein, E. H. (1978). *Career dynamics: Matching individual and organizational needs.* Reading, MA: Addison-Wesley.

Schneider, B. (1987). The people make the place. *Personnel Psychology, 14,* 437–453.

Settoon, R. P., & Adkins, C. L. (1997). Newcomer socialization: The role of supervisors, coworkers, friends, and family members. *Journal of Business and Psychology*, *11*, 507–516.

Snyder, M. (1974). The self-monitoring of expressive behavior. *Journal of Personality and Social Psychology*, *30*, 526–537.

Staw, B. M. (1981). The escalation of commitment to a course of action. *Academy of Management Review*, *6*, 577–587.

Triandis, H. C. (1995). *Individualism and collectivism.* Boulder, CO: Westview Press.

Van Maanen, J. (1976). Breaking in: Socialization to work. In R. Dubin (Ed.), *Handbook of work, organization, and society* (pp. 67–130). Skokie, IL: Rand McNally.

Van Maanen, J. (1984). Doing new things in old ways: The chains of socialization. In J. L. Bess (Ed.), *College and university organization.* New York: New York University Press.

Van Maanen, J., & Schein, E. H. (1979). Toward a theory of organizational socialization. *Research in Organizational Behavior*, *1*, 209–264.

Wanous, J. P. (1980). *Organizational entry: Recruitment, selection, and socialization of newcomers.* Reading, MA: Addison-Wesley.

Watson, D., & Clark, L. A. (1984). Negative affectivity: The disposition to experience aversive emotional states. *Psychological Bulletin*, *96*, 465–490.

White, R. W. (1959). Motivation reconsidered: The concept of competence. *Psychological Review*, *66*, 297–333.

CHAPTER 6

The Establishment Years
A Dependence Perspective
Terri A. Scandura

New employees often face a number of career problems in the establishment years. In a classic article on early career development, Webber (1976) identified a number of these issues based on interviews with hundreds of managers. He characterized the early years of one's career as being fraught with difficulties and dissatisfaction. First, conflicting expectations of what is taught in college and the actual content of the job may lead to dissatisfaction and job changing. Second, the employee may view the supervisor as incompetent, yet this supervisor plays an important role in the person's career development. As young adults struggle to cope with unmet expectations and disappointing role models, their attitudes toward their careers may become more negative and their career development in the establishment years stall.

To date, the literature on the establishment years is fragmented, ranging from models of occupational values and choice (career anchors), to the development of effective working relationships with supervisors and mentors, to the work-family interface. These lines of research are based on diverse perspectives from psychology, social psychology, management, and feminist theory. It has been difficult to identify unifying themes that might integrate the area. A framework is needed to address the core issues underlying these responses so that research can begin to address the psychological and social-psychological processes that occur during the establishment years.

159

Schein (1978) described the early career years as a series of up-ending experiences in which individuals are confronted with realities that are inconsistent with their expectations about the world of work. Individuals in early career may come to realize that organizations are more political than ever imagined, performance appraisals are not conducted with the rigor that was described in college textbooks, and the time spans differ greatly between academia and the workplace. In a study of new M.B.A. graduates, Clawson, Kotter, Faux, and McArthur (1992) found that many recent graduates were surprised by the ways in which they were asked to pay their dues. They also reported time management problems, difficulties in dealing with changes on the job, and frustrations with the level of disorganization at work. These authors reported that 62 percent of recent M.B.A. graduates just six months after graduation reported that they were less than happy with their job, employer, or career progress. In contrast, only 5 percent reported no adjustment problems at all. Thus, the gap between expectations and reality may create dissatisfaction and anxiety that negatively affect performance in the establishment years and result in turnover as well.

The Tasks of the Establishment Years

The literature on careers has addressed the issue of how difficult it often is for employees to adapt to the work setting during the establishment years. The establishment years have been described as a period in which there are a series of job trials, occupational changes, and periods of stabilization in which individuals attempt to settle into their careers (Super, 1957). Super suggested that the establishment stages spanned the age range of twenty-five to forty-four years, basing this framework on the work of the influential early adult life stage theoretician, Erik Erikson (1950). Tracing later work on careers back to Erikson's work reveals that adult development issues were a core aspect of his career theory, yet subsequent theoretical frameworks focused much more on developmental issues facing adolescents and young adults.

According to Erikson, the key psychological task that individuals face during the period from early adolescence to early middle age is balancing intimacy and isolation. Grappling with the ability to maintain one's unique identity in the development of relationships with others, then, is a key theme for the establishment years. Maintaining a balance between a sense of self and fitting in is a core issue for this period. Career theorists have also specified dependency as the core psychological state of the individual during the early career, or apprentice, years (Dalton, Thompson, & Price, 1977). During these years, this issue of dependence on others and the fear of isolation may drive the formation of career attitudes, behavior, and identity.

This chapter integrates issues of psychological dependence with current perspectives on careers. Important areas of research on the establishment years include developing career anchors, socialization, establishing developmental relationships (including mentoring), career-family issues, and occupational and job change; each will be discussed in terms of dependence issues. A dependence perspective on early careers may be particularly helpful in bringing together these diverse career research agendas into a more integrative framework to guide future research and theory. Finally, some potential implications for organizations, human resource professionals, supervisors, and managers to consider will be discussed.

Psychological Dependence

The struggle from adolescence to adulthood is marked by the declaration of psychological independence from parental authority. More often than not, adolescents use coping mechanisms to deal effectively with the issue of dependency and loosening ties to parents.

Blos (1979) summarized research on the impact of the environment on the development of the adolescent's well-being. When the environment impairs the healthy emergence of an adolescent's self-perception, the result may be forms of regression. Regression is defined as a controlled loss of autonomy characterized by reverting back to earlier behavior patterns, extreme behaviors, or emotional illness. Development is thus a pendular movement with regressive and progressive movements as adolescents mature.

Blos (1979) also stressed that regression is a defense mechanism that is necessary, at least in some form, for adult development. For example, the peer group may become a more important referent for the adolescent than the parents, even acting as a substitute for them. When dependence on peers simply substitutes for dependency on parents, however, these unresolved issues may result in permanent alterations in personality and behavior.

Bowlby (1969) studied the defense mechanisms that result from this struggle for independence during the adolescent years, focusing on the anxiety produced by separation. At one end of the continuum are adolescents who completely reject their parents, and at the other end are those who remain too closely attached. Most adolescents lie between these two extremes; they remain attached to parents but have the capacity to develop relationships with others as well. Bowlby specifically addressed the importance of resolving psychological defense issues for the ability of individuals to form healthy relationships as well as to endure separations in later life stages. These early issues of dependence emerge again during the establishment years due to the numerous serious career and life reappraisals that occur during this time period (Clawson et al., 1992; Levinson, Darrow, Klein, Levinson, & McKee, 1978; Schein, 1978; Super, 1957). Indeed, many young adults experience a fear of dependency on powerful others (Fromm, 1956).

By the end of the college years, most individuals have moved away from home, experienced independence, and begun to establish their unique identities. Graduation ceremonies serve as a ritual that celebrates the passage of the individual from the academic world into the working world. Thus, it is perhaps not surprising that newcomers to organizations often face the abrupt realization that dependence issues have returned and experience heightened frustration and anxiety. As the exuberance of graduation fades, the individual must cope with a new and often even more challenging set of demands by a new employer.

By definition, organizations are interdependent entities. Supervisors depend on employees, peers depend on one another, and many organizations now reinforce the interdependent nature of work through the formation of work teams. How the individual adjusts to this sudden loss of independence may have important implications for his or her early career development..

Moreover, during the establishment years, others in the workplace may become dependent on them at the same time they are trying to establish their own independent contributions and reputations. For example, they may have direct reports who look to them for guidance. They may get married and have children, which increases the demands on them for emotional support (Webber, 1976). Thus, those who may appear to deal with dependence effectively by compensating with their sense of independence may become overwhelmed by the large numbers of people who become dependent on them. They may even develop a behavioral pattern referred to as codependency at work, in which they exhibit excessive sensitivity to evaluation, responsibility for others' work, guilt, and low self-esteem (Davidhizar & Eshleman, 1992). It seems clear, then, that dependence issues have important implications for the study of the establishment years.

Individual Responses to Dependence Issues

For an organization to function effectively, its employees must conform to its culture and policies. At one extreme, the image of the organization man (Whyte, 1956), who lost his identity entirely to the organization, suggests that conformity was the price of success in many large organizations. At the other extreme, without at least compliance or consensus on the core behaviors in an interlocked set of jobs, organizations would surely experience chaos. More often than not, though, other role incumbents send newcomers strong messages regarding the appropriate role behaviors for the new employee to learn. Young adults then struggle to reconcile their personal identities with the demands of the organization for conformity.

The attitudinal responses to these demands range from compliance to identification to internalization (Kelman, 1961). With compliance, the individual merely adapts his or her outward behaviors to play the part but does not alter core identities or basic values. In the case of identification, the individual takes the cultural norms of the organization as important standards of behavior. The final stage, internalization, can several take months or even years. It represents the reconciliation of the individual's identity and that of the organization, as the organizational value system becomes the employee's own. Clearly, it benefits organizations to have employees who have internalized the organization's culture; however, less is known about the potential costs of that compliance to the individual's identity.

How individuals cope with these confrontations with the demands for conformity is an important social-psychological process that deserves further attention in career theory and research. These demands will most likely invoke responses that relate to an individual's reaction to authority figures. Unresolved issues from adolescence regarding parental authority may reemerge and impede the formation of career identity. A healthy resolution of this crisis would be the recognition that the self is unique, but yet is able to function effectively in a network of interdependent social relationships in pursuit of collective goals. There is also an acknowledgment that benefits to one's own career can result from the attainment of organizational goals.

Moreover, dysfunctional responses that may work at cross-purposes to the organizational goals are kept in check. The recent attention in the management literature to the concept of emotional intelligence (Goleman, 1995) can perhaps be thought of as an attempt to encourage self-regulation in emotional responses to events at work. The effective employee is now viewed as one who can manage his or her emotions in relation to a wide variety of persons and situations. More work is needed to understand why some people seem to be able to regulate their emotions more effectively than others. The answer, in part, may lie in how young adults are able to manage their reactions to other members of the organization who may be viewed as authority figures during their early career years.

Individuals in their twenties and thirties may respond to authority figures in ways that reflect the resolution of their dependence issues. These responses are summarized in Figure 6.1. The horizontal axis refers to whether a given response is functional (healthy) or dysfunctional (unhealthy). The vertical axis represents whether the individual is self- or other-focused in his or her responses. Thus, responses might fall into one of the four quadrants shown: anticonformity, independence, passivity, or interdependence.

Individuals may react in a rebellious manner (dysfunctional, low concern for others) by consistently resisting the authority figure's influence attempts and acting against the organization or the person making the requests. This response pattern is referred to as anticonformity by social psychologists (Hollander & Willis, 1967). A second response may also be independent (functional,

Figure 6.1. Responses to Dependence.

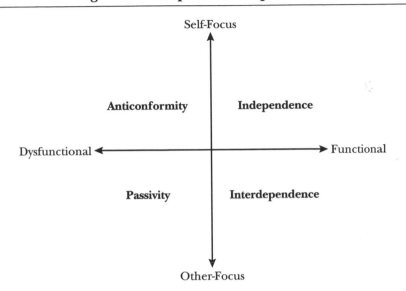

but low concern for others), simply ignoring the requests of the authority figure and defining their work as they see fit. They do not fight the directives of the organization; they are merely indifferent to them.

A third response is passivity (dysfunctional, high concern for others); the individual accepts the authority figure's requests without question. At the extreme, this response might be characterized as conformity, or yielding to group pressures, either real or imagined (Kiesler & Kiesler, 1969).

In this response, the individual complies with the demands of others in the work environment to avoid embarrassment or confrontation. The Milgram experiments (1965), in which subjects believed they were administering electrical shocks to confederates at the request of an authority figure (no actual shocks were administered), were a powerful reminder of the effects that passivity may have on behavior. Passive individuals may be the most dissatisfied of all three groups because their needs are not articulated and their ideas not heard. Over time, such individuals become ambivalent about the organization, the job, and their coworkers, and they may withdraw either psychologically or physically from the work environment (through absenteeism or turnover).

The fourth, and most effective, response to the demands for conformity is one of interdependence (functional, high concern for others). The individual recognizes that he or she must conform to a certain degree with the requests of those in the workplace, but still can maintain his or her own identity and value system. This response appears to be the logical and obvious choice over the others, and yet many people do not employ it in their daily work lives.

As Argyris (1990) noted, human beings develop programmed rules over time that govern their daily behavior. Some of these rules are defensive and dysfunctional to the organization and even to their own careers (for example, blaming others, concealing information, picking fights, and repeating errors). Argyris calls this "skilled unawareness and incompetence" (p. 23).

Career Anchors Revisited

Early research and theory on career development identified the important concepts of the external and the internal career (Van Maanen & Schein, 1977). The external career refers to salary, promotions, and other extrinsic benefits derived from working, which are viewed as rewards provided by society as its definition of success at work. The internal career refers to a person's subjective experience of work and perception of his or her role in the world of work. These two perspectives, external and internal, may be in agreement, or they may differ, since individuals define career success in their own terms.

Based on his research on alumni from the Massachusetts Institute of Technology, Schein (1990) developed the concept of career anchors. Career anchors are core values, interests, and abilities developed throughout early career that guide career decisions during the establishment years and subsequent career stages. Schein (1990) identifies eight of these career anchors: (1) technical-functional competence, (2) managerial competence, (3) autonomy-independence, (4) security-stability, (5) service-dedication, (6) pure challenge, (7) lifestyle integration, and (8) entrepreneurship.

Technical-functional competence refers to an individual's commitment to learning expertise within a profession, such as engineering. Managerial competence is the anchor that describes the person's desire to influence others and assume responsibility for the work of others. Autonomy-independence describes an individual's interest in working alone, without external supervision. Security-stability refers to a person's need for stable employment or a job situation that does not change frequently. The service-dedication anchor relates to an individual's predisposition to help others through choosing such occupations as nursing or social work. Pure challenge relates to work that offers interesting problems to solve every day. Individuals with a lifestyle integration seek to balance their career with their family responsibilities and leisure activities. Finally, those who are anchored in entrepreneurship are creative and may want to start their own ventures or organizations.

Schein holds that the career anchor is not something that a person easily changes and that is a relatively permanent aspect of an individual's value system. His career anchor framework views the early career years as a time of mutual discovery between the employer and the new employee, marked by a series of job challenges that enable the newcomer to learn more about his or her own career interests (Feldman & Bolino, 1997).

According to Schein (1990), the formation of the occupational self-concept has three components: (1) talents and abilities (based on success in the work setting), (2) motives and needs as the result of self-diagnosis from real work situations, and (3) attitudes and values based on interaction with the norms of the work setting. Thus, career anchors are formed as a result of the individual's reacting to real situations encountered in the workplace during the early career years. Career anchors both drive and constrain career choices, since individuals tend to seek out situations that have resulted in success in the past and avoid situations that may result in failure. Career anchors emerge over time as the individual experiences situations that are congruent or incongruent with his or her abilities, motives, and values (Schein, 1978).

Other theorists have elaborated on Schein's values framework, further linking psychological needs and interests to occupational choice and career decision making (Driver, 1980; Derr, 1980). Driver developed a model of the career self-concept and linked career choice to cognitive styles. Derr focused on key life events, examined times of transition in the course of adult development, and investigated how these events are interdependent with career change. Derr's framework included family issues, such as divorce or the birth of a child, that may initiate reappraisal of career choices. Recently, Schein (1990) revised career anchor theory to reflect the dramatic changes that individuals have been experiencing in their careers due to changes in organizational structures. Nevertheless, Schein maintains that the career anchor holds the internal career together in the midst of external change.

Career anchors may be closely related to dependency issues. The most obvious relationship is perhaps between dependency orientations and the autonomy-independence anchor. Those who are independent would be more likely to endorse this career anchor, compared with those who are passive. Similarly, those with technical-functional competence and entrepreneurship anchors may also be more independent.

Individuals who are anchored in security-stability, however, may have a more passive response and may not assert themselves in order to maintain a stable employment situation. These individuals may value the paycheck and benefits offered and not take risks on the job that might jeopardize their continued employment. For example, they may not challenge authority, even when decisions need to be challenged, for fear of losing their jobs.

Those with a service-dedication anchor or managerial-competence anchor may be more interdependent in their attitude toward dependence. These individuals value integration with others; working with others is what interests them most. Individuals having a challenge anchor are in need of interesting problems to solve at work. These individuals may be more likely to exhibit independent or even anticonforming behavior at work, since it is the challenge of the work itself (and not relationships with others) that is their primary motive for work.

Finally, dependency issues may affect work-family decisions. Those who are anchored in lifestyle integration may be either independent or anticonforming since they are interested in work that allows them to integrate their careers with family and leisure activities. The reexamination of career anchors from a dependency perspective may offer some interesting insight into why individuals gravitate toward certain career anchors. In addition, career anchors may facilitate coping with dependency issues during the establishment years, since such value systems may serve as guide-posts during times of upheaval.

The Socialization Process

Within this dependency perspective, the "joining-up" process appears to be another important dynamic with which to examine dependency issues. Socialization occurs in stages, first with anticipatory socialization, followed by encounter, and then change and acquisition (Feldman, 1976, 1981). Movement between these stages is viewed as a social-psychological process in which roles are sent to the employee followed by responses that indicate the degree to which the individual will accommodate to that role (Adkins, 1995). Depending on the degree of adjustment, individuals decide to stay with the employer and conform to organizational demands (to varying degrees) or to leave the organization and look for one that is a better fit (Ashforth & Saks, 1996; Baker & Feldman, 1990). The individual's basic approach to dependence issues with those in power may shape the outcomes of socialization as well as the socialization process itself.

Anticipatory Socialization

Even before the employee enters the organization, a job candidate is exposed to the organizational culture through the recruitment process. Major concerns at this stage center on the degree to which the individual holds realistic expectations about the organization and its members. Dependency issues may alter these expectations because of an individual's orientation toward authority figures. For example, those with an anticonformity stance may see large corporations as undesirable places to work due to a long recruitment process that often has multiple hurdles. These individuals may decide not to pursue employment with such organizations due to their discomfort with what they perceive as an inflexible structure.

In contrast, those who are passive may try to accommodate what the organization is looking for. Many self-help books on how to interview successfully, or second-guess what the interviewers want to hear, may actually reinforce the anticipatory socialization process by sending the person clear messages regarding what types of responses these organizations expect.

These self-help books focus on how to market oneself rather than how to choose a career that will be interesting and satisfying. For example, when the recruiter asks, "What is your biggest weakness?" the self-help books often suggest a response that has a positive spin such as, "I demand perfection in myself and others" or "I work long hours." These are clear messages to the individual regarding appropriate role-related behavior that are sent even before the person enters the organization. Passive individuals, for example, are likely to "talk the talk" during the employment interview despite their shyness in order to fit in and avoid rejection.

The Encounter Stage

The issue of dependency becomes even more salient during the encounter stage. Here, the new recruit begins to understand the organization he or she has chosen to work for and the attitudinal and behavioral expectations it will demand. In the work environment, supervisors, peers, and often customers send the new recruit messages regarding what are considered appropriate role behaviors (Fisher, 1986; Schein, 1964, 1978). Research has indicated that these early encounters significantly influence the process and outcomes of the socialization process (Bauer & Green, 1994).

These initial messages often relate to both work practices and norms (Chao, O'Leary, Wolf, Klein, & Gardner, 1994). This encounter stage may be very stressful to newcomers, as expectations about the organization and the reality of these messages clash (Louis, 1980). For example, norms may govern the appropriate way to dress, or where employees should live, or who they should socialize with after work. Work practice messages may be very different from those given to recruits during the interview process. New employees often feel that they are forced to do meaningless work or put up with other humiliating experiences, and sometimes even hazing (Van Maanen, 1976).

The employee's responses to these messages will be related in part to his or her orientation toward authority figures. Those who are passive in response to authority will respond by compliance with all of the requests made and lack of assertion, even when the demands made are unreasonable. They surrender their own identity in order to fit in with members of the organization and to be viewed as competent (Dix & Savickas, 1995). However, role senders often send conflicting messages, and then the passive individual experiences stress trying to reconcile these demands. The passive responder may end up losing influence with other organizational members due to inconsistent behavior or be characterized as a yes-man (or woman). Passive responses may result in resentment over the long term and lead to dysfunctional behavior or absenteeism and turnover.

Change and Acquisition

During the change and acquisition phase of socialization, the new-comer adjusts to the demands of those in the organization who are sending the messages regarding appropriate role behavior. At this phase, individuals need to master job requirements, integrate into the work group or other teams, learn role expectations, and understand organizational systems and values (Feldman, 1981; Schein, 1978; Wanous, 1992; Zahrly & Tosi, 1989). Dependency issues affect the degree to which individuals are able to reconcile their own identity with the demands of the organization. The modifications needed to fit in are made with the understanding that some personal sacrifices must be made if the employee is to be an effective member of the organization (Feldman, 1981).

Failure to comply with requests for new role behaviors may even result in failure to remain after the probationary period ends. New recruits who rebel against and reject the work practices and norms of the organization are not likely to be allowed to stay. An individual who has an independent response to authority figures will ignore all requests for behavior modifications.

In some circumstances, however, individuals' expertise makes them so valuable that their nonconformist behavior is tolerated, and it is the organization and its other members who must adjust. Such individuals will not be effective in teams and may have repeated conflicts with supervisors. Their noncompliance may eventually lead to career difficulties in the future should an alternative source for that expertise be found.

Schein (1978) described the interdependent response as "creative individualism" (p. 104). In this response, the newcomer accepts some of the core organizational values but retains the essential aspects of his or her own identity. These individuals continue to question important work practices and norms, and over time, they make innovative contributions to the organization. At the end of the socialization process, there is a reconciliation of person and system, resulting in a commitment to stay with the organization and contribute to its success. Those who respond by recognizing that they are interdependent with others and need to make some mutual adjustments, but not give up their identity, are most likely to be successful in the long term (Bauer & Green, 1994; Feldman, 1976, 1981; Ostroff & Kozlowski, 1993; Van Maanen, 1976; Van Maanen & Schein, 1977).

Work Relationships

In the establishment years, young adults balance independence and interdependence across a variety of groups and individuals in their lives. These include supervisors, mentors, spouses, and partners.

The First Supervisor

Reactions to the first supervisor are often an issue for new job incumbents (Clawson et al., 1992; Major, Kozlowski, Chao, & Gardner, 1995). The new employee may have unrealistic expectations regarding the supervisor's competence or ability to advance his or her career. The realization that the supervisor may not be as all-knowing or all-powerful as idealized by the new employee may be a source of frustration. Nevertheless, the first supervisor has an important impact on the newcomer's career because he or she assigns tasks, sends messages about appropriate attitudes and behavior, and conducts the newcomer's performance evaluations.

The individual's reactions to organizational demands for conformity may be played out within the context of this working relationship. Anticonformity, independence, or passivity may characterize these interactions, resulting in dysfunctional relationships and consequences. Hence, the encounter phase of socialization is the appropriate time to examine dependence issues, since the supervisor-subordinate relationship may reawaken unresolved issues about authority.

The importance of the first supervisor has been documented in research on the assimilation process (Graen, Orris, & Johnson,

1973). The supervisor fills a key role as a socialization agent and then as a vocational coach during the establishment years. When the newcomer's first supervisor sees his or her potential and offers additional challenging tasks, the newcomer develops his or her potential, acquires additional skills, and becomes more valuable to the organization. Beyond task assignment, the supervisor may offer support and coaching that enhances the learning of the newcomer. These initial relationships may have long-term career implications. Wakabayashi and Graen (1984) found that the initial working relationship with the first supervisor predicted career advancement seven years later in a study of large Japanese corporations. The first supervisor's impact may be due in part to the learning experiences that he or she sets up for the newcomer.

Hall (1996) found that early career challenge resulted in feelings of psychological success that enhanced newcomers' self-esteem, leading to a cycle in which these newcomers sought more challenge and attained more success. By providing supportive autonomy, supervisors give newcomers challenging assignments but also the freedom to make mistakes, to learn, and to grow. Baird and Kram (1983) reported that supervisors play an important part in meeting the newcomer's needs during the establishment period, including task needs (such as feedback on performance) and personal needs (such as offering acceptance and confirmation).

However, some initial reactions from the supervisor may be negative and result in newcomers' perceptions that they are being set up to fail (Manzoni & Barsoux, 1998). Rather than providing early career experiences that produce a sense of mastery and personal success, the supervisor gives tasks that are beyond the newcomer's capability. Early failures at these tasks result in a cycle that leads to frustration and, ultimately, organizational exit.

Newcomers' reactions to authority figures in general may influence their reactions to first supervisors in particular. If newcomers are passive, they may not tell their supervisors that the tasks assigned are beyond their capability and may not seek out additional challenging assignments after the task is completed. If the newcomer has a rebellious reaction, the supervisor will likely withdraw from the relationship and leave the newcomer to cope on his or her own. Independent newcomers may not recognize the supervisor's offers of help as good supervision and may ignore the help offered. Finally, the interdependent newcomer will accept the tasks assigned constructively by asking questions of clarification and seeking out guidance and coaching as needed.

In some cases, the supervisory relationship evolves into a mentoring relationship over time (Kram, 1985). In other cases, peers and other senior members of the organization mentor the newcomer in the work environment. The newcomer's disposition toward authority figures also helps to shape the evolution of mentoring relationships.

Mentoring and Developmental Relationships

Levinson et al. (1978) identified three major periods over the course of adult development: early adult transition, midlife transition, and late adult transition. The establishment years occur during the period between early adult and midlife transition.

The first phase of this period, *entering the adult world*, is marked by two tasks: exploration of adult living and the creation of a stable life structure. The end of this period is marked by the *age thirty transition* (age twenty-eight to thirty-three), a developmental crisis in which the existing life structure is deemed unsustainable, new choices are made, or old choices are reaffirmed. Next, a period of *settling down* occurs in which aspirations and goals of the earlier periods are realized. The major tasks of this period are to develop a specific competence or niche and pay increased attention to career advancement. Thus, during the establishment years, the individual undergoes dramatic changes and perhaps even periods of chaos and disorder as the novice identity becomes settled and then is challenged and altered during the age thirty transition.

Levinson et al. (1978) found that individuals who have mentors in work settings during the establishment years benefit from their contributions as teachers, advisers, and sponsors. Mentors may be particularly critical in helping to guide individuals through these periods of upheaval. Mentors may be bosses or other senior individuals in the workplace, but they are defined as individuals having advanced knowledge and skill who help junior colleagues become competent contributors to the organization. According to Levinson et al., the most crucial developmental function that the mentor plays is "to support and facilitate the realization of the Dream" (p. 98).

The image of the mentor as a good parent is evoked, yet the mentor role is considered to be a balance of parent and peer. Levinson et al. (1978) explicitly address dependency issues in mentoring relationships, noting that the age differential between mentor and protégé may result in conflicts for the junior colleague that may interfere with the mentoring relationship. Over time, mentoring relationships evolve and may become redefined as peer friendships, after the junior person becomes an autonomous contributor (Kram, 1985).

There has been a great deal of research in the years since the publication of Levinson et al. and Kram's initial work on mentoring relationships. Studies have shown that mentoring relationships can benefit both the protégé and the mentor and that informal mentoring appears to be more effective than formal mentoring. Peers have been found to provide certain mentoring functions, too, although they may be less instrumental to the protégé's career advancement (Kram & Isabella, 1985). Mentoring has also been linked to the effectiveness of the socialization process, with mentors providing important socialization information to the newcomer (Ostroff & Kozlowski, 1993).

Cross-gender issues and diversity have also been key themes in the mentoring literature (Noe, 1988; Ragins, 1989, 1997; Ragins & Scandura, 1994). This line of research suggests that women report having mentors, yet they may not be deriving the benefits to the same degree as men do (Dreher & Ash, 1990). Therefore, diversity variables, such as sex and race, should also be examined in this context, since dependency issues may differ for women and minorities.

Mentoring research has recently begun to examine some possible dysfunctional outcomes (Eby, McManus, Simon, & Russell, 1998; Feldman, 1999; Scandura, 1998). Some dysfunctional relationships may be traced back to the newcomer's orientation toward dependency. Those individuals with anticonformity orientations are more likely to have difficulty developing relationships with mentors. Also, mentoring relationships in which the protégé is passive ultimately would not develop into peer friendships or terminate productively. Protégés who are independent might not benefit from the coaching and support offered by the mentor.

In contrast, the protégé with an interdependent orientation should be able to retain his or her sense of self while benefiting from the advice of the senior person. Thus, a key individual difference in understanding the emergence of dysfunctional mentoring relationships may be the protégé's dependency needs.

Work-Family Issues

According to the most researched model of the work-family interface, the spillover model, satisfaction in one life domain creates positive affect in another (Kabanoff, 1980). Thus, positive experiences in family life may result in positive experiences at work, and vice versa (Kirchmeyer, 1992). Nonetheless, the ability to manage both work and nonwork domains during the early career years may be due in part to the ability to manage dependency relationships in both domains. It is possible that relationship skills learned in one domain might transfer to the other. Also, social support and advice from mentors, peers, and supervisors may assist the newcomer in balancing work and family concerns.

Dependency issues may affect the individual's ability to manage the domains of work and nonwork during the establishment years. As Levinson et al. (1978) noted, during the early career exploration phase the young adult typically dates and marries. Today, many marriages are two-career couples in which both spouses pursue careers in tandem, and more married couples now have two wage earners rather than one breadwinner.

Dependency issues will affect the ability of individuals to achieve integration between work and family roles. Those with anticonformity or independent orientations will not take into account the career of the spouse, and this may lead to marriage difficulties and perhaps even divorce. Those who are passive will go along with the career decisions of the spouse, which may result in geographical relocation or other career events that derail their own career. In addition, over time this passivity may lead to resentment and a deteriorating marital relationship. Those with an interdependent orientation, however, will more likely view spouses as equals and strive to develop collaborative career decision making with them. Although this is often difficult, the process of becoming aware of the spouse's career concerns and openly discussing these issues may help to alleviate misunderstandings and distress. When both parties take an interdependent posture toward the dependency issues in a two-career situation, working through challenges may enhance the quality of life of both parties (Hall & Hall, 1979).

Research has indicated gender differences in work-family conflict. Although many women now pursue careers, few have given up the role of wife and mother to achieve their career goals. Later in the establishment years, children may pose additional constraints on career decision making, as their needs must be considered as well. The birth of a child may cause an imbalance in the distribution of household tasks (Campbell, 1986). Hochschild (1989) found that women in two-career families reported working a "second shift" by doing cooking, cleaning, child care, and other household chores after they work an eight-hour day at a job. Dependency issues may affect these decisions regarding how work is distributed in the home. For example, passive women may be more likely to go along with the demands of their spouse, without asserting their own needs due to pervasive sex role stereotypes that the woman's role should be to support her husband's career.

Job Transitions During the Establishment Years

One of the outcomes of unsuccessful socialization and frustration during the first few months at work is turnover. In recent years, job transitions have become more common due to shifts in the expectations of younger workers (the so-called Generation X), organizational restructuring, and new technology that has eliminated many jobs. Job transitions and relocation may also occur because of family concerns (Brett & Reilly, 1988). Careers are now seen as a series of transitions rather than a clear trajectory of jobs with one employer (Arthur, 1994; Bird, 1994). Since many organizations can no longer promise long-term employment, the bonds between employers and employees have loosened (Rousseau & Wade-Benzoni, 1995; Robinson, Kraatz, & Rousseau, 1994). Given these trends in employment, movement across organizational boundaries has become more common, and in many cases expected.

Dependency issues may also play a role in how resilient an individual is in coping with numerous job transitions during the establishment years (Waterman, Waterman, & Collard, 1994). Those who are passive may experience more difficulty coping with job changes compared with those who are independent or interdependent. In contrast, individuals with an anticonformity approach to dependency may actually perform better and be more satisfied with temporary employment situations, which are becoming more common for professional and managerial work (Von Hippel, Mangum, Greenberger, Heneman, & Skoglind, 1997). How individuals respond to dependency may be important to understanding how young adults respond to job change, organizational change, and geographical mobility.

Implications for Research and Practice

Future research should assess the four responses to dependency (see Figure 6.1) and relate them to the key developmental issues that emerge in the five key areas during the establishment years. For example, studies of socialization might examine how dependency issues affect the various phases of socialization differentially (anticipatory, encounter, change, and acquisition). The dependency perspective may also help to integrate the diverse literatures on the establishment years, which range from work-family integration to mentoring and supervisory relationships. Dependence issues cut across all five of these areas, since young adults' orientations toward authority figures influence their worldview and coping strategies during the establishment years.

For decades, career anchors have been considered an important indication of an individual's core values and an important determinant of his or her occupational choice (Schein, 1985). These career anchors may also be related to how dependency issues are resolved and careers are chosen. Thus, career counselors might begin to view these tentative vocational choices as reflective of individuals' orientation toward authority, independence, and autonomy on the job. Since core values will not be easy to change, practitioners should focus on how to help the individual adapt or adjust to the demands of the job or career. From the perspective of person-environment fit, adults should be placed in positions that are suitable for both their individual developmental needs and organizational value systems.

Dependence issues affect how individuals interact with those they may view as authority figures at the workplace. Thus, research on supervisory relationships might begin to include the individual's response toward dependency to understand difficulties in leader-member relationships better. The mentoring literature also may be extended by adopting a dependence perspective as well. In-depth qualitative interviews might be an important first step in understanding how issues of dependence affect developmental relationships, since the mentoring literature has a rich tradition of uncovering important relationship functions and roles using interview methods (Kram, 1985; Levinson et al., 1978). For example, it may be that dependence is a moderator variable that affects the emergence of mentoring alliances and whether these relationships are functional or dysfunctional.

In the area of work and family, the spillover model might also be extended to examine the role that dependence issues play in the degree to which an individual separates work and family concerns in the establishment years. The individual's attitudes toward dependence and the work-family interface have not been studied, but there are some potentially rich research possibilities that might explore the degree to which passivity, for example, may affect an individual's willingness to put his or her own career on hold for the spouse. Research is needed on this issue because it may have important implications not only for careers but also for marital success and life satisfaction.

Research might also be conducted on attitudes toward dependence and job transitions. Those who are anticonforming or independent may have more job transitions than those who are interdependent or passive. In addition, the dependence perspective could be used to explain the varying degrees of individuals' abilities to cope with shifts in psychological contracts (Arthur, 1994; Robinson et al., 1994). Those who are passive, for example, may still expect employers to take care of them instead of managing their own career. Reactions to dependence may also influence how individuals' careers are anchored (Feldman & Bolino, 1997; Schein, 1985). In particular, dependency may affect the degree to which a person gravitates to entrepreneurship or autonomy anchors.

Human resource practices might benefit from considering dependence issues, too. Understanding an individual's basic orientation toward the demands for conformity may assist in better understanding reactions to the socialization process. Anticonformity responses are often particularly difficult for supervisors to deal with during the early career years. The socialization process for these individuals may be even more difficult than for those with independent or interdependent reactions. The coping mechanisms that anticonforming individuals employ may also be disruptive to the rest of the work group and impair work performance. An increased awareness of these basic developmental issues may assist supervisors, mentors, and human resource managers in more effectively responding to the reactions of the anticonformist.

Furthermore, there may be task assignments that are better suited to individuals with an anticonformist style, especially if they also value autonomy. For example, an anticonformist may be better suited to being a patient's advocate than a customer service representative. However, if the person must consistently collaborate with others in the course of work, mentoring and coaching may help him or her to adjust to the work demands better.

Many organizations realize that career decisions are made today in the context of two-career couples and that career transitions must now take into account the spouse's career. If both parties are independent or interdependent, accommodating the careers of both parties may be challenging. For example, some organizations offer assistance in finding a suitable job for the spouse when a career move requires relocation. The success of these job transitions may depend on how well adjusted the spouse is in the new location and the extent to which "family-friendly" work practices like flextime are available.

Another important avenue for future research is investigating the career issues facing blue-collar workers during the establishment years. Thomas (1989) argues that blue-collar workers' external careers are constrained by the limited vertical mobility opportunities available. However, these workers must make sense of their employment just as white-collar workers do. Dependence issues may be equally important for members of these occupations, since blue-collar workers may have to adopt different coping strategies to deal with the limited job opportunities available to them.

For example, some blue-collar workers adjust by using a "tourism" coping strategy (Pape, 1964), in which the individual moves between a series of jobs at the same skill level. When pay is low and benefits are similar across jobs, this may be viewed as a reasonable alternative to boredom, resulting in a horizontal series of career moves across jobs. In contrast, other blue-collar workers may respond to the lack of mobility and boredom in their jobs by creating games (Thomas, 1989). Blue-collar workers can accelerate the work pace so they can take off time later in the day, passing the time with internal competitions or chatting with coworkers (Roy, 1958). This game-playing response may be more likely to be adopted by those with an anticonformity approach to dependence.

There is also a need for career research to begin examining the career anchors of blue-collar workers. The framework presented by Schein (1990) may need to be amended to address different kinds of career trajectories. Along the same lines, balancing work and family may be different for blue-collar workers during the establishment years. They may not be able to afford nannies and other child care assistance, and the strain on these individuals may be even greater than in white-collar marriages. Frustrations and boredom at work may result in even more spillover from the workplace into the family setting (Thomas, 1989).

Conclusion

In keeping with the developmental perspective of this book, this chapter reexamined some key areas of research on the establishment years employing a dependency perspective. Since unresolved dependence issues from adolescence often affect relationships later in life (Bowlby, 1969), it is reasonable to assume that dependency issues will reemerge in the establishment years due to the numerous personal upheavals that occur during this critical period. Moreover, the resolution (or lack of resolution) of dependency issues at this time can significantly affect individuals' abilities to function effectively as superiors and subordinates in midcareer. I hope that this chapter offers some new ways of conceptualizing the establishment years from a developmental perspective and will guide future theory and research in useful and productive ways.

References
Adkins, C. (1995). A longitudinal examination of the socialization process. *Academy of Management Journal, 38,* 839–862.
Argyris, C. (1990). *Overcoming organizational defenses: Facilitating organizational learning.* Needham Heights, MA: Allyn & Bacon.

Arthur, M. B. (1994). The boundaryless career: A new perspective for organizational inquiry. *Journal of Organizational Behavior, 15,* 295–306.

Ashforth, B., & Saks, A. (1996). Socialization tactics: Longitudinal effects on newcomer adjustment. *Academy of Management Journal, 39,* 149–178.

Baird, L., & Kram, K. E. (1983). Career dynamics: Managing the superior/subordinate relationship. *Organizational Dynamics, 11,* 46–64.

Baker, H., & Feldman, D. (1990). Strategies of organizational socialization and their impact on newcomer adjustment. *Journal of Managerial Issues, 2,* 198–212.

Bauer, T., & Green, S. (1994). Effect of newcomer involvement on work-related activities: A longitudinal study of socialization. *Journal of Applied Psychology, 79,* 211–223.

Bird, A. (1994). Careers as repositories of knowledge: A new perspective on boundaryless careers. *Journal of Organizational Behavior, 15,* 325–344.

Blos, P. (1979). *The adolescent passage.* New York: International Universities Press.

Bowlby, J. (1969). *Attachment and loss.* New York: Basic Books.

Brett, J. M., & Reilly, A. H. (1988). On the road again: Predicting the job transfer decision. *Journal of Applied Psychology, 73,* 614–620.

Campbell, B. M. (1986). *Successful women, angry men.* New York: Random House.

Chao, G., O'Leary, A., Wolf, S., Klein, H., & Gardner, P. (1994). Organizational socialization: Its content and consequence. *Journal of Applied Psychology, 79,* 730–743.

Clawson, J. G., Kotter, J. P., Faux, V. A., & McArthur, C. C. (1992). *Self-assessment and career development* (3rd ed.). Upper Saddle River, NJ: Prentice Hall.

Dalton, G., Thompson, P., & Price, R. (1977). The four stages of professional careers: A new look at the performance of professionals. *Organizational Dynamics, 6,* 19–42.

Davidhizer, R., & Eshleman, J. (1992). Co-dependency at the workplace. *Hospital Topics, 70,* 15–20.

Derr, C. B. (Ed.). (1980). *Work, family, and career: New frontiers in theory and research.* New York: Praeger.

Dix, J. E., & Savickas, M. L. (1995). Establishing a career: Developmental tasks and coping responses. *Journal of Vocational Behavior, 47,* 93–107.

Dreher, G. F., & Ash, R. (1990). A comparative study of mentoring among men and women in managerial, professional, and technical positions. *Journal of Applied Psychology, 81,* 297–308.

Driver, M. J. (1980). Career concepts and organizational change. In C. B. Derr (Ed.). *Work, family, and career: New frontiers in theory and research* (pp. 5–17). New York: Praeger.

Eby, L., McManus, S., Simon, S. A., & Russell, J. (1998). The protégés' perspective regarding negative mentoring experiences: The development of a taxonomy. *Journal of Vocational Behavior, 57,* 1–21.

Erikson, E. H. (1950). *Childhood and society.* New York: Norton.

Feldman, D. C. (1976). A contingency theory of socialization. *Administrative Science Quarterly, 21,* 433–452.

Feldman, D. C. (1981). The multiple socialization of organization members. *Academy of Management Review, 6,* 309–318.

Feldman, D. C. (1999). Toxic mentors or toxic protégés? A critical reexamination of dysfunctional mentoring. *Human Resource Management Review, 9,* 247–278.

Feldman, D. C., & Bolino, M. C. (1997). Careers within careers: Reconceptualizing the nature of career anchors and their consequences. *Human Resource Management Review, 6,* 89–112.

Fisher, C. (1986). Organization socialization: An integrative review. *Research in Personnel and Human Resource Management, 4,* 101–145.

Fromm, E. (1956). *The art of loving.* New York: HarperCollins.

Goleman, D. (1995). *Emotional intelligence.* New York: Bantam Books.

Graen, G., Orris, D., & Johnson, T. (1973). Role assimilation process in a complex organization. *Journal of Vocational Behavior, 3,* 395–420.

Hall, D. T. (1996). Protean careers of the 21st century. *Academy of Management Executive, 10,* 8–16.

Hall, F. S., & Hall, D. T. (1979). *The two-career couple.* Reading, MA: Addison-Wesley.

Hochschild, A. (1989). *The second shift.* New York: Viking Press.

Holland, J. L. (1985). *Making vocational choices: A theory of vocational personalities and work environments.* Upper Saddle River, NJ: Prentice Hall.

Hollander, E. P., & Willis, R. H. (1967). Some current issues in the psychology of conformity and nonconformity. *Psychological Bulletin, 68,* 62–76.

Kabanoff, B. (1980). Work and nonwork: A review of models, methods, and findings. *Psychological Bulletin, 88,* 60–77.

Kelman, H. C. (1961). Three processes of social influence. *Public Opinion Quarterly, 25,* 57–78.

Kiesler, C. A., & Kiesler, S. B. (1969). *Conformity.* Reading, MA: Addison-Wesley.

Kirchmeyer, K. (1992). Nonwork participation and work attitudes: A test of scarcity vs. expansion models of personal resources. *Human Relations, 45,* 775–795.

Kram, K. E. (1985). *Mentoring at work: Developmental relationships in organizational life.* Glenview, IL: Scott, Foresman.

Kram, K. E., & Isabella, L. A. (1985). Mentoring alternatives: The role of peer relationships in career development. *Academy of Management Journal, 28,* 110–132.

Levinson, D. J., Darrow, C. N., Klein, E. B., Levinson, M. H., & McKee, B. (1978). *The seasons of a man's life.* New York: Knopf.

Louis, M. R. (1980). Surprise and sense making: What newcomers experience in entering unfamiliar organizational settings. *Administrative Science Quarterly, 25,* 226–251.

Major, D., Kozlowski, S., Chao, G., & Gardner, P. (1995). A longitudinal investigation of newcomer expectations, early socialization outcomes and the moderating effects of role development factors. *Journal of Applied Psychology, 80,* 418–431.

Manzoni, J., & Barsoux, J. (1998). The set-up-to-fail syndrome. *Harvard Business Review, 76,* 101–113.

Milgram, S. (1965). Some conditions of obedience and disobedience to authority. *Human Relations, 18,* 57–75.

Noe, R. A. (1988). Women and mentoring: A review and research agenda. *Academy of Management Review, 13,* 65–78.

Ostroff, C., & Kozlowski, S. (1993). The role of mentoring in the information gathering processes of newcomers during early organizational socialization. *Journal of Vocational Behavior, 42,* 170–183.

Pape, R. (1964). Touristry: A type of occupational mobility. *Social Problems, 11,* 336–344.

Ragins, B. R. (1989). Barriers to mentoring: The female manager's dilemma. *Human Relations, 42,* 1–22.

Ragins, B. R. (1997). Diversified mentoring relationships in organizations: A power perspective. *Academy of Management Review, 22,* 482–521.

Ragins, B. R., & Scandura, T. A. (1994). Gender differences in expected outcomes of mentoring relationships. *Academy of Management Journal, 37,* 957–971.

Robinson, S. L., Kraatz, M. S., & Rousseau, D. M. (1994). Changing obligations and the psychological contract: A longitudinal study. *Academy of Management Journal, 37,* 137–152.

Rousseau, D. M., & Wade-Benzoni, K. A. (1995). Changing individual-organizational attachments: A two-way street. In A. Howard (Ed.), *The changing nature of work* (pp. 290–322). San Francisco: Jossey-Bass.

Roy, D. (1958). Banana time: Job satisfaction and informal interaction. *Human Organization, 18,* 158–168.

Scandura, T. A. (1998). Dysfunctional mentoring relationships and outcomes. *Journal of Management, 24,* 449–467.

Schein, E. H. (1964). How to break in the college graduate. *Harvard Business Review, 42,* 68–76.

Schein, E. H. (1978). *Career dynamics: Matching individual and organizational needs.* Reading, MA: Addison-Wesley.

Schein, E. H. (1990). *Career anchors: Discovering your real values.* San Diego, CA: University Associates.

Super, D. E. (1957). *The psychology of careers.* New York: HarperCollins.

Thomas, R. J. (1989). Blue-collar careers: Meaning and choice in a world of constraints. In M. B. Arthur, D. T. Hall, & B. S. Lawrence (Eds.), *Handbook of career theory* (pp. 354–379). Cambridge: Cambridge University Press.

Van Maanen, J. (1976). Breaking in: Socialization to work. In R. Dubin (Ed.), *Handbook of work, organization and society.* Skokie, IL: Rand McNally.

Van Maanen, J., & Schein, E. (1977). Improving the quality of work life: Career development. In J. R. Hackman & J. L. Suttle (Eds.), *Improving life at work* (pp. 30–95). Santa Monica, CA: Goodyear.

Von Hippel, C., Mangum, S. L., Greenberger, D. B., Heneman, R. L., & Skoglind, J. D. (1997). Temporary employment: Can organizations and employees both win? *Academy of Management Executive, 11,* 93–104.

Wakabayashi, M., & Graen, G. B. (1984). The Japanese career progress study: A seven-year follow-up. *Journal of Applied Psychology, 69,* 605–614.

Wanous, J. P. (1992). *Recruitment, selection, orientation and socialization of newcomers.* Reading, MA: Addison-Wesley.

Waterman, R. H., Waterman, J. A., & Collard, B. A. (1994, July-Aug.). Toward a career resilient workforce. *Harvard Business Review,* 87–95.

Webber, R. A. (1976). Career problems of young managers. *California Management Review, 18,* 19–33.

Whyte, W. H. (1956). *The organization man.* New York: Simon & Schuster.

Zahrly, J., & Tosi, H. (1989). The differential effect of organizational process on early work role adjustment. *Journal of Organizational Behavior, 10,* 59–74.

CHAPTER 7

Career Development in Midcareer

Harvey L. Sterns, Linda M. Subich

The decision to pursue promotions, change jobs or careers, find new employment, or engage in career development activities may result from changes within the individual, the environment, or both in combination. The roles of the midcareer worker are being redefined in the rapidly changing work environment (Ciulla, 2000; Howard, 1995, 1998). Industrial and counseling psychologists also have redefined their views of midcareer development significantly since first examining this issue in the 1940s (Sterns & Huyck, 2001).

This chapter discusses the complexity of defining both the period of time that comprises midlife and the nature of the midcareer stage. We present an overview of a number of perspectives on the nature of the midlife period, examine theories and models of work choices and career development at midlife, and discuss how conceptualizations of work at midlife are continuing to evolve in careers research and practice.

Midcareer: Problems of Definition

The Age Discrimination in Employment Act (ADEA) of 1967 (amended in 1978 and 1986) defined any worker age forty and above as an older worker. At the same time, Lachman and Bertrand (2001) indicate that continuing controversy exists regarding the definition of the middle years. Midlife is usually thought of as beginning at age forty and ending at age sixty or sixty-five, the beginning of old age.

However, people hold varying views on the timing of midlife. The older the person is, the later he or she expects midlife to begin. This has been tied to the concept of subjective age in which people think of themselves as ten to fifteen years younger than their chronological age. For instance, almost half the respondents sixty-five to sixty-nine in a recent study by the National Council on the Aging (2000) considered themselves to be middle-aged. The use of flexible age ranges to represent middle age, then, reflects the current state of our understanding of the term. In addressing the issue of defining the adult life stages and career stages, Sterns and Doverspike (1989) suggested that five general approaches be considered: chronological-legal, functional, psychosocial, organizational, and life-span orientation.

In the chronological-legal approach, the distinction between older and younger workers rests most frequently on chronological age. Although little theoretical justification is offered for the age ranges, there is an implicit justification based on a legal definition of age. The ADEA protects workers over the age of forty. In recommending such a law, President Lyndon Johnson stated that approximately half of all private job openings were barred to applicants over age fifty-five, and a quarter were closed to applicants over age forty-five (Edelman & Seigler, 1978). Another commonly used cutoff point comes from the Job Training Partnership Act and the Older Americans Act: both recognize people aged fifty-five and older as adult and older adult workers.

The functional approach to defining age is performance based and recognizes that great individual variation exists in abilities and functioning at all ages. As chronological age increases, individuals go through various biological and psychological changes, including declines in physical abilities as well as increases in experience, wisdom, and judgment. Individuals can be identified as "younger" or "older" than their chronological age, based on objective measures of their performance.

The concept of functional age has been criticized from a number of dimensions, including definitional lack of clarity, problems with research designs assessing the construct, and underlying assumptions of decline (Avolio, Barrett, & Sterns, 1984; Salthouse,

1986). Despite these criticisms of the concept, different approaches and definitions of functional age continue to exert considerable influence on careers research.

Psychosocial definitions of middle-aged and older workers are based on social perceptions, including age typing of occupations, perceptions of the adult and older adult worker, and the aging of knowledge, skill, and ability sets. The individual's self-perception is also considered. How individuals perceive themselves and their careers at a given age may be congruent or incongruent with societal images. Relatively little research has addressed the quite basic question of how we know when workers will perceive themselves to be identified by others as middle-aged or older.

The organizational view of adult workers typically focuses on the joint effects of age and tenure. These two variables are usually related; adult workers often have spent substantially more time in a job and substantially more time in an organization. In the organizational view, then, the effects of aging often may be confounded by the effects of tenure and vice versa. Organizations also age (Schrank & Waring, 1981). Indeed, an organization may be perceived as old because of the average age of its members. As the average age of its members increases, new demands are placed on the organizational subsystems such as human resources.

Finally, the life-span approach borrows from a number of the previous approaches but adds its own unique emphasis. It advances the possibility for behavioral change at any point in the life cycle. Substantial individual differences in aging are recognized as critical in examining adult career patterns.

From this perspective, three sets of factors are seen as affecting behavioral change during the life cycle: biological and environmental determinants, which bear a strong relationship to chronological age; normative and history-graded influences that affect most members of a cohort in similar ways; and nonnormative determinants, which include career and life changes unique to each individual. According to this approach, there are more individual differences as people grow older (Baltes & Graf, 1996; Baltes, Reese, & Lipsitt, 1980).

In sum, the definitions of midcareer and midlife appear to vary from model to model, depending on the interests of various scholars and of those testing their models (Sterns & Hurd-Gray, 1998). Various models and theories have discussed the transition into midlife, how one gains awareness that one has become middle-aged (Neugarten, 1968), and the issues or crises that go along with this change (Baruch, Barnett, & Rivers, 1983; Jacques, 1965; Levinson, Darrow, Klein, Levinson, & McKee, 1978, Levinson & Levinson, 1996). The major issues in the first phase of midlife often revolve around recognizing the limits of career progress, deciding whether to shift gears or remain in place, and rebalancing work and family needs as children become more emotionally independent (but may need even more costly financial investment in higher education). During the second phase of midlife, the career issues revolve increasingly around the decisions about how much energy and ambition to invest in work and decisions about withdrawal from paid employment (Sterns & Huyck, 2001).

Midcareer and Midlife

Traditional linear career models bring together midcareer and midlife by tying career stages to chronological age. This approach has reinforced the interconnectedness of midcareer and midlife experiences. In contrast, life-span theory recognizes that career changes and events may take place at any point throughout the life span (Staudinger & Bluck, 2001; Sterns, 1986). Because career stages are not necessarily tied to any particular age, midcareer and midlife potentially may coincide. However, life-span theory does not require a co-occurrence of these events. This latter conceptualization suggests that non-age-specific variables may either positively influence midlife experiences or act as stressors that overwhelm individuals' coping resources.

In terms of midlife and work, Levinson et al. (1978) suggested that only 10 to 20 percent of middle-aged individuals experience moderate to high work satisfaction and that 20 to 30 percent receive minor gratification. In comparison, the largest group of middle-aged individuals (50 percent) experienced work as demeaning, empty, or damaging to the self. Although both women and men were presumed to be represented in all three groups, Levinson et al. (1978) felt that women were likely to be found disproportionately in the last group rather than in the first two.

In contrast to the potentially negative midlife work experiences suggested by Levinson et al. (1978), Chiriboga (1989) highlighted evidence that the middle years often are viewed as a time of challenge and reward in regard to work life. Furthermore, the positive relation between age and job satisfaction indicates that midlife can be a time of positive work experiences, too (Farr, Tesluk, & Klein, 1998).

Conceptualizations of Midlife

Erikson (1963) conceptualized psychosocial development as associated with age and predicted changes in adult personality throughout the life span. The developmental issue at midlife was viewed in terms of generativity versus stagnation. Successful resolution of this life period was characterized by a shift in focus to a concern for larger organizational or social issues and the development of the younger generation. Unsuccessful resolution of this developmental dilemma was believed to result in self-absorption that could hinder resolution of subsequent career stages.

Levinson (Levinson et al., 1978; Levinson & Levinson, 1996) also viewed developmental stages as connected to specific age periods. In Levinson's theory, the midlife transition was described as a period of self-evaluation, spanning ages forty to forty-five, and was emphasized as a universal experience. This transition was conceptualized as a time of severe crisis brought about by tensions and discrepancies between a person's actual and desired achievements. Although specific external stresses were thought to be important influences, internal events were considered to drive the developmental crisis as well. Increasing individuation and increased attention to the self were thought to be the major foci of this life period.

Levinson's original work was specifically based on the male experience at midlife. More recently, Levinson and Levinson (1996) suggested that both men and women experience the same periods of adult development at the same ages. The general structural framework of development was thought to be similar, but the specific life circumstances, coping resources, and existing constraints differ by gender. Especially at midlife, women's circumstances may become more complex. They may find themselves balancing job demands, career growth, care of children and the spouse, and elder care responsibilities for aging parents (Huyck, 1999).

Crisis and Development

Developmental theories emphasizing periods of transitions, particularly midlife transitions, also necessitate discussion of the meaning or nature of change and crisis. Riegel (1975) conceptualized developmental periods of both stability and change, noting that transition is not necessarily a negative experience. Similarly, Levinson and associates (Levinson et al., 1978; Levinson & Levinson 1996) and Sheehy (1976, 1995) suggested that crises are not necessarily negative because benefits as well as costs may result from such experiences. Crises can, in fact, be viewed as stimuli to further change (Riegel, 1975).

The equating of change with crisis exaggerates the importance of the first and weakens the connotations of the second (Chiriboga, 1989). Furthermore, it blurs the important distinction between constructive contradiction as part of normal development and imbalanced contradiction (Riegel, 1975). With imbalanced contradiction, an individual is unable to deal with his or her life situation. Environmental challenges surpass individual coping resources, resulting in deviations or blockages to normal development. Riegel (1975) labeled these developmental deviations catastrophes and considered their occurrences as inimical to normal, constructive development. This theme of situational conditions exceeding individual coping resources surfaces throughout much of the adult development literature.

Empirical evidence and popular literature present very different pictures of the prevalence of midlife crisis as a negative experience. For example, based on a summary of several studies, Chiriboga (1989) suggested that only 2 to 5 percent of middle-agers might actually experience serious midlife problems. More recently, findings from the Midlife Project funded by the McArthur Foundation suggest that significant life reevaluations during this period may be common but are not crises at all (Lachman, Lewkowicz, Marcus, & Peng, 1994). Although many respondents in this study believed that midlife crises exist, many also reported conceptualizing this period as an opportunity for growth and development rather than one of difficulty (Lachman & James, 1997). This finding is consistent with the conceptualization of midlife as a time for renewal by Bejian and Salomone (1995).

Similarly, within the framework of the Big Five personality traits (neuroticism, extraversion, openness to experience, agreeableness, and conscientiousness), the empirical data generally indicate continuity of personality traits over time. Consistent, replicated evidence of change in mean level or relative standing of personality factors is rarely found over time (Costa & McCrae, 1989). In contrast, both popular literature (for example, Sheehy, 1976, 1995) and case-study-oriented work (for example, Levinson et al., 1978; Levinson & Levinson, 1996) suggest the occurrence of universal predictable transition periods, with the majority of individuals reporting crisis experiences. Although empirical findings suggest consistency in general, this does not rule out the possibility of specific instances of change. For example, individuals who have poorly developed coping styles may experience more difficulties both at midcareer and throughout the life span (Vaillant, 1977).

Evidence of stability also may be contingent on the individual difference variable under investigation. Empirical investigations typically have focused on personality traits, which by definition are expected to be enduring. However, different traits may vary in terms of stability, and this stability itself may vary depending on the person's stage of the life span or environmental circumstances (Costa & McCrae, 1989). Thus, willingness (or ability) to change may be an intrinsic characteristic of some individuals who pursue change at midlife, and others may pursue change due to long-standing problems rather than just experiencing difficulties at their current stage (Costa & McCrae, 1989; Lachman & James, 1997; Lachman et al., 1994).

In addition, personality stability may be due in part to a stable and unchanging environment. This suggests the possibility that environmental factors might be related to changes or crises. In short, multiple factors are likely to influence midlife development (Lachman & James, 1997), and vectors of influence, such as career- and family-related issues and individual differences, may come together to affect individuals in unique ways.

Work Choices at Midlife

The life span orientation recognizes that behavioral change can occur over the entire life cycle. Over the course of a career, a person will be presented with increasingly complex work roles, which play a crucial role in stimulating the development of cognitive structures. Individuals begin with different potentials and improve at differing rates. A variety of theories have addressed work choices at midlife.

A Model of Career Progression

Patchett and Sterns (1984) and Sterns (1986) developed a model of adult career progression that assumes that transitions in work life occur many times throughout a career (see Figure 7.1). According to the model, the decision to change jobs or careers is influenced directly by attitudes toward mobility and success or failure in previous career development activities. Numerous factors are hypothesized to affect mobility attitudes, such as organizational tenure, career stage, growth needs, and job market conditions. The decision to change jobs or careers also may affect one's attitudes toward entering or reentering the workforce. Any of these variables also could be mediated by the effects of various personality variables.

This model incorporates Hall's model of career growth (1971), which conceptualizes career planning from a goal-setting perspective. Once a career goal decision—such as the decision to engage in training or retraining—is made, then goal attainment should lead to identity growth and enhanced self-esteem, which may lead to greater commitment to future career developmental goals, perceptions of self-efficacy, and future commitment to career development activities.

Especially for adults with doubts about their abilities to perform well in training or retraining programs, successes early in the program may be crucial. Not only do these successes enhance feelings of self-efficacy, but decisions to engage in future retraining may be enhanced as well. In contrast, early failures can result in decisions to drop out of the retraining programs or to avoid future programs, jeopardizing future career growth opportunities and decisions.

Mobility Models

Numerous models suggest that the mobility rates of younger persons (up to around age thirty) are much higher than are those of older

Figure 7.1. Career Progression in Middle and Later Adulthood.

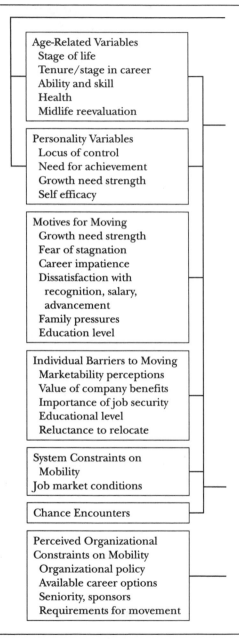

Source: From *Age, Health, and Employment* by Birren, Robinson, and Livingston, eds. Copyright © 1986. Reprinted by permission of Pearson Education, Inc., Upper Saddle River, NJ.

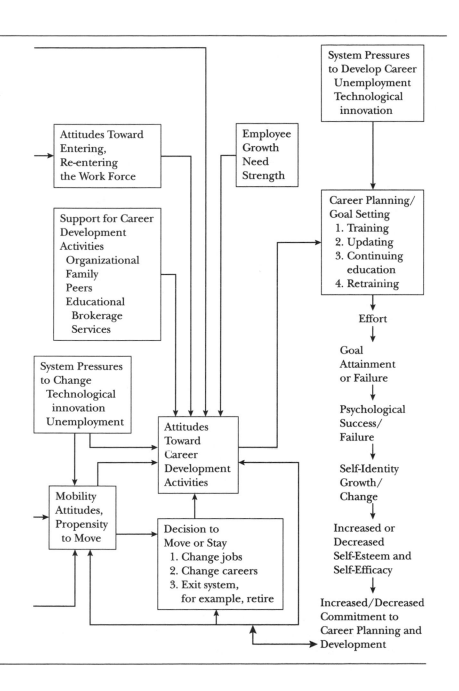

persons (Super, 1957; Veiga, 1983). As the younger generations move about seeking their niches in life, the older ones maintain theirs as they plan for retirement. Research on actual mobility rates seems to bear out these hypotheses (Veiga, 1983). Veiga (1983) also found that age correlated significantly and negatively with propensity to move.

Along similar lines, tenure (seniority) or stage in career has been a variable of interest in the mobility literature. Schein (1971) described three stages in a career: socialization, performance, and obsolescence (or the development of new skills). In the third stage, the obsolete person may be retained as deadwood with no options for mobility or be retrained, transferred into a lateral position, or forced into early retirement.

Although career development could be helpful to the employee in all three stages, it seems likely that the person who would most strongly desire such help would be in a third stage of Schein's model. Moreover, "mobility in the earliest stage of one's career bears an unequivocal relationship with one's later career" (Rosenbaum, 1979, p. 220; see also Veiga, 1981, 1983). Thus, the person who is mobile early on is most likely to favor career development programs later in his or her career (Sterns & Patchett, 1984).

Barriers to moving also bear some relationship to issues of aging and seniority. As Veiga (1983) suggested, perceptions of one's own marketability may strongly influence one's efforts to explore alternative career opportunities, either within or outside one's own organization. Holding a particular position within the same organization for an extended time period may reinforce one's feelings of specialization or obsolescence rather than one's feelings of marketability potential. Similarly, the longer a person remains within a company and the older that person gets, the more hesitant the individual will be about risking benefits accrued through the years in order to move to a new organization. The same may be true for the person who strongly values job security, regardless of age.

Mobility, then, implies a certain degree of risk to one's job security. Career development programs are likely to be seen as a waste of time for middle-aged or midcareer employees with little motivation to move.

Factors Influencing Mobility

Veiga (1983) identified five motives for moving that significantly influenced propensity to leave: fear of stagnation, career impatience, dissatisfaction with salary, dissatisfaction with recognition, and dissatisfaction with advancement.

Individuals who are self-managers of their careers will have an internal ideal about how growth and movement in their careers should take place. If they are not getting new assignments, opportunities for growth and training, recognition as important contributors, or salary increases and promotions, individuals may begin the process of seeking another position.

Personality variables also have been hypothesized to affect decisions about career mobility, especially internal locus of control. Neapolitan (1980) investigated occupational changes in midcareer and found that people who changed regardless of great obstacles tended to have more internal locus of control. A comparison group of people dissatisfied with their careers who did not change vocations tended to perceive greater risk beyond their control that might doom their efforts to change. According to Greenhaus and Sklarew (1981), exploration "is a pro-active attempt to understand and influence one's life" (p. 2). Thus, we might expect persons with an internal locus of control to engage in greater career planning activity than persons with external locus. Research by Gould (1979) tends to support this hypothesis.

Beehr, Taber, and Walsh (1980) also looked at locus of control and perceived channels of mobility. They found that employees who had not had a recent opportunity to change jobs were more likely to see mobility opportunities as controlled by external forces such as luck or favoritism. In contrast, employees with recent change opportunities tended to perceive mobility as contingent on performance (an internally controlled factor). We may conclude that persons believing that mobility opportunities are controlled by forces beyond their control (an external locus of control) would be less likely to view a career development program as beneficial to them, and thus less likely to participate in one.

Patchett and Sterns (1984) made three interesting observations about midcareer mobility in their development model. First, decisions to change jobs or careers, or decisions to engage in career development activities, may come about as a result of changes within the individual, the environment, or a combination of both. In contrast, other models have a tendency to concentrate on either the individual alone (an organismic perspective) or environmental factors that change and cause the individual to make career decisions (a mechanistic perspective). The Patchett and Sterns model can accommodate both a mechanistic and organismic perspective, but tends to emphasize the changing individual in a changing world.

Second, the Patchett and Sterns model recognizes that adults make multiple career transitions throughout the life span. These authors argue that there are people who are sixty and older who are still interested in working, changing jobs, and developing their careers. Unfortunately, past gerontological discussions have focused almost exclusively on the decision to retire; not enough attention has been given to multiple career transitions that may occur late in midlife or in old age.

Finally, previous models have tended to emphasize the usual career progressions of middle-aged and older adults and assumed fairly stable careers, particularly for white-collar workers. Patchett and Sterns's model allows for the occurrence of idiosyncratic career events that affect midcareer employees (such as unemployment and technological obsolescence), as well as for the normative events (such as promotions and lateral moves).

Current Theories from Vocational Psychology

Complementing these developmental and life span approaches to understanding midlife and midcareer behavior are two theories drawn from vocational psychology: developmental self-concept theory (Super, 1957; Super, Savickas, & Super, 1996) and social cognitive career theory (Lent, Brown, & Hackett, 1994).

Developmental Self-Concept Theory

Super's developmental self-concept theory, introduced formally in 1957, stressed the interaction of personal and environmental variables. As stated aims in formulating a theory of career and lifelong development, Super (1953) included a number of relatively standard issues related to vocational psychology: accounting for individual differences, acknowledging persons' occupational multipotentiality, incorporating occupational ability patterns, and addressing identification with (and importance of) role models. He also included foci more specific to life span development: the continuous nature of adjustment, the dynamic nature of life stages and career patterns, the importance of person- environment interactions, and the importance of job satisfaction to how one manages to play one's desired role in life through work. Although the former set clearly has relevance for persons at midlife, it is this latter set that seems most important to consider in theorizing about midlife adults.

In the original formulation of his theory, Super (1957) described persons of all ages as attempting to implement their self-concept through entering and working in a vocation permitting self-expression, with the specifics of the implementation behavior dependent on the person's life stage. Super also acknowledged the importance of contextual variables, such as socioeconomic status, in determining individuals' career patterns. Furthermore, he suggested that neither workers nor jobs are static; this view is entirely consistent with Sullivan's (1999) recent discussion of the changing and dynamic nature of the current work environment.

In sum, according to Super (1957, 1984; Super et al., 1996), vocational development at its core consists of ongoing growth and experimentation with self-concept, with work and life satisfaction dependent on the availability of adequate outlets for interests, abilities, and values. Thus, midlife career development is characterized less by specific tasks or attitudes than it is by complex, dynamic processes.

Nevertheless, Super (1957, 1984; Super et al., 1996) summarized the career development process as having five stages in its maxi-cycle: growth, exploration, establishment, maintenance, and disengagement. The stages most relevant to midlife would seem to be the establishment and maintenance stages.

In the establishment stage, individuals attempt to set themselves up in fields that seem appropriate to them. The individual stabilizes a pattern of working, attempts to become comfortable in his or her job, and makes some effort to advance in the chosen career in some way. In the maintenance stage, individuals become concerned about how to hold on to their place in the work world until retirement. Preserving status and gains previously made are an important part of this stage, but people vary in their manner of accomplishing this task. Some focus on holding their own in the organization, others pursue new learning and training, and still others work to innovate and make new contributions to their field.

Although these five states may represent a general direction of development, Super (1984; Super et al., 1996) posited that within the maxi-cycle, there occur mini-cycles that mirror the maxi-cycle. That is, in the maintenance stage, an individual may grow through becoming aware of his or her age-related gains and losses, may explore by seeking out new challenges, may establish new skills, may maintain status by prevailing against competitors, and may disengage from some activities that are less relevant as she or he ages.

This conceptualization of the development process suggests that change is constant and adaptation essential throughout the career. Indeed, Savickas (1997) recently proposed that the future relevance of Super's theory hinges on focusing more clearly on career adaptability—a construct that encompasses planful attitudes, ongoing exploration, and adaptive decisional skills. Savickas's perspective, too, suggests that career development at midlife is by definition concerned with change and the individual's ability to cope with it.

Furthermore, Super suggests that across the life span, persons play many roles simultaneously. These roles, which include child, student, worker, parent, and citizen, might wax and wane in importance over time. Super suggested the roles might be characterized by, and vary depending on, the life theaters in which they are played. He further suggested that persons vary in the amount of time, energy, and affect they invest in the set of roles they undertake. In 1980, he used the metaphor of a rainbow to elaborate on this point and to illustrate vividly how work is but one aspect of a person's life at midcareer (see Figure 7.2).

Super's rainbow expresses in a visual way the importance of considering career development in the context of other life roles and personal development, an issue especially salient at midlife, when it is recognized that persons play multiple roles in divergent theaters and can become overwhelmed by too many activities.

Figure 7.2. The Life-Career Rainbow: Nine Life Roles in Schematic Life Space.

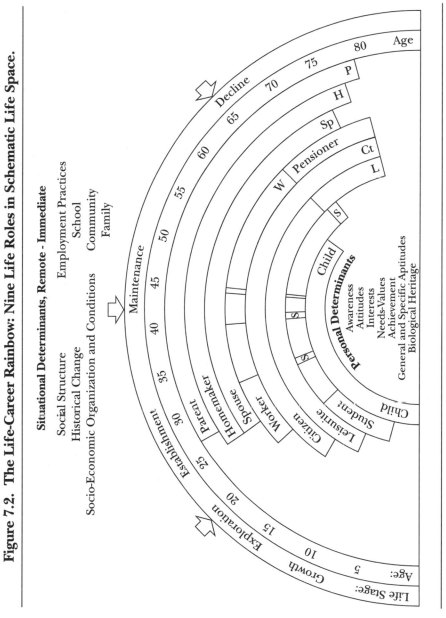

Situational Determinants, Remote - Immediate

Social Structure	Employment Practices
Historical Change	School
Socio-Economic Organization and Conditions	Community
	Family

Personal Determinants
Awareness
Attitudes
Interests
Needs-Values
Achievement
General and Specific Aptitudes
Biological Heritage

Source: From "A Life-Span, Life-Space Approach to Career Development" by D. E. Super, *Journal of Vocational Behavior,* 16, p. 289. Copyright 1980 by Academic Press, Inc.

Super reviewed some of the early research in support of his theory in a 1985 article in the *American Psychologist,* but recent research on his theory and postulates with adult samples has been sparse. Surveying some of these recent studies, however, suggests that the theory continues to have utility.

For example, Niles, Anderson, and Goodnough (1998) found that exploratory behavior was an important way in which a sample of adult career clients aged twenty-four to fifty-one coped with varied career development tasks, thereby supporting Super's ideas about the dynamic nature of career development and the relevance of growth and exploration into midlife. Smart and Peterson (1997) found similar results in a study of Australian adults (their mean age was approximately thirty years and all were under age fifty) who were considering or in the process of changing careers. These individuals were compared to similar persons without such intentions. Smart and Peterson (1997) found that individuals who were considering or in the process of actually changing their careers were characterized as having more exploration and implementation concerns than the comparison group.

Super's model also appears to be as relevant for women as for men. For example, Smart (1998) found that Australian women's satisfaction with different aspects of their career varied as predicted in Super's theory of life stages. Women were more satisfied with pay and more settled in their jobs in the establishment stage than at the exploration stage; professional commitment further solidified for women in the maintenance stage.

However, contextual factors such as poverty or access to labor market opportunities may moderate the manner and extent to which a person explores the world of work. Consequently, contextual factors should be used to supplement Super's theory as well (Blustein, 1997).

Social Cognitive Career Theory

Complementing Super's approach to understanding midlife career development is a promising recent theory that emerged from Bandura's (1986) social cognitive theory. Social cognitive career theory (SCCT), introduced by Lent et al. in 1994, has become a widely accepted framework for the study of the development of academic interests and vocational choices because of its comprehensiveness (Lent & Hackett, 1994) and strong empirical support (Betz & Voyten, 1997; Fouad & Smith, 1996). Although not originally conceptualized as such, SCCT seems to be a potentially productive framework from which to view midlife and midcareer development as well (see Figure 7.3).

SCCT is a cognitive approach that emphasizes anticipation, forethought, and the active construction of meaning by an individual (Lent & Brown, 1996). As already noted, it is based on three-way reciprocality between person, environment, and behavior (Bandura, 1986). The critical cognitive mechanisms that serve as the underpinnings to this theory are self-efficacy, outcome expectations, and goal representations.

Bandura defined self-efficacy as the self-evaluation of one's abilities to complete a certain task or attain a certain level of achievement or performance. In applying self-efficacy theory to vocational psychology, SCCT posits that individuals are more likely to pursue and be successful in occupational behaviors for which they have high self-efficacy (Lent et al., 1994).

In contrast, outcome expectations involve an individual's perceptions of the likely results of his or her actions toward a specific end (Bandura, 1986). According to SCCT, people are more likely to pursue occupations that they believe will result in positive outcomes, such as gainful employment, self-satisfaction, and admiration (Lent et al., 1994).

In SCCT, self-efficacy and outcome expectations are each hypothesized to influence educational success and vocational choices both directly and indirectly (Lent et al., 1994). The indirect links come through the influences of self-efficacy and outcome expectations on interest and exploratory behavior. More specifically, Figure 7.3 depicts the SCCT model of how a person makes occupational choices.

As Figure 7.3 suggests, a person's inputs consist of race, gender, health status, and background variables (such as socioeconomic status). These in turn lead to a unique set of learning experiences for the individual. Those learning experiences help develop self-efficacy and outcome expectations, which ultimately lead to career goals and actions. Choice behaviors predict performance, and performance attainments then become learning experiences that influence future choices. Like Super's theory (1957, 1980; Super et

Figure 7.3. Person, Contextual, and Experiential Factors Affecting Career-Related Choice Behavior.

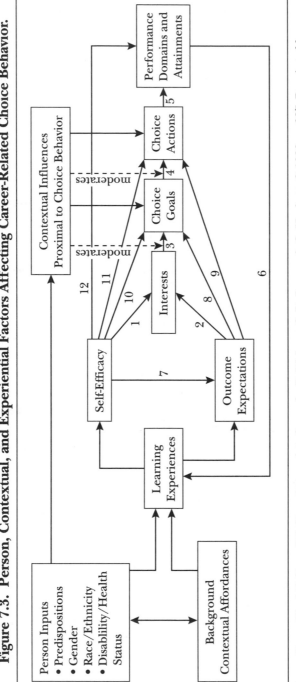

Source: From *The Life-Span, Life-Space Approach to Careers* by R. W. Lent, S. D. Brown, & G. Hackett, © 1993, p. 387. Reprinted by permission of John Wiley & Sons.

Note: Direct relations between variables are indicated with solid lines; moderator effects (where a given variable strengthens or weakens the relations between two other variables) are shown with dashed lines.

al., 1996), SCCT represents a dynamic approach to understanding career choice and development.

Although SCCT was conceptualized originally as a way to explain early occupational choice behavior, its dynamic nature and inclusion of a feedback loop to account for ongoing learning experiences suggest it may be applied productively to midlife and midcareer development as well. Its primary constructs—self-efficacy, outcome expectations, and goal representations—have been supported with persons of varying ages (Sadri & Robertson, 1993). Furthermore, the choice actions and performance attainments that SCCT targets as outcomes, such as choices of how much to invest in one's job at midlife or whether to alter one's career path, occur in varying forms across the life span. In addition, the midlife adult clearly has accumulated a rich history of learning experiences as a result of past goals, actions, and performance attainments. It is reasonable, therefore, to assume that this history informs his or her current career-related attitudes and behaviors as well.

Investigations involving applications of self-efficacy theory to vocational psychology consistently have shown it to be a significant predictor of career and academic choice and success in relevant fields, with results as predicted by SCCT (Fouad & Smith, 1996; Hackett, Betz, Casas, & Rocha-Singh, 1992; Lent, Lopez, & Bieschke, 1991; Lent, Lopez, & Bieschke, 1993; Multon, Brown, & Lent, 1991; Sadri & Robertson, 1993). Less research has focused on outcome expectations, goal setting, and vocational behavior (Hackett et al., 1992; Lent et al., 1991, 1993; Fouad & Smith, 1996). Unfortunately, most research on SCCT to this point has not moved beyond young adult samples (Betz & Voyten, 1997; Fouad & Smith, 1996; Tang, Fouad, & Smith, 1999).

In a rare study addressing some of the central SCCT constructs with employed adults, Donnay and Borgen (1999) examined the incremental validity (beyond interest) of self-efficacy in predicting tenure and satisfaction among employees above and beyond vocational interests. Interests alone predicted 20 percent of the variance in occupational group membership (that is, occupational choice), while 23 percent of the variance in group membership was predicted by self-efficacy alone. However, these variables together predicted 38 percent of the variance in group membership. Donnay and Borgen's research findings are consistent with the SCCT proposition that both self-efficacy and interest have direct effects on choice actions and performance attainments, and they begin to provide empirical support for the relevance of SCCT to midlife adults.

Recently, Lent, Brown, and Hackett (2000) elaborated on the SCCT model with regard to the issue of contextual factors and barriers. They argue that it is critical in understanding a person's current behavior to examine both the person's actual environment and interpretation of that environment in relationship to his or her unique learning history. This recent elaboration of SCCT expands the definition of environmental effects in the theory and highlights the importance of considering individual differences in relation to them.

Indeed, Lent et al. (2000) framed their discussion of individual differences in career-related cognitions and behaviors in terms of a concentric model of environmental context. In this model, they suggested that the impact of broader societal influences on cognitions and behavior is filtered through one's immediate social environment, such as friends and family, and perceptual schema. Consequently, all layers of the person's context must be considered in understanding midcareer and midlife issues.

This approach is also consistent with recent developments in the field of positive psychology (Seligman & Csikszentmihalyi, 2000). That is, objective environmental barriers (for example, ageist discrimination, rapid workplace change, and layoffs) may be perceived as career deterrents or challenges, depending on a person's unique context and learning history. This possibility expands traditional understanding of such career events and may enhance the explanatory power of our models of adult career development.

Models of Work at Midlife

Conceptualizations of work at midlife continue to evolve. For example, recent work by Hall and his colleagues (Hall & Mirvis, 1995a, 1995b; Hall & Associates, 1996) presents strong evidence regarding the protean career—one that is directed by the individual rather than by the employing organization. These authors stress the importance of career self-management in a dramatically changing work environment.

Sterns and Gray (1999) have also emphasized the challenges that midlife workers face in terms of self-management. As organizations move from pyramid shapes to flatter, more streamlined configurations, employees may experience job loss, job plateau-ing, and skills obsolescence (Farr et al., 1998; Sterns & Miklos, 1995). Middle-aged workers may be singled out in downsizing ef-forts on the basis of stereotypic traits, such as being unsuitable for retraining or fast-paced work environments (Hall et al., 1996; Hall & Mirvis, 1995a, 1995b). Furthermore, depending on age of ca-reer entry, middle-aged and older workers may be more likely to occupy the midlevel managerial positions that are often the focus of downsizing and restructuring strategies. In addition, slow com-pany growth may lead to less opportunity for advancement (Farr et al., 1998). These changes suggest that middle-aged and older workers may need to take increased responsibility for their own career management.

Organizational changes also are altering the nature of the re-lationships between organizations and employees (Hall & Mirvis, 1995a, 1995b). Employers' commitment to employees may last only as long as there is a need for their skills and performance. Simi-larly, employees' commitment to the employer may last only as long as their expectations are being met. These changes place greater emphasis on employees' adaptability and learning abilities (Hall & Mirvis, 1995a, 1995b).

These perspectives also highlight the artificiality of the distinc-tion between work and nonwork life. Personal roles and career roles are highly interrelated, and the boundaries between these roles tend to be fuzzy rather than clear-cut (Hall & Mirvis, 1995b).

One potential disadvantage of protean careers is that an indi-vidual's identity is not likely to be tied to any one organization. Problems of self-definition may result in that one's personal iden-tity is not connected to a formal organizational work role. More-over, middle-aged and older workers may be at a disadvantage in terms of moving toward greater career self-management. Making the transition from an organizational-driven career to a protean career may be a rather daunting task, particularly if an individual initially entered the workforce holding a one career–one employer ideal (Hall et al., 1996).

Conclusion

Chronological age is no longer the sole indicator of career stage due to increasing individual differences in career changes, work patterns (full-time or part-time work), and decisions to leave or reenter the workforce (Schaie, 1990). Furthermore, agreement is growing that how one views one's career, understands one's current circumstances, and plans future career moves is not necessarily related to a midlife crisis.

In fact, it may be more appropriate to conceptualize midlife as a period of reevaluation of commitment to one's current career. Individuals' abilities to understand the influences around them, the consequences of their choices, and their resources to take action all point to the importance of cognitive variables in understanding these issues.

In recent years, widespread downsizing, layoffs, and early buyouts have created considerable ambiguity for midlife and midcareer employees regarding future work opportunities and the need to seek new employment. Perhaps for midlife and midcareer employees more than for other groups, attitudes about work in general and mobility in particular will become increasingly important in determining whether they remain in the same career, change careers, or leave the workforce altogether.

References

Avolio, B. J., Barrett, G. V., & Sterns, H. L. (1984). Alternatives to age for assessing occupational performance capacity. *Experimental Aging Research, 10,* 703–724.

Baltes, P. B., & Graf, P. (1996). Psychology aspects of aging: Facts and frontiers. In D. Magnusson (Ed.), *The lifespan development of individuals: Behavioral, neurobiological and psychosocial perspectives* (pp. 427–460). Cambridge: Cambridge University Press.

Baltes, P. B., Reese, H. W., & Lipsitt, L. P. (1980). Life-span developmental psychology. *Annual Review of Psychology, 31,* 65–110.

Bandura, A. (1986). *Social foundations of thought and action: A social cognitive theory.* Upper Saddle River, NJ: Prentice Hall.

Baruch, G., Barnett, R., & Rivers, C. (1983). *Lifeprints: New patterns of love and work for today's women.* New York: McGraw-Hill.

Beehr, T. A., Taber, T. D., & Walsh, J. T. (1980). Perceived mobility channels: Criteria for intraorganizational job mobility. *Organizational Behavior and Human Performance, 26,* 250–264.

Bejian, D. V., & Salomone, P. R. (1995). Understanding midlife career renewal: Implications for counseling. *Career Development Quarterly, 44,* 52–63.

Betz, N. E., & Voyten, K. K. (1997). Efficacy and outcome expectations influence career exploration and decidedness. *Career Development Quarterly, 46,* 179–189.

Blustein, D. L. (1997). A context-rich perspective of career exploration across the life roles. *Career Development Quarterly, 45,* 260–274.

Byrne, J. J. (1975). *Occupational mobility of workers.* Washington, DC: U.S. Bureau of Labor Statistics, Special Labor Force.

Chiriboga, D. A. (1989). Mental health at the midpoint: Crisis, challenge, or relief? In S. Hunter & M. Sundel (Eds.), *Mid-life myths: Issues, findings and practice implications* (pp. 116–144). Thousand Oaks, CA: Sage.

Ciulla, J. B. (2000). *The working life: The promise and betrayal of modern work.* New York: Random House.

Costa, P. T., & McCrae, R. R. (1989). Personality continuity and the changes of adult life. In M. Storandt & G. R. VandenBos (Eds.), *The adult years: Continuity and change* (pp. 41–77). Washington, DC: American Psychological Association.

Donnay, D.A.C., & Borgen, F. H. (1999). The incremental validity of vocational self-efficacy: An examination of interest, self-efficacy, and occupation. *Journal of Counseling Psychology, 46,* 432–447.

Edelman, C. D., & Seigler, I. C. (1978). *Federal age discrimination in employment law: Slowing down the gold watch.* Charlottesville, VA: Michie.

Erikson, E. (1963). *Childhood and society* (2nd ed.). New York: Norton.

Farr, J. L., Tesluk, P. E., & Klein, S. R. (1998). Organizational structure of the workplace and the older worker. In K. W. Schaie & C. Schooler (Eds.), *Impact of work on older adults* (pp. 143–185). New York: Springer.

Fouad, N. A., & Smith, P. L. (1996). A test of social cognitive model for middle school students: Math and science. *Journal of Counseling Psychology, 43,* 338–346.

Gould, S. (1979). Characteristics of career planners in upwardly mobile occupations. *Academy of Management Journal, 22,* 539–550.

Greenhaus, J. H., & Sklarew, N. D. (1981). Some sources and consequences of career exploration. *Journal of Vocational Behavior, 18,* 1–12.

Hackett, G., Betz, N. E., Casas, J. M., & Rocha-Singh, I. A. (1992). Gender, ethnicity, and social cognitive factors predicting the academic achievement of students in engineering. *Journal of Counseling Psychology, 39,* 527–538.

Hall, D. T. (1971). Potential for career growth. *Personnel Administration, 34,* 18–30.

Hall, D. T., & Associates. (1996). *The career is dead: Long live the career: A relational approach to careers.* San Francisco: Jossey-Bass.

Hall, D. T., & Mirvis, P. H. (1995a). The new career contract: Developing the whole person at midlife and beyond. *Journal of Vocational Behavior, 47*, 269–289.

Hall, D. T., & Mirvis, P. H. (1995b). Careers as lifelong learning. In A. Howard (Ed.), *The changing nature of work* (pp. 323–361). San Francisco: Jossey-Bass.

Howard, A. (Ed.). (1995). *The changing nature of work*. San Francisco: Jossey-Bass.

Howard, A. (1998). Commentary: New careers and older workers. In K. W. Schaie & C. Schooler (Eds.), *Impact of work on older adults* (pp. 235–245). New York: Springer.

Huyck, M. H. (1999). Gender roles and gender identity in midlife. In S. L. Willis & J. D. Reid (Eds.), *Life in the middle: Psychological and social development in middle age* (pp. 209–232). Orlando, FL: Academic Press.

Jacques, E. (1965). Death and the mid-life crisis. *International Journal of Psychoanalysis, 66*, 502–515.

Lachman, M. E., & Bertrand, R. M. (2001). Personality and the self in midlife. In M. E. Lachman (Ed.), *Handbook of midlife development* (pp. 279–309). New York: Wiley.

Lachman, M. E., & James, J. B. (1997). Charting the course of midlife development: An overview. In M. E. Lachman & J. B. James (Eds.), *Multiple paths of midlife development* (pp. 1–17). Chicago: University of Chicago Press.

Lachman, M. E., Lewkowicz, C., Marcus, A., & Peng, Y. (1994). Images of midlife development among young, middle-aged and older adults. *Journal of Adult Development, 1*, 201–211.

Lent, R. W., & Brown, S. D. (1996). Social cognitive approach to career development: An overview. *Career Development Quarterly, 44*, 310–321.

Lent, R. W., Brown, S. D., & Hackett, G. (1994). Toward a unifying social cognitive theory of career and academic interest, choice, and performance. *Journal of Vocational Behavior, 45*, 79–122.

Lent, R. W., Brown, S. D., & Hackett, G. (2000). Contextual supports and barriers to career choice: A social cognitive analysis. *Journal of Counseling Psychology, 47*, 36–49.

Lent, R. W., & Hackett, G. (1994). Sociocognitive mechanisms of personal agency in career development: Pantheoretical prospects. In M. L. Savickas & R. W. Lent (Eds.), *Convergence in career development theories: Implications for science and practice* (pp. 77–101). Palo Alto, CA: CPP Books.

Lent, R. W., Lopez, F. G., & Bieschke, K. J. (1991). Mathematics self-efficacy: Sources and relation to science-based career choice. *Journal of Counseling Psychology, 38*, 424–430.

Lent, R. W., Lopez, F. G., & Bieschke, K. J. (1993). Predicting mathematics-related choice and success behaviors: Test of an expanded social cognitive model. *Journal of Vocational Behavior, 42*, 223–236.

Levinson, D. J., Darrow, C. N., Klein, E. B., Levinson, M. L., & McKee, B. (1978). *The seasons of a man's life.* New York: Knopf.

Levinson, D. J., & Levinson, J. D. (1996). *The seasons of a woman's life.* New York: Knopf.

Multon, K. D., Brown, S. D., & Lent, R. W. (1991). Relation of self-efficacy beliefs to academic outcomes: A meta-analytic investigation. *Journal of Counseling Psychology, 38,* 30–38.

National Council on the Aging. (2000, Mar.). *Myths and realities 2000 survey results.* Washington, DC: Author.

Neapolitan, J. (1980). Occupational change in mid-career: An exploratory investigation. *Journal of Vocational Behavior, 16,* 212–225.

Neugarten, B. L. (1968). The awareness of middle age. In B. L. Neugarten (Ed.), *Middle age and aging* (pp. 93–98). Chicago: University of Chicago Press.

Niles, S. G., Anderson, W. P., & Goodnough, G. (1998). Exploration to foster career development. *Career Development Quarterly, 46,* 262–275.

Patchett, M. B., & Sterns, H. L. (1984, Feb. 23–26). *Progression in middle and later adulthood.* Paper presented at the Tenth Annual Meeting of the Association for Gerontology in Higher Education, Indianapolis.

Riegel, K. F. (1975). Adult life crises: A dialectic interpretation of development. In N. Datan & L. H. Ginsberg (Eds.), *Life-span developmental psychology: Normative life crises* (pp. 99–128). Orlando, FL: Academic Press.

Rosenbaum, J. E. (1979). Tournament mobility: Career patterns in a corporation. *Administrative Science Quarterly, 24,* 220–241.

Saben, S. (1967). *Occupational mobility of employed workers.* Washington, DC: U.S. Bureau of Labor Statistics.

Sadri, G., & Robertson, I. T. (1993). Self-efficacy and work-related behaviour: A review and meta-analysis. *Applied Psychology: An International Review, 42,* 139–152.

Salthouse, T. A. (1986). Functional age: Examination of a concept. In J. E. Birren, P. K. Robinson, & J. E. Livingston (Eds.), *Age, health and employment* (pp. 78–91). Upper Saddle River, NJ: Prentice Hall.

Savickas, M. L. (1997). Career adaptability: An integrative construct for life-span, life-space theory. *Career Development Quarterly, 45,* 247–259.

Schaie, W. (1990). Intellectual development in adulthood. In J. E. Birren & K. W. Schaie (Eds.), *Handbook of the psychology of aging* (pp. 291–310). New York: Van Nostrand Reinhold.

Schein, E. H. (1971). The individual, the organization, and the career: A conceptual scheme. *Journal of Applied Behavioral Science, 7,* 401–426.

Schrank, H. T., & Waring, J. M. (1981). Aging and work organizations. In B. B. Hess & K. Bond (Eds.), *Leading edges: Recent research on psychological aging* (pp. 99–118). Washington, DC: U.S. Department of Health and Human Services, National Institute on Aging.

Seligman, M.E.P., & Csikszentmihalyi, M. (2000). Positive psychology: An introduction. *American Psychologist, 55,* 5–14.

Sheehy, G. (1976). *Passages.* New York: Dutton.

Sheehy, G. (1995). *New passages: Mapping your life across time.* New York: Random House.

Smart, R. (1998). Career stages in Australian professional women: A test of Super's model. *Journal of Vocational Behavior, 52,* 379–395.

Smart, R., & Peterson, C. (1997). Super's career stages and the decision to change careers. *Journal of Vocational Behavior, 51,* 358–374.

Sommers, D., & Eck, A. (1977). Occupational mobility in the American labor force. *Monthly Labor Review, 100,* 3–19.

Staudinger, U. M., & Bluck, S. (2001). A view on midlife development from life-span theory. In M. E. Lachman (Ed.), *Handbook of midlife development* (pp. 3–39). New York: Wiley.

Sterns, H. L. (1986). Training and retraining adult and older workers. In J. E. Birren & J. Livingston (Eds.), *Age, health, and employment* (pp. 93–113). Upper Saddle River, NJ: Prentice Hall.

Sterns, H. L., & Doverspike, D. (1989). Aging and the training and learning process in organizations. In I. Goldstein & R. Katzell (Eds.), *Training and development in work organizations* (pp. 299–332). San Francisco: Jossey-Bass.

Sterns, H. L., & Gray, J. H. (1999). Work, leisure, and retirement. In J. Cavanaugh & S. Whitbourne (Eds.), *Gerontology* (pp. 355–390). New York: Oxford University Press.

Sterns, H. L., & Hurd-Gray, J. (1998). Employment and potential mid-life career crisis. In I. H. Nordhus, G. R. VandenBos, S. Berg, & P. Fromholt (Eds.), *Clinical geropsychology* (pp. 147–153). Washington, DC: APA Books.

Sterns, H. L., & Huyck, M. H. (2001). Midlife and work. In M. E. Lachman (Ed.), *Handbook of midlife development* (pp. 447–486). New York: Wiley.

Sterns, H. L., & Miklos, S. M. (1995). The aging worker in a changing environment: Organizational and individual issues. *Journal of Vocational Behavior, 47,* 248–268.

Sterns, H. L., & Patchett, M. (1984). Technology and the aging adult: Career development and training. In P. R. Robinson & J. E. Birren (Eds.), *Aging and technology* (pp. 261–277). New York: Plenum Press.

Sullivan, S. E. (1999). The changing nature of careers: A review and research agenda. *Journal of Management, 25,* 457–484.

Super, D. E. (1953). A theory of vocational development. *American Psychologist, 8,* 185–193.

Super, D. E. (1957). *The psychology of careers.* New York: HarperCollins.

Super, D. E. (1980). A life-span, life-space approach to career development. *Journal of Vocational Behavior, 16,* 282–298.

Super, D. E. (1984). Career and life development. In D. Brown, L. Brooks, and Associates (Eds.), *Career choice and development* (pp. 192–234). San Francisco: Jossey-Bass.

Super, D. E., Savickas, M. L., & Super, C. M. (1996). The life-span, life-space approach to careers. In D. Brown, L. Brooks, and Associates (Eds.), *Career choice and development* (pp. 121–178). San Francisco: Jossey-Bass.

Tang, M., Fouad, N. A., & Smith, P. L. (1999). Asian Americans' career choices: A path model to examine factors influencing their career choices. *Journal of Vocational Behavior, 54,* 142–157.

Vaillant, G. E. (1977). *Adaptation to life.* New York: Little, Brown.

Veiga, J. F. (1981). Plateaued versus non-plateaued managers: Career patterns, attitudes, and path potential. *Academy of Management Journal, 24,* 566–578.

Veiga, J. F. (1983). Mobility influences during managerial career stages. *Academy of Management Review, 8,* 23–32.

CHAPTER 8

Career Issues Facing Older Workers

Terry A. Beehr, Nathan A. Bowling

Current trends lead to the almost certain prediction that the average age of the American workforce will increase during the first part of this century. Because of the growth in the proportion of older people and because older Americans are participating in the workforce at an increasing rate, the median age of the 2008 U.S. workforce is expected to be greater than it has ever been (Fullerton, 1999). This graying of the American workplace means that research on issues facing older workers is important today and will remain so for some time to come—and that older workers will have more impact on workplace issues than they have in the past.

This chapter covers issues confronted by workers and organizations toward and after the end of individuals' careers. These include age-related changes in abilities, values, performance, and well-being of older workers; the positive career opportunity most salient in late careers (promotion into senior-level management and leadership positions); and how workers decide to retire and adjust to life after their full-time careers are over.

The Abilities and Performance of Older Workers

A common assumption made about older workers is that sensory abilities and psychomotor abilities decline with age, and this could result in a negative age-job performance relationship. This view, however, is not necessarily supported by all research.

Age-Related Changes in Abilities

Several studies have examined the changes that occur in sensory, perceptual, psychomotor, and cognitive abilities as one ages. Based on decades of research, Forteza and Prieto (1994) concluded that aging is associated with a decline in sensory functions (such as hearing and sight), behavioral slowdown, decline in physical strength and endurance, decline in mental speed, decline in perceptual and spatial ability, increased tendency to become distracted, increased periods of time needed to learn a series of associated pairs, and decline in short-term memory.

Avolio and Waldman (1994) examined the relationship between age and scores on the General Aptitude Test Battery (GATB), which measures cognitive, perceptual, and psychomotor abilities. They found that relationships between age and scores on the general intelligence ($r = -.15$), verbal ($r = -.10$), and numerical ($r = -.17$) subtests were modest. The negative relationships between age and several other abilities, however, were substantially stronger. For example, correlations between age and the scores on form perception, motor coordination, finger dexterity, and manual dexterity subtests were $-.39$, $-.28$, $-.35$, and $-.28$. When education, experience, and occupational type were controlled, however, age explained relatively little of the variance in any of the GATB subscores, suggesting that non-age-related factors may account for much more of the variance. In sum, aging and the decline of various abilities do not necessarily go hand in hand.

Age-Related Changes in Job Performance

Many human abilities decline with age, and because abilities are related to job performance, it is logical to assume that such declines will translate into a negative age-performance relationship. Reviews of field research, though, have repeatedly concluded that there is little relationship between age and job performance (Warr, 1994; McEvoy & Cascio, 1989; Waldman & Aviolo, 1986; Rhodes, 1983).

If aging is associated with the decline of several different abilities, then why hasn't research consistently shown a negative age-performance relationship? Warr (1994) suggested that after older workers experience declines, they might move into different jobs that are more compatible with their abilities. This would have the effect of producing an age-performance relationship that is more positive or less negative than it would be if these workers were to continue with the jobs of their youth. In addition, older workers might leave the workforce entirely because of their declining performance. Many age-related declines in ability are not substantial until after one has reached the age at which most people have retired. Thus, the differences in abilities of the younger and the remaining older workers might not be significant due to these restriction-of-range problems.

Furthermore, adverse effects of aging on job performance can be partially counteracted by the experience gained with age. An illustrative experiment (Marrow, Leirer, Altieri, & Fitzsimmons, 1994) found that experience as a pilot reduced age differences in performance on a task designed to simulate the information exchange that takes place between aircraft pilots and air traffic control personnel. Therefore, age appears to be related to factors that can both improve and hinder job performance.

Overall, reviews that investigated the age-performance relationship have yielded mixed results. Rhodes's (1983) review concluded that roughly equal support exists for four different age-performance relationships: positive, negative, inverted U, and non-significant. She suggested that the age-performance relationship might depend on the manner in which performance is measured and the nature of the job, a position that has been supported by some subsequent research.

Moderators of the Age-Performance Relationship

In a meta-analysis by Waldman and Avolio (1986), the age-performance relationship depended on the way in which performance was measured. When performance was measured using objective indices, a positive age-performance relationship was found, but when supervisory ratings were used, there was a negative relationship. This finding raises issues concerning the age bias in performance ratings, which are addressed in a later section. However, a subsequent meta-analysis found that the type of performance measure did not moderate the age-performance relationship and that age-performance relationships were nonsignificant

(McEvoy & Cascio, 1989). The effects of the type of performance measure are therefore still unclear.

Rhodes's (1983) early review also suggested that job type moderates the age-performance relationship. Distinguishing between professional and nonprofessional jobs, the meta-analyses by Waldman and Avolio (1986) and McEvoy and Cascio (1989) tested this hypothesis. Waldman and Avolio found that the age-performance relationship was more positive or less negative for professionals than for nonprofessionals, regardless of whether objective or subjective performance measures were used. McEvoy and Cascio's later meta-analysis did not find that type of job moderates the age-performance relationship, however. As with effect of type of performance measure, the moderating effect of type of job is still an unsubstantiated hypothesis.

The professional-nonprofessional distinction is only one simple way of classifying jobs. There are obviously a great many dimensions along which jobs can vary. This dimension has probably become most salient in meta-analyses simply because it was consistently available in the data. It might make more sense to determine rationally which job dimensions might be age relevant and to examine the moderating effects of these.

Warr (1994) suggested a more general framework for examining job types in relation to this issue. His framework identifies two potentially age-related dimensions along which any given occupation might be classified. First, occupations vary in the extent to which job experience results in higher levels of job performance. For this dimension, of course, experience tends to covary with age. Second, occupations may vary in the extent to which specific skills required for successful performance decline with age. Jobs might vary on such dimensions as the extent to which they require computer literacy, the ability to influence others, or the ability to adapt to a quickly changing environment. Future research using a two-dimensional grid (relevance of experience by required skills that decline with age) might be needed to discover meaningful patterns of age-performance relationships.

The extent to which a job requires employees to update their training continuously is likely to moderate the age-performance relationship as well (Cascio, 1995). That is, a more negative or less positive age-performance relationship might be observed in jobs that require continuous training than those that require little or no training beyond what one initially receives. This proposition is based on the finding that older workers display less mastery of new training material and take longer to train than do younger workers (Kubeck, Delp, Haslett, & McDaniel, 1996).

For example, in order to keep pace with technological changes, individuals who are employed in jobs that involve the use of advanced technology are typically required to receive continuous training. Thus, we might expect older workers to perform less effectively than their younger counterparts in these types of jobs. Indeed, research has shown that age is associated with slower response times and more errors on a computer-based task (Czajka & Sharit, 1993). That study found, however, that age had a negative impact on performance on a computer-based task even when previous computer experience was held constant. Therefore, it would appear that the aging process itself, and not just the lack of computer experience, is associated with age-based differences in performance on computer tasks.

The age-performance relationship might also be moderated by the extent to which a job requires the ability to influence others. For example, individuals who hold leadership positions must be able to influence their subordinates in order to be effective at their jobs. To the extent that the ability to influence others is associated with age, the performance of leaders would also be associated with age. If a positive relationship between age and the ability to influence others is indeed found, then such a relationship might be due to the unwillingness of subordinates to follow the directions of a young leader because they assume that the leader lacks the experience, knowledge, and skills needed to make good decisions.

Criticisms of the Research on the Age-Performance Relationship

There are several potential weaknesses in the research on age-performance relationships. McEvoy and Cascio (1989) considered the possibility that a strong, positive age-performance relationship among very young workers might explain why some studies have found a weak positive age-performance correlation. That is, young entry-level workers might improve their skill and performance dramatically during the beginning stages of their careers, while there is little change in performance among older workers. However, the meta-analysis suggests that excluding very young workers from a sample has only small effects on the age-performance relationship.

As McEvoy and Cascio (1989) also noted, many studies might fail to test for a curvilinear age-performance relationship. One could argue that over a lifetime of working, an employee gets more proficient with experience until he or she reaches a plateau. Toward the end of a career, age-related decrements might emerge, resulting in a curvilinear relationship. This might happen only if both very early and very late stages of careers are included in the same study and would be detected only if the research examined potential nonlinear relationships.

When considering research findings concerning the age-performance relationship, it is important to note that older workers often hold jobs that differ from those held by younger workers. That is, workers often progress from entry-level to more advanced positions during their careers. In addition, individuals often take on a greater number of emergent task elements as they progress in their careers (Ilgen & Hollenbeck, 1991), and therefore there is little reason to assume that older workers perform the same tasks as younger workers simply because they hold positions with similar job titles. Even when studies control for job type, we cannot be fully confident about the conclusions drawn from research on the age-performance relationship.

Alternatively, one might argue that the age-performance relationship would tend to be positive because people generally hold jobs with increasing motivational potential throughout their careers (Hackman & Oldham, 1976). Thus, Rhodes's (1983) finding that older workers display higher levels of work motivation might be due to age-related differences in work environments rather than age-related differences in some human attribute associated with motivation. In sum, one could question whether it makes sense to compare the job performance of older workers with that of younger workers in many uncontrolled field settings and to conclude that aging itself is responsible for any relationships.

Another common criticism of the research on the age-performance relationship addresses the fact that these studies usually employ cross-sectional research designs (Warr, 1994). This

makes it impossible to determine whether the aging process accounts for any differences in job performance between younger
and older workers. One problem is that age differences in performance might be due to differences in historical influences experienced by people of different generations. For example, older
workers might perform at a different level from younger workers
because the older workers had been exposed to a different set of
cultural values. Limitations of cross-sectional designs do not allow
firm conclusions that older workers would have performed similarly to the younger workers when the older workers were the age
of the younger workers.

Selective attrition is another obvious problem with the cross-
sectional studies. Older workers eventually leave the workforce, for
example, through retirement. One way or another, they might leave
jobs in which they do not function well, and as a result older workers and younger workers are not equivalent samples of older and
younger people. Older people might not do as well on jobs in general, and yet they might serve their employers very well in the jobs
they occupy. This speculation has not yet been directly addressed
by research.

Job Performance and Age Discrimination

Society often has held negative perceptions of older workers. For
example, older workers in the past were viewed as being less productive, less motivated, and less efficient than their younger counterparts (Rosen & Jerdee, 1976). Such perceptions might have
several important effects. If research results are consistent with the
perception, has the public drawn a valid conclusion concerning
the age-performance relationship—or is it simply a negative self-
fulfilling prophecy?

Popular beliefs concerning the relationship between age and particular work criteria might be correct when individuals behave in a
way that confirms the expectations of others. In that case, age-based
differences in employee performance would be real, but these differences would emerge only after the general population has begun
to believe that such relationships exist. At present, however, the research does not consistently support a negative age-performance relationship in field settings. In addition, recent research suggests that

society's perceptions of older workers have become more favorable over time (Hassell & Perrewe, 1995). Thus, the self-fulfilling prophecy, which may have previously had a negative impact on performance of older workers, may no longer be an important determinant of their job performance.

It is also unclear whether the age-performance relationship is moderated by the type of performance measure used. If further research verifies Waldman and Avolio's finding (1986) that the age-performance relationship is less negative when objective measures are used, then one might conclude that older workers generally receive lower performance ratings on subjective measures than they deserve. This particular form of rating inaccuracy could be a result of age discrimination.

This assumes, however, that objective measures of performance are better representations of actual job performance than are subjective measures. Because objective measures are also vulnerable to the effects of contamination and deficiency, subjective measures are not necessarily inferior to objective measures. For example, if the number of traffic tickets written were used to assess the performance of police officers, then age-based differences in performance might be a result of age-based differences in the territories that officers patrol. That is, older officers might have more freedom than younger officers in choosing their beat. Knowing that their performance partly depends on the number of traffic tickets that they write, the older officers might choose to patrol high-traffic areas, leaving low-traffic areas for the younger officers to patrol.

In addition, objective measures of job performance, such as the numbers of traffic tickets written by a police officer, do not adequately measure all important aspects of job performance and by themselves represent a deficient measure of performance. Furthermore, all performance measures, whether based on objective performance or supervisor ratings, focus on in-role performance and typically fail to account for contextual performance, such as organizational citizenship behavior (Borman & Motowidlo, 1993). Excluding organizational citizenship behavior from the criterion domain has important implications for assessing the performance of older workers only if age is associated with the tendency to perform organizational citizenship behaviors. At this point, however, it appears that no such relationship exists (Schappe, 1998; Williams & Shiaw, 1999).

Thus, we should be cautious about interpreting findings, such as Waldman and Avolio's work (1986), as strong evidence of age bias in performance ratings. Furthermore, if additional research supports Hassell and Perrewe's finding (1995) that older workers are currently perceived more favorably than they once were, then age discrimination may not be as pervasive as it once was.

Age and Outcomes

A considerable amount of research has been conducted to investigate the relationship between age and job performance. These studies might imply that job performance is simply the extent to which an employee is effective and productive. In reality, however, job performance is a multidimensional construct (Seashore, Indik, & Georgopoulos, 1960). For this reason, we need to consider the relationships between age and several different types of outcomes. In the following discussion, we distinguish between organizational outcomes and individual outcomes, where organizational outcomes more directly affect the welfare of the organization and individual outcomes more directly affect the well-being of individual employees. Of the two, organizational outcomes appear to be more directly related to job performance.

Organizational Outcomes

Research indicates a negative relationship between age and turnover (Rhodes, 1983; Warr, 1994), with correlations about in the −.20s. Warr (1994) provides two explanations for this relationship. First, organizations are probably less willing to hire older workers, and therefore older workers stay with their jobs because they have relatively low expectations of finding work elsewhere. Second, because they generally earn higher wages, older workers are typically more satisfied with their jobs and more committed to their organizations.

It might also be the case that as people age and thus attain more tenure, they have more opportunities to move into jobs with their employer that they find enjoyable. Furthermore, the sunk costs associated with investing a significant portion of one's life in an organization might make one unwilling to leave that organization (Arkes & Blumer, 1985).

The relationship between age and absenteeism is different for avoidable absence than for unavoidable absence (Rhodes, 1983; Thomson, Griffiths, & Davison, 2000). Avoidable absences, which are negatively associated with age, are within one's control and are generally operationalized by absence frequency. Unavoidable absences, which are positively associated with age, are less within the individual's control and are often operationalized by absence duration. Perhaps older workers are less likely to be absent for voluntary reasons because they are more committed to their work than are younger workers, while younger workers are less likely to be absent from their work for involuntary reasons because they experience fewer health problems.

A negative relationship is typically found between age and workplace accidents (Warr, 1994; Rhodes, 1983). However, older workers tend to have longer average periods of disability when they do have accidents. They are also more likely to be permanently disabled or even die after having a workplace accident. It is possible that differences in the types of jobs held by younger and older workers result in age differences with respect to the amount of exposure to dangers at work and that these differences may explain many of the relationships of age with the frequency and severity of work accidents (Warr, 1994).

Individual Outcomes

The relationship between age and job satisfaction has gained a lot of attention from researchers. Rhodes (1983) and Warr (1994) each concluded that older workers are more likely to be satisfied with their jobs than younger workers are. However, Warr also notes that this relationship is usually not very strong; it typically falls between .10 and .20. Forteza and Prieto (1994) suggest, however, an inverted U relationship between age and job satisfaction.

In sum, the exact nature of the age-job satisfaction relationship has not been clearly determined. In general, age is associated positively with organizational commitment, job involvement, and Protestant work ethic and negatively with nonfinancial organizational commitment (Warr, 1994). In addition, older workers tend to place greater value on income and short working hours and less value on the opportunity for advancement (Rowe & Snizek, 1995).

There are many reasons that we might expect that the work values of older workers (in terms of commitment, involvement, and Protestant work ethic) are different from those of their younger counterparts. It is reasonable that a cohort effect causes older and younger workers to have differing work values. That is, the era in which one is born might shape one's work values. Work values might also differ with age because life experiences shape one's values. Thus, older workers could be expected to have different work values from those of younger workers, because older workers have more and probably different life experiences. These ideas about why work values might vary with age typify the problem of distinguishing whether age-based differences in a variable are due to a cohort effect or the developmental changes one experiences with age.

Making It to the Top

Promotion, particularly to senior management, is often viewed as a reward for doing good work. It is important to note, however, that multiple factors affect whether one gets promoted. Success at gaining a promotion is determined by both the characteristics of the individual and the organization in which the individual works. One's ability to obtain a promotion is likely due to both performance-relevant and performance-irrelevant behaviors, as well as to personal characteristics. Typically, however, aging and seniority are related to advancement. We now address factors affecting the ability to attain higher positions in the organizational hierarchy.

Individual Factors Affecting Promotions

Workers generally believe that both performance and nonperformance factors have an impact on who receives promotions (Beehr & Taber, 1993). That is, demographic characteristics and personal favoritism, as well as job performance, are perceived as influencing promotion decisions. Some workers believe that constructive contextual behaviors, such as organizational citizenship behaviors, also affect whether they receive promotions (Hui, Lam, & Law, 2000).

Several of these factors affect promotional opportunities for older workers. For example, task and contextual performance influence promotion decisions (Hui et al., 2000; Van Scotter, Motowidlo, & Cross, 2000). Task performance refers to behaviors that are directly related to the organization's core technical processes, and contextual performance involves behaviors that affect the context in which core activities are performed (Borman & Motowidlo, 1993). It appears, however, that tenure has the strongest effect of all factors on career advancement (Van Scotter et al., 2000), and tenure is positively related to age. Although many other factors can affect promotability, such as being similar to higher-level managers (Wayne, Graf, Ferris, & Liden, 1997) and physical attractiveness (Chung & Leung, 1988), it is unknown whether they interact with age of employee to predict promotions. It would be useful to know whether such nonperformance factors affect promotability as much for older workers as for younger ones. Overall, aging workers may have a good chance to obtain a high-level job in their organization if they have accumulated seniority and tenure, but their other characteristics and behaviors might also be important.

Career Systems and Promotion

Context factors also influence advancement opportunities for older and more senior workers. Career systems vary along two dimensions (Sonnenfeld & Peiperl, 1988): assignment flow, or the extent to which assignment and promotion decisions are based on individual performance versus the individual's contribution to the general group performance, and supply flow, or the extent to which nonentry-level (upper-level) positions are filled by individuals from outside rather than from within the organization.

Based on these two dimensions, Sonnenfeld and Peiperl (1988) assert that there are four basic career systems: fortresses, baseball teams, academies, and clubs. In fortresses, individuals from outside the organization fill positions at various levels of the organization, and individuals are promoted and assigned particular jobs based on their contributions to group performance. Baseball teams also recruit individuals from outside the organization to fill nonentry-level positions, but they base promotions and job assignments on individual contributions. Academies use individuals from within the organization to fill nonentry-level positions, and they base promotions and job assignments on individual contributions. Finally, clubs assign only individuals from within the organization to nonentry-level positions and promote and make job assignments based on group contributions.

It may be hypothesized that supply flow is related to the degree to which age and promotion are correlated in a given organization. When upper-level jobs are filled from within, older managers would be more likely to receive promotions, and seniority and tenure would be more likely to be rewarded with advancement.

Leader Emergence

Many researchers have confused the characteristics that cause a person to emerge as a leader with the characteristics that make an individual an effective leader (Lord, De Vader, & Alliger, 1986). Older workers are generally given more opportunities to lead and influence others within the workplace than are their younger counterparts, because with age comes job seniority, organizational tenure, and relevant work experience. There are a limited number of positions at the top of an organization's hierarchy, however, and thus only a few individuals can attain these positions. For this reason, having the requisite tenure and work experience is not always enough to guarantee that people will be able to climb to the top of their organization.

Leadership emergence is associated with intelligence, dominance, and masculinity-femininity, and these associations generalize across different kinds of jobs and situations (Lord et al., 1986). That is, individuals who are more intelligent, dominant, and masculine are more likely to become leaders. A recent study showed that emerging as a leader is also positively associated with cognitive ability, self-esteem, prior leadership experience, and scores on the Leader Potential Index of the California Psychological Inventory (Atwater, Dionne, Avolio, Camobreco, & Lau, 1999). Leader emergence, however, was not associated with conscientiousness, the ability to tolerate stress, and moral reasoning.

Leader Effectiveness

The degree to which a leader is effective may differ significantly from an individual's likelihood of emerging as a leader in a group situation. One recent study found that prior experience as a leader and physical fitness were associated with leader effectiveness (Atwater et al., 1999). Contrary to what would typically be expected, cognitive ability, self-esteem, conscientiousness, the ability to tolerate stress, moral reasoning ability, and scores on the Leader Potential Index were not related to leader effectiveness. Bass (1990), however, concluded that intelligence and other personal characteristics are indeed associated with leader effectiveness and that such relationships are dependent on situational contingencies. If we assume that leader effectiveness is associated with cognitive ability, then cognitive ability might mediate a negative relationship between age and leader effectiveness.

Although Atwater et al. (1999) found that cognitive ability and leader effectiveness were not correlated, cognitive resource theory (CRT) suggests that under certain situations, intellectual abilities, technical competence, and job-relevant knowledge can determine whether someone will be an effective leader (Fiedler, 1986). According to CRT, these cognitive characteristics should be associated with leader effectiveness when the leader is directive, has the support of the group that is being led, is working in a low-stress situation, and is working on tasks that are cognitively demanding.

CRT has potentially important implications for the relationship between age and leader effectiveness. We might expect that age has both positive and negative indirect effects on leader effectiveness. We might expect that age and leader performance are positively correlated because the tenure attained with age is associated with achieving technical competence and job-relevant knowledge. In contrast, age might have a negative indirect effect on leader effectiveness if aging has detrimental effects on the intellectual abilities needed to perform well as a leader. Thus far, empirical tests of CRT have yielded mixed results (Fiedler, 1986; Vecchio, 1990). CRT is a relatively new theory, however, and further research is warranted.

The Decision to Retire

Retirement, which marks a major milestone in the lives of older adults, offers individuals the opportunity to reflect on their life achievements. Traditionally defined as "withdrawal from the workforce altogether or the end of a person's working life" (Feldman, 1994, p. 287), the conceptualization of retirement is changing.

Because of the growing popularity of bridge employment (part- or full-time jobs between one's career job and total withdrawal from the paid workforce), it has become difficult to distinguish between who is and who is not retired (Beehr, Glazer, Nielson, & Farmer, 2000). For this reason, the more contemporary definition of retirement, offered by Feldman (1994), is "the exit from an organizational position or career path of considerable duration, taken by individuals after middle age, and taken with the intention of reduced psychological commitment to work thereafter" (p. 287). Beehr (1986) suggested that retirement can vary in the extent to which it is early versus on time, partial versus complete, and voluntary versus involuntary. Thus, there are different types of retirement.

The potential antecedents to retirement have been classified as pushes, which are negative considerations that drive individuals away from the workforce, and pulls, which are positive considerations that attract individuals to retirement or away from the workplace (Shultz, Morton, & Weckerle, 1998). Others have distinguished between work and nonwork antecedents to retirement (Beehr et al., 2000). Here, we identify three specific types of factors that can potentially influence an individual's decision to retire: individual factors, family factors, and institutional factors.

Individual Factors

Individual factors are personal factors that influence decisions to retire. Financial well-being and health appear to be two of the most well-established predictors of retirement (Taylor & Shore, 1995). Specifically, individuals are more likely to retire when they have the financial resources to maintain their preretirement lifestyles or when poor mental or physical health has made working excessively burdensome (Talaga & Beehr, 1989). Age has been found to be positively related to retirement (Kim & Feldman, 1998; Taylor & Shore, 1995), but gender has not been consistently associated with retirement age (Beehr et al., 2000; Adams, 1999).

Feldman (1994) suggests that organizational tenure (the number of years of continuous service with the same organization) is positively associated with early retirement. Consistent with the sunk costs effect (Arkes & Blumer, 1985), individuals might be unwilling to retire because they have invested a great deal of time and effort working for an organization. Career commitment (Adams, 1999) and organizational commitment (Taylor & Shore, 1995) have a positive relationship with planned retirement age, indicating that committed people are in fact less likely to retire.

However, research has also shown that after controlling for gender, wealth, and health, a psychological state of being tired of working is negatively associated with retirement age (Beehr et al., 2000). Adams (1999), too, found that occupational goal attainment was negatively correlated with planned retirement age. We might conclude that tenure is positively associated with both being tired of working and occupation goal attainment, and therefore tenure has an indirect positive effect on retirement.

Family Factors

Family factors include any characteristics of one's family, such as marital status, number of dependents, and spouse employment status. Because of the differences in gender roles, family factors may affect the decision to retire differently for men than for women. The number of dependents in one's family, for example, might be positively associated with retirement for women but negatively associated with retirement for men (Talaga & Beehr, 1995). One explanation is that men are expected to support their dependents by earning money through employment outside the home, while women are expected to support their dependents by directly caring for them.

Another family factor influencing the retirement decision in the same way for both sexes is whether one's spouse is retired (Kim & Feldman, 1998; Talaga & Beehr, 1995). Having a retired spouse is positively associated with one's own retirement. This makes sense, considering that many people plan retirements to coincide with retirement of their spouses (Feldman, 1994).

Research has generally shown that married workers retire earlier than their unmarried counterparts (Kim & Feldman, 1998). This finding is often explained in terms of the need for companionship. That is, married workers are drawn to retirement because they view retirement as an opportunity to spend time with their spouses. In contrast, many single workers might perceive retirement as undesirable because most of their social contacts are at work and retirement would lead to a sudden decrease in the amount of social interaction that they experience. Overall, family and social factors also appear important in retirement decisions.

Institutional Factors

Institutional factors in retirement refer to those characteristics of the organizational environment that can affect one's decision to retire, such as workforce cutbacks and layoffs (Beehr et al., 2000). It has been hypothesized that individuals tend to retire earlier when they work for organizations that flexibly manage older workers (Feldman, 1994). Whether an organization offers postretirement benefits interacts with gender to influence the decision to retire early, too (Fronstin, 1999). That is, men, but not women, are encouraged to retire early by the existence of pension plans and retiree health benefits.

Although it is reasonable to speculate that occupational labor markets play a role in the decision to retire, the exact nature of this relationship is unclear. For example, we might expect blue-collar workers to retire at younger ages than white-collar workers because blue-collar work is generally more physically demanding than is white-collar work. However, we might also expect white-collar workers to retire at a younger age than blue-collar workers because white-collar workers have more financial resources than do blue-collar workers. In a sample of administrative-clerical, managerial-supervisory, and technical-professional workers, though, Adams (1999) found that occupation was not associated with planned retirement age.

Overall, many research results on institutional predictors of retirement have been somewhat uncertain in the sense that most effect sizes are small or inconsistent and many of the predictors have not been studied very often. Financial and health predictors are the biggest exceptions. Comparisons of many personal and environmental predictors of retirement in the same study are also somewhat rare; one exception found that personal and work factors contribute similar amounts of variance in predicting retirement ages (Beehr et al., 2000).

Adaptation to Retirement

Retirement can be viewed as a period of change that requires some adaptive response on the part of the retiree (Carter & Cook, 1995). For those who have difficulty adjusting to a life without work, retirement can be a stressful process. For others, retirement represents a welcome event marked by freedom from the pressures of full-time employment. In fact, Beehr (1986) suggested that age-adjusted health improves on retiring. We next discuss the individual, social, and institutional factors that affect how well one adapts to retirement.

Individual Factors

It was once assumed that most individuals respond negatively to retirement. Instead, it appears that several personal characteristics are linked to the ease with which one adapts to retirement (Richardson & Kilty, 1991). Generally, retirees who held low-status yet high-paying jobs, are older, and had the greatest decrease in income after retiring tend to have the most problems adjusting to retirement. Carter and Cook (1995) identify several individual factors hypothesized to be associated with adaptation to retirement. Carter and Cook suggest that individuals adapt best to retirement when they have an internal locus of control, have high retirement self-efficacy, and are not highly attached to their employer or occupation.

Furthermore, it has been suggested that individuals are more likely to adjust satisfactorily to retirement when they currently earn high wages and expect to receive future pension plans, when self-identity is not strongly tied to work, and when they are certain about their retirement plans and macroeconomic trends (Feldman, 1994). Beehr (1986) suggested that postretirement physical health depends on retirees' financial status, preretirement jobs and health, and Type A behavior, while postretirement mental health depends on older workers' propensity to work, retirement planning, occupational goal attainment, and expectations about retirement.

The activities that retirees choose to engage in have important implications for life after retirement. In particular, participating in bridge employment and leisure activities has positive effects on retirement satisfaction (Kim & Feldman, 2000).

Social Factors

Close interpersonal relationships have been hypothesized to be associated with successful adaptation to retirement (Carter & Cook, 1995). Thus, we might expect that being happily married and having several close friendships would be helpful in acclimating one to retirement. On a similar note, participating in leisure activities and social groups such as clubs, churches, and volunteer organizations can provide access to satisfying interpersonal relationships and thus ease the transition into retirement. In many cases, organizations can provide opportunities for retirees to socialize with one another. For example, organizations could sponsor picnics for retirees either near the employment site or in retirement communities. Many communities also provide get-togethers and activities specifically aimed at older people.

Institutional Factors

It is often assumed that the decision to retire is completely voluntary. Perceived voluntariness of retirement can be an important variable when predicting retirement and retirement outcomes, however. In the United States, mandatory retirement is illegal. Nonetheless, in many instances, such as when an organization is downsizing, individuals feel forced into early retirement despite their desire to continue working (Isaksson & Johansson, 2000). Similarly, individuals who are forced to leave their careers because of poor health often perceive their retirement as involuntary (Shultz et al., 1998).

Perceiving one's retirement as involuntary has been linked with difficulties adapting to life as a retiree. Isaksson and Johansson (2000) found that satisfaction with outcomes of a downsizing process, psychological well-being and physical health, were both adversely affected by the perception of forced retirement. Furthermore, perceiving retirement as involuntary has been linked to life and retirement dissatisfaction, problems with physical and emotional health, and depression (Shultz et al., 1998). Also, Talaga and Beehr (1993) found that perceived voluntariness of retirement was linked to several affective outcomes, including satisfaction with health, finances, activities, life, marriage, and retirement.

These results could be due to a lack of retirement planning and perceived control among those who perceive their retirements as involuntary. In addition, Feldman (1994) suggested that individuals will adjust best to retirement when they do not perceive age discrimination in the workplace, when they receive preretirement counseling, and when their employers are flexible in their dealings with older workers.

Life After Retirement

Although retirement has traditionally referred to the end of work after a career of full-time employment has ended (Feldman, 1994), an active and productive life need not end with retirement. In fact, retirement can signal a new period of life in which individuals have the opportunity to pursue other life interests without being burdened by the responsibilities of a career. Retirement can be a time for individuals to engage in new vocational and leisure activities.

Because people are retiring at younger ages compared to decades ago (Feldman, 1994) and usually are not debilitated by age-related physical declines during the early retirement years, retirees are valuable resources who can contribute to society. Individuals might even engage in similar activities before and after retirement. A retired professional carpenter, for example, might take up woodworking as a hobby or volunteer in home repair projects for the needy.

Working in Retirement

Bridge employment refers to paid employment after one's career job ends and before permanent full-time retirement begins (Feldman, 1994). Retirement often looks like a transition from a semipermanent commitment to a job, career, or work to a permanent lifestyle of total and permanent unemployment. It has been suggested that a continuum exists in the extent to which an individual is retired (Beehr, 1986). Within such a continuum, bridge employment would represent a form of partial retirement (Beehr et al., 2000).

Feldman (1994) suggested that demographic variables, career tracks, organizational-level variables, and macroeconomic and external environmental variables all affect individuals' decisions to seek or accept bridge employment. These variables can be considered as either pushes or pulls that increase or decrease the probability an individual will accept bridge employment. Kim and Feldman (2000) found that good health, high organizational tenure, having a currently employed spouse, and having financially dependent children were all positively associated with participation in bridge employment. In this study, bridge employment was negatively related to age and salary at time of retirement.

Weckerle and Shultz (1999) found that voluntariness of retirement, job flexibility, and anticipated financial reward were each positively associated with employees' decisions to accept bridge employment. Others found that employees are more likely to accept early retirement incentives when opportunities for bridge employment are available (Kim & Feldman, 1998).

Postretirement Leisure Activity

With retirement comes the paradox of increased opportunities to engage in leisure activities but a decrease in disposable income that can be spent on leisure activities. A spillover effect best describes the relationship between the type of leisure activities people engage in before and after retirement. In fact, research supports the notion that preretirement and postretirement activities are similar (Kremer & Harpaz, 1982). Kremer and Harpaz's study of Israeli retirees (1982) revealed several interesting patterns. Public entertainment activities, which include attending movies and the theater, were found to be less important during postretirement than during preretirement. In contrast, religious activities and reading became more important after retirement.

More research is needed to determine which variables can predict consistent patterns of activities and interests before and after retirement. Most retirees are likely to benefit from leisure activities, given that participation in such activities is associated with both retirement and life satisfaction (Kim & Feldman, 2000).

Postretirement Volunteer Activities

Volunteer work, which can be defined as "helping behavior that is nonobligatory and is not done for monetary compensation"

(Fischer, Mueller, & Cooper, 1991, p. 192), can serve as an opportunity for retirees to feel useful, needed, and productive (Omoto, Snyder, & Martino, 2000). We might expect that because they are no longer burdened by the responsibilities of full-time employment, retirees would participate in volunteer work at a higher rate than those who have full-time jobs. Research indicates, however, that participating in volunteer work tends to decrease with age (Fischer et al., 1991).

Several reasons have been given for this decline, including poor health and disability among older people and an inability to obtain transportation to and from the volunteer site. It also might simply be the case that many older workers do not volunteer because they are unwilling to work without being paid (Chambre, 1993). Chambre's work suggests, however, that because of emerging policies and programs aimed at increasing the number of older volunteers, we might expect that many more older individuals will volunteer at a higher rates in the future. Interestingly, recent research suggests that older individuals tend to participate in volunteer work for different reasons than do younger individuals (Omoto et al., 2000). Older people generally are motivated to volunteer as a means of serving their communities, while younger people typically participate in volunteer work as a means of networking and developing social relationships.

It is unfortunate that more retirees do not participate in volunteer activities, because several important outcomes have been associated with volunteering. When compared with employees who do similar work, volunteers are more satisfied and report their jobs as being more praiseworthy (Pearce, 1983). Furthermore, engaging in volunteer activities is positively associated with life satisfaction (Kim & Feldman, 2000). Of particular interest to managers is the finding that volunteers report less intent to leave their organizations than do employees. The performance of volunteers, however, is less predictable than that of paid employees (Pearce, 1982).

Several characteristics predict whether older individuals are likely to volunteer (Fischer et al., 1991). For example, having a high income, being well educated, having good health and the absence of disability, being married, and having some means of transportation were all associated with volunteerism among older individuals.

Implications for Career Management

With the growth in the population of older people in the workplace (Fullerton, 1999), it has become increasingly important for organizational scientists, practitioners, and elderly people themselves to become familiar with the career issues that face older workers. The late-career years present myriad challenges and opportunities to organizations and individuals alike.

People at the top of large organizations are likely to be somewhat older than the average employee, but the process by which they work their way to the top is a complex one. All employees cannot get to the top of their organizations, and many do not wish to—but what can they do instead? Although it appears that older individuals generally experience mild physical and mental declines during the later stages of their careers (Forteza & Prieto, 1994), these declines do not necessarily result in poor job performance among older workers (see Waldman & Avolio, 1986; McEvoy & Cascio, 1989).

For the majority whose performance has not declined, their wealth of experience, skills, and important contacts can be useful inside or outside the organization. Inside the organization, their experience, contacts, knowledge, and abilities can make them valuable potential mentors to aid newer employees. In addition, these same characteristics can allow older employees to serve as advisers and sounding boards for the decision makers in the organization's hierarchy. Alternatively, if older workers should retire or otherwise leave their employers, their personal resources can be valuable outside the organization—working for either another organization or for themselves in consulting roles. Despite the fact that many people hold negative attitudes toward older workers (Rosen & Jerdee, 1976), then, it appears that even when employees are in the later stages of their careers, organizations can take advantage of their numerous contributions.

Age discrimination is, of course, illegal in the United States, but aside from the law, it may not be in the organization's best interest to discriminate against older workers in general anyway. It does not appear that their performance is generally worse than when they were younger. Some of the discriminatory actions against older workers appear to be driven by a desire to cut costs. Even this motivation can be reduced by pay-for-performance policies. If employees' pay (a cost to the organization) is related more to their performance than to their seniority, there is less incentive to discriminate against more senior, older workers by trying to force them to retire. This suggests that pay-for-performance compensation might reduce temptation for organizations to discriminate against older workers by illegally trying to force them to retire.

We have discussed the complexities that surround the decision to retire and adaptation to retirement. It appears that these issues involve an interplay among individual, family, social, and institutional factors. Although there is evidence that people might engage in various postretirement activities a little less than they had expected before they retired (Beehr & Nielson, 1995), the discussion on postretirement employment and leisure activities suggests that life after one's career has ended need not be inactive and nonproductive. Both older individuals and their employers can benefit from retirement transitions resembling bridge employment if they can be worked out on a cost-effective basis. Working part time prior to full retirement, perhaps with assignments suitable for someone who is experienced and senior, might be a possible first step to that end.

References
Adams, G. A. (1999). Career-related variables and planned retirement age: An extension of Beehr's model. *Journal of Vocational Behavior, 55,* 221–235.
Arkes, H. R., & Blumer, C. (1985). The psychology of sunk cost. *Organizational Behavior and Human Decision Processes, 35,* 124–140.
Atwater, L. E., Dionne, S. D., Avolio, B., Camobreco, J. F., & Lau, A. W. (1999). A longitudinal study of the leadership development process: Individual differences predicting leader effectiveness. *Human Relations, 52,* 1543–1562.
Avolio, B. J., & Waldman, D. A. (1994). Variations in cognitive, perceptual, and psychomotor abilities across the working life span: Examining the effects of race, sex, experience, education, and occupational type. *Psychology and Aging, 9,* 430–442.
Bass, B. M. (1990). *Bass and Stogdill's handbook of leadership.* New York: Free Press.
Beehr, T. A. (1986). The process of retirement: A review and recommendations for future investigation. *Personnel Psychology, 39,* 31–55.

Beehr, T. A., Glazer, S., Nielson, N. L., & Farmer, S. J. (2000). Work and non-work predictors of employees' retirement ages. *Journal of Vocational Behavior, 57,* 206–225.

Beehr, T. A., & Nielson, N. L. (1995). Descriptions of job characteristics and retirement activities during transition to retirement. *Journal of Organizational Behavior, 16,* 681–690.

Beehr, T. A., & Taber, T. D. (1993). Perceived intra-organizational mobility: Reliable versus exceptional performance as means to getting ahead. *Journal of Organizational Behavior, 14,* 579–594.

Borman, W. C., & Motowidlo, S. J. (1993). Expanding the criterion domain to include elements of contextual performance. In N. Schmitt & W. C. Borman (Eds.), *Personnel selection in organizations* (pp. 71–98). San Francisco: Jossey-Bass.

Carter, M.A.T., & Cook, K. (1995). Adaptation to retirement: Role changes and psychological resources. *Career Development Quarterly, 44,* 67–82.

Cascio, W. F. (1995). Whither industrial and organizational psychology in a changing world of work? *American Psychologist, 50,* 928–939.

Chambre, S. M. (1993). Volunteerism by elders: Past trends and future prospects. *Gerontologist, 33,* 221–228.

Chung, P. P., & Leung, K. (1988). Effects of performance information and physical attractiveness on managerial decisions about promotion. *Journal of Social Psychology, 128,* 791–801.

Czajka, S. J., & Sharit, J. (1993). Age differences in the performance of computer-based work. *Psychology and Aging, 8,* 59–67.

Feldman, D. C. (1994). The decision to retire early: A review and conceptualization. *Academy of Management Review, 19,* 285–311.

Fiedler, F. E. (1986). The contribution of cognitive resources and leader behavior to organizational performance. *Journal of Applied Social Psychology, 16,* 532–548.

Fischer, L. R., Mueller, D. P., & Cooper, P. W. (1991). Older volunteers: A discussion of the Minnesota Senior Study. *Gerontologist, 31,* 183–194.

Forteza, J. A., & Prieto, J. M. (1994). Aging and work behavior. In H. C. Triandis, M. D. Dunnette, & L. M. Hough (Eds.), *Handbook of industrial and organizational psychology* (2nd ed., Vol. 4, pp. 447–483). Palo Alto, CA: Consulting Psychologists Press.

Fronstin, P. (1999). Retirement patterns and employee benefits: Do benefits matter? *Gerontologist, 39,* 37–47.

Fullerton, H. N. (1999). Labor force projections to 2008: Steady growth and changing composition. *Monthly Labor Review, 122,* 19–32.

Hackman, J. R., & Oldham, G. R. (1976). Motivation through the design of work: Test of a theory. *Organizational Behavior and Human Performance, 16,* 250–279.

Hassell, B. L., & Perrewe, P. L. (1995). An examination of beliefs about older workers: Do stereotypes still exist? *Journal of Organizational Behavior, 16,* 457–468.

Hui, C., Lam, S.S.K., & Law, K.K.S. (2000). Instrumental values of organizational citizenship behavior for promotion: A field quasi-experiment. *Journal of Applied Psychology, 85,* 822–828.

Ilgen, D. R., & Hollenbeck, J. R. (1991). The structure of work: Job design and roles. In M. D. Dunnette & L. M. Hough (Eds.), *Handbook of industrial and organizational psychology* (2nd ed., Vol. 2, pp. 165–209). Palo Alto, CA: Consulting Psychologists Press.

Isaksson, K., & Johansson, Q. (2000). Adaptation to continued work and early retirement following downsizing: Long-term effects and gender differences. *Journal of Occupational and Organizational Psychology, 73,* 241–256.

Kim, S., & Feldman, D. C. (1998). Healthy, wealthy, or wise: Predicting actual acceptance of early retirement incentives at three points in time. *Personnel Psychology, 51,* 623–642.

Kim, S., & Feldman, D. C. (2000). Working in retirement: The antecedents of bridge employment and its consequences for quality of life in retirement. *Academy of Management Journal, 43,* 1195–1210.

Kremer, Y., & Harpaz, I. (1982). Leisure patterns among retired workers: Spillover or compensatory trends? *Journal of Vocational Behavior, 21,* 183–195.

Kubeck, J. E., Delp, N. D., Haslett, T. K., & McDaniel, M. A. (1996). Does job-related training performance decline with age? *Psychology and Aging, 11,* 92–107.

Lord, R. G., De Vader, C. L., & Alliger, G. M. (1986). A meta-analysis of the relation between personality traits and leadership perceptions: An application of validity generalization procedures. *Journal of Applied Psychology, 71,* 402–410.

Marrow, D., Leirer, V., Altieri, P., & Fitzsimmons, C. (1994). When expertise reduces age differences in performance. *Psychology and Aging, 9,* 134–148.

McEvoy, G. M., & Cascio, W. F. (1989). Cumulative evidence of the relationship between employee age and job performance. *Journal of Applied Psychology, 74,* 11–17.

Omoto, A. M., Snyder, M., & Martino, S. C. (2000). Volunteerism and the life course: Investigating age-related agendas for action. *Basic and Applied Social Psychology, 22,* 181–197.

Pearce, J. L. (1982). Leading and following volunteers: Implications for a changing society. *Journal of Applied Behavioral Science, 18,* 385–394.

Pearce, J. L. (1983). Job attitude and motivation differences between volunteers and employees from comparable organizations. *Journal of Applied Psychology, 68,* 646–652.

Rhodes, S. R. (1983). Age-related differences in work attitudes and behavior: A review and conceptual analysis. *Psychological Bulletin, 93,* 328–367.

Richardson, V., & Kilty, K. M. (1991). Adjustment to retirement: Continuity vs. discontinuity. *International Journal of Aging and Human Development, 33,* 151–169.

Rosen, B., & Jerdee, T. H. (1976). The nature of job-related age stereotypes. *Journal of Applied Psychology, 61,* 180–183.

Rowe, R., & Snizek, W. E. (1995). Gender differences in work values: Perpetuating the myth. *Work and Occupations, 22,* 215–229.

Schappe, S. P. (1998). The influence of job satisfaction, organizational commitment, and fairness perceptions on organizational citizenship behavior. *Journal of Psychology, 132,* 277–290.

Seashore, S. E., Indik, B. P., & Georgopoulos, B. S. (1960). Relationships among criteria of job performance. *Journal of Applied Psychology, 44,* 195–202.

Shultz, K. S., Morton, K. R., & Weckerle, J. R. (1998). The influence of push and pull factors on voluntary and involuntary early retirees' retirement decision and adjustment. *Journal of Vocation Behavior, 53,* 45–57.

Sonnenfeld, J. A., & Peiperl, M. A. (1988). Staffing policy as a strategic response: A typology of career systems. *Academy of Management Review, 13,* 588–600.

Talaga, J. A., & Beehr, T. A. (1989). Retirement: A psychological perspective. In C. L. Cooper & I. Robertson (Eds.), *International review of industrial and organizational psychology* (pp. 185–211). New York: Wiley.

Talaga, J. A., & Beehr, T. A. (1993, June). *Retirement types differ in predicting retirement adjustment.* Paper presented at the meeting of the American Psychological Society, Chicago.

Talaga, J. A., & Beehr, T. A. (1995). Are there gender differences in predicting retirement? *Journal of Applied Psychology, 80,* 16–28.

Taylor, M. A., & Shore, L. M. (1995). Predictors of planned retirement age: An application of Beehr's model. *Psychology and Aging, 10,* 76–83.

Thomson, L., Griffiths, A., & Davison, S. (2000). Employee absence, age and tenure: A study of nonlinear effects and trivariate models. *Work and Stress, 14,* 16–34.

Van Scotter, J. R., Motowidlo, S. J., & Cross, T. C. (2000). Effects of task performance and contextual performance on systemic rewards. *Journal of Applied Psychology, 85,* 526–535.

Vecchio, R. P. (1990). Theoretical and empirical examination of cognitive resource theory. *Journal of Applied Psychology, 75,* 141–147.

Waldman, D. A., & Aviolo, B. J. (1986). A meta-analysis of age differences in job performance. *Journal of Applied Psychology, 71,* 33–38.

Warr, P. (1994). Age and employment. In H. C. Triandis, M. D. Dunnette, & L. M. Hough (Eds.), *Handbook of industrial and organizational psychology* (2nd ed., Vol. 4, pp. 485–550). Palo Alto, CA: Consulting Psychologists Press.

Wayne, S. J., Graf, I. K., Ferris, G. R., & Liden, R. C. (1997). The role of upward influence tactics in human resource decisions. *Personnel Psychology, 50,* 979–1006.

Weckerle J. R., & Shultz, K. S. (1999). Influences on the bridge employment decision among older USA workers. *Journal of Occupational and Organizational Psychology, 72,* 317–329.

Williams, S., & Shiaw, W. T. (1999). Mood and organizational citizenship behavior: The effects of positive affect on employee organizational citizenship behavior intentions. *Journal of Psychology, 133,* 656–668.

PART 3

The Changing Context of Career Development

Public Policy and the Changing Legal Context of Career Development

Jon M. Werner

Given the widespread turbulence facing individuals, organizations, and society as a whole (Jacoby, 1999; Leana & Feldman, 2000; Watts, 1996), it is imperative that researchers and practitioners take a more holistic approach to career issues. This means, first and foremost, looking at career issues throughout the various stages of life and work (Levinson, 1986; Greenhaus, Callanan, & Godschalk, 2000). This also means focusing more explicitly on legal and public policy issues than has generally been the case in the career management and development literature.

Legal and public policy issues have received relatively little attention in the careers literature to date (Watts, 2000a). Nonetheless, government actions have a pervasive influence on individuals' career decision making throughout their lives. While public policy is often viewed primarily as a means of mitigating career failures, public policy can also be used to advance individual career opportunities. A critical question to address here, then, concerns the proper role of government and public policy in career development (Hiebert & Bezanson, 2000).

I thank Ronald Crabb, James Malloy, and Daniel Feldman for their assistance with drafts of this chapter.

In this chapter, I use the career stage framework from Green-haus et al. (2000) to highlight public policy issues and initiatives that influence individual career decisions over the course of a life-time. I then discuss the implications of a developmental perspective on the interface between public policy and career development and the implications of government policies for individuals' careers and organizations' career development strategies. This section suggests that the careers literature must move beyond individually oriented and organizationally oriented models of career development to include a focus on societal-level models as well (Collin & Young, 2000a). A developmental perspective provides a valuable framework with which to integrate public policy decisions with career decisions made across the life span.

A Larger Role for Public Policy Issues in Careers Research

In most discussions of career development, legal and public policy issues have played a secondary or background role. Although I discuss only two examples in this regard, I believe they are representative of the current state of the careers literature as a whole.

Attention to Public Policy and Careers

In most texts on career development, a career stage, or developmental, perspective is used to discuss many critical career-related issues. However, public policy issues receive only cursory attention. There are minor references to significant legislation and regulations with an impact of careers (including Title VII and the Family and Medical Leave Act), and some attention is devoted to the topic of managing diversity (such as affirmative action and sexual harassment). Yet even in major work in the field, legal and public policy issues receive only minimal coverage.

As my second example, consider the Careers Division Program at the 2001 National Academy of Management. At the 2001 meetings, the Careers Division had thirty-two papers and sixteen sessions where careers papers and topics were presented. One joint symposium session was on affirmative action, another on women and minorities in the information technology field, and a third on race and gender issues. Only one paper accepted by the Careers Division distinctly covered legal or public policy issues (Foley & Kidder, 2001). The winner of the Best Paper Award (Thompson, 2001), though, did discuss the transition of many physicians from private practitioners to employees, although the public policy implications were largely left implicit. Thus, despite the fact that the theme for the conference was "How Governments Matter," public policy issues received little attention.

Public Policy Issues in Career Development Research

Even a cursory discussion of the changes in the legal protections offered to employees in the United States over the past seventy-five years highlights the prominent place that law and public policy decisions play in the employment setting. Depression-era legislation, such as the Social Security Act of 1935 and the Fair Labor Standards Act of 1938, provided income maintenance protection and a federal minimum wage, respectively. The Wagner Act of 1935 firmly established the legal right of U.S. workers to organize and bargain collectively over wages and working conditions.

Beginning in 1963, a large body of civil rights laws and executive orders were passed, providing a variety of protections for U.S. workers from discrimination based on numerous protected categories (see Table 9.1). Besides the federal laws and orders highlighted in Table 9.1, states and municipalities have passed laws covering other bases for discrimination; for example, discrimination on the basis of height, weight, and marital status are all addressed under Michigan law. In addition, there have been myriad court decisions focusing on employment issues, as well as rules and regulations set forth by regulatory agencies such as the Equal Employment Opportunity Commission (EEOC) and the Office of Federal Contract Compliance Programs (Werner, 1998). In total, a significant amount of U.S. public policy affects career-related issues. It is shortsighted, even self-defeating, to give only modest or glancing attention to this rather massive body of material.

It is no exaggeration to suggest that the influence of public policy on U.S. citizens is evident from cradle to grave. School-to-work programs, as well as college loan and tax incentives, are intended to increase the skill and education levels of young people entering

Table 9.1. Significant Legislation Concerning
the U.S. Workplace Since 1930.

Legislation or Executive Order	Major Provisions
Social Security Act (1935)	Income provisions for older citizens, plus those injured, disabled, or otherwise unable to work, and their dependents
Wagner Act (1935)	Gave workers the legal right to organize and bargain collectively
Fair Labor Standards Act (1938)	Established federal minimum wage and overtime pay and placed restrictions on child labor
Equal Pay Act (1963)	Men and women doing substantially equal work should receive substantially equal pay
Title VII, Civil Rights Act (1964)	Employers may not base employment decisions on race, color, religion, sex, or national origin
Executive Order 11246 (1965)	Covers federal agencies and government contractors with contracts of $10,000 or more; employment decisions may not be based on race, color, religion, sex, or national origin; stronger requirements concerning affirmative action than included in Title VII
Age Discrimination in Employment Act (1967, amended)	Covers individuals forty and older; for most jobs, age may not be used as a basis for an employment decision
Employee Retirement Income Security Act (1974)	Minimum vesting and funding requirements set for most U.S. private pension funds
Job Training Partnership Act (1983)	Provided federal funds to private industry councils to secure skills training for unemployed, displaced, or disadvantaged individuals
Worker Adjustment and Retraining Notification Act (1988)	Employers with one hundred or more employees must provide at least sixty days of advance notice of a plant closure or layoff affecting fifty or more full-time employees

Table 9.1. Significant Legislation Concerning
the U.S. Workplace Since 1930, Cont'd.

Americans with Disabilities Act (1990)	Employment decisions may not be based on physical or mental disability or chronic illness; reasonable accommodations must be offered to disabled individuals (unless this would cause an undue hardship on the employer)
Family and Medical Leave Act (1993)	Employees must be given up to twelve weeks of unpaid leave per year for certain covered events (childbirth; adoption; serious health condition for the employee, a spouse, parent, or child)
School-to-Work Opportunities Act (1993)	Provided federal grants to states to implement school-to-work programs (such as youth apprenticeships and co-op education programs)
Health Insurance Portability and Accountability Act (1996)	Increased the portability of employee health coverage
Tax Relief Act (1997)	Established Hope tax credit to offset up to $1,500 per year in tuition expenses for college freshmen and sophomores and lifetime learning credit (currently $1,000 or 20 percent of the first $5,000 of family tuition expenses); income limits reduce the amounts that can be claimed by families with higher incomes
Workforce Investment Act (1998)	Consolidated over seventy federal education and training programs (including the Job Training Partnership Act); provides block grants to states to meet the educational and training needs of youths, adults, and displaced workers
Economic Growth and Tax Relief Reconciliation Act (2001)	Increased the amount of contributions that can be made to education IRAs from $500 to $2,000 per year; allowed individuals to withdraw funds from state-sponsored IRS Section 529 plans tax free if the funds are used to pay for college expenses.

the workforce. Federal structures such as America's Job Bank, maintained by the U.S. Department of Labor, seek to promote the efficient linking of applicants with available jobs. In addition to providing benefits to retired workers, Social Security provides payments to the dependents of workers who die or are unable to work. These payments are intended to provide a replacement for some of the wages lost by the wage earner's death or disability. Finally, beyond Social Security, legislation concerning health coverage (for example, Medicare) and pension protection (for example, Employee Retirement Income Security Act) focus particularly on the needs of older citizens.

Virtually every citizen is aware of the widespread impact of the law on modern U.S. life. The more contentious question is what role government and public policy should play in career development. What is the proper role of public policy in this area? Here the prescriptions may vary from those deemed politically liberal to conservative, especially concerning the proper amount of government regulation of the employment relationship.

Changes in the Legal Context Surrounding Career Development

The most extensive writing on the topic of public policy and careers has been done by A. G. Watts, a British researcher (Watts, 1996, 1999, 2000a, 2000b, 2001a, 2001b; Watts & Kidd, 2000). Furthermore, an edited volume recently appeared from a 1999 symposium on this topic held in Ottawa, Canada (Hiebert & Bezanson, 2000). These authors addressed a number of important issues:

- *The proper role of government versus the market in the employment relationship.* For instance, Watts (2000b, p. 259) argued that "the USA . . . has been concerned to restrict labor-market regulation and to trust the free flow of market forces. Although deregulation has created jobs, many have been low-skill in nature. Combined with low levels of social-welfare expenditure, this has resulted in marked social disparities." Watts contrasts this with the stronger employment regulations (and higher unemployment) found in most continental European countries.

- *A changing or new employment relationship* (Arthur & Rousseau, 1996; Capelli, 1999). For instance, Littleton, Arthur, and Rousseau (2000, p. 101) state that "the new environment suggests a shift from pre-ordained and linear development to perpetually changing career paths and possibilities. As a result, a shift from 'bounded' careers—prescribed by relatively stable organizational and occupational structures—to 'boundaryless' careers—where uncertainty and flexibility are the order of the day—is increasingly common."

- *Issues of agency versus structure in individual careers.* Using the terminology of Giddens (1993), this debate deals with the extent to which individuals are agents with responsibility for their own career issues and decisions and the extent to which corporate and governmental structures have primary responsibility for enhancing career success (Watts, 2001b). Much of the careers literature has emphasized the agency and responsibility of individuals in achieving career success (for example, "Pack your own parachute!"). Yet many career "failures" (for example, individuals who drop out of school or who otherwise never make it into the paid workforce) are attributed to flaws in macroeconomic policies and structural unemployment, particularly for those on the margins of poverty.

- *The role of publicly funded guidance services for non-school-age individuals.* Career guidance services have primarily been aimed at young people and have generally been conducted within schools. Watts (2000b) argues that such guidance should be available to individuals throughout their lives. However, as Watts and Kidd (2000, p. 494) point out, "The term 'guidance' has proved difficult to market to adults outside educational settings, partly because many people do not know what it means and partly because they associate it with something done unto them at school." The goal, they argue, is to connect career guidance with popular discussions of lifelong learning (DeSimone, Werner, & Harris, 2002).

Integrating Public Policy and Career Development

Applying a developmental perspective to the careers situation highlights a number of important legal and public policy issues. Greenhaus et al. (2000) suggest that five career stages can be used to understand individual careers: career preparation (up to age twenty-five), organizational entry (generally ages eighteen to twenty-five), early career (ages twenty-five to forty), midcareer (ages forty to fifty-five), and late career (age fifty-five and older). I use this framework to discuss important legal and public policy issues across the span of an individual's life.

Salient Public Policy Issues Related to Career Preparation (to Age Twenty-Five)

Approximately 7 million Americans receive survivor benefits through the Social Security system and the Old Age Survivors and Disability Insurance (OASDI) program, and this number includes almost 2 million children under age nineteen (U.S. Social Security Administration, 2001). The aim of this program is to provide a form of government-sponsored life insurance in order to make up for the wages lost by the death of a wage-earning parent. According to the Social Security Administration, Social Security pays more benefits to children than any other federal program (U.S. Social Security Administration, 2000). Such payments make it easier for survivors' children to complete their high school education, a necessary prerequisite for most work careers.

In the United States, the vast majority of career guidance efforts have occurred within schools. Social and educational reforms have played a dominant role in shaping the role of vocational counseling (Lapan, 2001). For instance, Herr (2001) describes several federal initiatives and laws that have enhanced career guidance efforts within schools. These range from the National Defense Education Act of 1958, which sought to identify and counsel students with high levels of scientific talent (a response to the cold war with Russia), to federally funded comprehensive guidance and counseling programs that seek to address the full developmental needs of young people (Gysbers & Henderson, 2001).

Two concerns that have been expressed concerning U.S. public education are the apparent lack of connection between education and job opportunities and the lack of assistance for students who are not pursuing bachelor's degrees in college (Guest, 2000; Imel, 1991). In response, many states have initiated programs that fall under the heading of school-to-work programs, which frequently include apprenticeships and co-op educational opportunities for high school students (DeSimone et al., 2002). The School-to-Work Opportunities Act was passed in 1993 to provide grants to states to carry out such programs. However, funding for the act sunset in October 2001.

Limited empirical evidence exists to date concerning the effectiveness of such programs (Guest, 2000). A recent study of seven organizations with active school-to-work programs, for example, failed to establish that the benefits to employers were greater than the costs of running such programs (Bassi & Ludwig, 2000). This raises concerns about the future viability of such programs. In addition, Guest (2000, p. 619) argues that such efforts must be better grounded in the existing body of theory concerning career issues: the "concepts of career assessment, career development, and career exploration must be integral and not optional components to any vocational program."

A final career issue relating to public policy geared to young adults is the financing of college education. Federal initiatives, such as the Tax Relief Act of 1997 and the Economic Growth and Tax Relief Reconciliation Act of 2001, have been passed to encourage parents to set money aside to pay for their children's college expenses (Brenner, 2001; Huntley, 2001). These laws have led to the establishment of numerous plans and approaches to saving money for college (for example, Roth IRAs, Coverdell Education Savings Accounts, and IRS section 529 plans run by individual states; Dugas, 2001; Quinn, 2001). Although the details vary, the basic idea is to minimize the amount of taxes paid on money set aside for college education. To date, there has been little empirical evidence on the effects of these programs on the rates of entry or completion of college.

Tax exemptions for students in college (or their parents) are also designed to promote college attendance (Quinn, 2001). Huntley (2001) reports that IRS section 529 plans have been established in California, Florida, Kansas, New Hampshire, and Wisconsin (see also Barney, 2001; Hurley, 2001). Hebel (2000) reported IRS data that suggested that approximately $3.5 billion was claimed on 1999 U.S. tax returns for 1998 college expenses. However, these other reports suggest that little of these tax savings are being claimed by low- and middle-income families (Hebel, 2000; Reid, 2001; Reynolds, 2000). The rules for use of these plans are quite complicated (Stockman, 2001).

In addition to tax incentives, college loans, such as Stafford and PLUS loans, are plentiful and relatively easy to obtain (Cropper, 2001), though the public policy implication of this last point has been strongly criticized. For example, Fossey and Bateman (1998) edited a volume that describes the substantial negative consequences to young people of starting out their careers with large amounts of student loans outstanding. Clearly, the federal government has been active in many ways to encourage the increased participation of young people in career preparation activities, most directly in terms of encouraging college attendance.

Public Policy Issues Related to Organizational Entry (Ages Eighteen to Twenty-Five)

A major goal of the Civil Rights Act of 1964 was to provide greater and more equal access to school and work opportunities for racial minorities, especially African Americans. This act and other equal employment opportunity (EEO) legislation and government regulations have significantly improved the options for minorities to gain access to jobs without regard to race, religion, gender, or other categories protected by law (see Table 9.1).

While lawsuits concerning employment discrimination remain at a high level, with almost eighty thousand charges filed with the EEOC in fiscal year 2000, the majority of these cases pertain to issues other than organizational entry (Charge Statistics, 2001). Given the number of organizations that also pursue affirmative action goals of actively recruiting and hiring more women and minorities, greater equality of access to organizational entry is probably one of the most observable outcomes from the civil rights efforts that began in the 1960s.

Current laws and regulations allow for complaints and investigations of alleged employment discrimination and hold out the potential for judicial redress in many cases. However, the legal route is a slow and largely reactive process. Overreliance on litigation can foster the notion that public policy is primarily a means of redressing real or perceived career failures, such as not getting a job offer because of one's race or gender.

Recently, there has been an increased amount of governmental activity designed to promote successful career entry and development. In addition to the school-to-work efforts, the U.S. Department of Labor has greatly increased the number of one-stop career centers that it operates (Barkume, 1998–1999). These centers go beyond the notion of the unemployment office and typically include career libraries, free computer and Internet access, and opportunities to meet with career counselors (Mariani, 1997).

The Internet has provided another means of linking job seekers and employers. The Department of Labor has expanded its efforts through sites such as America's Job Bank, a no-cost means of posting or seeking full-time employment, primarily in private sector jobs. In October 2001, the job bank listed over 1 million job openings and had over 400,000 resumés available for employers to search (America's Job Bank, 2001). A related site, America's Career InfoNet, allows individuals to engage in career exploration activities on-line (Barkume, 1998–1999).

Public Policy Issues Related to Early-Career Issues (Ages Twenty-Five to Forty)

Equal employment opportunity and affirmative action laws and guidelines apply to other career stages as well. At the early career stage, the focus is not only on recruitment and selection, but also on promotion and retention issues. A sizable body of EEO case law concerns the promotion and retention of women and minorities, especially those in the early career stage (Werner, 1998).

The career impact of childbirth and child care is salient for many individuals in the early career stage. This led to the passage of the Family and Medical Leave Act (FMLA) of 1993, which provides up to twelve weeks of unpaid leave for various personal activities, including the birth or adoption of a child. The employee's existing health coverage must be maintained during the time in which FMLA leave is granted.

Unemployment compensation is provided to workers at this career stage (and others) who are terminated through no fault of their own (Bergman & Scarpello, 2001). Unemployment compensation was originally mandated by the Social Security Act of 1935; it is now administered by the individual states. Employers pay into the state funds based on their experience ratings, that is, according to the number of former employees who have successfully filed for unemployment claims. To receive unemployment benefits, the unemployed worker must be actively looking for work. For example, a former employee may not collect unemployment benefits if he or she is enrolled as a full-time student.

More support for individuals at the early career stage can be seen in tax credits available to organizations that provide tuition reimbursement for the continuing education of their employees. Although such plans are widely popular among young adults, these tax credits remain unevenly available to individuals in different jobs and different states. For example, in 2001, the Wisconsin State Assembly proposed legislation that would give corporations tax credits for 50 percent of employee tuition expenses that are paid for by an employer. If passed, this bill would have cost the state an estimated $12 million in lost tax revenue (Weier, 2001). In the wake of widespread state budget problems, this bill was defeated in March 2002. To address particular skill shortages, Virginia, Maryland, and Pennsylvania offer targeted tuition assistance or tax credits to students in information technology programs (Thibodeau, 1999).

Public Policy Issues Related to Midcareer Issues (Ages Forty to Fifty-Five)

Additional legal protection is provided for those age forty and older under the Age Discrimination in Employment Act (ADEA). Age discrimination claims constitute a sizable portion of the EEOC caseload, comprising 20 percent of the total charges in fiscal year 2000 (Charge Statistics, 2001). In addition, individuals in mid- and late-career stages are also making increased use of the Americans with Disabilities Act (ADA) to challenge undesired job changes and terminations. For example, back problems are the leading cause of wrongful termination claims filed under the ADA (Grossman, 2001), and these are most likely to be filed by individuals age forty or older.

Mid- and late-career individuals are also more likely to use leave under the FMLA to care for themselves, a spouse, or a parent. One survey of FMLA leave takers found that the largest percentage of leave-takers (40.8 percent) were between the ages of thirty-five and forty-nine and that 58.8 percent had taken leave to address their own serious health conditions (Commission on Family and Medical Leave, 1996).

On a more proactive note, the Workforce Investment Act of 1998 provides potential governmental support for worker retraining. This act supersedes the Job Training and Partnership Act of 1983, which was criticized as expensive, ineffective, and confusing to both employers and those seeking assistance (Judy & D'Amico, 1997; Pantazis, 1996). This Workforce Investment Act consolidated more than seventy existing federal education and training programs. Block grants are available to states to fund particular programs. This act was aimed at providing training opportunities to those who are unemployed, displaced, or economically disadvantaged and has particular relevance for midcareer individuals in need of new or updated technical skills (DeSimone et al., 2002). Although it is still too early to determine the success of the consolidations brought on by the Workforce Investment Act, anecdotal evidence suggests that some successful implementations have occurred (Nilsen, 2001; "Six States Eligible," 2001).

Public Policy Issues Related to Late-Career Issues (Age Fifty-Five and Older)

The elimination of mandatory retirement ages for most jobs in the United States has been a significant development brought on by the ADEA. More older Americans are working past the traditional age retirement age of sixty-five. Some of this is by choice, and some is due to necessity. Serious weaknesses in the funding and protection of private pension funds led to the passage of the Employee Retirement Income Security Act in 1974. This law increased the funding levels committed to private pension funds, in particular to defined-benefit plans that promise retirees a specific dollar amount per month based on a formula for earnings, years worked, and age of retirement.

Recently, there has been a major shift in pensions towards the provision of defined-contribution plans. These include IRAs, KEOGH plans, and 401(k) plans. In such plans, money is set aside in an individual's account. The individual typically has much greater choice and responsibility concerning how the money will be invested. Conversely, in such plans, the individual also bears greater personal risk (Jacoby, 1999; Severson, 2001).

Concerns have been expressed that self-directed defined-contribution plans have a disparate impact on women and minorities. Zanglein (2001) argues that on average, women and minorities earn lower wages during their careers than white males. Women live longer than men; however, Zanglein argues that both women and minorities make more conservative investments than white men do. Consequently, women and minorities are particularly at risk that they will earn lower returns on their investments. In fact, all individuals covered by defined-contribution plans have less certainty and security concerning how much money will be available to them when they retire.

Added to this situation are the widely publicized problems concerning current and future funding levels for government programs such as Social Security, Medicare, and Medicaid. For instance, Social Security Trust Fund expenditures are expected to exceed income around the year 2016, with insolvency projected for roughly twenty years after that (Forman, 2001). Clearly, major changes are needed soon to protect the future viability of government-provided benefits to older individuals.

Implications for the Interface Between Public Policy and Career Development

Much of this discussion of current U.S. public policy relevant to career issues has highlighted reactive governmental policies or actions: laws, lawsuits, or investigations of alleged discriminatory or otherwise unlawful actions by organizations against applicants or employees. However, there are also proactive initiatives, such as Roth education IRAs, America's Job Bank, tax credits for employees taking additional college courses, and initiatives under the Workforce Investment Act. An important follow-up issue to address is how public policy decisions can more effectively mitigate career failures as well as advance opportunities for career success.

Both individuals and employers often experience something of a love-hate relationship with government. This also holds true concerning attitudes toward the legal profession (Werner, 1998). That is, employment legislation, regulations, and executive orders are often seen as constraining influences on employment practices (Lee, 2001; Martin, Bartol, & Kehoe, 2000; Wells, 2001; Werner & Bolino, 1997). However, employees believe that public policy decisions can and should also promote career success. In the following section, I discuss how public policy can be used more proactively to encourage career success.

Implications for Individuals

Hall and Mirvis (1996) proposed the notion of a protean career as a fitting picture for many careers today. As the Greek god Proteus was said to be able to change his shape at will, so individuals are increasingly being asked to "reinvent" their careers over time. This puts increased emphasis on individual choices and flexibility. Some of the popular writing on this topic has tended toward overstatement, for example, "You are absolutely, positively on your own" (Morin, 1996, p. 22). Despite such exaggerations, however, it is clear that individuals today do have to bear a greater responsibility for managing their own careers from education through retirement (Arthur & Rousseau, 1996; Capelli, 1999; Greenhaus et al., 2000).

One of the rights and responsibilities of citizen and employees is to make use of the various laws, policies, and programs available to them, including those already discussed in this chapter. However, it seems that in many cases, there is a general lack of use of available governmental programs and regulations. For example, both applicants and employers often neglect state employment agencies, despite a recognition among experts that the services of such agencies are of generally high quality (Rosse & Levin, 1997). Similarly, a sizable number of employment discrimination complaints never move forward because they were not filed within the deadlines established for such complaints (Gordon, 2000–2001).

Two surveys of FMLA leave usage found that despite the widespread popularity of the FMLA, employers reported usage rates for their employees that were less than 4 percent (Commission on Family and Medical Leave, 1996; Tompson & Werner, 1997). Finally, none of the 316 taxpayer returns studied by Reynolds (2000) claimed any educational tax credits, and Reynolds attributed this to both ineligibility and unawareness of the provisions of the Tax Relief Act of 1997.

Taken together, these data suggest a need for broad citizen education concerning individual rights under existing laws and guidelines. Such education might include information about how to contact appropriate agencies, how to file complaints, and how to avail oneself of the many positive options available, for example, America's Job Bank and retraining programs. A broader and deeper form of citizen education is needed so that all citizens can better avail themselves of the legal protections and career-related resources available. This could start in high schools and extend to colleges and universities. Government, law, political science, and career preparation classes are all potential vehicles for disseminating information about the work-related legal remedies that are available in the United States.

More research is needed to ascertain the effectiveness of various state initiatives, such as school-to-work programs (Guest, 2000). Although hope has been expressed concerning a bright future for career guidance services (Gysbers & Henderson, 2001), there appears to be considerable room for improvement in the manner in which the guidance needs of those of high school and college age are met (Watts, 2001a).

Another implication at this level is that individuals should be more proactive in their career development efforts by making greater use of work portfolios, which are similar to work samples. Besides submitting resumés, college students are increasingly being encouraged to submit a portfolio of their student work, such as papers and projects, to demonstrate to potential employers examples of the type and quality of their work (Pool, 2001). Cohen and Mallon (1999) suggest that a strong work portfolio might be critical in obtaining jobs in the future. This would be similar to what is currently done by individuals in the film industry (Jones & DeFillippi, 1996), though for a much wider array of jobs and industries.

There are obvious proprietary issues that must be addressed if individuals are to share work samples from previous or current employers with other potential employers. These issues have been addressed by professional service firms and do not seem insurmountable (Malos & Campion, 1995). Furthermore, the infrastructure already exists to carry out such an effort on a national scale. For instance, individuals can maintain their own work portfolios, can do so electronically, and can control access to them on Web sites. In this way, individuals can control the information shared with any particular organization.

Another linking mechanism between organizations and individuals could be a for-profit organization, such as Monster.com or the America's Job Bank Web site maintained by the Department of Labor. In fact, there is now a related Department of Labor Web site that would be a prime candidate for this endeavor. Called America's Talent Bank, it provides electronic matches between the applicant characteristics (skills, education, and preferences) and organizational demands. Once matches are discovered, both parties are notified (Barkume, 1998–1999). The work portfolio could then be used as a means for applicants to demonstrate (electronically) that they possess the necessary knowledge or skills to perform a given job successfully. Given the many positive opportunities for individuals to take greater control of their own careers, a more active use of updated work portfolios would seem a natural way to promote individual career development.

Implications for Organizations

A focus on the individual has dominated career research and theorizing, especially in North America (Collin & Young, 2000b). Some recent efforts have included more organizationally focused theories and models of career management (Greenhaus et al., 2000). However, as Harris-Bowlsbey (1996, p. 54) stated, "Career theories, and particularly career guidance practice in the United States, have tended to focus on the individual's power and right to forge a self-actualizing career that emanates from personal interests, abilities, and values. Far more emphasis has been placed on the individual in this process than on the environment that surrounds the individual."

Given the dramatic changes occurring in society and in organizations, it seems clear that expanded notions of career management are needed. This should not remove the emphasis on the individual, but should increase the attention paid to organizational and societal influences (Super, 1990). For both organizations and individuals, this suggests that greater focus should be placed on the future employability of individuals, that is, on the portability of learning from one organizational setting to another (Watts, 2000b). In this regard, there are several strategies that organizations and human resource professionals can employ to assist in this process.

For example, Rousseau and Arthur (1999, p. 12) write, "To forestall future failure, the responsible firm needs to create new learning mechanisms, such as greater information sharing and exposure to new skills through training and active practice. All of these can make employability a more meaningful concept to current yet boundaryless employees." These authors then describe six features that they believe will characterize future HR practices:

- Voluntarism: Encouraging employees to participate in the design of their particular employment arrangements
- Market discipline: Promoting the links between current work skills and external job opportunities
- Leveraging career competencies: Expecting employees to use some portion of their time, say, 15 percent, on new markets or innovative endeavors
- Resiliency: Maintaining each employee's ability to respond to job career and life changes (moving into and out of the workforce based on current life issues)
- Collaboration: Developing relationships and networks both inside and outside one's organization
- Civility: Providing such safety nets and supports as portable benefits and skill credentials to deal with market changes

As an example of collaboration, Rousseau and Arthur (1996) cite Cap Gemini Ernst & Young. Cap Gemini is a large provider of information technology services and consulting. Its IT consultants may work on external assignments for months at a time but return periodically to their home office to share what they have learned, discuss problems, and maintain their personal ties within Cap Gemini.

To assist employees in dealing with a more dynamic work environment, organizations can also provide employees with greater choices concerning benefits. While employee choices concerning benefits options have increased in the past twenty years, true cafeteria-style or flexible benefits plans remain relatively rare (Hirschman, 2001). Rarer still are situations where employees have portability of benefits, that is, the ability to carry benefits from one employer to another (Nordlinger, 2001). The Health Insurance Portability and Accountability Act of 1996 mandated that covered employees have the right to maintain their existing health coverage when they change jobs, although the number of individuals affected by this provision of the act is low (Stroupe, Kinney, & Kneisner, 2001).

Other potential dramatic changes on the organizational front would be reducing or eliminating the time periods required before employee pension benefits are vested or guaranteed to the employee or increasing the portability of pension benefits. Both changes could be accomplished if employees are allowed to place employer contributions from various employers into IRAs they themselves control. However, for employer-controlled pensions (whether defined benefit or defined contribution), employees frequently must wait five to seven years before their employer-contributed pension benefits are fully vested. Furthermore, the decision to allow employees to take their pension benefits with them when they change employers rests with the employer; portability of pension benefits is an option under the Employee Retirement Income Security Act, but it is not mandatory (Bohlander, Snell, & Sherman, 2001).

Given that pension reform does not seem imminent (Bernstein, 2001), it would appear that concerted actions by employees and employee advocacy groups will be needed to persuade employers to decrease vesting requirements and increase the portability of individual employee pension funds. Concerning portability, there are several advantages to employees of building up one consolidated (defined contribution) pension fund over time versus maintaining multiple smaller funds. Consolidated pension funds can eliminate the loss of unvested pension benefits because funds are immediately under the control of the employee. Furthermore, if an individual has multiple plans and some of the earlier plans are defined-benefit plans, this can substantially affect the monthly payments that the individual receives at retirement (given that years of service and salaries are frozen in the earlier plans even if those funds are fully vested).

A discussion of public policy implications for organizations includes not only legal issues but also considerations of the managerial and ethical dimensions of organizational decision making. For example, the Worker Adjustment and Retraining Notification Act of 1988 requires large employers to give at least sixty days' notice to workers who are being downsized. As Van Buren (2000) has argued, downsizing is not just a legal issue but a moral one as well; that is, there are both legal and ethical elements to the organizational decisions that affect individual careers (Preston & Post, 1975). Feldman and Leana (2000), for example, document the lowered salaries and job responsibilities of executives who found reemployment after recent downsizing. Although many executives expressed satisfaction with their new positions, many others expressed lower trust and greater cynicism concerning organizations. It can be argued that organization's redefinition of employment contracts to absolve themselves of any responsibility for assisting their employees in finding meaningful future employment after downsizing is unethical as well.

Implications for Government and Public Policymakers

Many of the implications explored here must be implemented by (or at least in conjunction with) those who establish public policy. A recent forum of career professionals and public policymakers in Canada is an encouraging development in terms of seeing positive interaction between the parties necessary to such a discussion (Hiebert & Bezanson, 2000). Here, I highlight the most pressing issues that must be addressed at the societal and public policy level.

Besides the citizen education initiatives already discussed, another far-reaching implication is the need to develop a stronger role for career guidance services throughout life. Rather than primarily focusing services provided in schools to teenagers and young adults (Watts, 2001b), such services should go beyond the educational arena and could include roles for work organizations, intermediary organizations (such as professional associations or trade unions; see Sunoo, 1999), public libraries (Watts, 2000a), and other governmental agencies (Watts, 2000b). In Great Britain, for example, the National Advisory Council for Careers and Educational Guidance seeks to bring together the major stakeholders "within a coherent strategic framework" (Watts, 2000b, p. 271). More efforts along these lines are needed in the United States.

Making career guidance services more readily available to individuals throughout their lives would certainly promote increased self-management of careers, too. There are a number of other ways to increase the public policy support for self-managed careers (see Watts, 1996). One idea is to provide financial incentives for lifelong learning. This could be in the form of "individual learning accounts" (Watts, 2000b). Watts (2000b, p. 265) recommends that contributions for such a fund come from government, organizations, and individuals, in order to provide "a mechanism for recognizing mutuality of interest by sharing the costs." Given the success of IRAs, the idea of supporting lifelong learning in a similar fashion should be vigorously pursued.

The past two decades have seen dramatic job creation among entrepreneurial and small business organizations. Government support for such efforts is already available through the U.S. Small Business Administration (SBA), as well as the many Small Business Development Centers set up around the country. However, further governmental support for entrepreneurial activity is sorely needed. Blann (2000) spoke to the U.S. Congress about how entrepreneurs are frequently unaware of existing programs in their geographical area and recommended that a nationwide Web site be created (perhaps linked to the SBA) where such information and best practices could be shared.

There has been much recent discussion of a skills gap in the U.S. economy—a sizable gap between the skills possessed by those seeking employment and the skills now required by organizations (Rauschenberger, 2001). Some of the most severe shortages of qualified applicants are in computer-related and other high-tech fields. This has led to many public policy initiatives to strengthen governmental support for technological skills and knowledge work. As one example, despite cuts in other areas, Wisconsin recently increased the funding provided to technology training and education programs by $18 million (Conference Committee, 2001). This money was allocated to existing programs at universities and technical colleges.

Finally, there is much that can be learned from the ongoing collaborations among career researchers, career professionals, and public policymakers from multiple nations. In the Canadian forums that have been mentioned (Hiebert & Bezanson, 2000), issues such as unemployment, social exclusion, underemployment and dislocation have been addressed. More research is needed to learn from the best career practices of other nations and to follow up on the initiatives that have already been started (Watts, 2000a). Harris-Bowlsbey (1996) has called for a consistent U.S. national policy concerning career development. She states that the United Kingdom has already taken positive steps in this direction, but then contrasts this with the situation in the United States: "Herr (1996) provides insight into the reasons why prospects for positive change seem bleaker in the United States. These reasons include the facts that our national policy typically (a) is not mandated; (b) is not integrated into a broader program of educational reform; (c) allows spotty implementation; (d) is construed and promoted by different federal agencies, resulting in noncohesive services, and (e) changes dramatically from administration to administration" (p. 57).

Conclusion

The concerns raised by Herr (1996) and summarized by Harris-Bowlsbey (1996) remain salient. Given this situation, the need for stronger U.S. public policy support for career development is evident. Career researchers can contribute to this dialogue by more explicitly including public policy issues within their theory and research. In particular, there is a need to move beyond an individualized view of careers. Greater attention needs to be paid to individual careers within organizational and societal contexts (Collin & Young, 2000b). As Watts and Kidd (2000, p. 496) have argued, "In order to better inform guidance practice over the lifespan, theory needs to be more interactive, in the sense of taking account of the relationship between the individual and economic and social institutions." Collaborations between researchers with backgrounds in psychology and sociology are most likely to address the twin pillars of individual and environment that Super (1990) depicted as crucial to the concept of career.

In the current political climate, it is easy for individuals and organizations to react negatively to extant law and public policy. As Redmond (2000, p. 319) framed it so succinctly, the focus is often primarily on, "Are you breaking some sort of law?" This chapter has highlighted not only the ways in which public policy can address career disruptions and failures but also the many ways in which public policy can be used proactively to promote greater individual career success.

Many individuals and organizations view public policy and the law as something to be resisted or reacted against. Recently, however, Edelman and her colleagues made a strong argument concerning the endogeneity of legal regulation (Edelman, Uggen, & Erlanger, 1999). They argue that the law is more than an exogenous entity outside organizations. Laws and regulations become endogenous to individuals and organizations as both entities interact with them over time. Edelman's argument is that the interpretations of law made by lawyers and human resource professionals are subsequently adopted by organizations and serve to shape the manner in which courts and regulatory institutions construe those same laws and regulations.

As one example, Edelman et al. (1999) present the argument that judges would be more likely to defer to companies that have internal grievance procedures in place, in part because these procedures should provide the same types of fairness and due process that are held up as the ideal in judicial proceedings (Werner & Bolino, 1997). However, this was not strictly true (from a legal perspective) until after the U.S. Supreme Court's decision in *Meritor Savings Bank* v. *Vinson* (1986). This doctrine was then strengthened by the Supreme Court decision in *Faragher* v. *City of Boca Raton* (1998). That is, for many years, human resource authors promoted the claim that employers may avoid legal liability when they have an internal grievance procedure in place and an employee fails to use it. However, it was over a decade before this claim was subsequently accepted and adopted by the court system.

The larger point here is that legal issues are not strictly exogenous to individuals and organizations. Rather, they permeate our daily lives. While careers research has often been ideological (for example, heavily pro-education), careers researchers have largely avoided many issues that are explicitly political. School-to-work initiatives are generally accepted by those on both the political right and left because of the prospects of providing higher-level skills (and better-paying jobs) for those unlikely to pursue a bachelor's degree. However, what options and recommendations are to be made for those who are socially excluded, that is, those whose backgrounds are marked by poverty, inequality, and disadvantage (Watts, 2001a, 2001b)? Efforts to address social welfare and welfare-to-work programs are much more controversial. Recent efforts by career professionals to work with public policymakers (Hiebert & Bezanson, 2000; Watts, 2001a) suggest that we can no longer afford to be unengaged in public policy debates about career issues. My hope is that this chapter has promoted a greater understanding of these issues, as well as a greater commitment to include public policy issues in future careers research.

References

America's Job Bank. (2001). Available online: http://www.ajb.dni.us/.

Arthur, M. B., & Rousseau, D. M. (1996). *The boundaryless career.* New York: Oxford University Press.

Barkume, M. (1998–1999). Career guidance from the federal government: Helping workers help themselves. *Occupational Outlook Quarterly, 42,* 8–11.

Barney, L. (2001, Mar. 15). States beef up their college savings plans. *TheStreet.co.* Available on-line: http://www.thestreet.com/funds/investing/1346723.html.

Bassi, L. J., & Ludwig, J. (2000). School-to-work programs in the United States: A multi-firm case study of training, benefits, and costs. *Industrial and Labor Relations Review, 53,* 219–239.

Bergman, T. J., & Scarpello, V. G. (2001). *Compensation decision making* (5th ed.). Fort Worth, TX: Harcourt.

Bernstein, M. C. (2001). The future of private pensions: It is not pretty. *Employee Rights and Employment Policy Journal, 5,* 385–389.

Blann, J. (2000, Sept. 28). *Future of small business in America.* Testimony to the House Small Business Subcommittee. FDCH Congressional Testimony.

Bohlander, G., Snell, S., & Sherman, A. (2001). *Managing human resources* (12th ed.). Cincinnati, OH: South-Western.

Brenner, L. (2001, Oct. 14). Family finance: Affordable options put college within reach. *Newsday*, F04.

Capelli, P. (1999). Career jobs are dead. *California Management Review, 42,* 146–167.

Charge Statistics. (FY 1992–FY 2000). Available on-line: http://www.eeoc. gov/stats/charges.html/.

Cohen, L., & Mallon, M. (1999). The transition from organizational employment to portfolio working: Perceptions of "boundarylessness." *Work, Employment and Society, 13,* 329–352.

Collin, A., & Young, R. A. (Eds.). (2000a). *The future of career.* Cambridge: Cambridge University Press.

Collin, A., & Young, R. A. (2000b). The future of career. In A. Collin & R. A. Young (Eds.), *The future of career* (pp. 276–300). Cambridge: Cambridge University Press, 2000b.

Commission on Family and Medical Leave. (1996). *A workable balance: Report to Congress on Family and Medical Leave policies.* Washington, DC: U.S. Department of Labor.

Conference Committee. (2001). Available on-line: http://www.legis.state. wi.us/lfb/2001–03budgedocuments/ConferenceCommittee/ ConferenceCommittee.htm/.

Cropper, C. M. (2001, July 9). O.K. students, lock in those loans. *Business Week,* 114.

DeSimone, R. L., Werner, J. M., & Harris, D. M. (2002). *Human resource development* (3rd ed.). Fort Worth, TX: Harcourt.

Dugas, C. (2001, Nov. 9). Don't let college savings flunk during downturn; Options remain if slump has taken toll on tuition funds. *USA Today,* p. B03.

Edelman, L. B., Uggen, C., & Erlanger, H. S. (1999). The endogeneity of legal regulation: Grievance procedures as rational myth. *American Journal of Sociology, 105,* 406–454.

Faragher v. City of Boca Raton. (1998). 524 U.S. 775.

Feldman, D. C., & Leana, C. R. (2000). A study of reemployment challenges after downsizing. *Organizational Dynamics, 29,* 64–75.

Foley, S., & Kidder, D. (2001, Aug.). *Hispanic law students' perceptions of discrimination, justice, and career prospects.* Paper presented at the Academy of Management, Washington, DC.

Forman, J. B. (2001). Comparing apples and oranges: Some thoughts on the pension and social security tax expenditures. *Employee Rights and Employment Policy Journal, 5,* 297–326.

Fossey, R., & Bateman, M. (Eds.). (1998). *Condemning students to debt: College loans and public policy.* New York: Teachers College Press.

Giddens, A. (1993). *New rules of sociological method* (2nd ed.). Cambridge: Polity Press.

Gordon, M. P. (2000–2001). Title VII: Survey of recent decisions (Timely filing of state claims). *Cumberland Law Review, 31,* 431–434.

Greenhaus, J. H., Callanan, G. A., & Godschalk, V. M. (2000). *Career management* (3rd ed.). Fort Worth, TX: Harcourt.

Grossman, R. J. (2001). Back with a vengeance. *HR Magazine, 46,* 36–46.

Guest, C. L., Jr. (2000). School-to-work program. *Education, 120,* 614–620.

Gysbers, N. C., & Henderson, P. (2001). Comprehensive guidance and counseling programs: A rich history and a bright future. *Professional School Counseling, 4,* 246–256.

Hall, D. T., & Mirvis, P. H. (1996). The new protean career: Psychological success and the path with a heart. In D. T. Hall (Ed.), *The career is dead: Long live the career* (pp. 15–45). San Francisco: Jossey-Bass.

Harris-Bowlsbey, J. (1996). Synthesis and antithesis: Perspectives from Herr, Bloch, and Watts. *Career Development Quarterly, 45,* 54–57.

Hebel, S. (2000, Apr. 21). In year 2 of tuition tax credits, colleges cope better, but still complain. *Chronicle of Higher Education,* p. A34.

Herr, E. L. (1996). Perspectives on ecological context, social policy, and career guidance. *Career Development Quarterly, 45,* 5–19.

Herr, E. L. (2001). The impact of national policies, economics, and school reform on comprehensive guidance programs. *Professional School Counseling, 4,* 236–245.

Hiebert, B., & Bezanson, L. (Eds.). (2000). *Making waves: Career development and public policy.* Ottawa: Canadian Career Development Foundation.

Hirschman, C. (2001). Kinder, simpler cafeteria rules. *HR Magazine, 46,* 74–79.

Huntley, H. (2001, Aug. 5). Congress gives college savers a boost. *St. Petersburg Times,* p. 3H.

Hurley, J. F. (2001). *The best way to save for college; A complete guide to 529 plans (2001 edition).* Pittsford, NY: BonaCom Publications.

Imel, S. (1991). *School to work transition: Its role in achieving universal literacy* (Digest No. 106). Columbus, OH: ERIC Clearinghouse on Adult, Career, and Vocational Education. (ERIC Document Reproduction Service No ED 329 806)

Jacoby, S. M. (1999). Are career jobs headed for extinction? *California Management Review, 42,* 123–145.

Jones, C., & DeFillippi, R. J. (1996). Back to the future in film: Combining industry and self-knowledge to meet career challenges in the 21st century. *Academy of Management Executive, 10,* 89–103.

Judy, R. W., & D'Amico, C. (1997). *Workforce 2020: Work and workers in the 21st century.* Indianapolis: Hudson Institute.

Lapan, R. T. (2001). Comprehensive guidance and counseling programs: Theory, policy, practice, and research. *Professional School Counseling, 4,* IV-V.

Leana, C. R., & Feldman, D. C. (2000). Managing careers. In E. E. Kossek & R. N. Block (Eds.), *Managing human resources in the 21st century: From core concepts to strategic choice* (pp. 24.1–24.19). Cincinnati, OH: South-Western.

Lee, B. A. (2001). The implications of ADA litigation for employers: A review of federal appellate court decisions. *Human Resource Management, 40,* 35–50.

Levinson, D. J. (1986). A conception of adult development. *American Psychologist, 41,* 3–13.

Littleton, S. M., Arthur, M. B., & Rousseau, D. M. (2000). The future of boundaryless careers. In A. Collin & R. A. Young (Eds.), *The future of career* (pp. 101–114). Cambridge: Cambridge University Press.

Malos, S. B., & Campion, M. A. (1995). An options-based model of career mobility in professional service firms. *Academy of Management Review, 20,* 611–644.

Mariani, M. (1997). One-stop career centers: All in one place and everyplace. *Occupational Outlook Quarterly, 41,* 3–16.

Martin, D. C., Bartol, K. M., & Kehoe, P. E. (2000). The legal ramifications of performance appraisal: The growing significance. *Public Personnel Management, 29,* 379–405.

Meritor Savings Bank v. Vinson. (1986). 477 U.S. 57.

Morin, W. J. (1996, Dec. 9). You are absolutely, positively on your own. *Fortune,* 222.

Nilsen, S. R. (2001, Oct. 4). Job training. Testimony to the Senate Health, Education, Labor and Pensions Committee. FDCH Congressional Testimony.

Nordlinger, P. (2001). Corporate disconnect. *Working Woman, 26*(3), 14–16.

Pantazis, C. (1996). The state of lifelong learning. *Training and Development, 50*(8), 36–40.

Pool, S. W. (2001). Designing and measuring educational outcomes utilizing student portfolios for business management education. *Journal of Instructional Psychology, 28,* 50–58.

Preston, L. E., & Post, J. E. (1975). *Private management and public policy: The principle of public responsibility.* Upper Saddle River, NJ: Prentice Hall.

Quinn, J. B. (2001, Aug. 5). Planning for college takes some homework. *San Diego Union-Tribune,* p. H–1.

Rauschenberger, J. (2001). Finally, a cure for the skills gap. *Techniques: Connecting Education and Careers, 76*(6), 46–47.

Redmond, J. L. (2000). Are you breaking some sort of law? Protecting an employee's informal complaints under the Fair Labor Standards Act's anti-retaliation provision. *William and Mary Law Review, 42,* 319–351.

Reid, K. S. (2001, May 23). Report: HOPE offers little help to poor students. *Education Week, 2,* 5.

Reynolds, R. G. (2000). Use of the new education tax credits by selected income filers. *International Advances in Economic Research, 6,* 592.

Rosse, J., & Levin, R. (1997). *High impact hiring: A comprehensive guide to performance-based hiring.* San Francisco: Jossey-Bass.

Rousseau, D. M., & Arthur, M. B. (1999). The boundaryless human resource function: Building agency and community in the new economic era. *Organizational Dynamics, 27,* 7–18.

Rucnicki, B. A. (1996). *Pack your own parachute: The three secrets to being successful no matter who you work for.* Naples, FL: Sebastian Productions.

Severson, S. (2001). 401(k) plans turn 20. *Credit Union Magazine, 67*(2), 32.

Six states eligible for WIA incentive awards. (2001). *Techniques: Connecting Education and Careers, 76*(6), 11.

Stockmal, K. M. (2001). EGTRRA adds new tax benefits to planning for higher education expenses under Section 529. *Journal of Taxation, 95,* 238–247.

Stroupe, K. T., Kinney, E. D., & Kneisner, T. J. (2001). Chronic illness and health-related job loss. *Journal of Policy Analysis and Management, 20,* 525–544.

Sunoo, B. P. (1999). Labor-management partnerships boost training. *Workforce, 178*(4), 80–84.

Super, D. E. (1990). A life-span, life-space approach to career development. In D. Brown & L. Brooks (Eds.), *Career choice and development* (2nd ed., pp. 197–261). San Francisco: Jossey-Bass.

Tang, T.L.-P., Sutarso, T., Tang, D.S.-H., & Luna-Arocas, R. (2001, Aug.). *Career choice, experience, and demographic variables as related to income, money ethic, pay equity comparison, and pay satisfaction.* Paper presented at the Academy of Management, Washington, DC.

Thibodeau, P. (1999, Sept. 6). States seek to grow own IT workforces. *Computerworld,* 16.

Thompson, J. A. (2001, Aug.). *Commitment shift during organizational upheaval: An analysis of physicians' transitions from private practitioner to employee.* Paper presented at the Academy of Management, Washington, DC.

Tompson, H. B., & Werner, J. M. (1997). The Family and Medical Leave Act: Assessing the costs and benefits of use. *Employee Rights and Employment Policy Journal, 1,* 125–151.

U.S. Social Security Administration. (2000, Aug.). *Survivors benefits.* Washington, DC: U.S. Government Printing Office. Available on-line: http://www.ssa.gov/pubs/10084.html/.

U.S. Social Security Administration. (2001, Jan.). *Basic facts.* Washington, DC: U.S. Government Printing Office. Available on-line: http://www.ssa.gov/pubs/10080.html/.

Van Buren, H. J., III. (2000). The bindingness of social and psychological contracts: Toward a theory of social responsibility in downsizing. *Journal of Business Ethics, 25,* 205–219.

Watts, A. G. (1996). *Careerquake: Policy supports for self-managed careers.* London: Demos.

Watts, A. G. (1999). *Reshaping career development for the 21st Century.* Derby, England: Centre for Guidance Studies, University of Derby.

Watts, A. G. (2000a, June). Career development and public policy. *Journal of Employment Counseling, 37,* 62–75.

Watts, A. G. (2000b). The new career and public policy. In A. Collin & R. A. Young (Eds.), *The future of career* (pp. 259–275). Cambridge: Cambridge University Press, 2000b.

Watts, A. G. (2001a, Mar.). *Career development and social exclusion: A challenge for public policy and for the future of the career guidance profession.* Keynote address at the International Association for Educational and Vocational Guidance, Vancouver.

Watts, A. G. (2001b). Career guidance and social exclusion: A cautionary tale. *British Journal of Guidance and Counselling, 29*(2), 157–176.

Watts, A. G., & Kidd, J. M. (2000). Guidance in the United Kingdom: Past present and future. *British Journal of Guidance and Counselling, 28,* 485–502.

Weier, A. (2001, Oct. 5). Assembly OKs tax credits for tuition; business would pay costs, get breaks. *Madison Capital Times,* 2A.

Wells, S. J. (2001). Is the ADA working? *HR Magazine, 46*(4), 38–46.

Werner, J. M. (1998). Employment discrimination cases in U.S. courts of appeals: A brief commentary on Mollica. *Employee Rights and Employment Policy Journal, 2,* 255–265.

Werner, J. M., & Bolino, M. C. (1997). Explaining U.S. courts of appeals decisions involving performance appraisal: Accuracy, fairness, and validation. *Personnel Psychology, 50,* 1–24.

Zanglein, J. E. (2001). Investment without education: The disparate impact on women and minorities in self-directed defined contribution plans. *Employee Rights and Employment Policy Journal, 5,* 223–272.

CHAPTER 10

The Changing Organizational Context of Careers

Carrie R. Leana

If there is one conclusion to be drawn from the literature on organizational context and careers over the past two decades, it is that organizations simply do not matter as much as they used to. One need not be an academic researcher or even a practicing manager to arrive at this conclusion; it has been heralded in nearly every popular press or other mass media outlet in the United States that covers contemporary social patterns. Employees, we are told, no longer need employers to structure their careers but instead may act as free agents, selling their talents and time in a series of short-term arrangements that bear little resemblance to any conventional models of careers. This phenomenon has been articulated so convincingly and with such frequency (see, for example, Pink, 2001) that it has now entered into the canon of conventional wisdom in the United States and, to a lesser degree, other parts of the world as well.

American workers in most professions and jobs can no longer count on their employers for job stability, much less job security, and instead will work for a greater number of employers for a shorter average duration over the course of their careers. This assertion is bolstered by evidence of declining job tenure in many professions (Mishel, Bernstein, & Schmitt, 2001) and evidence in national surveys of decreased organizational attachment or commitment by employees (reviewed in Cappelli, 1999a). Phenomena like the large-scale downsizings experienced by shop floor and professional workers alike in the 1980s and 1990s, as well as the "broken" career ladders within organizations (Osterman, 1994), have been cited as the impetus driving these changing attitudes and employment patterns (Bluestone & Harrison, 1982; Cappelli, 1999b; Leana & Feldman, 1992; *New York Times,* 1996).

That organizational context matters less today than in the heyday of the much-maligned organization man (Whyte, 1956) is generally not disputed. Rather, the questions for researchers and managers alike center on the role of organizational context in shaping individual careers. In this chapter these issues will be discussed and the following three questions addressed: What are the major changes in organizational practice and context over the past two decades regarding employees' career management? What have been the effects of such changes on employee attitudes and behavior? What do the changes in employee-employer attachments mean for future research on the organizational context of careers? These three questions parallel the three major changes in organizational context and practice regarding careers: the ascendancy of the external market as the primary basis for organizational decision making, the transfer of risk for career management from employer to employee, and the increased role of networks in understanding employees' attachments to organizations.

The Changing Nature of Employment

Most analysts cite technological change, deregulation, and the rise in international competition in many industries as the major factors driving the changing nature of employment in the United States (see, for example, Cappelli et al., 1997). Many writers are also quick to note that these changes have been experienced most profoundly in managerial and professional jobs (Jacoby, 1999; Osterman, 1994).

Individuals in these jobs historically have enjoyed the greatest benefits from internal labor markets, where individuals could rely on their employers for relatively stable employment, opportunities for advancement, skill development, and pay tied to job category. Lower-level workers, those with fewer skills, and women and minority workers generally did not reap the benefits of such employment stability unless they were represented by a labor union, and even this group was decidedly white and male in composition (Conroy & Castells, 1997). Thus, the traditional career as it has often been described was one that was enjoyed in the past by a relatively small and homogeneous segment of the labor pool. It was only when the protections to this category of workers were threatened by the white-collar downsizings of the 1990s that the popular and business press began to register alarm over the changing nature of work (see Jacoby, 1997; Leana, 1996).

The erosion of the traditional career, even if experienced by a relatively elite group, has implications beyond the number of individuals personally affected. In many ways, this traditional model of careers represented an ideal that was sought, if not achieved, by a large number of American workers. It also defined in many ways what it meant in the United States to be a "good" employer that offered "good" jobs (Jacoby, 1997). Thus, it may have come to shape the expectations of many American workers and the psychological contracts and commitments that were the foundation of organizational loyalty and career satisfaction for individuals.

Cappelli (1999a, 1999b) nicely describes the primary attributes of the ideal traditional career as an ideal for managers and other professionals in the United States. First, traditional careers were bolstered by a system that economists have labeled internal career ladders. These career management systems are characterized by stable tenure within the organization, investments by both employer and employee in firm-specific knowledge and skills, internal opportunities for advancement, pay and benefits tied to the job rather than to the individual, and high exit costs to deter individuals from leaving their employer. He then contrasts this model with one that exists for these same managers and professionals today. Instead of stability and long tenure, managers and professionals now commonly experience ongoing job insecurity and more involuntary and voluntary turnover.

Similarly, investments in knowledge and skills are now more often made solely by the individual rather than by the organization and individual in concert (Pil & Leana, 2000), and promotions are sometimes nonexistent due to the compression of hierarchy that characterized much of the organizational restructuring of the past two decades. Pay is more commonly tied to individual performance today, and benefits such as pensions more frequently take the form of 401(k) plans that follow the individual from organization to organization. Due in part to these factors, the costs to the individual of leaving a particular employer have been greatly reduced in terms of potential losses in compensation and benefits, the individual's reputation, and opportunities in the external job market. In short, the career ideal has lost many of its traditional boundaries and has instead become what Arthur and Rousseau (1996) describe as boundaryless.

These changes have a number of implications for how individuals perceive their careers and how these perceptions shape their behavior at work and in other areas of their lives. Of these changes, foremost in terms of its effects is the ascension of external market forces as the primary determinants of the nature of jobs, the form and level of compensation and advancement opportunities for the individual, and the organizational contexts in which careers are played out.

Second, as Jacoby (1999) and others have pointed out, there has been a large-scale transfer of risk from the organization to the individual in terms of managing careers. The individual, rather than the organization, may now bear primary responsibility for everything from receiving training to obtaining intrinsic rewards to negotiating extrinsic compensation and benefits.

Third, the processes by which individuals become attached to their jobs have changed, too. Commitment to any one organization has declined. In its place are such network attributes as job embeddedness (Lee, Mitchell, Sablynski, Burton, & Holtom, 2001) and social attachments to peers and supervisors (Leana & Van Buren, 1999).

The Expanding Role of the External Market

Perhaps no other factor has shaped contemporary career management more than external markets' becoming the primary factor in decisions about nearly every aspect of careers: compensation, benefits, training opportunities, and even the very existence of jobs themselves. The external markets approach is based on the general assumption that individuals should be rewarded in proportion to the demand for their skills externally and their contribution to organizational performance. Those who have valued skills and contribute a great deal should expect to receive greater rewards, ranging from compensation to promotions to enhanced intrinsic aspects of their jobs, and those who contribute little should be least rewarded and most vulnerable to reductions in compensation and even job insecurity. This performance-reward link is a building block of classic motivation theory (Vroom, 1964) and fundamental to many Americans' sense of basic fairness in the workplace.

This approach to careers based on market demand has always been present and indeed encouraged in many quarters. Today, however, fewer and fewer employees are insulated from it, and more and more aspects of career decision making and organizational practice are based on it. Now, for example, instead of pay being tied primarily to some combination of factors like job grade, position, or tenure, organizations of all kinds have instituted pay-for-performance systems that individualize compensation based on how much the employee contributes to the achievement of organizational goals (Rynes & Gerhart, 2000).

Similarly, other forms of compensation such as benefits and pension plans have been individualized so that benefits are based in part on the choices individuals make (for example, cafeteria-style benefit plans) and their own financial contributions (for example, 401(k) retirement accounts). Base pay and bonuses are often also tied to the external market for the individual's talents. Thus, large raises are given to employees who are able to generate external job offers. Those who may perform equally well but do not test the external market are penalized through such practices (Feldman, 1985).

In the past, this external market approach to compensation, advancement opportunity, and other aspects of careers was most salient to two very different groups of workers: those who had talents and skills that were rare or in high demand, such as professional athletes, and those whose talents and skills could be easily purchased elsewhere or whose work could be accomplished by other means, such as dishwashers.

The employees in the middle—managers, professionals, unionized industrial workers, and craft workers, for example—were not immune from market forces. However, they could count on a reasonable degree of stability in compensation and job characteristics, regardless of fluctuations in market demand for their talents and services (Jacoby, 1997). For managers and professionals, the social contract in many organizations protected them from the vagaries of the external market, and unionized workers were protected by contracts that penalized organizations for responding too quickly or dramatically to market changes.

Many writers have extolled the virtues of a more market-based approach to career management where employees are hired, compensated, and terminated based on the demand for their skills and services elsewhere and their contribution to the organization's success (see Sullivan, 1999). Other writers, though, have not been so sanguine about market-based approaches, particularly when they are used to the near exclusion of all other criteria.

Writers such as Frank and Cook (1995) have argued that the external market has become such a dominant force in career decision making within organizations that it now works against the long-term interests of individuals and society as a whole. They describe a phenomenon whereby growing segments of the workforce are operating in winner-take-all markets, characterized by enormous rewards for those at the top, often at the expense of those in the middle or even those just slightly below the top tier. Such markets operate like those for professional athletes where the difference between being in first place or second is enormous in terms of the rewards received, even if there are no real discernable differences between the two in actual skill and talent.

Frank and Cook (1995, p. 4) argue that occupations ranging from "law, journalism, consulting, medicine, investment banking, corporate management, publishing, design, fashion, and even the hallowed halls of academe" now operate like winner-take-all markets. Thus, bankers in the "best" investment firms are compensated at a rate perhaps far greater than their actual merit compared to those at second-tier firms. Celebrity journalists, medical doctors, and academics now operate in labor markets that are not so different from those for athletes and rock stars. They are a part of a popular culture and market that lavishly rewards a few while paying little heed (or relative compensation) to those whose talents and skills are only marginally less than those at the top.

According to Frank and Cook (1995), one detrimental effect of this expanding winner-take-all phenomenon is to pervert people's thinking about their careers and career choices. Thus, gaining admission to the "best" universities, for example, becomes a pre-requisite for even being considered for competition at the top of some professions, despite the fact that the candidates from "just-below-best" universities are not discernibly different in terms of talent and training. Moreover, these huge rewards for big winners result in too many people being attracted to professions in which they have little chance of achieving success. Although this was always true in some occupations (for example, many more people aspire to be professional tennis players than will ever make the circuit), today more and more occupational categories operate like winner-take-all markets and more and more individuals become losers in favor of a small elite.

Winner-take-all markets also explain the ever-expanding gap in pay between those at the top and the bottom of many organizations. In the United States, this difference has grown exponentially over the past few decades, with chief executive officers now being paid at over two hundred times the rate of workers at the bottom of these same organizations (Mishel et al., 2001). Frank and Cook cite the winner-take-all phenomenon as partially responsible for the growing income inequalities in the United States and elsewhere. Indeed, analysis of income data in the United States supports this view. Mishel et al. (2001), for example, show evidence that the growing difference between haves and have-nots in the U.S. economy is due more to the spectacular rise in the income of the top 1 to 5 percent rather than to a substantial decline at the bottom.

There are several consequences of the market-driven approach to careers on individuals' perceptions and behaviors. Some, such as the effect on career choices for individuals, have already been described. Beyond that, though, there are important implications for employee motivation. Some of these consequences are quite positive and reflect the beneficial effects of competition on employees' motivation at work. Several researchers, for example, have described the relationship between stress and performance as a curvilinear one. That is, neither very low nor very high levels of stress will result in good performance; rather, some medium point is optimal. Thus, goal-setting theory admonishes managers to set attainable but challenging targets for employees (Locke, 1996).

Similarly, one of the major reasons behind the widespread application of pay-for-performance and pay-for-knowledge programs is a motivational one. A basic tenet of motivation theory is that individuals can be expected to behave in ways that help them to attain valued rewards. Designed properly, such systems should not only direct behavior but also increase individual effort toward reaching organizational goals (see Ambrose & Kulik, 1999, for a recent review of the motivation literature).

At the same time, organizational decision making based on external market considerations can have demotivating effects on employees. A basic tenet of expectancy theory, for example, is that individuals must feel efficacious in their ability to attain, or at least maintain, desired rewards (Vroom, 1964). This is the instrumentality dimension of the theory and an essential component of many classic theories of motivation. However, if employees' pension benefits can be reduced or their jobs eliminated, based not on their level of skill, performance, or tenure but rather due to market forces beyond their control, the logical conclusion for employees is that how they behave at work does not matter (Leana, 1996). This realization is a demotivating one that should negatively affect employee attitudes, motivation, and perhaps job performance as well.

Furthermore, because winner-take-all markets disproportionately reward a few at the expense of others, they may challenge individuals' feelings of equity. As Frank and Cook (1995, p. 17) explained, "In winner-take-all markets . . . pay distributions will be more spread out—often dramatically so—than the underlying distributions of effort and ability. It is one thing to say that people who work 10 percent harder or have 10 percent more talent should receive 10 percent more pay. But it is quite another to say that such small differences should cause pay to differ by 10,000 percent or more." If employees see the distribution of rewards and career opportunities as fundamentally unfair, equity theory predicts a decline in effort and performance on the part of disadvantaged employees (Adams, 1965; Mowday, 1991).

A final effect of the external market on organizational context and practice is that it inevitably shifts responsibility for career management toward employees themselves and away from the organizations employing them. The benefits of such a shift in terms of enhanced employee control and efficacy have been described elsewhere (see Pink, 2001, for a particularly positive account). At the same time, with this responsibility comes added risk, the subject of the second major change in organizational context and careers.

Transfer of Risk from the Organization to the Individual

In the traditional model of careers, the organization assumed most of the risks associated with market fluctuations in product demand and changes in the business cycle. Employees, conversely, were protected from such risk; in exchange, they offered their loyalty and talents to the organization over the long term. The market, to the extent it mattered at all, operated within the organization. Thus, while employees might have to worry about other potential competitors within the firm for a coveted promotion, they did not have to worry much about external market forces.

Much has been written about the basis for this arrangement, with questions centered on why organizations are no longer willing to assume this external market risk and why they ever did so. Several writers have attributed this change in practice to a change in the social compact between employee and employer (Pink, 2001). Because of changing norms, businesses and the executives who run them no longer feel compelled to create a family model whereby the organization is socially, and perhaps morally, obligated to provide for the welfare of its employees. Others have explained the change in terms of organization self-interest (Cappelli, 1999a, 1999b; Jacoby, 1999). For these authors, organizations were willing to assume additional risk because the returns, in the form of firm-specific capital and lower turnover, justified the costs. Some elements of both explanations are probably true.

Few would argue, however, that the costs to organizations of assuming market risk were lower in the past than they are today. When organizations operate in business environments where technology is predictable and there are substantial entry barriers to new competitors (such as high capital investment requirements and restricted access to capital markets), the risks that organizations assume are much smaller and more predictable. Thus, protecting employees from market fluctuations was not so costly. Employees were not only assured of maintaining their positions in all but the most dire circumstances for the organization, but they could also count on a predictable salary, specified promotional opportunities, and defined-benefit plans.

Thus, employees could not only feel secure in their jobs, but they also knew what to expect in the future, all the way up through retirement. In this way, a balance was achieved with tacit agreement from both employee and employer about what each would give and what each could expect to receive in exchange.

This balance was disrupted by the changes to how careers were conceptualized and managed by both individuals and organizations over the past two decades. As articulated by Feldman (1989) and others (Arthur & Rousseau, 1996; Sullivan, 1999), with the changes in the competitive structure of many industries in the 1970s and 1980s, organizations were no longer willing to assume what had become the escalating risk and associated costs for securing employees' jobs and futures. Welfare capitalism, as it came to be known, was dead.

At the same time, Feldman (1985) and others argued that individuals were no longer willing to accept the paternalism and limitations imposed on them by the traditional career model. Moreover, the entry of women into the workforce in large numbers in the United States over the past three decades almost ensured that the nature of the employment relationship had to change to accommodate career patterns that were, in many cases of necessity, nonlinear and less predictable than the traditional career stage models (Super, 1957).

With the change in the traditional career ideal came a shift in the way employees viewed their relationships with their employers and what they viewed as right and fair with regard to the exchange of risk and reward. Recent research on psychological contracts (and their breach) addresses these adjustments and how employees may alter their attitudes and behavior to accommodate changes in employment relations.

Rousseau (1995, p. 9) defines psychological contracts as "individual beliefs, shaped by the organization, regarding terms of an exchange agreement between individuals and their organizations." Because employees rely on these implicit contracts in making career decisions not just today but tomorrow as well, according to Rousseau, "psychological contracts have the power of self-fulfilling prophesies: they can create the future." Psychological contracts are often described along a transactional-relational continuum, based on the degree of flexibility and the expected longevity of the relationship. Traditional employment relations have been described as more relational in nature, whereas current employment, particularly for workers who are not considered core, is more often transactional and based on quid pro quo exchanges.

Given the downsizings and restructurings that have taken place in U.S. industry over the past two decades, it is not surprising that much of the recent research on psychological contracts has focused on contract breach. As Perrow (1996, p. 297) observed, while some may benefit from the changing organizational context in which individuals enact their careers, "for every boundaryless career that opens up, there are five to ten dead-end and degrading ones created, and one or two people left unemployed for a long stretch." Such violations can be the product of observation rather than direct experience. Downsizing has been described as the workplace equivalent of capital punishment, and even if a given employee is spared the ax, he or she may feel a sense of violation by witnessing the termination of friends and colleagues (Brockner, 1988).

Work by Robinson (1996) and her colleagues (Robinson, Kraatz, & Rousseau, 1994; Robinson & Rousseau, 1994) has shown that psychological contract breach is associated with several career-related outcomes, such as high turnover, lower job performance, and greater intentions to quit. It is also negatively related to employee satisfaction at work, trust in the employer, and the employee's own sense of what she owes the organization. Thus, the shifting of risk from employer to employee may fundamentally change the way employees view their exchange relationships with the organization, generating feelings of unfairness and corresponding negative reactions in the form of work behaviors and willingness to remain with the organization.

Other research that addresses shifting of risk from employer to employee for career management has focused on specific aspects of careers, such as promotions, training, and compensation (Tsui, Pearce, Porter, & Tipoli, 1997). In an influential study, Greenberg (1990) found that when employees' wages were decreased as a way for the organization to cut costs, theft of organizational property increased. This suggests that employees may use their own devices to restore a sense of rough justice when implicit contracts are broken.

There has also been a good deal of research on variable compensation practices and their effects on not just employee behavior but also employee attachment and attitudes (Rynes & Gerhart, 2000). Here, issues like distributive and procedural justice are found to be quite important. When employees believe that market-based compensation programs offer not just risks but corresponding opportunities for increased personal rewards, such as bonus systems, they are more accepting of the new systems and often find them motivating as well. Similarly, stock option programs that offer employees a share of ownership in addition to potential compensation may be viewed favorably if the risk-reward trade-off is seen as fair.

In the area of training and development, Pil and Leana (2000) describe the movement in the United States to establish skill standards in response to the changing employment contract. If employees are expected to move from job to job over the course of their careers, skill standards would attempt to certify the knowledge that employees carry with them, thereby making each individual's skills more transparent to potential future employers. This not only helps speed the process of employment for individuals but also saves organizations the time and expense of testing and screening for skills.

The skill standards approach implicitly accepts the shift of responsibility for training and skill development to the employee rather than the potential employer. However, as Pil and Leana (2000) articulate, an alternative approach is to certify workplaces in addition to workers. Not only would a potential employer know what it was getting regarding a potential employee's skills and knowledge, but that same potential employee would know what he or she could look forward to in terms of future training and development.

Thus, the risks and rewards for training would be more balanced than they are under a strict free agent model or a traditional career model. However, because the traditional implicit contract between employee and employer has been so widely breached over the past two decades, employees have perhaps shown a decided shift of their own in terms of the focus of their loyalty and organizational attachment.

Commitment Focused on People Rather Than Firms

Organizational commitment has been a mainstay topic of research in the fields of organizational behavior and industrial/organizational psychology for over thirty years. Organizational commitment has been described in many forms—for example, affective, continuance, and normative (Meyer & Allen, 1997)—and has been empirically associated with a wide range of employee attitudes and behaviors. For instance, organizational commitment has been shown to predict turnover intentions and turnover behavior negatively (Allen & Meyer, 1996) and predict job performance, satisfaction, and citizenship behavior positively (Organ & Ryan, 1995; Ostroff, 1992).

With the decreasing expectation of longevity with any one employer, organization-based commitment may not be as powerful a predictor of individuals' behavior or as useful a guide for management practice as it has in the past. Indeed, recent research on organizational attachment has broadened its scope. Today, it focuses not just on organizational commitment but also on factors like social exchange, social capital, and job embeddedness as predictors of why people remain in particular jobs or organizations.

This emerging literature recognizes the shift away from the traditional career model while offering a more realistic and comprehensive set of predictors of organizational attachment. As Lee et al. (2001) noted, researchers have focused a good deal of attention on why people leave jobs but perhaps not enough on why they stay. In the light of the career chaos of the past two decades, this question seems more relevant now than ever before.

The argument made by Mitchell, Lee, and their colleagues is that individuals remain in jobs not just because they are emotionally or practically attached to organizations but also because they are emotionally and practically attached to coworkers, colleagues, and communities (Mitchell & Lee, in press; Mitchell, Holtom, Lee, Sablynski, & Erez, in press). These attachments, in fact, may be more powerful predictors of retention than the classic constructs of organizational commitment or identity. That individuals have broadened the focus of their attachments (and in the process weakened their attachments to organizations) can be explained as a rational response to the organizational upheavals of the past two decades.

Mitchell et al. (in press) have developed the construct of job embeddedness that seeks to capture this broadened sense of attachment. According to their model, three factors comprise job embeddedness: links, fit, and sacrifice. Links are social connections between a person and other persons and groups. These links can be directly tied to a job, or they can be personal links to family and friends that bind a person to a particular location or vocation. Fit is the individual's perception of his or her compatibility with the work itself and with the values of the organization, coworkers, and supervisors. Sacrifice consists of potential losses that might be incurred if the employee leaves the job. These sacrifices are broadly defined and include factors ranging from financial security to status to on-site child care support.

In a series of studies, Mitchell and his colleagues have found support for the construct of job embeddedness and its ability to predict retention and on-the-job behaviors (Mitchell & Lee, in press). What is most interesting about this line of research for the purposes of this chapter is how little the organization context itself figures into the embeddedness construct. Instead, much of the focus is on social ties both inside and outside work; the individual's level of comfort with the organization and its mission may be less important than affiliations with colleagues and communities. Thus, the previously described movement away from the traditional career model may have also implicitly shifted individuals' priorities in terms of what they value in a particular job and whether they value it enough to stay when they have other choices.

Another emerging line of research that implicitly incorporates attachments other than to the organization itself in determining individuals' career decisions is work on social capital (Leana & Rousseau, 2000). Leana and Van Buren (1999), for example, discuss the importance of a sense of community at work as a determinant of employees' decisions about where and how much to contribute their efforts and talent. Here, factors like trust and associability among coworkers are the dominant mechanisms for individual attachment to particular jobs or organizations. Again, the focus of affective commitment in the social capital model is not the organization but rather the people who work within it. Thus, downsizings and restructurings, such as those experienced within so many organizations over the past two decades, may have a detrimental impact on individuals' motivation at work, not just because they challenge individuals' concepts of fair exchange but also because of the disruptions to social networks on the job.

A third line of research that moves the focus away from the organization and toward social relations in explaining individual attachment is the recent work on social exchange within teams of workers (Seers, 1989; Seers, Petty, & Cashman, 1995). In this research, employee attitudes and behavior are seen as being shaped by relationships with colleagues rather than employer-employee attachments or even employer-supervisor attachments. Empirical studies have shown that team member exchange is significantly associated with a variety of career-related outcomes, including turnover intentions and actual job exit (Liden, Wayne, & Sparrow, 2000).

Thus, organizational context may affect how individuals make basic career choices not so much due to the direct effect of organizational policies and practices (as in the past, for example, internal career ladders), but because of the indirect effect of organizational context in influencing social relations. This movement away from the organization as the focus of attachment and toward other factors such as colleagues and community is a relatively new development in the careers research and one that may be largely a reflection of changes in the way employees and employers alike view career management.

Future Directions in Practice

Several writers have predicted the continuance of many of the current trends regarding market-based approaches to decision making about career practices and benefits. (The recent discussions about privatizing government-provided Social Security benefits are an example of this continuing trend.) Moreover, there is little reason to believe that the trends regarding skill-based and market-based compensation will reverse themselves, although much of the growth in the use of these systems may already have taken place. Perhaps the setting that will experience the largest future growth will be in the public sector. Here, programs such as paying public school teachers bonuses for improvements in students' test scores and various programs for reinventing government have been proposed over the past decade.

Few writers expect income inequality in the United States to lessen in the near future, due in part to the growth of winner-take-all markets. This suggests that the "winners" and "losers" in a free agent economy may become more pronounced, with economic class playing a growing role in determining career opportunities for individuals. Mishel et al. (2001) and others present evidence of a dwindling middle class in the United States as the winners who take all pull further away from the rest of the society. Despite the recent business press stories about the excesses of winner-take-all markets in escalating CEO pay (Colvin, 2001), there is little evidence of change in these compensation practices.

Jacoby (1999) is most likely right in the view that there are limits to the burdens employers can shift to employees regarding career management. These limits are political, in the form of threatened regulation if organizational practices become too extreme. At the same time, the shifting of risk will be managed least well by those who have the fewest skills and resources to begin with. This suggests a further distancing between those at the top and those at the bottom of U.S. society.

Future Directions in Research

Work on psychological contracts, organizational embeddedness, and social capital should continue to gain in popularity as individuals focus their commitments on others rather than on organizations. There should also be a further research interest in the boundaryless career based largely on its promise of being an interesting new way of thinking about careers.

Nonetheless, researchers may be unwittingly relying on conventional management ideology in this regard. Despite evidence that many individuals are not faring well in the "free agent nation" (Pink, 2001), many researchers again seem to be following the lead of managers and their consultants in extolling the benefits of the changing career model. As Hirsch and Shanley (1996, p. 219) have noted, discussions of careers without boundaries are generally couched in very positive terms, "depicted as being filled with opportunities for personal development and fulfillment—indeed,empowerment—as well as for enhanced value creation and productivity." Furthermore, "even as we look forward to a boundaryless world that has not yet unfolded, its report card seems to have already arrived, with an impressive chorus of almost uniformly high evaluations."

At the same time, there is a growing body of research on the difficulties faced by segments of the workforce that have not benefited from the new market-reliant approach to careers and have not adjusted well to the shifting of risk for career management from organizations to individual employees. This stream of research focuses on segments of the workforce such as transitional and contingent employees (Callaghan & Hartmann, 1991), older workers trying to make transitions to new careers (Leana & Feldman, 1995), women (Fondas, 1996), and those moving from the rolls of government assistance to full-time employment (Kossek, 2000). One hopes that future research will incorporate both positive and negative models of the new career realities into a more comprehensive analysis of the effects of the widespread changes in organizational context and career development.

A final direction for future research is the issue of attachment and its manifestations and effects. Sennett (1998) recently wrote about the detrimental psychological effects of the "flexibility at all costs" approach to work and career management that seems to characterize contemporary practice. In his view, we (as researchers but also as organizational citizens) have too quickly accepted change as both an inevitable aspect of organizational life and a uniformly desirable one as well. In the process, we have tended to overestimate the benefits of mobility and underestimate its toll on human development and civil society. For Sennett, it is difficult to understand how individuals will manage to have lives of meaning without also having attachments. Better understanding the nature of these attachments and how organizational context strengthens or undermines them in the new workplace is surely an interesting and useful direction for future research on career development.

References

Adams, J. S. (1965). Inequity in social exchange. In L. Berkowitz (Ed.), *Advances in experimental psychology* (Vol. 2, pp. 267–299). Orlando, FL: Academic Press.

Allen, N., & Meyer, J. (1996). Affective, continuance, and normative commitment to the organization: An examination of construct validity. *Journal of Vocational Behavior, 49,* 252–276.

Ambrose, M., & Kulik, C. (1999). Old friends, new faces: Motivation research in the 1990s. *Journal of Management, 25,* 231–292.

Arthur, M., & Rousseau, D. (1996). *The boundaryless career.* New York: Oxford University Press.

Bluestone, B., & Harrison, B. (1982). *The deindustrialization of America.* New York: Basic Books.

Brockner, J. (1988). The effect of work layoffs on survivors: Research, theory and practice. In B. Staw & L. Cummings (Eds.), *Research in organizational behavior.* Stamford, CT: JAI Press.

Callaghan, P., & Hartmann, H. (1991). *Contingent work.* Washington, DC: Economic Policy Institute.

Cappelli, P. (1999a). *The new deal at work: Managing the market-driven workforce.* Boston: Harvard Business School Press.

Cappelli, P. (1999b). Career jobs are dead. *California Management Review, 42,* 146–167.

Cappelli, P., Bassi, L., Knoke, D., Katz, H., Osterman, P., & Useem, M. (1997). *Change at work.* New York: Oxford University Press, 1997.

Colvin, G. (2001, June 25). The great CEO pay heist. *Fortune,* 64–68, 70.

Conroy, M., & Castells, M. (1997). *Sustained flexibility.* Paris: Organization for Economic Cooperation and Development.

Feldman, D. C. (1985). The new careerism: Origin, tenets, and consequences. *Industrial Psychologist, 22,* 39–44.

Feldman, D. C. (1989). Careers in organizations: Recent trends and future directions. *Journal of Management, 15,* 135–156.

Fondas, N. (1996). Feminization at work: Career implications. In M. Arthur & D. Rousseau (Eds.), *The boundaryless career.* New York: Oxford University Press.

Frank, R., & Cook, P. (1995). *The winner-take-all society.* New York: Penguin.

Greenberg, J. (1990). Employee theft as a reaction to underpayment inequity: The hidden costs of pay cuts. *Journal of Applied Psychology, 75,* 561–568.

Hirsch, P., & Shanley, M. (1996). The rhetoric of boundaryless—or, how the newly empowered managerial class bought into its own marginalization. In M. Arthur & D. Rousseau (Eds.), *The boundaryless career.* New York: Oxford University Press, 1996.

Jacoby, S. (1997). *Modern manors: Welfare capitalism since the New Deal.* Princeton, NJ: Princeton University Press.

Jacoby, S. (1999). Are career jobs headed for extinction? *California Management Review, 42,* 123–145.

Kossek, E. (2000). Learning from the working poor and welfare reform: Paradoxes in promoting employability. In C. Leana & D. Rousseau (Eds.), *Relational wealth: The advantages of stability in a changing economy.* New York: Oxford University Press, 2000.

Leana, C. (1996). Why downsizing won't work. *Chicago Tribune Magazine,* pp. 14–16, 18.

Leana, C., & Feldman, D. C. (1992). *Coping with job loss: How individuals, institutions and communities deal with layoffs.* San Francisco: New Lexington Press.

Leana, C., & Feldman, D. C. (1995). Finding new jobs after a plant closing: Antecedents and outcomes of the occurrence and quality of reemployment. *Human Relations, 48,* 1381–1401.

Leana, C., & Rousseau, D. (Eds.). (2000). *Relational wealth: The advantages of stability in a changing economy.* New York: Oxford University Press.

Leana, C., & Van Buren, H. (1999). Organizational social capital and employment practices. *Academy of Management Review, 24,* 538–555.

Lee, T., Mitchell, T., Sablynski, C., Burton, J., & Holtom, B. (2001). *The effects of job embeddedness on voluntary turnover, voluntary absences, job performance, and organizational citizenship* (Working Paper). Seattle: University of Washington.

Liden, R., Wayne, S., & Sparrow, R. (2000). An examination of the mediating role of psychological empowerment on the relations between the job, interpersonal relationships, and work outcomes. *Journal of Applied Psychology, 83,* 407–416.

Locke, E. A. (1996). Motivation through conscious goal setting. *Applied and Preventive Psychology, 5,* 117–124.

Meyer, J., & Allen, N. (1997). *Commitment in the workplace.* Thousand Oaks, CA: Sage.

Mishel, L., Bernstein, J., & Schmitt, J. (2001). *The state of working America: 2000–2001.* Ithaca, NY: Cornell University Press.

Mitchell, T., Holtom, B., Lee, T., Sablynski, C., & Erez, M. (in press). The retention of employees: The role of organizational embeddedness. *Academy of Management Journal.*

Mitchell, T., & Lee, T. (in press). The unfolding model of voluntary turnover and job embeddedness: Foundations for a comprehensive theory of attachment. In B. Staw & R. Sutton (Eds.), *Research in organizational behavior.* Stamford, CT: JAI Press.

Mowday, R. (1991). Equity theory predictions of behavior in organizations. In R. M. Steers & L. W. Porter (Eds.), *Motivation and work behavior* (5th ed., pp. 11–131). New York: McGraw-Hill.

New York Times. (1996). *The downsizing of America.* New York: New York Times Company.

Organ, D., & Ryan, K. (1995). A meta-analytic review of attitudinal and dispositional predictors of organizational citizenship behavior. *Personnel Psychology, 48,* 775–802.

Osterman, P. (1994). How common is workplace transformation and who adopts it? *Industrial and Labor Relations Review, 47,* 173–188.

Ostroff, C. (1992). The relationship between satisfaction, attitudes, and performance: An organizational level analysis. *Journal of Applied Psychology, 77,* 963–974.

Perrow, C. (1996). The bounded career and the demise of the civil society. In M. B. Arthur & D. M. Rousseau (Eds.), *The boundaryless career* (pp. 297–313). New York: Oxford University Press.

Pil, F. K., & Leana, C. R. (2000). Free agency versus high involvement approaches to skill development. In C. R. Leana & D. M. Rousseau (Eds.), *Relational wealth* (pp. 116–129). New York: Oxford University Press.

Pink, D. (2001). *Free agent nation.* New York: Warner Business Books.

Robinson, S. L. (1996). Trust and breach of the psychological contract. *Administrative Science Quarterly, 41,* 574–599.

Robinson, S. L., Kraatz, M. S., & Rousseau, D. (1994). Changing obligations and the psychological contract: A longitudinal study. *Academy of Management Journal, 37,* 137–152.

Robinson, S., & Rousseau, D. (1994). Violating the psychological contract: Not the exception but the norm. *Journal of Organizational Behavior, 15,* 245–259.

Rousseau, D. (1995). *Psychological contracts in organizations: Understanding written and unwritten agreements.* Thousand Oaks, CA: Sage.

Rynes, S. L., & Gerhart, B. (2000). *Compensation in organizations.* San Francisco: Jossey-Bass.

Seers, A. (1989). Team member exchange quality: A new concept for role-making research. *Organizational Behavior and Human Decision Processes, 43,* 118–135.

Seers, A., Petty, M., & Cashman, J. (1995). Team-member exchange under team and traditional management. *Group and Organization Management, 20,* 18–38.

Sennett, R. (1998). *The corrosion of character: The personal consequences of work in the new capitalism.* New York: Norton.

Sullivan, S. (1999). The changing nature of careers: A review and research agenda. *Journal of Management, 25,* 457–484.

Super, D. (1957). *Psychology of careers.* New York: HarperCollins.

Tsui, A., Pearce, J., Porter, L., & Tripoli, A. (1997). Alternative approaches to the employee-organizational relationship: Does investment in employees pay off? *Academy of Management Journal, 40,* 1089–1121.

Vroom, V. (1964). *Work and motivation.* New York: Wiley.

Whyte, W. H. (1956). *The organization man.* New York: Simon & Schuster.

CHAPTER 11

International Careers as Repositories of Knowledge
A New Look at Expatriation
Gregory K. Stephens, Allan Bird,
Mark E. Mendenhall

Expatriation as a major component of staffing in multinational corporations has received considerable attention over the past twenty years. In particular, that research has focused on expatriate adjustment (Black & Mendenhall, 1991; Church, 1982; Deshpande & Viswesvaran, 1992; Mendenhall & Oddou, 1985), cross-cultural training (Black & Mendenhall, 1990; Kealey & Protheroe, 1996), selection and recruitment of expatriates (Miller, 1973; Spreitzer, McCall, & Mahoney, 1997; Tung, 1982), and repatriation of expatriates (Black, Gregersen, & Mendenhall, 1992; Feldman & Tompson, 1993). Despite the significant increase in scholarly investigations on this topic, relatively few studies have systematically studied the expatriation from a career theory perspective.

Scholars have investigated some specific aspects of expatriate careers. For example, studies have explored repatriate attrition after global assignments have been completed (Adler, 1981), the initial effects of repatriation on careers of recently returned expatriates (Feldman & Thomas, 1992; Harvey, 1989), the relationships between expatriation and career success and achievement (Birds-

---

Grateful acknowledgment is given for financial support provided by the Charles Tandy American Enterprise Center at Texas Christian University.

eye & Hill, 1995; Feldman & Thomas, 1992) and repatriation adjustment (Gomez-Meija & Balkin, 1987), and the degree to which expatriate assignments aid in the development of skills that can enhance future career success (Oddou & Mendenhall, 1991).

Nonetheless, although expatriation is embedded in the overall career experience of many managers and professionals, relatively little research has integrated theoretical models of international management and careers scholars on the expatriate phenomenon. This chapter begins to usher in just such integration, with the hope that recent theoretical, conceptual, and definitional developments in the study of careers may be of help in delineating the phenomenon of expatriation.

While several career theories have been used to understand expatriation, this chapter uses the perspective of careers as repositories of knowledge as its main integrating mechanism (Bird, 1994). We discuss this perspective in detail and illustrate how it can help synthesize previous research on expatriation within a new framework and serve as a heuristic for guiding future research on expatriate careers.

Careers as Repositories of Knowledge

Within the varied social science disciplines of psychology, sociology, political science, economics, history, and geography, Arthur, Hall, and Lawrence (1989) identify eleven separate descriptions of what constitutes a career. Social psychologists define career as an "individually mediated response to outside role messages." By contrast, economists define it as a "response to market forces," and political scientists view careers as "the enactment of self interest" (Arthur et al., 1989, p. 10). Common to all of these perspectives, however, are characteristics of work experiences occurring over some span of time. In its broadest sense, then, a career is "the evolving sequence of a person's work experiences over time" (Arthur et al., 1989, p. 8).

Within these definitions, there is no clear agreement on the essential substance of a career. Differences in type, duration, length, and sequence of work experiences are viewed as important dependent and independent variables in studying careers. However, these are outward manifestations of external careers. A more comprehensive conception of careers must explicitly encompass internal careers as well, that is, the inflows, outflows, and transformations of individual and organizational knowledge that result from sequences of work experiences.

For our purposes, we will characterize careers as accumulations of information and knowledge (for example, skills, expertise, and relationship networks) acquired through an evolving sequence of work experiences over time. From this perspective, changes in work experiences constitute the primary mechanism by which careers develop, though they are not themselves careers. Rather, the nature or quality of a career is defined by its accumulated information and knowledge. Viewing careers as repositories of knowledge allows for the possibility that in addition to being accumulated, knowledge may also be removed, modified, shared, guarded, rearranged, improved, or replaced.

Syntax of Careers

The relationship between knowledge and work experiences can be illustrated by borrowing two concepts from grammar: syntax and semantics. Syntax refers to "the way in which words are put together to form phrases, clauses, or sentences" (Merriam-Webster, 1977, p. 1183), whereas semantics refers to meaning or content.

The syntactic aspect of a career is its structure. Just as sentences comprise words that can be classed as verbs, subjects, or objects, careers comprise work experiences that can be classed in terms of duration, sequence, or occupational type. Much of the research on careers focuses on measuring their syntax and the relationship of syntax to a variety of individual and organizational variables. A representative example of this approach can be found in Rosenbaum's study of careers (1984) of a cohort of workers in a single large organization. He analyzed roughly four thousand careers, indexing them in terms of such metrics as number of hierarchical levels advanced and length of stay at each level.

Semantics of Careers

The semantic aspect of careers, by contrast, considers the significance of work as reflected in accumulated knowledge. It is concerned with the content and meaning of work experiences.

Semantic aspects of careers are often idiosyncratic and have different meanings in different contexts. Just as the meaning of sentences, regardless of syntax, may change depending on context, careers, too, are inextricably embedded in context.

The contents of a career are located in what is learned from experiences—in the information, knowledge, and perspectives that are acquired or changed over time as a result of a series of work experiences. For example, two employees might both work for three years as tellers in the same bank. The syntactic aspects of their careers are similar: the same position, the same bank, the same length of time. In semantic terms, however, there may be substantial differences as a result of the specific relationship networks developed, skills acquired, and expertise accumulated.

Careers and Organizations as Knowledge Creators

The notion of careers as repositories of knowledge cannot be untangled from a view of organizations as knowledge creators (Argote & Ingram, 2000; Inkpen & Dinur, 1998) or from the notion that the substance from which knowledge is created is the experiences of individuals (Nonaka, 1991). Whether firms compete on the basis of cost, quality, or service, a firm's strategy is aimed at distinguishing its products or services from that of its competitors. A firm's ability to differentiate itself from others is embedded in an invisible asset: its knowledge base (Prahalad & Hamel, 1994) and, by extension, the individuals from whom the firm's knowledge base emerges (Nurasimha, 2000).

Increasingly, all advantages are becoming informational in nature. To remain competitive and to ensure an ongoing ability to differentiate, firms must develop their human resources in ways that enhance the supply of information and knowledge available to them. Through knowledge creation and transfer, firms revitalize themselves and set themselves apart from competitors (Argote & Ingram, 2000).

An important way in which organizations create knowledge is by shaping the firsthand work experiences of employees and then drawing out this experiential learning in ways that allow it to be shared throughout the organization and lead to the accomplishment of organizational objectives. Under this conceptualization, a key activity of managers is to give direction to the knowledge-generating activities of employees by creating meaning, that is, by making sense of seemingly senseless data (Louis, 1980; Weick, 1996).

Explicit Knowledge and Tacit Knowledge

Organizations and individuals transmit knowledge in two ways. Explicit, or articulable, knowledge can be transmitted to others through formal, systematic language (Polanyi, 1966). It is impersonal and independent of context. A mathematical equation, for example, is explicit knowledge because it conveys knowledge by means of an impersonal (it is not rooted in any person or situation), formal (there are rules governing the structure of equations), systematic language (mathematical symbols).

In contrast, tacit knowledge refers to information embedded in people's experiences that may be difficult to communicate to others. Tacit knowledge is necessarily personal because it is attained through firsthand experiences and is deeply rooted in action and commitment (Nonaka, 1991). It is accessible to its possessor primarily in the form of intuition, speculation, and feeling. Tacit knowledge is the sum of an individual's understanding as described by Polanyi (1966) when he states, "We know more than we can tell" (p. 4).

Two aspects of tacit knowledge are relevant to its application to careers. First, tacit knowledge has a cognitive dimension that is reflected in traditional beliefs, paradigms, schemata, or mental models (Nonaka, 1990). The cognitive dimension helps us to make sense of the world around us, influencing how we perceive and define it. The second aspect is the technical dimension, which consists of skills, crafts, and know-how that are situation-specific. Much of tacit knowledge, particularly the cognitive dimension, remains beyond our ability to make it explicit (Winogard & Flores, 1986).

Types of Knowledge Creation

The interplay between these two types of knowledge—tacit and explicit—gives rise to knowledge creation (Nonaka, 1990). There are four types of knowledge creation (see Figure 11.1).

Figure 11.1. Typology of the Knowledge Creation Process.

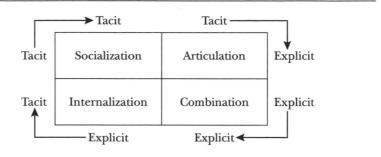

Source: Adapted from Nonaka, I. 1990. *Managing Innovation as a Knowledge Creation Process.* Paper presented at New York University, Stern School of Business, International Business Colloquium.

Tacit-to-Tacit Knowledge Creation

One form of knowledge creation involves the transmittal of tacit knowledge between individuals. An apprentice who studies under a master craftsman learns not only through spoken words or instructions, but through observation and imitation as well. Socialization of the apprentice leads to knowledge creation through the expansion of his or her knowledge; the newcomer imbues or modifies what is learned from agents of socialization through the filter of his or her own understanding. Notwithstanding this process, however, little new knowledge is created through socialization. To paraphrase Polanyi (1966), it remains as more than can be told. Furthermore, transmission of knowledge through socialization is time-consuming and difficult to manage among large numbers of people.

Explicit-to-Explicit Knowledge Creation

In contrast to its tacit counterpart, knowledge that is explicit in nature can be easily transmitted. Its very explicitness often makes combination transparent and easy. Consequently, we refer to bringing explicit knowledges together as combination. For example, collecting information about the financial performance of various overseas business units (explicit knowledge) brings about the creation of new knowledge: how the firm as a whole is performing in overseas markets (explicit knowledge).

Nevertheless, although combination can create new knowledge through synthesis, as with socialization (tacit-to-tacit knowledge creation), the new knowledge created tends to be minimal in its scope. The most profound knowledge creation occurs when knowledge spans tacit-to-explicit or explicit-to-tacit forms. It is also at this nexus individuals' careers and work experiences hold the potential to make their largest contribution to the organization.

Tacit-to-Explicit Knowledge Creation

The conversion of tacit knowledge to explicit knowledge—articulation—is significant for the organization because it makes possible the sharing of knowledge that was previously inaccessible. In a furniture company, when a master cabinetmaker is able to articulate the thinking and techniques behind his particular style of woodworking, that information can be widely disseminated within the organization. Designers can incorporate the newly created knowledge into future products. Also, the information can be shared with other cabinetmakers so that they can produce pieces of comparable workmanship.

Explicit-to-Tacit Knowledge Creation

When employees acquire explicit knowledge and then apply it to their own unique situations, the result is an expansion of their tacit knowledge base. Internalization leads to a reframing of knowledge that constitutes knowledge creation in its own right. Perhaps most important, the transference from explicit to tacit can lead to self-renewal of the employee and a deepening commitment to the work itself. In addition, self-renewal of individual employees, taken in larger groups, can constitute a self-renewal of the overall organization.

Tacit-to-tacit and explicit-to-tacit knowledge creation types appear similar in several ways. The difference between socialization and internalization in this typology lies in the primary informational source contributing to knowledge creation. In the tacit-to-tacit quadrant (socialization), the primary information source contributing to new knowledge creation is the master or the role model. New knowledge is created through replication, with the receiver's knowledge base contributing little to the newly created knowledge. By contrast, in the explicit-to-tacit quadrant, it is the receiver's knowledge base that contributes the bulk of information. Here, the explicit knowledge stimulates learning by obliging the receiver to see things in a different light or think in a different way—both forms of new knowledge.

Career Paths as Spirals of Knowledge Creation

The sequencing of knowledge creation modes may be thought of as defining a career path. Different experiences lead to shifts from one mode to another. Nonaka (1991) outlines the nature of experiences in each mode, as well as shifts across modes in his description of how a product development team at Matsushita Electric Company created a new home bread-making machine.

Although a prototype had been developed, the bread that the machine produced was considered unacceptable. The crust was hard and the inside doughy. One member of the development team, Ikuko Tanaka, suggested they study the technique of Osaka International Hotel's baker, who had a reputation for making the best bread in Osaka. While working as an apprentice with the baker, Tanaka noticed that the baker used a distinctive technique of stretching the dough when kneading it. Upon returning to the product development team, Tanaka shared her insights with coworkers. After making several modifications in the design of the bread maker, Matsushita developed the "twist dough" method and came out with a new machine that set a sales record for kitchen appliances.

As Nonaka (1991) suggests, the emergence of the solution to the problem involved all four types of knowledge creation:

1. Ikuko Tanaka learns the tacit secrets of the Osaka International Hotel baker (socialization).
2. She translates these secrets into explicit knowledge that she can communicate to her team members and others at Matsushita (articulation).
3. The team standardizes this knowledge, putting it together into a manual or workbook and embodying it in a product (combination).
4. Through the experience of creating a new product, Tanaka and her team members enrich their own tacit knowledge base (internalization). In particular, they come to understand in an

extremely intuitive way that products like home bread-making machines can provide genuine quality. That is, the machine must make bread that is as good as that of a professional baker.

The use of project team experiences as the basis for this illustration is noteworthy for several reasons. First, the sequencing of experiences is laid bare (Nonaka, 1994). Although individuals usually begin getting socialized when they enter a firm or move from one position to another, socialization intensifies when they join a project or work team. Rounds of dialogue and discussion among team members trigger the shift to an articulation mode. As concepts generated by the team are pieced together or joined with existing data, there is often a modal shift to the combination mode. Experimentation with various new combinations results in a change to the internalization mode, as members of the team engage in learning by doing that results in the translation of explicit knowledge into various types of tacit knowledge.

As individuals reiterate this sequence of work experiences, their store of knowledge grows. A career, then, can be understood as the path of an individual's work experiences through the various knowledge creation modes. The sequences of modes between the tacit and explicit forms of knowledge can be visualized as an outwardly expanding spiral.

Four Types of Knowing

Although the knowledge creation cycle provides a description of the trajectory that a career traces across work experiences, it fails to delineate the content of that career. In other words, realizing that work experiences involve progressing through cycles of knowledge creation still tells us very little about the types of knowledge embedded in the career. Kidd and Teramoto (1995) propose a four-class taxonomy of "knowings" that is useful in dissecting the knowledge content of a career.

Know who refers to a person's social capital, that is, the actual and potential resources embedded within, available through, and derived from the network of relationships an individual possesses. Examples of know who include such knowledge as having a contact in a Japanese bank willing to make introductions on one's behalf to local firms or being acquainted with key individuals in the

Hong Kong Trade Development Agency. Knowing who involves not only an acquaintanceship with others, but also an ability to draw on various resources through those relationships.

Know how relates to a person's set of skills and knowledge about how to accomplish tasks or do work. Methods for structuring invoicing schedules to offset the effects of hyperinflation in Russia represent one type of know how. Giving one's adversary some opportunity to save face in negotiations in China would be another.

Know what relates to the nature and extent of a person's understanding about specific projects, products, services, or organizational arrangements. A knowledge of the firm's product offerings in Brazil and an understanding of structure of the Brazilian subsidiary constitute types of know what.

Know why relates to the nature and extent of a person's identification with the firm's culture and strategy, for example, knowing why the firm chose to sct up an overseas operation in Brazil rather than Argentina. Knowing why gives meaning and purpose to organizational and individual action.

Through time, the volume and value of each type of knowing may increase or decrease. In addition, specific types of knowledge may be acquired, lost, and recovered. Figure 11.2 presents a prototypical depiction of an idealized career developing over time.

Figure 11.2. Four Types of Knowing over Time.

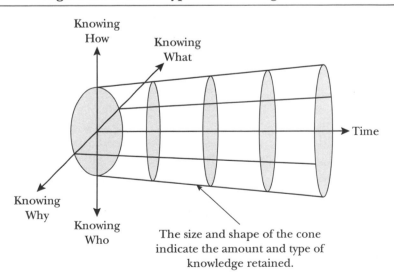

Knowing How

Knowing What

Time

Knowing Why

Knowing Who

The size and shape of the cone indicate the amount and type of knowledge retained.

Types of Knowing in International Contexts

Although the perspective of careers as repositories of knowledge offers significant value for the study of all careers, we believe it is particularly useful for enhancing our understanding of international
careers. A recurring theme of research on international careers has
been the dramatic impact that the wealth of new experiences, both
work and nonwork, has on people's understanding.

The essential element in knowledge creation is personal experience, the basis for all tacit knowledge. However, not all experiences contribute equally to knowledge creation. Those that are
repeated frequently, for example, filing expense reports, provide
little grist for new knowledge creation. Experiences likely to lead
to significant knowledge creation share three facets in common:
variety, quality, and self-knowledge (Nonaka, 1994). All three are
present in the experiences associated with international careers.

Variety of experience refers to the range of experiences acquired
over a period of time. International careers are striking in this regard because they are unlike most other work experiences. Working and living in a host country and traveling overseas present a
wide range of new experiences. There is often a mixture of customs,
norms, beliefs, and attitudes to be encountered across a vast array
of situations and circumstances. The new environment often has a
different climate, terrain, and weather. There are new foods and
beverages to sample. There may be a new language to learn. And
at the core of the experience, there is a new job with new colleagues
in a part of the company not previously experienced.

A consequence of these varied novel experiences is that the
quality of an overseas experience is richer and deeper than a
domestic job change. Expectations about anticipated outcomes,
which people carry into all experiences, are more likely to be un-
dermet or overmet in overseas assignments (Black, Mendenhall, &
Oddou, 1991), forcing expatriates to pay greater attention to the
international experience itself. Failures are likely to be more frequent (Mendenhall, 2001), causing people in international careers
to reevaluate assumptions. Individuals are also more likely to experience unexpected successes (Mendenhall, 2001), filling them
with surprise.

The heightened quality of overseas experience increases the
probability that individuals will develop greater *self-knowledge*. That

is, overseas assignments create more self-knowledge because they evoke stronger affective reactions than domestic assignments do (Mendenhall, 2001). Moreover, the challenge of adapting and adjusting within international careers is often intensely stressful, heightening the impact of emotions, positive or negative.

In short, international job changes can be characterized as rare occasions during which managers are likely to acquire extraordinary volumes of tacit-knowledge experience. This explains why international careers are often characterized as a transformative experience for many managers (Osland, 1995). They have no obvious comparison within a work career context and few comparisons outside. The profundity of such experiences—the extent of variety, the depth of quality, and the intense emotionality—may also help explain why careers researchers have had difficulty in coming to terms with how to study them.

Application to International Careers

When understood within the context of knowledge creation, international careers possess unique properties, with implications for career theory and research.

Syntactic and Semantic Issues

If international assignments (IAs) are to lead to significant knowledge creation beneficial to the firm, then human resource managers must address the syntactic and semantic dimensions of careers. Syntactic dimensions include duration, sequence, and structure.

For example, the duration of IAs tends to be arbitrarily established. Short-term assignments of nine months or less are usually based on the completion of a particular task or project. Long-term assignments often follow a standard length, three years being the typical tenure. These durations are set with little regard for the impact on knowledge acquisition or dissemination (Black, Gregersen, Mendenhall, & Stroh, 1999). Similar cultures, legal regulations, and a common language make it possible for a U.S. manager to learn how to get a new plant up and running in Australia quickly. By contrast, it may take that same manager considerable time to learn how to set up a similar plant in China.

The difference is not simply one of cultural distance, but involves the challenges of acquiring the right sorts of experiences through which useful new knowledge can be created. Whether a particular culture is characterized by high- or low-context communication preferences, for example, may influence whether the most effective knowledge creation methods will be tacit or explicit (Dulek & Fielden, 1991).

Chinese culture is high context; much of the communication essential to understanding what is going on is embedded in the situation rather than in explicit written documents or verbal exchanges (Hall, 1966). Consequently, U.S. managers working in China may need to acquire a substantial range of local experiences before they can make sense of what is going on around them. In other words, the most effective knowledge creation in the early stages of the assignment may take place through a tacit-to-tacit exchange—socialization—whereby a newly arriving manager might work closely with a local Chinese manager or an experienced expatriate. By contrast, U.S. managers in Australia may be able to create knowledge through a process of combination (explicit-to-explicit) in which they and their local counterparts share their understanding of plant set-up and management.

Sequence is also an issue when considering the use of IAs in developing global business leaders. Work by Gunz (1989) suggests that although many large organizations carry out career planning to identify logical sequencing of positions and promotions for managerial personnel, it is not clear that such planning factors into the knowledge creation process. An IA may be appropriate as the next step on a career path headed to the top of the organization, but may not be appropriate for moving a manager through the next phase of the knowledge creation cycle. For example, after eighteen months in a domestic department focused on mortgaged-based securities, one manager at a U.S. investment bank was transferred to Tokyo, where his new position was to oversee a Japanese securities trading operation. There was little, if any, room within the new assignment for internalization of knowledge he had acquired in the previous position.

This kind of disruption in the knowledge creation process also occurs when managers return from IAs (Gupta & Govindarajan, 1991; Black et al., 1999; Stroh, 1995). Adler (2002) notes that repatriates experience xenophobia from their colleagues and supervisors, who may fear or reject the foreign knowledge brought back by the former expatriate. Such reactions inhibit the transfer of knowledge from the repatriate.

It is often difficult for firms to gain a deep understanding of what expatriates have learned or to position the manager so that his or her IA experiences can be used effectively in new knowledge creation activities. In one typical instance, a manager returning from five years in Germany was placed in a holding pattern: a six-month temporary assignment assisting in the training of new employees in the United States. His superiors had no idea how to capitalize on his German experiences within the context of existing training programs, nor could he identify ways to apply his hard-won insights in this assignment. By the time he received a longer-term assignment working with African subsidiaries, his German know who, so critical to the knowledge base, had already begun to dissipate. Key contacts had moved or were no longer in a position to help him.

Finally, firms are only just beginning to recognize that the structure of IAs must be tied to knowledge growth for both the individual and the organization. There has been a long-standing appreciation that foreign work assignments are an opportunity for expatriates to acquire knowledge and skills that are rarely available in their home country (Tung, 1998) and that this personal growth can have a positive payoff for the firm as a whole (Oddou & Mendenhall, 1991). However, few firms consciously consider the knowledge creation process in making such assignments. For example, mentoring is widely recommended as a means of helping to train and counsel managers on IA (Feldman and Thomas, 1992). Focused mentoring can also be used effectively to help managers make sense of their IA experiences in terms of what they can contribute to the firm or accomplish within it (use of tacit-to-explicit to create know why and know what).

Ironically, although firms send managers on IAs to get experience and develop new insights, few firms seem to appreciate how successful they have been, often underestimating the growth in knowledge that managers experience in IAs. Returning managers report that their work takes on broader significance. Moreover, they have a changed perspective of their role within the firm and within the world, as well as a changed understanding of where the firm fits in the world.

Employee Transformation

Three aspects of the IA experience help to explain why managers undergo significant transformations. First, both short- and long-term assignments often result in a co-mingling of work and non-work experiences. When the IA involves moving a manager's family to a new location, the manager often becomes caught up in a host of nonwork experiences in the host country, which also lead to learning and insight about oneself, one's family, and the world in general. These insights inevitably extend to a changed view of the work setting. Even in the case of shorter assignments not requiring the relocation of family, extended absences or the need to develop social support systems in the host country often lead to a new perspective on work, the company, and larger life issues.

Second, IAs are often characterized by the compression of myriad novel and intense experiences into a short time span. Consequently, managers' repertoire of schema and scripts for dealing with a multitude of commonplace and not-so-commonplace events grows. One obvious example relates to the proper way to greet people in a business setting. Prior to an IA in Japan, a typical U.S. manager would employ a handshake as the common form of greeting and introduction. After working in Japan for several months or years, that same manager would return home with an expanded set of greetings and introductions that would include bows of various depths and rigidity, as well as handshakes of varying strength and duration.

Finally, IAs can also lead to significant losses of knowledge. Some friendships, acquaintances, and relationship networks wane; knowledge of some products and services or specific aspects of some organizational arrangements is forgotten, becomes outdated, or is no longer relevant. One's identification with the firm or its culture may ebb, and knowledge of certain techniques or the ability to use some skills may wither. IAs are not only a time of knowledge growth and development; they are also a time of loss.

Problems with Sharing Tacit Knowledge

The potential for organizational knowledge creation from international assignments is substantial. Unfortunately, finding ways to elicit individual managers' tacit knowledge is problematic. The conditions under which effective knowledge creation is most likely to occur are usually missing in the case of managers on, or returning from, IAs. Moreover, expatriates and repatriates themselves often do not possess enough self-awareness or knowledge sufficient to initiate organizational learning on their own.

Given the volume of tacit knowledge acquired on IAs, efforts at organizational knowledge creation can focus on two modes: socialization (tacit-to-tacit) and articulation (tacit-to-explicit). Socialization, requiring as it does the one-on-one participation of an apprentice, is costly, time-consuming, and, in the case of IAs, difficult to foster. Most socialization involves an understudy who observes and mimics a "master." This may be straightforward in the case of a cabinetmaker or a mechanic. However, it is hard to envision how one observes and mimics a master of IA. Effective socialization as a form of knowledge creation requires that the knowledge be observable through action or outcome, something that is virtually impossible to do with highly idiosyncratic IAs.

Articulation may not be much easier to facilitate. Nonaka (1994) suggests that the most effective vehicle for articulation involves dialogue in which participants enjoy a common frame of experience. Such interaction affords participants with occasions for explicit sense making in which one's understanding (knowledge) is made explicit through the stimulation that others provide (Weick, 1996). Dynamics of dialogue give rise to new understandings as participants react to one another's statements. Recall the bread-maker example in which Tanaka's insight is elicited through interaction with fellow team members.

The difficulties for organizations are fixing a location for this information sharing and assembling participants with the right set of shared experiences. To be useful, the knowledge must be created in ways that make it consistent with an organization's vision, mission, and strategy. However, in the case of IAs, the process of knowledge sharing cannot be easily controlled or shaped by the organization. Most IA managers engage in sense making and dialogue in local social groups in the host country. Alternatively, where there are sufficient numbers, IA managers may gather within the local subsidiary, but usually outside the office, in more social settings.

The conceptualization of new knowledge, then, is likely to be on a more personal level, connecting tacit knowledge to family and self, relating to work primarily in terms of career. Without the influence of the organization, and outside a peer group of fellow managers within the firm, there is little chance that tacit knowledge will be developed in ways that meaningfully contribute to organizational goals. Even when the articulation process elicits knowledge valuable to the firm, there is little possibility that it will be accessed, tested, applied, or retained by the firm because it was created externally.

One option for organizations is to bring IA managers together on a regular basis, through knowledge retreats or under the guise of training seminars. For example, one Japanese multinational corporation holds a regional semiannual gathering for its human resource managers in Europe. As part of this gathering, Japanese expatriates frequently congregate to talk among themselves. The result is new explicit knowledge. The current challenge, however, is for the company to find ways to codify and transfer this newly created and fleeting explicit knowledge to others.

Problems in Organizational Control of Knowledge Creation

Beyond the more basic structural challenges of shaping the tacit-to-explicit knowledge creation activities of IA managers are several additional challenges that face multinational corporations. Extended involvement with overseas subsidiaries and host country personnel may lead to a shifting of employee commitment to the local operation or the emergence of a dual commitment to both parent and subsidiary. A greater commitment to the host country subsidiary may lead to the development of knowledge that is overly localized. The old epithet, "He's gone native," may be appropriate for describing the direction of individual knowledge growth for the IA manager who has developed a strong allegiance to the host country operation. In such cases, there is often a perceived rift on the part of the IA manager—a belief that knowledge of the IA cannot be blended with organizational knowledge or systems.

On return from an IA, some repatriates may be less committed to the organization and more committed to their individual careers or personal lives and families. Repatriates may be unwilling to invest themselves in the organization's knowledge creation process or become disillusioned with efforts to transfer the knowledge they have obtained to others in the organization.

Even when the returning manager is committed and the organization can structure the repatriate position to facilitate knowledge creation to work in its favor, shifts in the types of knowing within the organization's and repatriate's repositories of knowledge may be too significant for effective transmission to take place. For example, a repatriate's broadened and more philosophical view of the firm's place in the world may create difficulties in his or her ability to see connections between tacit knowledge and organizational mission. Similarly, repatriates may find it difficult to use their expanded network of host country contacts effectively in new initiatives when the composition or reach their network of headquarters relationships and acquaintances has altered or diminished as a consequence of the IA experience (Burt, 1997; Ibarra, 1993).

In a related vein, some of the most personally compelling learning and knowledge acquisition on IAs may not be firm specific at all. Managers often acquire non-work-related living and coping skills when adjusting to a new country and culture. Such skills may lead to improved interpersonal effectiveness, enhanced self-confidence, and heightened self-awareness. Nevertheless, it may be difficult for repatriates to change how they are viewed by colleagues back at headquarters. Indeed, many repatriated managers, having undergone a transformational IA, confront difficulties in fitting back into the home country organization (Osland, 1995). If managers do not share a sense of community, they cannot effectively share the tacit knowledge they have acquired.

Exploiting the Knowledge Creation Potential in International Assignments

Viewing organizations as knowledge creators and careers as repositories of knowledge alters our perceptions of IAs and their value in developing global business leaders. The conventional wisdom has long been that IAs are invaluable in developing skills and knowledge essential to becoming an effective global manager. What has been missing is a framework for understanding why and how IAs contribute to management development. Career planning takes on a different character when it is directed at providing opportunities for acquiring the right sorts of experience and creating organizationally useful types of knowledge.

If firms are to capitalize on the experiences that managers acquire from IAs, they must take action in two areas. First, they must structure assignments to enhance the individual learning and growth that lead to tacit knowledge creation. Second, they must construct fields of interaction for IA managers in ways that will encourage conceptualization and crystallization of new knowledge of practical value to the firm. For actions in these two areas to be effective, firms must adopt a knowledge organization mind-set in which learning and the acquisition of new knowledge is valued as one of their central goals.

Enhancing Tacit Knowledge

Through thoughtful career planning and assignment management, firms can capitalize on the enhanced levels of tacit knowledge acquired by IA managers. Managing the expectations held by soon-to-be or current expatriates and repatriates is key to this goal (Feldman & Tompson, 1993; Stroh, Gregersen, & Black, 2000).

For example, predeparture briefings provide occasions during which clear learning expectations can be established. A typical briefing might encourage a manager to consider what aspects of past experience and current knowledge might be applicable in the new assignment—and even whether they should accept or reject the offer of a foreign work assignment at all (Stroh, Varma, & Valy-Durbin, 2000).

In planning and managing IAs, firms too often do not, but should, take a strategic approach to the variety in experiences that expatriate managers receive (Forster, 1999). As many as 40 percent of repatriated managers have reported that their firms have not taken advantage of the skills they had learned during their foreign work assignments (Oddou & Mendenhall, 1991). On a more positive note, a Japanese multinational corporation with which one of us has worked has used the occasion of short-term assignments of three to six months in the United Kingdom to provide its managers with additional learning opportunities by incorporating visits to affiliated subsidiaries on the Continent. Although such visits were not necessary for completing the assignment, Japanese managers were able to acquire additional insights into the company's worldwide operations that were useful in their positions back in Tokyo.

Firms may also want to incorporate additional tasks or projects specifically designed to foster the development of tacit knowledge in an IA. For example, an IA manager in a marketing position might be asked to write a sales prospectus to be used in the host country or design a seminar for host country nationals.

Sharing Tacit Knowledge

Having provided managers with fertile IA experiences, the next challenge for firms is in finding ways to help managers share their tacit knowledge, thereby creating new knowledge and simultaneously developing global business leaders. Firms can facilitate sharing in three ways.

First, they can construct heterogeneous project teams and managerial groups. Returning managers often complain of being isolated or being placed in work units where they have little in common with others. Sharing requires a frame of reference that is at least partially held in common among group members. When IA managers are placed in units where they alone have international experience (or those with international experience are in a small minority), sharing is constrained and the knowledge gained from IAs is either suppressed or dismissed. These situations parallel those associated with groupthink.

Not surprisingly, recommendations for overcoming groupthink may also enhance the IA knowledge creation and transfer process: ensuring full focus on areas of doubt and uncertainty, tenaciously challenging assumptions and presenting the fullest possible information, soliciting and receiving feedback and criticism regarding organizational members' judgments, and appointing group members (for example, former IA managers) to evaluate critically the popular ideas and sentiments of the group. Including IA managers in decision making and strategic planning groups can help maximize the knowledge creation process within the firm.

Sharing of tacit knowledge gained through IA experience can also be accomplished by establishing formal and informal reporting and briefing opportunities that focus explicitly on what has been learned. Most IA managers prepare reports on a regular basis about their progress on a particular project or assignment or on the performance of their units. However, it is unusual for them to report on what experiences they had, what they learned from those experiences, or how what was learned might be applied elsewhere in the organization.

Nonetheless, these learning reports are far more likely to lead to knowledge creation useful to the development of effective global leadership, for both the individual and the organization. In a related practice, some firms have returning managers give learning briefings for groups of colleagues and superiors. The briefings themselves and the accompanying question-and-answer sessions often lead to new insights for presenter and audience alike. IA managers' tacit knowledge can also be shared through systematic journaling made available to others in the organization, interviews with IA managers, preparation and dissemination of IA case studies, and simulations debriefed by IA managers.

A third step firms can take is enlisting returning IA managers in the preparation and subsequent mentoring of new IA managers. To the extent that IA managers' assignments overlap in time, the effectiveness of such mentoring may be enhanced. Aside from the benefits new managers can gain from this type of wisdom sharing, former managers themselves are often transformed as they internalize the very wisdom that they share.

An additional benefit of assigning returning IAs to work with new IAs is that it encourages the creation of informal networks for sharing IA tacit knowledge. Although not always formally supported, informal networks of IA managers develop naturally within most global firms. By bringing together new and returning IA managers, firms can support informal group formation, thereby expanding and influencing the fields in which knowledge is shared and created.

Implications for Future Research

In addressing a variety of implications that derive from taking a perspective of careers as repositories of knowledge, we begin by returning to a long-standing dichotomy in the careers literature: the distinction between objective careers and subjective careers. From there we proceed to a consideration of the current gaps in our understanding of international careers, specifically addressing the potential for this new framework to fill those gaps and possibly uncover others not previously considered.

The False Dichotomy of Objective Versus Subjective Careers

The distinction between objective and subjective conceptions of careers surfaced early in the field's history (Hall, 1966; Stephens, 1994). The objective conception focused on outwardly, independently measurable aspects of a career—for example, positions held, tenure in positions, or frequency of promotion. By contrast, the subjective conception directed attention to how people perceived their work experiences over time. The concern was not with tracing work experiences through positions held within an organization, but rather on how people adopt new and different orientations to existing work roles—that is, how they make sense of their work experience (Stephens, 1994). These two approaches have often been seen as relatively distinct from one another, due in part to the fact that researchers in the two streams were interested in answering very different questions and adopted very different methodologies.

Adopting the perspective of careers as repositories of knowledge does not eliminate the validity or the value of considering objective and subjective aspects of an individual's career. Instead, it illuminates the interconnectedness of these two perspectives by uncovering the impact that individual perception and sense making have on the essential element that constitutes a career: the knowledge that is created, transformed, or lost due to specific career experiences. The subjective understanding of one's career necessarily has an effect on knowing why.

Theoretical Issues and Gaps

The integrating theme of this book is a developmental perspective on careers, and our view of a career as a repository of knowledge sheds new light on this perspective. It has important implications for how career development activities geared to international job changers themselves (like selection, training, socialization, and mentoring) are implemented and evaluated. Additional theoretical work is needed, however, to help us understand the antecedents, processes, and outcomes of knowledge creation in IAs. Related research domains, such as social learning theory, information technology, and knowledge systems management, have much to say regarding careers as repositories of knowledge. Certainly, we have raised more questions than answers, but they are questions that we believe are critical for understanding how to use more effectively (or avoid misusing) international job changers.

Much of the current research on international careers has focused on issues of adjustment (and, to a lesser extent, expatriate performance) both during and after the international assignment. Future work addressing issues of knowledge creation and transfer might fruitfully consider the other side of the coin:

- The extent to which expatriate and repatriate assignments entail development of new skills and how those skills can be codified and transferred to create new organizational knowledge
- How organizational knowledge systems should be structured and managed to foster knowledge creation and transfer
- Differences in stages of knowledge creation in the overseas assignment—that is, whether knowledge creation is best accomplished at preassignment, during assignment, or postassignment
- How cultural differences (especially behavioral and assumptive differences) between knowledge holders and knowledge receivers influence knowledge creation and transfer
- How knowledge codification may influence the success or adjustment of expatriates and those with whom they work
- The extent to which different types of international job changers (expatriates and repatriates) experience knowledge assimilation, creation, and transfer in different ways
- How different characteristics of international assignments affect the knowledge creation and transfer process (for example, assignment length, hierarchical level of the assignee, job characteristics, experience of the expatriate)
- How the tacit knowledge of the returning or experienced expatriate is best accessed, codified, transferred, and used
- The role of nonexpatriate international experiences in knowledge creation (for example, bringing foreign country nationals to the home country headquarters)

- The "lost" expatriate—that is, the expatriate who has co-opted and gone native or left the firm altogether

In particular, we know little about the differential effects of sequencing work experiences in international careers. This raises two future research questions in particular. The first involves the impact of sequencing in terms of work experiences leading up to and following international assignments. Although there is some writing in this area, it focuses mainly on adjustment issues rather than on knowledge flows. For example, do certain prework experiences improve or impede an individual's ability to create new knowledge in the area of know who?

The second involves the sequencing of work experiences within the international assignments. Again, there is some literature that focuses on adjustment, and to a lesser extent performance, but an examination of the literature reveals little focus on the sequencing of work experiences in international careers as it relates to knowledge creation or transfer. Work on the transformational nature of international assignments (Osland, 2001) is one notable exception, but much remains to be accomplished in this area. In particular, we believe that examinations of differences between international and noninternational careers in terms of how people make sense of their careers—that is, subjective careers—would be a beneficial area of research.

In this postindustrial age, where the knowledge work paradigm is becoming increasingly preeminent, the ability to create and transfer critical knowledge resources is likely to distinguish competitive from uncompetitive organizations (Bennis, 1999). Ensuring that organizational visits and international job changes alike take advantage of new knowledge gained overseas will be a critical element in the success or failure of today's global corporations.

References

Adler, N. J. (1981). Re-entry: Managing cross-cultural transitions. *Group and Organization Studies, 6,* 341–356.

Adler, N. J. (2002). *International dimensions of organizational behavior* (4th ed.). Cincinnati, OH: South-Western.

Argote, L., & Ingram, P. (2000). Knowledge transfer: A basis for competitive advantage in firms. *Organizational Behavior and Human Decision Processes, 82,* 150–169.

Arthur, M. B., Hall, D. T., & Lawrence, B. S. (1989). *Handbook of career theory.* Cambridge: Cambridge University Press.

Bennis, W. (1999). The leadership advantage. *Leader to Leader, 12,* 18–23.

Bird, A. (1994). Careers as repositories of knowledge: A new perspective on boundaryless careers. *Journal of Organizational Behavior, 15,* 325–344.

Birdseye, M., & Hill, J. S. (1995). Individual, organizational/work and environmental influences on expatriate turnover tendencies: An empirical study. *Journal of International Business Studies, 26,* 787–813.

Black, J. S., Gregersen, H. B., & Mendenhall, M. E. (1992). Toward a theoretical framework of repatriation adjustment. *Journal of International Business Studies, 23,* 737–760.

Black, J. S., Gregersen, H. B., Mendenhall, M. E., & Stroh, L. (1999). *Globalizing people through international assignments.* Reading, MA: Addison-Wesley.

Black, J. S., & Mendenhall, M. E. (1990). Cross-cultural training effectiveness: A review and a theoretical framework for future research. *Academy of Management Review, 15,* 113–136.

Black, J. S., & Mendenhall, M. E. (1991). The U-curve adjustment hypothesis revisited: A review and theoretical framework. *Journal of International Business Studies, 22,* 225–247.

Black, J. S., Mendenhall, M. E., & Oddou, G. (1991). Toward a comprehensive model of international adjustment: An integration of multiple theoretical perspectives. *Academy of Management Review, 16,* 291–317.

Burt, R. S. (1997). The contingent value of social capital. *Administrative Science Quarterly, 42,* 339–365.

Church, A. T. (1982). Sojourner adjustment. *Psychological Bulletin, 91,* 540–572.

Deshpande, S. P., & Viswesvaran, C. (1992). Is cross-cultural training of expatriate managers effective: A meta analysis. *International Journal of Intercultural Relations, 16,* 295–310.

Dulek, R. E., & Fielden, J. S. (1991). International communication: An executive primer. *Business Horizons, 34,* 20–29.

Feldman, D. C., & Thomas, D. C. (1992). Career management issues facing expatriates. *Journal of International Business Studies, 24,* 507–529.

Feldman, D. C., & Tompson, H. B. (1993). Expatriation, repatriation, and domestic geographical relocation: An empirical investigation of adjustment to new job assignments. *Journal of International Business Studies, 24,* 507–530.

Forster, N. (1999). Another "glass ceiling"? The experiences of women professionals and managers on international assignments. *Gender, Work and Organization, 6*(2), 79–90.

Gomez-Meija, L., & Balkin, D. (1987). The determinants of managerial satisfaction with the expatriation and repatriation process. *Journal of Management Development, 6,* 7–17.

Gunz, H. (1989). The dual meaning of managerial careers. *Journal of Management Studies, 26,* 225–250.

Gupta, A., & Govindarajan, V. (1991). Knowledge flows and the structure of control within multinational corporations. *Academy of Management Review, 16,* 768–792.

Hall, E. T. (1966). *The hidden dimension.* New York: Doubleday.

Harvey, M. C. (1989). Repatriation of corporate executives: An empirical study. *Journal of International Business Studies, 20,* 131–144.

Ibarra, H. (1993). Network centrality, power, and innovation involvement: Determinants of technical and administrative roles. *Academy of Management Journal, 36,* 471–501.

Inkpen, A. C., & Dinur, A. (1998). Knowledge management processes and international joint ventures. *Organization Science, 9,* 454–468.

Kealey, D. J., & Protheroe, D. R. (1996). The effectiveness of cross-cultural training for expatriates: An assessment of the literature on the issue. *International Journal of Intercultural Relations, 20,* 141–165.

Kidd, J. B., & Teramoto, Y. (1995). The learning organization: The case of the Japanese RHQs in Europe. *Management International Review, 35*(2, Special issue), 39–56.

Louis, M. R. (1980). Surprise and sense making: What newcomers experience in entering unfamiliar organizational settings. *Administrative Science Quarterly, 25,* 226–251.

Mendenhall, M. E. (2001, Mar. 15). *Global assignments, global leaders: Leveraging global assignments as leadership development programs.* Paper presented at the Research Colloquium on Expatriate Management, Cranfield Business School, Cranfield, U.K.

Mendenhall, M. E., & Oddou, G. R. (1985). The dimensions of expatriate acculturation: A review. *Academy of Management Review, 10,* 39–47.

Merriam-Webster. (1977). *Webster's new collegiate dictionary.* Springfield, MA: Merriam.

Miller, E. L. (1973). The international selection decision: A study of some dimensions of managerial behavior in the selection decision process. *Academy of Management Journal, 16,* 239–252.

Nonaka, I. (1990). *Managing innovation as a knowledge-creation process: A new model for a knowledge-creating organization.* Paper presented at New York University, Stern School of Business, International Business Colloquium, New York.

Nonaka, I. (1991). The knowledge-creating company. *Harvard Business Review, 69*(6), 96–104.

Nonaka, I. (1994). A dynamic theory of organizational knowledge creation. *Organization Science, 5,* 14–37.

Nurasimha, S. (2000). Organizational knowledge, human resource management, and sustained competitive advantage: Toward a framework. *Competitiveness Review, 10,* 123–135.

Oddou, G., & Mendenhall, M. E. (1991). Succession planning in the 21st century: How well are we grooming our future business leaders? *Business Horizons, 34,* 26–34.

Osland, J. S. (1995). *The adventure of working abroad.* San Francisco: Jossey-Bass.

Osland, J. S. (2001). The quest for transformation: The process of global leadership development. In M. E. Mendenhall, T. Kuhlmann, & G. Stahl (Eds.), *Developing global business leaders: Policies, processes and innovations* (pp. 137–158). Westport, CT: Quorum Books.

Polanyi, M. (1966). *The tacit dimension.* London: Routledge & Kegan Paul.

Prahalad, C. K., & Hamel, G. (1994). Strategy as a field of study: Why search for a new paradigm? *Strategic Management Journal, 15,* 5–16.

Rosenbaum, J. E. (1984). *Career mobility in a corporate hierarchy.* Orlando, FL: Academic Press.

Spreitzer, G. M., McCall, M. W., Jr., & Mahoney, J. D. (1997). Early identification of international executive potential. *Journal of Applied Psychology, 82,* 6–29.

Stephens, G. K. (1994). Crossing internal career boundaries: The state of research on subjective career transitions. *Journal of Management, 20,* 479–501.

Stroh, L. K. (1995). Predicting turnover among repatriates: Can organizations affect retention rates? *International Journal of Human Resource Management, 6,* 443–456.

Stroh, L. K., Gregersen, H. B., & Black, J. S. (2000). Triumphs and tragedies: Expectations and commitments upon repatriation. *Journal of Human Resource Management, 11,* 681–697.

Stroh, L. K., Varma, A., & Valy-Durbin, S. (2000). Why are women left at home: Are they unwilling to go on international assignments? *Journal of World Business, 35,* 241–255.

Tung, R. L. (1982). Selection and training procedures of US, European and Japanese multinationals. *California Management Review, 25,* 57–71.

Tung, R. L. (1998). American expatriates abroad: From neophytes to cosmopolitans. *Journal of World Business, 33,* 125–144.

Weick, K. (1996). *Sensemaking in organizations.* Thousand Oaks, CA: Sage.

Winogard, T., & Flores, F. (1986). *Understanding computers and cognition.* Reading, MA: Addison-Wesley.

PART 4

Directions for Industrial/ Organizational Practice and Research

Organizational Assistance in Career Development

Manuel London

In general, organizations support career development to ensure that employees, managers, and senior executives are ready to meet immediate business needs and are prepared for future challenges. Moreover, organizations support career development because it contributes to organizational learning: the firm's capability to respond to changing technological, economic, and competitive forces.

Firms vary in their approach to career development, depending on organizational competitive strategies and environmental forces (such as competition) that affect the need for employees with different types of skills and experiences. For example, the organization's structure and processes impose demands for certain individual competencies. Flexible multinational organizations, for instance, require adaptable, self-managing, collaborative employees who value diversity. Similarly, the external labor market in which the organization operates influences the importance of employee training and development—for example, whether to hire or develop employees with required skills and what resources to put into continuous learning for older employees.

Career development programs can be classified into those that focus on organizational, individual, and interpersonal processes. Organizational processes link career development to broader performance management programs. A comprehensive, integrated system of selection, development, performance appraisal, and rewards may be based on a common set of competencies relevant to a particular group, such as managers. Individual processes include exploring career options, making decisions about one's career, overcoming barriers, and adapting to transitions. Individual-level career exploration entails self-assessment of strengths and weaknesses, career values, interests, goals, and getting input from counselors, coworkers, friends, and family members (Colquitt, LePine, & Noe, 2000). Interpersonal processes include mentoring, counseling, coaching by the supervisor or an external coach, and role modeling.

Career development programs established by the organization vary in intensity, the extent to which employees are required to participate, the integration of multiple career development activities, the extent to which career development activities are self-controlled, the commitment required, and the time horizon for their impact (Hall, 1987). The greater the organizational need and belief in the importance of the career development program and the greater the employees' need for the program, the more likely it is that the program will be beneficial to the organization and its employees alike. Such programs are likely to produce more positive outcomes for both individual employees (career satisfaction, productivity, preparedness for new opportunities, continuous learning) and organizations (talented people in the organization ready to assume positions as they arise, individual learning that contributes to organizational learning, and high performance).

This chapter explores the organizational conditions that drive career opportunities and development experiences for employees. It considers individual characteristics affecting needs for organizational assistance, reviews career development programs appropriate for various organizational conditions and individual characteristics, and offers a model and propositions to predict the evolution and effects of career development programs.

Organizational Trends Influencing Career Development

Ideally, career development programs balance organizational needs with individuals' desires for career stability and opportunities (Schmidt, 1994). However, the downsizing, mergers, and attention to productivity and quality improvement between 1985 and 1995 caused some organizations to emphasize organizational concerns over individual goals. Downsizing and mergers meant employee dislocations. Many employees lost their jobs, and others faced opportunities that were more limited than they anticipated. Employees recognized that a thirty-year career with the same organization was becoming an anachronism and that they needed to take responsibility for their own careers.

The Need for Self-Directed, Continuous Learning

Self-directed career development and organizational support for continuous learning became strong during the 1990s as changing business conditions resulted from rapidly emerging technologies, global competition, and a strong economy. The focus of career development shifted from training and promotion for young people to a recognition that development is continuously needed for everyone regardless of age and career stage. New organizational approaches included making use of day-to-day assignments to encourage learning through novel experiences, helping people recognize developmental activities and opportunities, communicating organizational strategies and skill requirements, and providing tools for self-assessment and development planning like feedback and coaching (Schmidt, 1994).

Today, employees face unfamiliar pressures resulting from new technology, intense e-commerce competition, and new organizational forms, such as flexible organizational structures and global business ventures. Advancing technologies affect the way work is done and how people communicate and interact with each other using virtual networks, e-mail, videoconferencing, and wireless telephone to manage geographically dispersed teams and manage remote employees in virtual offices (Sullivan, 1999). This environment requires continuous expansion of knowledge and abilities.

Discontinuous, Boundaryless Careers

The notion of a career has changed from a traditional sequence of positions in a single large organization, with success defined in terms of movement to higher levels of responsibility in the organizational hierarchy, to a protean career with diverse disciplines, functions, and even industries (Hall & Moss, 1998). Careers across multiple firms and boundaries are discontinuous and boundaryless (Arthur & Rousseau, 1996). They require portable skills, knowledge, and abilities. Individuals need to be motivated to learn, aware of the skills and knowledge they acquire while working on an assignment, able to develop multiple networks and peer learning relationships, and willing to take responsibility for their own careers (Sullivan, 1999).

Learning is critical for people who move quickly across multiple boundaries within and between firms. Organizations need to accelerate socialization of newcomers and develop career opportunities for short-term, contract, and temporary employees. In the process, organizations need to avoid discrimination in availability of, and support for, career development. For instance, women and minorities outside the formal organizational structure may have trouble finding sponsors and networks to give them career advice (Sullivan, 1999).

Learning Organizations

Another organizational trend affecting support for career development is the concept of learning organizations: companies that are capable of adapting to changes in the external environment by practicing continuous renewal of their structures and processes. In contrast to large, centralized bureaucracies, learning paradigm companies have small, flexible divisions and decentralized control structures (Lei, Slocum, & Pitts, 1999). They have integrated communications systems designed to share and transfer knowledge and make decisions.

Moreover, much of the major work in learning organizations is accomplished by using cross-functional teams. Cross-division transfers break down narrow thinking that can be a barrier to cooperation. This is important for general managers and technical specialists alike, helping them recognize divisional priorities and customer requirements. In contrast to traditional organizations, the learning organization encourages individual learning, risk-taking behaviors, and growth for members of all groups.

A concept related to the learning organization is the J-form (Japanese-style) organization, that is, one that integrates the efficiency and stability of a bureaucracy with flexibility and team dynamics (Nonaka & Takeuchi, 1995). This is an organic, non-hierarchical system melded together by a strong corporate culture reinforced by embedded shared values. The J-form organization is adaptive and innovative with a capacity to accumulate tacit knowledge (Lam, 2000). Being exposed to diverse challenges in multiple settings increases employees' flexibility.

Feedback Systems

Feedback is integral to performance improvement and career development. It is the basis for setting development and performance goals and evaluating progress. Learning organizations use performance information as part of ongoing experimentation and innovation (Wishart, Elam, & Robey, 1996).

London and Smither (in press) define a feedback organizational culture in terms of the organization's support for feedback, including providing nonthreatening and behaviorally oriented feedback, coaching to help interpret and use feedback to set performance goals, and rewards for performance improvement. They then outline three types of organizational interventions that contribute to a feedback culture: (1) processes that enhance the quality of feedback, such as rater training and clear performance dimensions; (2) policies that communicate the importance of ratings and feedback in the organization, such as top executives' involvement in the process; and (3) help in using feedback, such as coaching and the availability of courses on the competencies and performance dimensions measured by the feedback.

A feedback, learning-oriented organizational culture and the attendant support for career development are driven by the changing nature of organizations. Internal and external pressures determine the importance of human resources to the organization and the extent to which the organization wants to help employees develop and learn. Employees, too, need to understand and be receptive to their roles as self-developers.

Individual Characteristics and Trends Influencing the Use of Career Resources

Organizational support for career development cannot ignore individual differences in motivation to participate in developmental activities. Recognizing key individual differences, organizations provide support that enables employee development and increases employees' desire for development. Here, I consider employees' motivation for training and development, expansive personality characteristics, and the tendency to be a continuous learner as prime individual characteristics influencing the use of career resources.

Motivation for Training and Development

Career motivation is a function of insight, direction, and persistence (London, 1985). Career insight is the spark that ignites motivation. It is awareness of one's strengths and weaknesses, needs and interests, and recognition of career opportunities. A concept related to career insight is feedback orientation—an individual's overall receptivity to feedback, including comfort with feedback, desire for feedback, tendency to seek feedback, and the use of feedback to increase performance over time (London & Smither, in press). Feedback orientation is also influenced by the organization's support for feedback. As the feedback culture becomes stronger, individuals seek and receive feedback more often, deal with it mindfully, and use it to calibrate and adjust their behavior to improve performance.

Career identity is the direction of motivation. It centers on one's career goals, such as the desire to lead, be a functional expert, or achieve balance in work and family life. It is the structure of meanings to which people link their own motivation, interests, and competencies with acceptable career roles.

Career resilience is the persistence component of motivation. It is a function of one's self-efficacy, internal control, willingness to take reasonable risks, and need for personal and professional growth. It is the readiness to maintain motivation even in the face of career transitions and barriers to one's career goals. Individual characteristics related to resilience are career maturity (Super, 1980) and hardiness (Kobasa, Maddi, & Kahn, 1982). While managers influence employees' career insight and identity by providing feedback, they influence employees' career resilience by providing rewards, such as recognition, financial bonuses, and chances for promotion.

In confronting career barriers such as job loss, individuals with strong insight, identity, and resilience are able to appraise the situation, determine possible actions and likely outcomes, evaluate resources, and set goals. The stronger the individual's career motivation is, the more likely the individual will adopt proactive, realistic coping strategies, including seeking needed support (Leana & Feldman, 1992).

Expansiveness

People with expansive personalities show continued growth of their dedication, learning, and involvement in technological discovery and enterprise development. Expansive individuals have high ability, energy, and ambition (Kaplan, Drath, & Kofodimos, 1991). They want to achieve, are willing to take risks, and have a sense of what they can accomplish (Shaver & Scott, 1991). They are driven and passionate, self-regulated, and naturally proactive (Deci & Ryan, 1991; Kaplan ct al., 1991). Expansiveness is especially important in today's e-commerce organizations, in which the pressures and rewards of technological development seem to be greater and open to more people than ever before.

Continuous Learners

Fast-paced organizational changes require people who can take advantage of organizational resources for continuous learning. The organizational changes already described, particularly the emergence of the learning organization, suggest the value of an empowering work environment—one that provides informational feedback, offers choices with clear consequences, recognizes the problems facing employees, and provides reasons to act (London & Smither, 1999b).

Career-related continuous learning (CRCL) is a deliberate and sustained effort to learn and a readiness and desire to acquire new knowledge and skills. It is understanding one's own capabilities, being sensitive to those of others, engaging in activities that foster learning, and applying increased knowledge and skills toward performance improvement. Continuous learners recognize the need for CRCL, acquire new skills and knowledge as needed, and apply their learning in organizational settings on a regular basis (London & Smither, 1999a).

In summary, individuals vary in their motivation to participate in career development. Organizations, though, can design career development programs that enhance the likelihood that various kinds of employees will take advantage of opportunities for learning and advancement.

Career Development Programs and Processes

As a prelude to articulating a model of how organizational and individual factors influence investment in career development programs, this section examines examples of organizational, individual, and interpersonal career development processes. The programs selected for review here are prominent in organizations today because they most directly address the trends already described.

From an organizational standpoint, the first element of career development is identifying competencies that the organization needs. These competencies become the foundation for measuring employees' strengths and weaknesses, assessing development gaps, providing feedback, making training available, and establishing directions for long-term career development. Assessment of competencies often entails the use of self-paced, Internet-based career planning tools and 360-degree feedback surveys.

Competency Identification and Assessment

The design of career development programs to prepare people for specific organizational needs begins with an identification of competencies required for success. Competencies are individual characteristics that cause effective job performance (Briscoe & Hall, 1999). Employees use information about competencies as a guide for their own self-assessment and development, and organizations use competencies as a guide for assessment and development methods that support career growth in line with organizational ambitions. The competencies become a common language in the organization for communicating and discussing performance expectations, accomplishments, and directions for improvement and growth.

There are several approaches to competency development: (1) research-based (studying high-performance managers), (2) strategy-based (asking top executives to describe current and future strategies and their implications for needed competencies), (3) values-based (identifying values in the organization, perhaps those expounded by the chief executive officer or norms prevalent in the organization), and (4) a combination of the three (Briscoe & Hall, 1999).

The research approach is grounded in employees' actual behaviors but may miss behaviors that could have been even more successful but were not exhibited. Also, it does not address future career development needs. The strategic approach focuses on organizational transformation in the light of predicted or desired future attributes. However, this view of the future may not ultimately emerge, creating both substantial sunk costs and opportunity costs. Competencies identified in this way are based on speculation rather than actual behavior. The values approach has strong motivating power and focus but may lead to misguided competencies or attention to a few values over all others. In addition, a single value can be interpreted differently by different people, and values are difficult to translate into behaviors.

Overall, two competencies are needed for successful continuous learning. First, employees need adaptability (for example, flexibility, exploration, openness to new ideas and diverse people). Second, employees need to formulate their career identity (for example, seeking feedback, engaging in a variety of personal development activities, and being willing to modify self-perceptions as one's abilities and roles change) (Briscoe & Hall,1999).

Succession Planning and Pools

Succession planning is the process of periodically reviewing managers' potential for advancement and slotting several managers as possibilities to fill each executive position. This process would typically be conducted annually by a human resource department executive working with the CEO and other top officials. In many organizations, however, this process has limited value, as shifting job requirements make job rotation and promotion from within less viable as the sole source of executive talent. Organizations seek to hire new blood at all levels as business conditions change. Also, managers increasingly are willing to change employers because they recognize that the days of secure thirty-year careers and structured career paths are gone.

Given the dynamic nature of organizational positions and structures, organizations often establish high-potential management development programs (London & Stumpf, 1982). Byham (2000, p. 30) calls these "acceleration pools." Rather than pinpointing one or more managers for particular executive positions in a succession planning process, the organization selects a pool of talented managers who receive the experiences they need to advance to higher levels of responsibility. Often, the focus is on preparing generalists—people who can take over high-level jobs regardless of the specific function or business unit.

A company may have several pools at different organizational levels for different regions of the world or different functional areas. For instance, there may be a pool of early career managers. The number of people in the pool is targeted to the number of mid-level managers projected to be needed in five years or so and the retention and advancement rates of talented managers in the program (that is, their likelihood of staying in the company). Selection criteria are based on the current and anticipated future leadership competencies required by the business. The projection of competencies and numbers of managers needed in the future is derived from interviews with top executives.

A principal vehicle for development of acceleration pool participants is on-the-job training. Program participants are rotated into a new assignment every six to eighteen months to learn the business. They are assigned to key projects as a means of testing their abilities, expanding their knowledge, and exposing them to higher-level managers. They attend organizational events and conferences during which they hear from top executives as they discuss business strategies. They are sent to special leadership training programs and are often assigned to mentors—higher-level managers, possibly in other departments—who meet with them periodically to discuss their progress and give them task advice and social support. Also, they may be assigned to external coaches, who help them understand business problems, analyze performance feedback, and establish development plans.

In some companies, the names of managers in the pool are confidential. Even the participants may not know they are in the pool, except, of course, that they are likely to recognize the greater range of opportunities available to them. Secrecy is intended to prevent the self-fulfilling prophecy that those in the program will succeed if nothing untoward happens. In other cases, the names of participants are known. Participants are evaluated annually on their performance and developmental progress. In companies that use up-or-out programs, those who do not do well are asked to leave the company altogether. Alternatively, they may be offered a functional specialist position, which may still have advancement opportunities but at a slower pace. Those who stay in the program advance further on a fast track.

Action Learning Methods

Individuals learn as they perform their jobs. Indeed, on-the-job experiences can produce more learning than classroom training. Such experiences include temporary assignments (projects and task forces), major increases in responsibilities, moving from line to staff (or vice versa), establishing a start-up operation, and fixing a failing operation (Baird, Holland, & Deacon, 1999). Called action learning, this training is low cost and of high benefit to the individual and organization.

An example of action learning might be leading a multicultural, geographically dispersed team or working on a special assignment abroad. Action learning is all the more valuable because the tacit knowledge required on the job has a personal quality that is hard to communicate and cannot be taught in brief off-site training programs. Tacit knowledge is intuitive and unarticulated and can be gained only through practical experience in the situation—that is, learning by doing and reflecting on what was learned (Nonaka, 1994).

A variety of techniques can be used to enhance the value of on-the-job learning (Seibert, 1999). Coached reflection is the process of providing employees with structured questions and one-hour reflection sessions to think about their experiences and their value for self-development. Reflection-in-action is teaching employees to reflect on their actions while confronting challenging experiences so that the reflection can still make a difference (a technique originally developed by Schön, 1983). Conditions that promote reflection-in-action include job autonomy, performance feedback, and having supervisors, peers, mentors, or friends who can provide emotional support for learning. It also helps to have brief periods away from work, too (Seibert, 1999).

Internet-Based Delivery of Self-Managed Career Resources

Numerous Internet-based career services are available for free, often through university and corporate career centers. These can be useful for finding a job, posting a resumé, networking, and discovering information about careers. These Web sites provide job search tips, relocation information, articles about careers, self-assessment inventories with instant scoring and score interpretation, salary ranges, cost-of-living indicators, company benefits and conditions, and even on-line career counseling (usually for a fee).

An interesting example is the Talent Alliance, an Internet-based resource cosponsored by member companies and available only to employees in those firms. This alliance lets a company purchase high-quality resources that provide support for self-initiated, self-paced career exploration. Web pages on career coaching explain the value of coaching, ways to identify competent coaches, and how to be a career coach to others. Personal inventory tools prompt self-discovery of leadership style, motivation, technical skills, and work context.

Some modules in the Web site present information and ideas. Others are interactive, requiring input like self-assessments. Still others provide forms for career planning and guidelines for holding discussions about career planning with one's supervisor or subordinates. An informal learning module helps employees understand how to learn from their daily experiences. A personal development module allows employees to design their own feedback survey, select the items, list colleagues to complete the survey, and send the survey by e-mail. The computer automatically scores the results and prepares a feedback report. Other modules focus on options for changing jobs or careers, methods for networking, balancing careers with personal lives, and surviving organizational change (mergers, restructuring, and downsizing).

Multisource Feedback Surveys

Multisource feedback surveys, also referred to as 360-degree feedback, have become a popular tool to support job and career development, especially for managers and executives (London,

1997). They ask managers' subordinates, peers, supervisors, customers, and often the managers themselves, for performance ratings on a series of items reflecting competencies that are important to the organization. The popularity of this technique stems from the organizational philosophy that individuals need to take responsibility for their own development while the organization provides the enabling resources. The assumption is that managers need feedback in order to guide their behavior for performance improvement and development. Multisource feedback recognizes that the complexity of managers' jobs requires input from diverse perspectives, and managers' supervisors cannot be expected to have direct knowledge of each constituency with whom their subordinates interact.

Multisource feedback should be viewed not as a stand-alone, one-time tool, but as part of an ongoing performance management and career development process (London & Tornow, 1998). People tend to shy away from giving and receiving feedback, whether the feedback is positive or negative. For this reason, items on 360-degree or upward feedback surveys focus on behaviors rather than personality characteristics (DeNisi & Kluger, 2000). The resulting reports provide specific, nonthreatening feedback that can be translated into goals for development.

Research on multisource ratings has shown that while self-ratings tend to be inflated, there is reasonably high interrater agreement among peer, subordinate, and supervisor ratings (Harris & Schaubroeck, 1988). Other research has shown that 360-degree feedback is correlated with external measures of performance and improvements in performance over time (Martineau, 1998; Walker & Smither, 1999).

Coaching

The focus of this executive development tool varies in complexity. Coaches can address some simple issues, such as helping the executive-manager assess staff needs and set priorities. Somewhat more difficult issues coaches assist in are establishing action plans for career development and adapting to new jobs. Even more complex or sensitive issues coaches advise on are improving interpersonal relationships with teams and peers, enhancing one's appearance and personal style, and improving relationships with one's boss and senior managers (Hall, Otazo, & Hollenbeck, 1999).

The underlying assumption is that coaching encourages self-knowledge, which in turn helps those who are being coached to recognize the effect they have on others and the need to vary their behavior to meet situational demands. Coaching is potentially valuable because it is customized to the manager's needs, sensitive to the manager's time, and not more expensive than attending off-site, generic leadership development programs.

There are several stages in the coaching process (Smither & Reilly, 2001). The first is establishing the coaching relationship, which includes clarifying expectations and roles (for example, the manager agrees to prepare for the coaching sessions and do follow-up work). The second is assessing the manager's job situation by reviewing feedback data (for instance, results of a 360-degree feedback survey, information gathered by the coach in meetings with the manager's colleagues, and immediate business challenges that need to be addressed). The third stage is establishing plans for development and behavior changes consistent with those development goals. The fourth is tracking progress on plans. The coach may meet with the manager two or more times during the first month. This may continue for one or two more months as a plan of action is established and implemented. The coach may follow up with telephone calls periodically.

Coaches are usually external consultants who were trained in counseling or were executives themselves. They may also be internal to the organization—either organizational development or human resource experts or executives who are expected to coach their subordinate managers. Making coaching part of executives' and managers' roles is a way to cascade the benefits of coaching down through the organizational hierarchy.

Mentoring

Professionals with multiple sources of mentors have higher levels of career success and feelings of career satisfaction than those with a single mentor or no mentor at all (Peluchette & Jeanquart, 2000). Moreover, professionals use different sources of mentors at different career stages.

Formal assigned mentoring programs can be catalysts for ensuring that some mentoring occurs. Such programs are especially useful for minorities or others who need more support early in their career. Mentors can be sources of psychosocial support, information and guidance, and role modeling (Kram, 1985) and can contribute to higher work satisfaction (Higgins, 2000).

Career Counseling

Career counseling is a method to increase psychological well-being, decrease stress, and help overcome career barriers (Young & Chen, 1999). Most organizations do not provide this type of professional help. Often, employees must go outside the organization, and sometimes they turn to clinicians or outplacement counselors in private practice. Many supervisors do not have the skills, motivation, or personality to be effective career counselors or coaches to their subordinates.

Furthermore, employees may have issues they would prefer not to discuss with their boss, such as career moves to competing firms and performance problems. Indeed, the boss may be part of the problem. Career counselors, particularly outplacement counselors, can help increase employees' self-efficacy and cope with career barriers (Albert & Luzzo, 1999). For example, they can help clients distinguish between barriers that can be controlled and those that cannot. Counselors can also assist clients in focusing on solutions rather than placing blame, help clients consider possible career barriers before they arise, and discover some new directions for career renewal (Bejian & Salomone, 1995).

Toward a Model of Organizational Support for Career Development

An important question facing researchers is how human resource requirements in the organization, in conjunction with individual competencies and motivation, drive the types and nature of the organization's support for career development. This section fleshes out the relationships that predict the type and degree of support that organizations provide for career development. Figure 12.1 provides a model for predicting the type and degree of support

Figure 12.1. Factors Predicting Organizational Support for and Employee Involvement in Career Development.

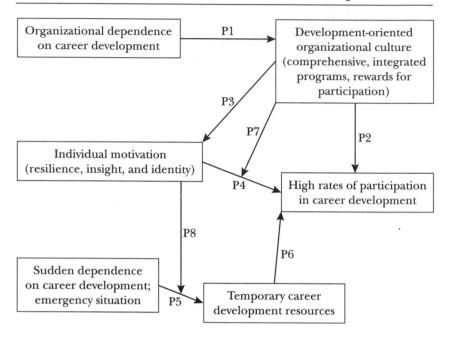

that organizations will provide for career development. In this section, I also provide testable propositions (labeled P1 through P8) to guide research along these lines.

The first variable to consider here is the dependence on having employees who are ready to contribute to complex and changing organizational strategies. As Proposition 1 suggests, the more the organization requires employees who understand the business and its strategies and have the skills needed to meet changing business conditions (such as a rapid shift from domestic to multinational production and marketing), the more the organization will focus on human resource programs that emphasize career development. To do so, it will develop career programs that are comprehensive (cover assessment, goal setting, training, performance appraisal, and career planning) and integrated (based on a common set of competencies) in nature.

Such career programs clarify needed competencies and identify pools of high-potential employees at different career stages, functions, and levels. These programs also provide comprehensive assessment, feedback, training, and job movement options. The participants learn the importance of continuous learning to meet long-term business demands, and they internalize this philosophy of career development in guiding their own subordinates.

Proposition 1: The more organizations depend on human resource development as a strategic advantage, the more likely they will: establish career development programs that are organization-wide, comprehensive, and integrated; closely guide individuals' participation in development and track their progress; focus on long-term outcomes (having the people who will meet anticipated future competency requirements); and reward continuous learning.

Organizations that invest in continuous learning, career development, and meeting long-term goals can become flexible learning organizations in the process. The members of these organizations understand the value of development. As Proposition 2 suggests, a development-oriented culture increases employees' participation in jobs and special assignments that have a critical role in establishing new organizational strategies. Career policies and practices of continuous learning organizations attract recruits who have the motivation to develop and reinforce this proclivity in current employees. Development-oriented corporations may also be more successful in developing employees' career motivation (Proposition 3) and in getting those people involved in career development (Proposition 4).

Proposition 2: The more developmentally oriented the organizational culture is, the more that employees at all career stages are likely to participate in career development and learn in the process of working (action learning).

Proposition 3: The more developmentally oriented the organizational culture is, the more employees will receive positive reinforcement for learning and accomplishment (contributing to their career resilience), feedback about their performance (contributing to their career insight), and information about career opportunities that fit their abilities and interests (contributing to their career identity).

Proposition 4: Individuals who have high career motivation are likely to use career programs that are self-initiated and self-paced, seek feedback for performance improvement and development through available resources, and participate actively in their own career development.

Individuals' work situations may change their attitudes toward career development, particularly in the short run. Rapid organizational changes may mean that paths to advancement are new, unclear, and uncertain. Job security may be undermined as organizations shift directions and discover needs for people with different skills. As Proposition 5 suggests, organizations in this situation may establish rapid action programs (such as outplacement counseling) to address these immediate needs. As Proposition 6 suggests, these programs, in the long term, are likely to provoke individuals into greater awareness of the need for self-development and a stronger motivation to participate in the organization's career development programs.

Proposition 5: Sudden needs arising from a crisis, such as an actual or impending downsizing, lead organizations to establish emergency action career programs for immediate use; examples are outplacement career counseling and training in new functional areas.

Proposition 6: Emergency career programs increase employees' short-term involvement in development activities and may stimulate ongoing career development.

Organizational and individual variables may interact to affect the rate of participation in long- and short-term career development activities. Organizational requirements for development (because of long-term goals or immediate business needs) may or may not match the value that individuals place on development because of personal characteristics that were ingrained before the individual was hired, because of needs and interests that were developed while working in the organization, or because of the sudden realization of need prompted by recent events. Propositions 7 and 8 suggest that employees with high career motivation are especially likely to participate in career development programs whether these career development programs are temporary or ongoing.

Proposition 7: Individuals who are high in career motivation are more likely to participate in developmental activities when the organizational culture is developmentally oriented.

Proposition 8: Organizations that experience a sudden dependence on human resource development are more likely to provide temporary career development resources to individuals with high levels of career motivation.

Conclusion

The model and propositions presented here assume that career development will lead to positive individual and organizational outcomes. This assumption begs the question of whether career programs are effective in accomplishing what the organization intends. In terms of individual outcomes, do the programs affect employees' career satisfaction, productivity, readiness for new opportunities, and motivation for continuous learning? In terms of organization outcomes, does the organization develop a coterie of talented people who are ready to assume critical positions? Does individual learning contribute to organizational learning (for instance, work groups that are able to work collaboratively)?

Answering these questions poses a variety of challenges for action research: establishing reliable measures that tap meaningful outcomes, identifying the unique effects of various development initiatives (for example, the effects of 360-degree feedback supported by coaching and counseling), and measuring changes in attitudes as performance standards and expectations change over time. For example, regression models are needed to examine the additive and configural effects of organizational conditions, individual characteristics, and program dynamics on key career development outcomes.

The proposed model can be used to design career program content and form to meet the organization's goals and employees' expectations. Human resource practitioners can ask questions such as the following: What is the press for human resource development? Do existing career programs support the competencies that top executives and individual experts feel that the organization will need in the future? Do existing career programs need to be linked together better than they are? Are the career programs too structured relative to the need for organizational flexibility? Should the organization be more aggressive in establishing a cohort of managers to meet future leadership needs? Are employees learning as they engage in new activities, such as adopting new technologies, working in multifunctional teams, and communicating across cultures? Should the organization expect, train, and reward supervisors to be coaches and mentors to their subordinates? Basic research addressing these questions can inform how organizations diagnose career development needs, implement career interventions, and assess the effectiveness of their efforts in this area.

References

Albert, K. A., & Luzzo, D. A. (1999). The role of perceived barriers in career development: A social cognitive perspective. *Journal of Counseling and Development, 77,* 431–441.

Arthur, M. B., & Rousseau, D. M. (1996). The boundaryless career as a new employment principle (pp. 3–20). In M. G. Arthur & D. M. Rousseau (Eds.), *The boundaryless career.* New York: Oxford University Press.

Baird, L., Holland, P., & Deacon, S. (1999). Learning from action: Embedding more learning into the performance fast enough to make a difference. *Organizational Dynamics, 27,* 19–32.

Bejian, D. V., & Salomone, P. R. (1995). Understanding midlife career renewal: Implications for counseling. *Career Development Quarterly, 44,* 52–63.

Briscoe, J. P., & Hall, D. T. (1999). Grooming and picking leaders using competency frameworks: Do they work? *Organizational Dynamics, 27*(3), 37–52.

Byham, W. C. (2000). How to create a reservoir of ready-made leaders. *Training and Development Magazine, 54*(3), 29–33.

Colquitt, J. A., LePine, J. A., & Noe, R. A. (2000). Toward an integrative theory of training motivation: A meta-analytic path analysis of 20 years of research. *Journal of Applied Psychology, 85,* 678–707.

Deci, E. L., & Ryan, R. M. (1991). A motivational approach to self: Integration in personality. In R. Dienstbier (Ed.), *Nebraska Symposium on Motivation: Perspectives in Motivation* (Vol. 38, pp. 237–288). Lincoln: University of Nebraska Press.

DeNisi, A. S., & Kluger, A. N. (2000). Feedback effectiveness: Can 360-degree appraisals be improved? *Academy of Management Executive, 14*(1), 129–139.

Hall, D. T. (1987). *Career development in organizations.* San Francisco: Jossey-Bass.

Hall, D. T., & Moss, J. (1998). The new protean career contract: Helping organizations and employees adapt. *Organizational Dynamics, 26*(3), 22–37.

Hall, D. T., Otazo, K. L., & Hollenbeck, G. P. (1999). Behind closed doors: What really happens in executive coaching. *Organizational Dynamics, 27*(3), 39–53.

Harris, M., & Schaubroeck, J. (1988). A meta-analysis of self-supervisor, self-peer, and peer-supervisor ratings. *Personnel Psychology, 41,* 43–61.

Higgins, M. C. (2000). The more the merrier? Multiple developmental relationships and work satisfaction. *Journal of Management Development, 19,* 277–296.

Kaplan, R. E., Drath, W. H., & Kofodimos, J. R. (1991). *Beyond ambition: How driven managers can lead better and live better.* San Francisco: Jossey-Bass.

Kobasa, S. C., Maddi, S. R., & Kahn, S. (1982). Hardiness and health: A prospective study. *Journal of Personality and Social Psychology, 42,* 168–177.

Kram, K. E. (1985). Improving the mentoring process. *Training and Development Journal, 39*(4), 40–43.

Lam, A. (2000). Tacit knowledge, organizational learning and societal institutions: An integrated framework. *Organization Studies, 21,* 487–513.

Leana, C. R., & Feldman, D. C. (1992). *Coping with job loss: How individuals, organizations, and communities respond to layoffs.* San Francisco: New Lexington Press.

Lei, D., Slocum, J. W., & Pitts, R. A. (1999). Designing organizations for competitive advantage: The power of unlearning and learning. *Organizational Dynamics, 27*(3), 24–38.

London, M. (1985). *Developing managers: Preparing and motivating people for successful managerial careers.* San Francisco: Jossey-Bass.

London, M. (1997). *Job feedback: Giving, seeking, and using feedback for performance improvement.* Mahwah, NJ: Erlbaum.

London, M., & Smither, J. W. (1999a). Career-related continuous learning: Defining the construct and mapping the process. In G. R. Ferris (Ed.), *Research in Human Resources Management, 17,* 81–121.

London, M., & Smither, J. W. (1999b). Empowered self-development and continuous learning. *Journal of Human Resource Management, 38,* 3–16.

London, M., & Smither, J. W. (in press). Feedback orientation, feedback culture, and the longitudinal performance management process. *Human Resource Management Review.*

London, M., & Stumpf, S. A. (1982). *Developing managers.* Reading, MA: Addison-Wesley.

London, M., & Tornow, W. W. (1998). 360-degree feedback—More than a tool! In W. W. Tornow & M. London (Eds.), *Maximizing the value of 360-degree feedback: A process for successful individual and organizational development* (pp. 1–8). San Francisco: Jossey-Bass.

Martineau, J. W. (1998). Using 360-degree surveys to assess change. In W. W. Tornow & M. London (Eds.), *Maximizing the value of 360-degree feedback: A process for successful individual and organizational development* (pp. 217–248). San Francisco: Jossey-Bass.

Nonaka, I. (1994). A dynamic theory of organizational knowledge creation. *Organization Science, 5,* 14–37.

Nonaka, I., & Takeuchi, H. (1995). *The knowledge creating company.* New York: Oxford University Press.

Peluchette, J.V.E., & Jeanquar, S. (2000). Professionals' use of different mentor sources at various career stages: Implications for career success. *Journal of Social Psychology, 40,* 549–564.

Schmidt, S. (1994). The new focus for career development programs in business and industry. *Journal of Employment Counseling, 31*(1), 22–28.

Schön, D. (1983). *The reflective practitioner.* New York: Basic Books.

Seibert, K. W. (1999). Tools for cultivating on-the-job learning conditions. *Organizational Dynamics, 27*(3), 54–65.

Shaver, K. G., & Scott, L. R. (1991). Person, progress, choice: The psychology of new venture creation. *Entrepreneurship Theory and Practice, 16*(2), 16–20.

Smither, J. W., & Reilly, S. P. (2001). Coaching in organizations. In M. London (Ed.), *How people evaluate others in organizations* (pp. 221–252). Mahwah, NJ: Erlbaum.

Sullivan, S. E. (1999). The changing nature of careers: A review and research agenda. *Journal of Management, 25,* 457–484.

Super, D. E. (1980). A life-span, life-space approach to career development. *Journal of Vocational Behavior, 16,* 282–298.

Walker, A. G., & Smither, J. W. (1999). A five-year study of upward feedback: What managers do with their results matters. *Personnel Psychology, 52,* 393–423.

Wishart, N. A., Elam, J. J., & Robey, D. (1996). Redrawing the portrait of a learning organization: Inside Knight-Ridder, Inc. *Academy of Management Executives, 10,* 7–20.

Young, R. A., & Chen, C. P. (1999). Annual review: Practice and research in career counseling and development—1998. *Career Development Quarterly, 48*(2), 98–141.

CHAPTER 13

Advancing Research on Work Careers

A Developmental Perspective on Theory Building and Empirical Research

Daniel C. Feldman

For a variety of reasons, practitioner advice on career development has often outstripped empirical research on the topic; the self-assured convictions of career mavens have far outpaced the consistency and magnitude of empirical findings. First and foremost, there are millions of dollars to be made from purveying career advice in best-selling books. Second, as the authors of the chapters in this book have highlighted, there is considerable career anxiety about "swimming with the sharks" among all segments of the population. Young adults are having trouble finding the right path to start out on, while older adults are having trouble adjusting to a world of increased downsizing and decreased job security (Feldman, 1999b). Third, we live in a time in which prolonged self-analysis and self-examination are widely promoted in our culture. The existential "finding oneself" of the 1960s has transmuted itself into "finding one's market niche" in this decade.

Each of the chapter authors in this book has sought to sift fact from fiction and empirical truth from mere assertion about some portion of the literature on career development. In this final chapter, we explore directions for future theory building and empirical research using a developmental perspective. The chapter integrates the ideas and findings presented by the chapter authors and sets out an agenda for future explorations of work careers—an agenda that will be useful to academics and practitioners alike.

Building Theory

There are two slippery slopes that researchers face as they try to advance their understanding of work careers. On one hand, theoretical frameworks and constructs may be so broad that it is nearly impossible to frame testable (and refutable) hypotheses. On the other hand, career theories can become so population specific or context specific that research efforts become balkanized. If academics are separately researching careers of women, blacks, the disabled, doctors, and M.B.A.s, independently examining careers in the manufacturing, health care, government, and service sectors, and focusing on the idiosyncrasies of careers in Japan, Mexico, Australia, Singapore, Nigeria, and Poland, we will end up with a gumbo of noncomparable, nongeneralizable findings.

In *Social Theory and Social Structure,* Merton (1968) advocates the increased use of middle-range theories as a way to advance social science. Such theories "lie between the minor but necessary working hypotheses that evolve in abundance during day-to-day research and the all-inclusive systematic efforts to develop a unified theory that will explain all the observed uniformities of social behavior, social organization, and social change" (1968, p. 39). Although Merton does not give a comprehensive list of criteria on which to classify theories as middle range, his writings make salient four key characteristics of such theories:

1. Middle-range theories involve abstract concepts.
2. These abstractions are close enough to observable data so that empirical testing of propositions may occur; middle-range theories involve more than just organized descriptive data or empirical generalizations.
3. Middle-range theories involve sets of confirmed hypotheses; the hypotheses must not be logically disparate or unconnected.
4. Middle-range theories cut across micro- and macrolevels of analysis and have some implications for practice.

Given the diverging paths in theory building in careers research—the emergence of very broad theoretical constructs like boundaryless organizations on one hand, very micro-oriented studies of specific populations (like career challenges facing Hong Kong bank managers) on the other hand—some move to the middle might make sense for the careers research area (Feldman, 1980). Merton suggests that middle-range theories will ultimately evolve into a broader and more useful scientific base, building on "the strategic importance of a graded series of empirically confirmed theories" (1968, p. 58). Based on the findings and conclusions of the chapter authors in this book, we consider six ways in which theory development in the area of career development might be rebalanced to head toward the middle.

Within-Person Versus Within-Context Change

Career scholars have looked at change from a variety of perspectives. Some seminal research has looked at within-individual change over time; for example, the work of Levinson (1978), Valliant (1977), and Gould (1978) examines how individuals' career needs and values change over the course of a lifetime. Other researchers have looked at within-career-path changes over time. For instance, several researchers have examined individuals' decisions to switch careers, organizations, and jobs (Dalton & Todor, 1993; Whitener & Waltz, 1993) or how managers have changed the ways in which they plan their careers in occupations with decreasing job security and fewer opportunities for promotions (Leana & Feldman, 1992). Still other researchers have looked at changes in the context in which careers unfold over time; studies of boundaryless organizations exemplify this approach to career development (Arthur & Rousseau, 1996). Yet another group of authors has focused on changes in career behaviors and attitudes across generations. The work of Brooks (2001), for instance, investigates how changing values among members of Generation X and Generation D (that is, the digital generation) have altered the ways careers are perceived and managed in different cohorts.

In terms of both bulk and influence, most of the recent research on careers has focused on changes in career paths and organizational contexts over time. As Leana and London point out in their chapters (Chapters Ten and Twelve, respectively), careers researchers have paid a great deal of attention to how the breakdown in the traditional employment contract has altered the ways in which individuals and organizations manage careers. By way of contrast, developmental changes within individuals and changes across generations have received considerably less attention. Simply the logistics of following individuals across time, never mind following large cohorts across time, is a monumental undertaking. For scholars like Levinson, Gould, and Valliant, such undertakings were literally a life's work.

Nonetheless, to advance career theory from a developmental perspective, much more research tracking individuals longitudinally is needed. While undertaking large-scale panel studies across the entire life span might be career suicide, more middle-range theories of within-individual change are certainly possible. In Chapter Five, on the school-to-work transition, for instance, Elizabeth Wolfe Morrison highlights ways in which shorter-term changes in early career development can be studied over time. Similarly, in Chapter Eight on late-career issues, Terry Beehr and Nathan Bowling highlight some ways in which the transitions from full-time work to bridge employment to full-time retirement can be studied longitudinally. As Chapter Seven by Sterns and Subich on midcareer issues highlights, it is also possible that archival data on family background, educational experiences, and work history could be used to understand the impact of early life events on subsequent career behaviors.

Thus, while studying changes across the entire life span might not be feasible, studying changes during significant career transitions that occur in shorter time periods is an important and realistic goal. Such an approach would also allow us to examine within-person changes across a broad array of occupations, organizational contexts, and cultures—and in so doing, move us toward more consistent and generalizable findings.

Change Versus Stability

As the chapter authors make clear, each career stage presents its own special incentives and barriers to change. Moreover, as

Stephens, Mendenhall, and Bird point out in Chapter Eleven, many changes in context (for example, moving overseas for an expatriate assignment) force individuals to develop in new and different ways.

The research on change not withstanding, though, there is more stability in career preferences than might otherwise be expected. As Bradley, Brief, and George point out in Chapter Two, basic personality traits and vocational interests are formed relatively early in life and remain quite stable, at their core, across the life span. For all the talk of mobility, the 2000 Census reports that 80 percent of Americans are still living in the same state in which they were born.

This suggests, then, that much more research is needed on why people do *not* change careers, organizations, and jobs over time even when it would be rational for them to do so. Certainly, money plays a major role; people will not quit their jobs if there are no alternative jobs available (Dalton & Todor, 1993; Whitener & Waltz, 1993). However, even when money is not a major concern, many individuals perseverate in career paths that they intellectually know are no longer appropriate for them and from which they no longer derive much pleasure.

With the exception of some research on image theory and postdecision dissonance (Bobocel & Meyer, 1994; Dunegan, 1993), most researchers have largely ignored why people do not redirect their careers even in the wake of major within-individual (for example, declining health) and within-context (for example, declining job security) changes. Why do so many people stay the course despite numerous opportunities to leave and virtually no barriers to exit? Despite all the rhetoric about "packing your own parachute," why do so many people still go down with the plane? Is it the degree of difficulty associated with acquiring new skills, as Ostroff, Shin, and Feinberg might suggest in Chapter Three? Are there personality traits (such as low openness to new experience) that hamper not only the ability to change but also the ability to perceive opportunities for change, as Bradley, Brief, and George suggest? These questions about stability are as critical to our understanding of career development as are questions about change itself.

Career Interests Versus Work Skills

Perhaps no other topic has dominated the careers literature as much as the development of career interests and their role in shaping important career decisions. The voluminous literature on early career development suggests that career interests are a major predictor of which occupations individuals gravitate toward, how much they like those occupations, and how long they remain in those vocations (Holland, 1985). Although the issue has not yet been fully tested, it is likely that these career interests subsequently feed into, and help form, career anchors as well (Schein, 1990). That is, individuals with social personal orientations may be more likely to develop managerial career anchors, while individuals with investigative personal orientations may be more likely to develop technical-functional career anchors (Feldman & Bolino, 1997).

By way of contrast, skills have been relatively understudied in the formation and development of careers. As both Morrison and Ostroff, Shin, and Feinberg highlight in their chapters, much more research has been conducted on person-environment fit in terms of career interests than of work skills. Yet the research presented in this book suggests that lack of skills may be the most important impediment to individuals getting out of declining occupations and organizations. Moreover, continuous learning may be the most important predictor of ability to get promoted, get hired by other firms, and receive other significant career rewards (see Chapter Twelve). If, in fact, individuals need to be more adaptable and flexible to survive in boundaryless careers and organizations, then that adaptability and flexibility has to go beyond simple attitudes. It has to include the learning and retention of additional skills, too.

There are several directions for future research in the area of skill development that could be productive. First, we know surprisingly little about the emergence of skills in children and adolescents. Most of the research in this area has investigated how parents and schools reinforce (or extinguish) early interests in various pursuits, but we know much less about how those initial skills and abilities develop. Second, how do individuals learn that they need to learn more? That is, what energizes individuals to monitor the environment carefully for the need to increase skills—and what motivates them to overcome inertia to do so? Third, to what extent does early career counseling geared to identifying vocational interests ("likes and dislikes") desensitize individuals to the importance of skills in subsequent career decisions? Fourth, as Werner suggests in Chapter Nine, how can federal and state governments create incentives for organizations to invest in workers and for workers to invest in themselves? As important as the role of career interests may be, perhaps it is time that more attention is paid to the role of work skills as well.

Career Stages Versus Life Stages

Over the years, the careers literature has produced multiple models of career stages that help explain how careers unfold across time. Illustrative of these kinds of models is the one presented by Dalton and his colleagues (Dalton, 1989; Dalton, Thompson, & Price, 1977). It suggests that there are four stages of career development, ranging from the apprentice stage to the sponsor stage. Each stage has its own set of psychological demands (for example, dependence or independence), and each has its own set of work demands (for example, the ability to perform routine, detailed work or the ability to think strategically). Although the empirical evidence demonstrating that these stages are separate, distinct, and nonoverlapping is mixed, the evidence that there are major differences between individuals at various career stages is stronger (Feldman, 1988).

From a developmental perspective, perhaps the most important direction for future research is the link between career stages and life stages. While proponents of these stage models argue that career stages are not age related per se, empirical testing of these models has been scant. Moreover, the restriction of range problem in this research area is significant; for example, the average age of professionals in each of Dalton's four stages (Dalton, 1989) fell within a narrow range. Perhaps most critical, it is important to discover to what extent the differences in stages are due to the unfolding of careers themselves (apprentice versus colleague responsibilities) or due to the aging process. For example, is the desire to mentor tied to being midcareer or middle-aged?

Although the interplay of career stages and life stages is frequently discussed, it is much less frequently researched. One place where the differential impact of career stages and life stages on personal development might be more easily seen is in cases where the career stage is out of sync with the typical life stage with which it is associated. For example, how do adults who graduate from college at age thirty experience the school-to-work transition? How do prodigies who get through school very young and get promoted very quickly deal with being a mentor for individuals older than themselves? It may be through empirically examining these out-of-sync cases that we can better understand the independent effects of career stages and life stages and the interplay among them.

Work Life Versus Family Life

It has almost become axiomatic that individuals' careers are inextricably linked with events in their personal lives. With the increase in females' labor force participation rates, more and more couples are having to balance their career needs with those of their partners. Moreover, it is clear that there is spillover from the work setting to the home setting, and vice versa. Problems on the home front decrease individuals' abilities to absorb or tolerate as much stress at work; problems at work decrease individuals' abilities to absorb or tolerate as much stress at home (Doby & Caplan, 1995; Stephens & Feldman, 1997; Thomas & Ganster, 1995).

While these general spillover effects have been well documented, the pattern of results on family status in many areas of careers research is often inconsistent. When looking at the amount of variance that variables like marital status and minor children account for in career decisions, frequently the results are insignificant or weak in magnitude (see Powell & Butterfield, 1994, and Williams & Alliger, 1994, for some reviews of this literature).

One major possibility is that we are not capturing the complexities of non-nuclear families; fewer than 50 percent of children in the United States live with both their biological parents. Thus, simple dichotomies between married couples and single individuals (or between those who have minor children in the household and those who do not) may not capture the diversity of family relationships today. Family responsibilities now include a much broader array of relationships: stepparenting; adult children still living at home; gay and lesbian couples; nonmarried couples living together in committed relationships; custodial responsibilities for nieces, nephews, and grandchildren; elder care responsibilities; and joint custody arrangements. Thus, it is not only careers and organizations that have become boundaryless; families have become more boundaryless, too.

An interesting approach to understanding the interplay of work and family dynamics has been suggested by Eby, Allen, and Douthitt (1999) in their work on family power theory. They propose that power over career decisions in the family unit derives from the percentage of income that one partner in a relationship generates relative to the other. In other words, it is not simply the raw amount of money earned that influences career decision making; rather, it is the relative amount of money earned that matters. This approach of relative power could also be expanded to understand such other constraints (or freeing factors) as size of the extended family, attachment and involvement in family affairs, and level of commitment to the career itself on career decisions (Ayree, 1999).

Another important avenue for future research along these lines has been suggested by the work of Hochschild (1997, 1989). Hochschild persuasively argues that more and more managers and professional workers are now working fifty to sixty hours per week. As noted above, the traditional approach to this development has been to examine the adverse spillover effects of work overload on quality of family relationships. Hochschild turns that argument on its head and argues that the complexity of family relationships and the ensuing conflicts they entail entice workers to put in even more hours at work. Indeed, in many cases, employees perceive working with colleagues as a source of support and enjoyment and participating in family activities as work.

As we try to gain a deeper understanding of career development, we need to move away from simply considering the effects of family dynamics on career decisions and career investments. Instead, we need to consider the ways in which the boundaries between work lives and outside lives are blurring and how work, in some cases, may be providing the psychological support that decaying, stressful families have failed to do.

Immediate Versus Distal Influences on Career Behaviors

As the chapters in this book make clear, there are major external forces (such as the robustness of the economy or societal values) that influence how individuals feel about their jobs and plan for their careers. While the ultimate impact of these distal forces has been heavily documented (for example, the effects of economic depressions on level of education attained), the roles of siblings, friends, and coworkers as forces in career development have been relatively understudied. Because groups are so important in cueing individuals to which environmental factors should be noticed and taken seriously—and because groups are so important as filters and interpreters of incoming information (Salancik & Pfeffer, 1978)—it is critical to examine the ways in which peers (broadly defined as siblings, friends, and coworkers) affect individuals' career development (Schmitt, Sacco, Ramey, Ramey, & Chan, 1999).

There is some literature, for example, suggesting that younger siblings model the career interests of older siblings rather than those of their parents, while oldest children are more influenced by parents than by younger siblings. The explanation offered for these results is that individuals tend to conform to the expectations of those in higher-status positions; therefore, children model "up" to either older siblings or parents, depending on birth order (McHale, Updegraff, Helms-Erikson, & Crouter, 2001).

There are several other ways, though, in which siblings may influence career development. While younger children may indeed model their older siblings, there is also evidence that younger children may choose completely separate interests to differentiate themselves from other family members. Siblings can play a role in influencing levels of aspiration and attitudes toward school and work in general; siblings can also present role models of appropriate (or inappropriate) work habits and ways of behaving toward authority figures. In addition, younger children may learn vicariously about effective (and ineffective) career strategies from looking at the successes and failures of their older siblings. Thus, older siblings may be not only an important source of career information but also an important filter of parental influence (Fuligni, Eccles,

Barber, & Clements, 2001; Hamm, 2000). From a developmental perspective, much more research is needed along these lines.

The role of friends in career development has not received much research attention, either. Indirectly, friends have been studied as an inducement not to relocate geographically (Eby et al., 1999; Feldman & Bolino, 1998); more directly, they have been studied as a source of social support after layoffs and other negative career events (Brockner, Grover, Reed, DeWitt, & O'Malley, 1987; Leana & Feldman, 1992). However, research on nonwork friends as sources of information about careers and as sources of career advice has been scant.

Certainly in early career, the role of friends can be a major factor in setting aspiration levels and involvement in deviant behaviors (Hamm, 2000). Perhaps more critical, though, friends may be particularly important in cueing each other about environmental trends and appropriate ways of responding to them (Salancik & Pfeffer, 1978). For example, if one looks at the career decisions of graduating M.B.A. students, it is not unusual to see annual swings of 25 percent or more in students' choices of finance, marketing, operations, e-commerce, and accounting as majors. Given that most students are exposed to much of the same environmental information (and assuming there are no major genetic mutations from year to year), it is logical to look at peers as an important factor in understanding these rapid shifts in career preferences. Peers may make salient which trends in the environment are most critical to consider and may bolster classmates in their commitment to act accordingly.

As recent research on psychological contracts and the new employment model has indicated, the sense of attachment that individuals have to their organizations has been declining. In its stead, attachment to members of the immediate work group has become a larger factor in individuals' career decisions (see Chapter Ten). Attachment to members of the immediate work group may decrease individuals' propensity to quit; it may also motivate individuals to engage in more citizenship behaviors, which help the immediate work group succeed (Konovsky & Pugh, 1994). As Chapter Six on the establishment years by Terri Scandura highlights, the work group also serves as a major source of career advice, social support, and task information. If, in fact, organizations are becoming more boundaryless, then understanding the impact of immediate work groups on individuals' career behaviors and career attitudes becomes even more essential.

Conducting Empirical Research

As Bradley, Brief, and George point out in Chapter Two on personality, advances in theory building can occur only in the context of advances in empirical research. Theory building and conducting empirical research are recursive processes. The ability to test and refine theory is strongly influenced by the sample, methods, and instruments used; the samples, methods, and instruments used guide us toward, or away from, important theoretical questions. In the following section, we explore six important avenues for advancing empirical research on careers from a developmental perspective.

Sampling Biases

As several chapter authors pointed out, careers research on developmental issues has been influenced by a rather limited set of employee populations. In terms of demographic status, those samples have been largely white male, largely middle class, and largely managerial or professional in terms of occupational group. We know considerably less about the career experiences of racial and ethnic minorities than we do about those of whites, much less about females' careers than males' careers, and much less about the careers of blue-collar workers than we do about graduates of elite M.B.A. programs.

Part of the reason for this sampling bias is historical. Because the term *career* was originally used to refer to the experiences of full-time employees and especially the experiences of individuals in high-status occupations and organizations, the underrepresentation of nonwhite, nonmale, non-middle-class workers is unsurprising.

However, the changes in the nature of the labor force have outpaced researchers' attention to these emerging additions to the labor force. As just one example of this sampling bias, the amount of research done on female expatriates is quite modest. The experiences of females living overseas are usually studied in terms of their adjustment as "trailing spouses"; much less frequently do we examine their own experiences in the overseas workforce, despite their increased representation as expatriates. Similarly, although we have developed a substantial body of knowledge about the experience of balancing work and family among the upper middle class, we know considerably less about the experiences of poor blue-collar workers and single mothers struggling to hold down two jobs while juggling child care responsibilities.

The most obvious drawback of the current sampling bias is the lack of generalizability of research findings from existing research to unstudied or understudied populations. However, a potentially more important problem to face concerns whether we are missing major theoretical questions or drawing incorrect conclusions because of those biases. For example, do poor and blue-collar workers even think in terms of careers, or do they simply think of work? While much of the careers literature has focused on choice, many in the underclass may view their environments as much more strictly constrained. As Scandura points out in Chapter Six, the concept of mentoring is central to the thinking of the managerial and professional class; however, do blue-collar workers think in terms of mentoring or just in terms of having good supervisors and apprentice teachers? Thus, the problems with sampling go beyond simply those of external validity; they open up to question whether major constructs that we use regularly are meaningful and capture the reality of understudied populations.

Clarification of Constructs

Another area for future empirical investigation is clarifying major constructs that are central to the career development literature. The careers literature is not alone in facing problems of construct definition, but neither is it immune from criticisms of underspecified terms and overly inclusive concepts.

At the intraindividual level or analysis, for example, the concept of career stage is itself somewhat fuzzy. For example, does the term refer to years since graduation? Level of advancement in one's occupation or organization? Years away from retirement? As noted earlier, it is also quite difficult to disentangle career stage from age. For instance, if an individual returns to get a Ph.D. when he or she is fifty-five years old and gets tenure at age sixty-two, is that person early career, midcareer, or late career? Is career stage defined in terms of internal careers, external careers, or both—and if so, how do differences between these definitions resolve themselves?

At the level of organizational context, the concept of boundarylessness has also been somewhat underspecified. For instance, in terms of boundaryless careers, does boundarylessness refer to the fact that individuals change occupations, make the transition between full-time and part-time work, or change direction of hierarchical position (vertical, horizontal, downward)? Do all changes contribute to boundarylessness—that is, does any change in a career path make a career boundaryless, or is there some threshold of change that has to be met? When the term *boundaryless* is used to describe organizations, does it refer to the extent the organization outsources, downsizes, partners with external firms, uses flexible staffing policies, or some of all of these? Are there degrees of boundarylessness, and how can they be reliably assessed?

As challenging as the task of specifying and operationalizing constructs can be, there are hopeful signs that scholars are being more attentive to just such research concerns. At the individual level of analysis, for instance, Cleveland and Shore (1992) have examined the differential roles that employees' chronological age, subjective age (self-perceptions of age), and relative age (age relative to the mean age of group members) play in influencing various work outcomes. This approach nicely integrates both internal and external definitions of age and addresses both objective and subjective differences among employees at different life and career stages.

Another recent contribution in this area is the work of Boh, Slaughter, and Ang (2001), who hypothesized that information technology (IT) professionals with low occupation-specific human capital would have more mobility into other occupations, while IT professionals with high occupation-specific human capital would have more mobility across organizations. The authors used longitudinal data from 412 IT professionals from the National Longitudinal Survey of Youth data set. They found that of those who were formally trained in IT, 82 percent undertook a sequence of jobs primarily within IT. In contrast, of those who were not formally trained in IT, 89 percent moved into and out of IT positions. Studies such as these address the thornier issues of boundarylessness in creative ways and materially add to our understanding of career development in changing times.

Balancing Self-Report and Multisource Data

Social scientists have long had considerable reservations about using self-report data. Some of those reservations are based on respondents' perceptual distortions of themselves and their environments. Another source of those reservations derives from the attributional biases of respondents and the defense mechanisms individuals use to cope with negative career events. Other major contributing factors to researchers' skepticism about self-report data include failures and distortions of memory, respondents' attempts to achieve consistency of answers within questionnaires, and research participants' efforts to confirm the investigators' hypotheses (Kerlinger, 1986). Over the past ten years, in particular, journals have become increasingly reluctant to publish research reports that rely heavily or exclusively on self-report data.

This reluctance to take self-report data seriously has important implications for careers researchers. If experiences of careers are truly amalgams of external events and internal perceptions, then ignoring self-report data significantly undervalues the internal component of careers. As Bradley, Brief, and George suggest in Chapter Two on personality, such a constraint on research strategy would make idiographic research using a life task approach virtually impossible.

Moreover, some of the research strategies being widely used as substitutes for self-report data have their own significant drawbacks. For example, multisource data (getting peers to provide evaluations of an individual's performance) is ideally a better measure a focal employee's productivity—assuming that researchers, rather than study participants, are choosing the peer evaluators. However, if, as in several recent studies, research subjects provide the names of peer evaluators or distribute evaluation forms themselves, it is not clear how much objectivity is being gained.

Similarly, is a supervisor's global Likert rating more accurate than an individual's own self-report of performance? Both suffer from important response biases, and neither is independently verifiable. By the same token, while policy-capturing studies have the advantage of procuring individuals' responses to multiple stimuli, they also often suffer from the use of naive research subjects. It is hard to argue that college students' responses to thirty-two scenarios about how they would respond if they worked and they were laid off have greater external validity than laid-off workers' self-reports of their own personal experiences.

As empirical research on career development moves forward, a more moderate middle ground may prove beneficial to the quality of quantitative work. Exclusive reliance on self-report data may present too many problems of interpretation, but bans on all self-report data deny the importance of internal career phenomena.

For example, a series of recent studies on bridge employment has helped illuminate the experiences of older workers as they consider retirement. Bridge employment refers to the jobs older workers take between their exit from long-held, full-time jobs and their total workforce withdrawal (Doeringer, 1990; Feldman, 1994). Several authors have combined archival data (for example, on salary, years of service, age, and early retirement incentives) with participants' self-report data to explain when and why older workers choose to work in bridge jobs before their complete withdrawal from the workforce (Kim & Feldman, 1998, 2000; Isaksson & Johansson, 2000; Weckerle & Shultz, 1999). Such studies help us understand not only the objective environments that older workers face, but also how individuals' own experiences shape their perceptions of late-career opportunities.

Creative Use of Archival Data

Because collecting self-report data longitudinally presents significant difficulties, such as loss of study participants over time and long time frames for publication, collecting archival data may be an appealing alternative for gaining longitudinal information about individuals' careers. Archival data can be used in three ways to this end: to provide past data on current research subjects, verifiable measures of current research subjects' career status, and follow-up data on past subjects' subsequent career trajectories.

For instance, Harvey (1999) has examined the short-term and long-term effects of early parental employment using data from the National Longitudinal Survey of Youth. Archival data on mother's employment status and speed of return to work after childbirth were studied as predictors of children's subsequent cognitive development. Similarly, Fuligni et al. (2001) used students' archival school records as dependent variables in their studies of the long-term effects of adolescents' orientation toward peers.

One of the most creative uses of archival data can be seen in Boris Groysberg's "The Drivers of Star Knowledge Workers' Performance: Evidence from a Ranked Analyst Market" (2001). Groysberg uses panel data ranking equity research analysts in investment banks from 1988 to 1996, as well as analysts' changes of employers. By using this rich data set, Groysberg can test whether star knowledge workers continue to be stars even after they change firms (thereby confirming a human-capital approach to employee mobility) or whether star performers' success declines after changing firms (thereby confirming an organizational-capital approach to employee mobility). Groysberg's results suggest that star analysts' performance declines after changing firms, giving greater credence to the firm-specific nature of star knowledge workers' career success.

As Groysberg's study highlights, the use of archival data can be used to test competing hypotheses in rigorous ways. Moreover, archival data can also be used to separate out ideology from reality in understanding career dynamics. For example, there has been a great deal of attention paid recently to the "free agent" model of careers, in which employees sell their services to the highest bidder (see Leana's chapter for a more detailed commentary on this approach). Groysberg's data indicate that star performers who move alone often suffer significant productivity losses. However, analysts tend to reach higher levels of achievement when they bring other employees from their previous firms with them. Thus, the ideology that organizations will perform better by recruiting away stars is not completely accurate; rather, firms would do better to recruit away whole teams instead.

Creative uses of archival data extend beyond merely mitigating against self-report biases. Depending on the nature of the data set, archival data can be used to increase the size and diversity of the sample, add a time dimension to cross-sectional studies, and address research questions not easily answered by self-report or idiographic methodologies alone.

The Criterion Problem

A related methodological issue concerns the use of criterion variables in careers research. Developmental researchers are often caught on the horns of a dilemma. If they rely on criteria of internal career success (such as career motivation, job involvement, professional identification, organizational commitment, or life satisfaction), they are accused of ignoring the self-report biases from which such measures may suffer. On the other hand, if they rely on indicators of external career success (such as rate of promotions, amount of salary, hierarchical position, size of budget, or number of subordinates), then the internal component of careers is undervalued. For instance, one highly compensated vice president may leave her position because it has always been her dream to be a chief executive officer; another equally compensated vice president may be ecstatic because he has achieved far more than he ever expected.

The facile answer, of course, is to collect both types of data—and, in fact, many of the scholars cited in this book have done so. Perhaps more critical, though, is ensuring that the criteria used in the research flow logically from the theory being tested and are operationalized in ways that make sense.

For example, if we are considering the impact of delayering organizations on rates of vertical mobility, then the actual number of promotions received seems like a reasonable criterion variable. On the other hand, using rates of advancement as the criterion variable in mentoring research may or may not make sense. If the mentoring provided is in the form of social support, there is no reason to expect it to have a positive impact on promotion rates. In the latter case, measures of internal career success may be more appropriate. The nature of the theory, rather than beliefs about the goodness of various types of data, should drive the choice of criteria.

Another area where more thoughtful attention to criterion variables is needed is research on career plateaus (see Chapter Seven by Sterns and Subich on midcareer issues). At the level of external careers, certainly rates of mobility can be appropriate criteria. However, as Feldman and Weitz (1988) point out, being plateaued is not simply a matter of promotions; it entails failure to receive assignments of increasing responsibility as well. A brand manager who retains that title for five years but manages brands of increasing importance (in terms of market share, profit contribution, and budgets) is not experiencing the same career hurdles as someone who is a brand manager on the same small brand for five years. Thus, archival measures, no matter how objective, may themselves be incomplete or misleading.

Similarly, operationalizations of internal career criteria need to map better on to theories being tested. For instance, in studying the affective reactions of layoff survivors to their organizations, measuring job satisfaction may miss some of the major career dynamics associated with downsizing. Such survivors may be happy to be working at all, but not necessarily happy in the real sense of that word. Instead, it may make more sense to look at differences in survivors' affective, continuance, and normative commitment (Meyer & Allen, 1991). That is, are survivors genuinely emotionally committed to remaining with their firms, remaining for lack of identifiable alternatives, or remaining due to pressure from others? Again, it is not necessarily the case that one type of criterion is superior to another. Instead, one type of criterion may be a more logical outcome of a specific career dynamic than another.

One-Way Versus Two-Way Influence

Certainly, the idea of mutual influence in career development has been discussed for close to fifty years. In his classic book, *Integrating the Individual and the Organization,* Argyris (1964) stresses the importance of integrating individuals' needs with organizational demands. He argues that by creating more challenging work assignments and a culture of mutual respect and openness, organizations can meet employees' needs for psychological growth at the same time productivity is increased.

As several of the chapter authors in this book suggest, there has also been considerable research testing various fit models of careers (see, for example, Chapter Two on personality and vocational interests and Chapter Three on skill acquisition). While the operationalizations of fit and congruence have varied somewhat from author to author, research using fit models to understand the integration of individuals and organizations has generally yielded positive, if modest, results.

What have not received as much attention, though, are feedback (or recursive) models of career dynamics. More specifically, we need to examine more fully the extent to which employees, individually and collectively, shape the character of the environments they inhabit. Does organizational job insecurity lead to a free agent response to managing careers, or do greater desires for interfirm mobility on the part of individuals lead to fewer organizational guarantees of job security? Have companies increased the amount of training they provide because they have become more enlightened, or have low levels of employee literacy and numeracy forced them to do so? Have high school and college guidance counselors become more affirming and esteem building as a result of their own professional socialization, or have adolescents' lack of direction and self-confidence forced counselors to respond to students in new ways?

The literature on mentoring niccly illustrates this need for recursive models (see Chapter Six for a review of these studies). Most of the literature on mentoring has investigated the impact of senior colleagues on protégés (Levinson, 1978), although there has also been some examination of the types of services and support protégés can provide in exchange (Kram, 1985; Scandura & Schriesheim, 1994). However, "dysfunctional" (insufficient, ineffective, and/or destructive) mentoring has typically been attributed to the inappropriate behaviors and motives of senior colleagues. Failure of junior colleagues to thrive later in their careers has been assumed to result from inadequacies of the part of their mentors (Missirian, 1982).

There is an alternative perspective to be considered here, though: the ways junior colleagues create opportunities for themselves to be mentored and the ways protégés influence the quality of mentoring they receive (Feldman, 1999a). For example, the work of Green and Bauer (1995) suggests that junior colleagues' skills and reputation at time of entry have a major impact on the quantity and quality of mentoring they receive. That is, the best newcomers are most likely to attract the best potential mentors and to receive more constructive assistance from them. Rather than determining which junior colleagues become successful, then, it may be that newcomers' base rate skills matter more. In other words, mentors may change the slope, but not the trajectory, of their protégés' future careers.

Moreover, by sabotaging their mentors, using deceptive impression management techniques, and free-riding on their mentors' coattails, protégés may evoke hostile responses from their senior colleagues in return. Thus, junior colleagues may create disincentives for senior coworkers to mentor them or create conditions for distrustful or distant guidance (Feldman, 1999a). Only by examining two-way influences can such important career dynamics be disentangled and understood.

Linking Research with Practice

In this final section, we examine some ways in which practitioners and researchers can collaborate more effectively, not only in terms of generating new knowledge but also in terms of improving the design and delivery of career development services. If it is indeed the case that practitioner advice on careers has outpaced empirical research, that speaks as much to the lack of relevant information being generated by researchers as it does to the rush to judgment of practitioners.

Data Sources

Even within the constraints of confidential and proprietary information, organizations running career development programs for their employees, consulting firms specializing in career development issues, and universities running placement and career guidance centers are fertile sources of data for careers researchers. Nonetheless, many organizations are highly reluctant to allow researchers either access to archival data or direct contact with employees.

Both parties suffer as a result of such mistrust. Researchers are forced to resort to using student and alumni samples, and practitioners are forced to operate without firm justifications for their programs. Think about some of the following questions: What types of career counseling models work best with high school and college students? How effective are organizational orientation programs in facilitating the school-to-work transition? What types of outplacement services have the greatest impact on laid-off employees' abilities to get rehired? Despite the huge potential samples with which to examine these questions, the amount of empirical data specifically addressing these issues is surprisingly thin. Failure to collaborate in empirical research impedes the progress of scholars and practitioners alike.

Identification of Research Questions

A second avenue for collaboration is the identification of mutually interesting research questions. When one looks at the academic and practitioner journals in the careers area, the difference in topical focus is striking. Academics are more prone to study changes in context; practitioners are more prone to study changes within individuals. Academics are more likely to study molar career strategies like information search; practitioners are more likely to study microcareer behaviors like the use of college placement offices and interview tactics.

All in all, one gets the sense that careers researchers often fail to frame their research in ways that practitioners find useful or are unsuccessful in translating their results in ways practitioners find helpful. By working more closely with each other, practitioners and scholars can shape a more interesting and relevant research agenda for the future. If careers scholars are serious about their research having an impact on organizational practice and public policy, at some level they need to address the issues that matter most to the people who deliver and use career development services.

Design and Assessment of Programs

Finally, a vital direction for collaboration between academics and practitioners lies in the design and assessment of career development programs. Collaboration with practitioners may also help researchers gather better predata by which to judge postintervention success and control for exogenous variables likely to make interpretation of study results difficult. Collaboration with researchers may help practitioners customize career development programs for different groups of employees and develop new kinds of career development interventions. Through efforts such as these, both researchers and practitioners would gain a better understanding of the important interaction effects that are so prominent in our theories yet are so infrequently studied empirically in practice.

In the long run, then, a closer relationship between practitioners and academics could result in the identification of best practices in career development and a framework for understanding when and how career development practices should be used. Ultimately, such an outcome would be valuable not only to academics and practitioners themselves, but more important, to the individuals whose careers we study or manage on a daily basis.

References

Argyris, C. (1964). *Integrating the individual and the organization.* New York: Wiley.

Arthur, M. B., & Rousseau, D. M. (1996). *The boundaryless career: A new employment principle for a new organizational era.* Cambridge: Cambridge University Press.

Ayree, S. (1999). An examination of the moderating influence of breadwinner role salience on the pay-life satisfaction relationship. *Human Relations, 52,* 1279–1290.

Bobocel, D. R., & Meyer, J. P. (1994). Escalating commitment to a failing course of action: Separating the roles of choice and justification. *Journal of Applied Psychology, 79,* 360–363.

Boh, W. F., Slaughter, S., & Ang, S. (2001, Aug.). *Is information technology a boundaryless career?* Paper presented at the Annual Academy of Management, Washington, DC.

Brockner, J., Grover, S., Reed, T., DeWitt, R., & O'Malley, M. (1987). Survivors' reactions to layoffs: We get by with a little help from our friends. *Administrative Science Quarterly, 32,* 526–541.

Brooks, D. (2001). The organization kid. *Atlantic Monthly, 287,* 40–55.

Cleveland, J. N., & Shore, L. M. (1992). Self- and supervisory perspectives on age and work attitudes and performance. *Journal of Applied Psychology, 77,* 469–484.

Dalton, D. R., & Todor, W. D. (1993). Turnover, transfer, and absenteeism: An interdependent perspective. *Journal of Management, 19,* 193–219.

Dalton, G. W. (1989). Developmental views of careers in organizations. In M. B. Arthur, D. T. Hall, & B. S. Lawrence (Eds.), *Handbook of career theory* (pp. 89–109). Cambridge: Cambridge University Press.

Dalton, G. W., Thompson, P. H., & Price, K. L. (1977). The four stages of professional careers: A new look at performance by professionals. *Organizational Dynamics, 6,* 19–42.

Doby, V. J., & Caplan, R. D. (1995). Organizational stress as threat to reputation: Effects on anxiety at work and at home. *Academy of Management Journal, 38,* 1105–1123.

Doeringer, P. (1990). *Bridges to retirement: Older workers in a changing labor market.* Ithaca, NY: Cornell University ILR Press.

Dunegan, K. J. (1993). Framing, cognitive modes, and image theory: Toward an understanding of a glass half full. *Journal of Applied Psychology, 78,* 491–503.

Eby, L. T., Allen, T. D., & Douthitt, S. S. (1999). The role of nonperformance factors on job-related relocation opportunities: A field study and laboratory experiment. *Organizational Behavior and Human Decision Processes, 79,* 29–55.

Feldman, D. C. (1980). On research in organizational socialization: The case for middle range theory. In C. C. Pinder & L. F. Moore (Eds.), *Middle range theory and the study of organizations* (pp. 315–325). Boston: Martinus Nijhoff.

Feldman, D. C. (1988). *Managing careers in organizations.* Glenview, IL: Scott, Foresman.

Feldman, D. C. (1994). The decision to retire early: A review and conceptualization. *Academy of Management Review, 19,* 285–311.

Feldman, D. C. (1999a). Toxic mentors or toxic protégés? A critical reexamination of dysfunctional mentoring. *Human Resource Management Review, 9,* 247–278.

Feldman, D. C. (1999b). What everyone knows to be true about careers, but isn't: Why common beliefs about managing careers are frequently wrong. *Human Resource Management Review, 9,* 243–246.

Feldman, D. C., & Bolino, M. C. (1997). Careers within careers: Reconceptualizing the nature of career anchors and their consequences. *Human Resource Management Review, 6,* 89–112.

Feldman, D. C., & Bolino, M. C. (1998). Moving on out: When will employees follow their organization during corporate relocation? *Journal of Organizational Behavior, 19,* 275–288.

Feldman, D. C., & Weitz, B. A. (1988). Career plateaus reconsidered. *Journal of Management, 14,* 69–80.

Fuligni, A. J., Eccles, J. S., Barber, B. L., & Clements, P. (2001). Early adolescent peer orientation and adjustment during high school. *Developmental Psychology, 37,* 28–36.

Gould, R. (1978). *Transformations: Growth and change in adult life.* New York: Simon & Schuster.

Green, S. G., & Bauer, T. N. (1995). Supervisory mentoring by advisers: Relationships with doctoral student potential, productivity, and commitment. *Personnel Psychology, 48,* 537–561.

Groysberg, B. (2001, Aug.). *The drivers of star knowledge workers' performance: Evidence from a ranked analyst market.* Paper presented to the Academy of Management, Washington, DC.

Hamm, J. V. (2000). Do birds of a feather flock together? The variable bases for African American, Asian American, and European American adolescents' selection of similar friends. *Developmental Psychology, 35,* 445–459.

Harvey, E. (1999). Short-term and long-term effects of early parental employment on children of the National Longitudinal Survey of Youth. *Developmental Psychology, 35,* 445–459.

Hochschild, A. R. (1989). *The second shift.* New York: Avon Books.

Hochschild, A. R. (1997). *The time bind.* New York: Holt.

Holland, J. L. (1985). *Making vocational choices: A theory of careers* (2nd ed.). Upper Saddle River, NJ: Prentice-Hall.

Isaksson, K., & Johansson, G. (2000). Adaptation to continued work and early retirement following downsizing: Long-term effects and gender differences. *Journal of Occupational and Organizational Psychology, 73,* 244–256.

Kerlinger, F. N. (1986). *Foundations of behavioral research* (3rd ed.). Orlando, FL: Harcourt.

Kim, S., & Feldman, D. C. (1998). Healthy, wealthy, or wise: Predicting actual acceptances of early retirement incentives at three points in time. *Personnel Psychology, 51,* 623–642.

Kim, S., & Feldman, D. C. (2000). Working in retirement: The antecedents and consequences of bridge employment and its consequences for quality of life in retirement. *Academy of Management Journal, 43,* 1195–1210.

Konovsky, M. A., & Pugh, S. D. (1994). Citizenship behavior and social exchange. *Academy of Management Journal, 37,* 656–689.

Kram, K. E. (1985). *Mentoring at work.* Glenview, IL: Scott, Foresman.

Leana, C. R., & Feldman, D. C. (1992). *Coping with job loss: How individuals, organizations, and communities respond to layoffs.* New York: Lexington Press.

Levinson, D. J. (1978). *The seasons of a man's life.* New York: Knopf.

McHale, S. M., Updegraff, K. A., Helms-Erikson, H., & Crouter, A. C. (2001). Sibling influences on gender development in middle childhood and early adolescence: A longitudinal study. *Developmental Psychology, 37,* 115–125.

Merton, R. K. (1968). *Social theory and social structure* (2nd ed.). New York: Free Press.

Meyer, J. P., & Allen, N. J. (1991). A three-component conceptualization of organizational commitment. *Human Resource Management Review, 1,* 61–89.

Missirian, A. K. (1982). *The corporate connection: Why executive women need mentors to reach the top.* Upper Saddle River, NJ: Prentice-Hall.

Powell, G. N., & Butterfield, D. A. (1994). Investigating the "glass ceiling" phenomenon: An empirical study of actual promotions to top management. *Academy of Management Journal, 37,* 68–86.

Salancik, G. R., & Pfeffer, J. (1978). A social information processing approach to job attitudes and task design. *Administrative Science Quarterly, 23,* 224–253.

Scandura, T. A., & Schriesheim, C. A. (1994). Leader-member exchange and supervisor career mentoring as complementary concepts in leadership research. *Academy of Management Journal, 37,* 1588–1602.

Schein, E. H. (1990). *Career anchors: Discovering your real values.* San Diego, CA: Pfeiffer.

Schmitt, N., Sacco, J. M., Ramey, S., Ramey, C., & Chan, D. (1999). Parental employment, school climate, and children's academic and social development. *Journal of Applied Psychology, 84,* 737–753.

Stephens, G. K., & Feldman, D. C. (1997). A motivational approach for understanding work versus personal life investments. *Research in Personnel and Human Resource Management, 15,* 333–378.

Thomas, L. T., & Ganster, D. C. (1995). Impact of family-supportive work variables on work-family conflict and strain: A control perspective. *Journal of Applied Psychology, 80,* 6–15.

Valliant, G. (1977). *Adaptation to life.* New York: Little, Brown.

Weckerle, J. R., & Shultz, K. S. (1999). Influences on the bridge employment of older USA workers. *Journal of Occupational and Organizational Psychology, 72,* 317–329.

Whitener, E. M., & Waltz, P. M. (1993). Exchange theory determinants of affective and continuance commitment and turnover. *Journal of Vocational Behavior, 42,* 265–281.

Williams, K. J., & Alliger, G. M. (1994). Role stressors, mood spillover, and perceptions of work-family conflict in employed parents. *Academy of Management Journal, 37,* 837–868.

Name Index

A

Ackerman, P. L., 13, 35
Adams, G. A., 228–230
Adams, J. S., 281
Adkins, C. L., 130, 169
Adler, N. J., 294, 306
Albert, K. A., 12, 99, 337
Allen, N. J., 286, 364
Allen, T. D., 354
Alliger, G. M., 226, 353
Altieri, P., 15, 216
Ambrose, M., 281
Amsel, R., 108
Anderson, W. P., 202
Ang, S., 359
Angleitner, A., 40
Arbona, C., 72
Argote, L., 297
Argyris, C., 163, 166, 364
Arkes, H. R., 222, 228
Arthur, M. B., 3, 6, 27, 28, 103, 111,
    117, 138, 177, 179, 251, 259, 262,
    277, 283, 295, 326, 348
Asama, N. F., 36
Asch, S. E., 142
Ash, R., 175
Ashford, S. J., 126, 127, 129–131,
    133, 134, 138, 139, 142, 145, 146,
    149
Ashforth, B. E., 126, 127, 141–143,
    150, 169
Ashton, M. C., 51
Assouline, M., 32, 49
Astin, A. W., 32
Atanasoff, L., 31
Atwater, L. E., 226, 227
Austin, J. T., 16, 74

Avolio, B. J., 14, 187, 188, 215–217,
    221, 222, 226, 236
Axelrad, S., 28
Axelrod, W., 94
Ayree, S., 354

B

Baird, L., 173, 333
Baker, H. E., 150, 169
Balkin, D., 294, 295
Baltes, P. B., 188
Bandura, A., 202, 203
Barber, B. L., 11, 111, 355, 356
Barkume, M., 255, 261
Barling, J., 11, 12, 100, 102, 114
Barnard, C. I., 144
Barnett, R., 189
Barney, L., 253
Baron, A., 36
Baron, J. N., 136, 137
Barrett, G. V., 187, 188
Barrick, M. R., 13, 38, 68
Barsade, S. C., 13
Barsoux, J., 173
Bartley, D. F., 95, 106
Bartol, K. M., 259
Baruch, G., 189
Bass, B. M., 227
Bassi, L. J., 253
Bateman, M., 254
Bauer, T. N., 126, 135, 170, 172, 365
Beach, L. R., 104
Becker, H. J., 16
Beehr, T. A., 19, 72, 74, 197, 214,
    224, 228–233, 237, 349
Bejian, D. V., 191, 337
Bell, L., 79

Bem, D. J., 4, 95, 96
Bennis, W., 317
Bergman, T. J., 255, 256
Bernstein, J., 274
Bernstein, M. C., 263
Berra, L. P., 93
Bertrand, R. M., 186
Betz, N. E., 4, 12, 30, 53, 76, 94, 97, 104, 106, 203, 205
Bezanson, L., 245, 250, 264, 266, 268
Bies, R. J., 133
Bieschke, K. J., 205
Bird, A., 20, 177, 294, 295, 350
Birdseye, M., 294, 295
Black, J. S., 294, 304–306, 312
Black, S. S., 129–131, 138, 139, 146
Blake, R. J., 16, 72, 73
Blann, J., 265
Block, J., 39
Bloom, A., 93, 99, 106, 107
Blos, P., 161
Bluck, S., 4, 94, 106, 107, 189
Bluestone, B., 275
Blumer, C., 222, 228
Blustein, D. L., 16, 202
Bobocel, D. R., 350
Boh, W. F., 359
Bohlander, G., 263
Bolino, M. C., 4, 167, 179, 259, 267, 351, 356
Bolles, R. N., 4, 112
Bond, N. A., Jr., 31
Borgen, F. H., 76, 109, 205
Borman, W. C., 221, 225
Borow, H., 53, 73
Bowlby, J., 162, 181
Bowling, N., 19, 214, 349
Bradley, J. C., 17, 27, 350, 356, 360
Brass, D. J., 136, 139
Brehm, J. W., 144
Brenner, L., 253
Brett, J. M., 129–131, 177
Brewer, G. A., 102
Brief, A. P., 17, 27, 38, 46, 48, 350, 357, 360
Briscoe, J. P., 330, 331

Brockner, J., 145, 284, 356
Brooks, D., 11, 99, 101, 348
Brooks, L., 29, 80
Brousseau, K. R., 3–4, 10, 67
Brown, D., 29
Brown, S. D., 12, 34, 69, 97, 198, 203–206
Burger, J. M., 13, 109
Burke, M. J., 38
Burkhardt, M. E., 139
Burt, R. S., 136, 137, 311
Burton, J., 277
Butterfield, D. A., 353
Byham, W. C., 332
Bynner, J., 77

C

Cable, D., 46
Caldwell, D. F., 13, 36, 67
Calister, R. R., 126
Callaghan, P., 290
Callanan, G. A., 245
Camobreco, J. F., 226
Camp, C. C., 76
Campbell, B. M., 177
Campion, M. A., 261
Cantor, N., 29, 41–44
Capelli, P., 259, 282
Caplan, R. D., 353
Cappelli, P., 77, 274, 275
Carter, M.A.T., 231, 232
Casas, J. M., 205
Cascio, W. F., 15, 215–219, 236
Cashman, J., 288
Caspi, A., 4, 40, 95, 96
Castells, M., 276
Catalano, M., 32, 66
Chambre, S. M., 235
Chan, D., 10, 111, 355
Chao, G., 127, 170
Chartrand, J. M., 36, 76
Chatman, J. A., 142, 144, 149
Chen, C. P., 337
Chiriboga, D. A., 189–191
Christal, R. E., 27
Christensen, P. R., 31

Chung, P. P., 225
Church, A. T., 294
Ciulla, J. B., 186
Clark, L. A., 36, 132, 133
Clawson, J. G., 160, 162
Clements, P., 11, 111, 355, 356
Cleveland, J. N., 359
Coatsworth, J. D., 96
Cochran, L., 11, 97, 101
Cohen, L., 260
Cohen, P., 11, 99
Cole, N. S., 32
Collard, B. A., 177
Collin, A., 246, 261, 266
Colquitt, J. A., 324
Colvin, G., 289
Conroy, M., 276
Conyers, L. M., 108
Cook, K., 231, 232
Cook, P., 279–281
Cooper, P. W., 234, 235
Cornelius, A., 11, 80
Costa, P. T., Jr., 27, 35–37, 39, 40, 51, 192
Craik, K. H., 46
Crites, J. O., 6
Crittendon, A., 40, 53, 54
Cropper, C. M., 254
Cross, T. C., 225
Crouter, A. C., 110, 355
Csikszentmihalyi, M., 206
Cummings, L. L., 134
Curtis, G., 36
Czajka, S. J., 218

D
Dalton, D. R., 348, 350
Dalton, G. W., 7, 9–10, 15, 161, 352
D'Amico, C., 257
Darley, J. G., 34, 35
Darrow, C. N., 162
Davidhizer, R., 163
Davison, S., 223
Dawis, R. V., 29, 30, 41, 42, 46, 49, 65, 66, 145
De Fruyt, F., 72

de Raad, B., 51
De Vader, C. L., 226
Deacon, S., 333
Deci, E. L., 329
DeFillippi, F. J., 260
Delp, N. D., 218
DeNisi, A. S., 68, 335
Derr, C. B., 167, 168
Deshpande, S. P., 294
DeSimone, R. L., 251, 253, 257
Desmarais, L. B., 16, 73
DeWaard, R. J., 36
DeWitt, R., 356
Digman, J. M., 12, 40, 106
Dinur, A., 297
Dinur, C., 74
Dionne, S. D., 226
Dix, J. E., 171
Dixon, J., 10
Doby, V. J., 353
Doeringer, P., 361
Doerpinghaus, H. I., 102
Donnay, D.A.C., 109, 205
Dougherty, T. W., 138, 139
Douglas, J. W., 102
Douthitt, S. S., 354
Doverspike, D., 187
Drath, W. H., 329
Dreher, G. F., 175
Driver, M. J., 3–4, 167
Dulek, R. E., 306
Dunegan, K. J., 105, 350
Dunnette, M. D., 5, 6
Dustmann, C., 114
Dweck, C. S., 134
Dye, D. A., 36

E
Eby, L. T., 81, 175, 354, 356
Eccles, J. S., 11, 111, 355, 356
Eccles, R. G., 138
Edelman, C. D., 187
Edelman, L. B., 267
Edwards, J. R., 16, 50, 64
Ekeberg, S., 32
Elam, J. J., 327

Elder, G. H., 4, 95, 96
Elliott, T. R., 36
Emmons, R. A., 43
Eneroth, K., 3–4
England, G. W., 29
Enright, M. S., 108
Epperson, D., 76, 77
Erez, M., 286
Erikson, E. H., 160, 190
Erlanger, H. S., 267
Eshleman, J., 163
Ethington, C. A., 79
Exberg, S. E., 66
Eyler, J., 80

F

Fain, J. R., 112
Fallick, B. C., 113
Farmer, S. J., 228
Farr, J. L., 190, 207
Fassinger, R. E., 11, 14, 100
Faux, V. A., 160
Feehan, P. F., 76
Feinberg, B., 18, 350, 351
Feldman, D. C., 3–5, 8, 9, 12, 15, 18,
    21, 28, 93, 102, 103, 112, 116,
    129–131, 135, 140, 143, 150, 167,
    169, 171, 172, 175, 179, 227–231,
    233–235, 264, 275, 278, 283, 290,
    297, 307, 312, 329, 346, 348,
    351–353, 356, 361, 363, 365, 366
Feldman, K. A., 79
Ferris, G. R., 225
Fichten, C. S., 108
Fiedler, F. E., 227
Fielden, J. S., 306
Finkelberg, S. L., 16
Fischer, A. R., 35
Fischer, L. R., 234, 235
Fisher, C. D., 127, 141, 142, 148, 170
Fitzgerald, L. F., 30
Fitzsimmons, C., 15, 216
Fleenor, J., 52
Flores, F., 298
Foley, S., 247
Folks, W. R., 12, 102

Fondas, N., 290
Forman, J. B., 258
Forret, M. L., 138, 139
Forster, N., 312
Forteza, J. A., 215, 223, 236
Fossey, R., 254
Fouad, N. A., 79, 81, 203, 205
Frank, R., 279–281
Fricko, M.A.M., 72, 74
Frieze, I. H., 105
Fromm, E., 162
Fronstin, P., 230
Fuligni, A. J., 11, 14, 111, 355, 356,
    362
Fullerton, H. N., 214, 236
Furnham, A., 31, 35, 46, 49

G

Ganster, D. C., 353
Gardner, P., 170
George, J. M., 17, 27, 34, 38, 47, 48,
    350, 357, 360
Georgopoulos, B. S., 222
Gerhart, B., 278, 285
Giddens, A., 251
Gilliland, S. W., 67, 78
Gini, A., 29
Ginzberg, E., 28, 30, 94, 106
Ginzberg, S. W., 28, 94
Glazer, S., 228
Godschalk, V. M., 245
Goh, D. S., 35
Goldberg, L. R., 27, 40, 45, 51
Goldin, D., 8
Goldstein, H. W., 52
Goleman, D., 164
Gomez-Meija, L., 294, 295
Goodnough, G., 202
Gordon, M. P., 259
Gottfredson, D. C., 38, 101
Gottfredson, G. D., 66, 73, 75
Gottfredson, L. S., 16, 53, 73–76
Gould, R., 7, 348, 349
Gould, S., 197
Govindarajan, V., 306
Graen, G., 172

Graf, I. K., 225
Graf, P., 188
Gray, J. H., 206
Green, S. G., 170, 365
Greenberg, J., 284
Greenberger, D. B., 146, 178
Greenberger, E., 4, 12, 101, 114
Greenfield, D., 80
Greenhaus, J. H., 197, 245, 246, 251, 259, 261
Gregersen, H. B., 294, 305, 312
Grensing-Pophal, L., 101
Griffith, J., 11, 99, 111
Griffiths, A., 223
Griliches, Z., 94, 114
Grossman, R. J., 256
Grover, S., 356
Groysberg, B., 362
Guest, C. L., Jr., 252, 253, 260
Guilford, J. P., 31
Guion, R. M., 50
Gunz, H., 306
Gupta, A., 306
Gysbers, N. C., 252, 260

H

Habermas, T., 4, 94, 106, 107
Hackett, G., 12, 34, 69, 97, 198, 203–206
Hackman, J. R., 219
Hadas, C., 46
Hagenah, T., 35
Hall, D. T., 6, 27, 28, 177, 193, 206, 207, 259, 295, 324, 330, 331, 336
Hall, E. T., 306, 315
Hall, F. S., 177
Hamel, G., 297
Hamm, J. V., 111, 355, 356
Hanish, K. A., 16, 74
Hanley-Maxwell, C., 98
Harlow, R. E., 43
Harmon, L. W., 76
Harpaz, I., 234
Harper, L., 8, 99
Harris, D. M., 251
Harris, M., 335

Harris-Bowlsbey, J., 261, 266
Harrison, B., 275
Hartmann, H., 290
Harvey, E., 100, 361
Harvey, M. C., 294
Haslett, T. K., 218
Hassell, B. L., 221, 222
Hayes, E. L., 54
Hebel, S., 253, 254
Heesacker, R. S., 53
Heggestad, E. D., 35
Helms-Erikson, H., 110, 355
Helwig, A. A., 79
Henderson, P., 252, 260
Heneman, R. L., 178
Henry, P., 78, 79
Hepburn, C. G., 100
Herna, J. L., 28, 94
Herr, E. L., 252, 266
Hiebert, B., 245, 250, 264, 266, 268
Higgins, C. A., 38, 68
Higgins, E. T., 133
Higgins, M. C., 136–138, 337
Hill, J. S., 294, 295
Hill, R. E., 30
Hirsch, P., 289
Hirschman, C., 263
Hitchings, W. E., 106
Hochschild, A. R., 9, 107, 177, 354
Hofstede, G., 111, 146, 147
Hofstee, W.K.B., 51
Hogan, J., 12
Hogan, R., 12, 16, 39, 72, 73
Holland, J. L., 4–6, 13, 16, 27, 29–38, 41, 42, 49, 51, 52, 65, 66, 72, 82, 96, 107, 113, 117, 351
Holland, P., 333
Hollander, E. P., 163
Hollenbeck, G. P., 336
Hollenbeck, J. R., 219
Holtom, B., 277, 286
Hopkins, C., 12, 101
Hopkins, N., 73, 74
Hotchkiss, L., 53
Hough, L. M., 37
Howard, A., 186

Hui, C., 224, 225
Huntley, H., 253
Hurd-Gray, J., 188
Hurley, J. F., 253
Huyck, M. H., 186, 189, 190

I

Ibarra, H., 136, 137, 311
Ickes, W., 29
Ilgen, D. R., 219
Imel, S., 252
Indik, B. P., 222
Ingram, P., 297
Inkpen, A. C., 297
Isabella, L. A., 175
Isaksson, K., 232, 361

J

Jablin, F. M., 128–131
Jackson, D. N., 13, 35, 45
Jackson, S. E., 67
Jacoby, S., 245, 258, 275–277, 279, 282, 289
Jacques, E., 189
James, J. B., 191, 192
Janis, I. L., 97, 104, 105, 117
Jeanquar, S., 336
Jerdee, T. H., 220, 236
Jobin-Davis, K., 16
Johansson, G., 232, 361
John, O. P., 40
Johnson, J., 11, 99
Johnson, T., 172
Johnston, J. A., 36, 76
Jones, C., 260
Jones, G., 128, 132, 139, 140, 150
Jones, G. R., 34
Jones, R. G., 67
Joseph, R., 80
Judge, T. A., 38, 46, 55, 68
Judy, R. W., 257
Juntunen, C. L., 74, 78, 79

K

Kabanoff, B., 175, 176
Kahn, S., 328

Kanfer, R., 13
Kanter, R. M., 138
Kantrowitz, T. M., 13
Kaplan, R. E., 329
Kasen, S., 11, 99
Kay, G. G., 36
Kealey, D. J., 294
Kehoe, P. E., 259
Kelloway, E. K., 12, 102
Kelman, H. C., 163
Kerckhoff, A. C., 79
Kerlinger, F. N., 360
Kerr, M., 97
Kidd, J. B., 302
Kidd, J. M., 250, 251, 266
Kidder, D., 247
Kiesler, C. A., 165
Kiesler, S. B., 165
Kilty, K. M., 231
Kim, S., 8, 228, 229, 231, 234, 235, 361
Kinney, E. D., 263
Kirchmeyer, K., 176
Kirkham, K. L., 10
Klein, E. B., 162
Klein, H., 127, 170
Klein, S. R., 190
Klimoski, R., 67
Kluger, A. N., 335
Kneisner, T. J., 263
Kobasa, S. C., 328
Kofodimos, J. R., 329
Kokko, K., 95, 96
Konovsky, M. A., 356
Kossek, E., 290
Kotter, J. P., 160
Kozlowski, S.W.J., 127, 129, 136, 175
Kraatz, M. S., 177, 284
Kraimer, M. L., 39
Kram, K. E., 15, 81, 136, 140, 141, 174, 175, 179, 337, 365
Kremer, Y., 234
Kristof, A., 16, 47, 65
Kristof, A. L., 66–67
Krumboltz, J. D., 79–81
Kubeck, J. E., 218

Kuder, G. F., 30
Kulik, C., 281
Kush, K., 11, 97, 101

L

Lachman, M. E., 186, 191, 192
Lam, A., 327
Lam, S.S.K., 224
Langer, E., 104
Langston, C. A., 44
Lapan, R. T., 252
Larsson, R., 3–4
Lau, A. W., 226
Law, K.K.S., 224
Lawrence, B. S., 6, 27, 295
Leana, C. R., 20, 264, 274, 276, 277,
  281, 285, 287, 290, 329, 348, 349,
  356, 362
Lee, B. A., 259
Lee, S., 146
Lee, T., 277, 286, 287
Leggett, E. L., 134
Lei, D., 326
Leirer, V., 15, 216
Lent, R. W., 12, 34, 69, 76, 81, 97,
  104, 113, 198, 202–206
Leong, F. T., 35
LePine, J. A., 324
Leung, K., 225
Levin, R., 259
Levinson, D. J., 15, 162, 348, 349,
  365
Levinson, J. D., 189–192
Levinson, M. H., 162, 174–176, 189,
  190, 192
Lewin, K., 128
Lewko, J. H., 11, 100
Lewkowicz, C., 191
Liden, R. C., 225, 288
Lipke, D. J., 101
Lipsitt, L. P., 188
Little, B. R., 43
Littleton, S. M., 251
Locke, E. A., 280
Lofquist, L. H., 29, 41, 42, 65, 66,
  145

London, M., 3–4, 21, 95, 323, 328,
  329, 332, 334–335, 349
Lopez, F. G., 205
Lord, R. G., 226
Loughlin, C. A., 102
Louis, M. R., 131, 135, 141, 170, 298
Ludwig, J., 253
Luzzo, D. A., 12, 81, 99, 104, 106,
  337

M

Maddi, S. R., 328
Mael, F., 141, 142
Magnusson, D., 37
Mahoney, J. D., 294
Major, D. A., 129
Mallon, M., 260
Malos, S. B., 261
Mangum, S. L., 178
Mann, L., 97, 104, 105, 117
Manzoni, J., 173
Marcus, A., 191
Mariani, M., 255
Marmarosh, C., 36
Marriner, A., 103
Marrow, D., 15, 216
Martin, D. C., 259
Martineau, J. W., 335
Martino, S. C., 235
Maslow, A. H., 99
Masten, A. S., 96
McArthur, C. C., 160
McBride, J. R., 74
McCall, B. P., 75
McCall, M. W., Jr., 294
McClelland, D. C., 134
McCormick, E., 68
McCrea, R. R., 27, 35, 36, 39, 40, 51,
  192
McDaniel, M. A., 218
McEvoy, G. M., 15, 215–217, 219,
  236
McFadden, K. L., 76
McHale, S. M., 110, 355
McKee, B., 162
McMahon, M., 30

McManus, S., 175
McMillion, M., 12, 66, 101
Meir, E. I., 32, 46, 49, 66, 74
Melamed, S., 74
Mendenhall, M. E., 20, 294, 295, 304, 305, 307, 312, 350
Merton, R. K., 347, 348
Mervielde, I., 72
Meyer, J. P., 286, 350, 364
Mickelwright, J., 113, 114
Miklos, S. M., 207
Milgram, S., 165
Miller, E. L., 294
Miller, V. D., 128–131
Mirvis, P. H., 206, 207, 259
Mishel, L., 274, 280, 289
Missirian, A. K., 365
Mitchell, T., 104, 286, 287
Monahan, C. J., 47, 63
Mone, E. M., 95
Moon, H., 50
Morin, W. J., 259
Morrison, E. W., 18, 126–129, 133, 136, 137, 349, 351
Mortimer, J. T., 80
Morton, K. R., 228
Moss, J., 325, 326
Moss, M. K., 105
Motowidlo, S. J., 225
Mount, M. K., 13, 38
Mowday, R., 281
Muchinsky, P. H., 46, 47
Mueller, D. P., 234, 235
Multon, K. D., 205

N

Nauta, M., 76, 77
Neapolitan, J., 197
Neugarten, B. L., 189
Ng, K., 72, 106
Nicholson, N., 131, 147
Nielson, N. L., 228, 237
Niles, S. G., 202
Nilsen, S. R., 257
Noe, R. A., 175, 324
Nonaka, I., 297–299, 301, 302, 304, 309, 326, 333

Nordlinger, P., 263
Noyfeld, M., 46
Nurasimha, S., 297

O

O'Brien, K. M., 11, 14, 100
Oddou, G. R., 294, 295, 304, 307, 312
O'Hara, R. P., 97
Oldham, G. R., 219
O'Leary-Kelly, A., 127, 170
O'Malley, M., 356
Omoto A. M., 235
O'Reilly, C., 143, 148
O'Reilly, C. A. III, 67, 144, 149
Organ, D., 286
Orris, D., 172
Osipow, S. H., 81, 95
Osland, J. S., 305, 311, 317
Ostendorf, F., 40, 51
Osterman, P., 275
Ostroff, C., 18, 127, 136, 175, 286, 350, 351
Otazo, K. L., 336
Overton, T. D., 105

P

Palmer, S., 101
Pantazis, C., 257
Pape, R., 180
Parsons, F., 29, 30
Pascarella, E. G., 78
Patchett, M. B., 193, 196–198
Patton, W., 30
Paunonen, S. V., 45, 51
Pautler, K. J., 11, 100
Pearce, J. L., 235, 284
Peidmont, R. L., 39
Peiperl, M. A., 225
Peluchette, J.V.E., 336
Peng, Y., 191
Perone, M., 36
Perrewe, P. L., 221, 222
Perrow, C., 284
Pervin, L. A., 68–70
Peterson, C., 202
Petty, M., 288

Pfeffer, J., 355, 356
Phillips, S. D., 16
Pil, F. K., 276, 285
Pink, D., 274, 281, 282, 289
Piotrowski, C. S., 11, 100
Pitts, R. A., 326
Plata, M., 106
Podolny, J. M., 136, 137
Polanyi, M., 298, 299
Pool, S. W., 260
Porter, L., 284
Posner, B. Z., 135
Post, J. E., 264
Post-Kammer, P., 107
Powell, G. N., 135, 353
Prahalad, C. K., 297
Prediger, D. J., 73, 76, 77
Preston, L. E., 264
Price, R., 7, 46, 161, 352
Prieto, J. M., 215, 223, 236
Protheroe, D. R., 294
Pugh, S. D., 356
Pulkkinen, L., 95, 96

Q
Quinn, J. B., 253

R
Ragins, B. R., 175
Rajah, N., 113, 114
Ramey, C., 10, 111, 355
Ramey, S., 10, 111, 355
Rauschenberger, J., 265
Rayman, J., 31
Redmond, J. L., 267
Reed, T., 356
Reese, H. W., 188
Reichers, A. E., 138
Reid, K. S., 253, 254
Reilly, A. H., 177
Reilly, S. P., 336
Reskin, B., 53
Retish, P., 106
Reutefors, D. L., 105
Reynolds, R. G., 253, 254, 260
Rhodes, S. R., 215–217, 219, 222, 223

Richards, J. M., Jr., 32, 73, 74
Richardson, V., 231
Richmond, J., 80
Riegel, K. F., 191
Rivers, C., 189
Roarke, A. E., 16
Roberts, B. W., 12, 40
Robertson, I. T., 205
Robey, D., 327
Robinson, S. L., 177, 178, 284
Robitshek, C., 95, 106
Rocha-Singh, I. A., 205
Roe, A., 5, 30, 93, 94
Roese, N. J., 97
Rogers, K. A., 12, 102
Rose, M. L., 36
Rosen, B., 220, 236
Rosenbaum, J. E., 196, 296
Ross, S., 103
Rosse, J., 259
Rothstein, M., 13
Rounds, J. B., 66
Rousseau, D. M., 3, 28, 103, 111, 117, 138, 177, 251, 259, 262, 277, 283, 284, 326, 348
Rowe, R., 223
Roy, D., 181
Rumsey, D. J., 38
Russell, J., 175
Ryan, E. S., 78
Ryan, K., 286
Ryan, R. M., 329
Rynes, S. L., 278, 285
Rysiew, K. J., 95

S
Sablynski, C., 277, 286
Sacco, J. M., 10, 111, 355
Sackett, P. R., 16, 73, 75
Sadri, G., 205
Saks, A. M., 126, 127, 150, 169
Salamone, P. R., 11, 100, 191, 337
Salancik, G. R., 355, 356
Salomone, P. R., 100
Salthouse, T. A., 187, 188
Sanderson, C. A., 44
Sands, M. M., 74

Saucier, G., 45, 51
Saunders, L., 54
Savickas, M. L., 34, 80, 171, 198, 200
Scandura, T. A., 19, 159, 175, 356, 358, 365
Scarpello, V. G., 255, 256
Schacter, D. L., 15, 97, 105
Schaie, W., 208
Schank, R. C., 104
Schappe, S. P., 221
Schaubroeck, J., 335
Schein, E. A., 4, 114, 115, 127, 139, 141–143, 150, 160, 162, 166–168, 170, 171, 172, 178, 179, 181, 196, 351
Schinka, J. A., 36
Schmidt, S., 324, 325
Schmitt, J., 274
Schmitt, N., 10, 111, 355
Schneider, B., 6, 47, 50–52, 68
Schneider, L. J., 105
Schneider, R. J., 37
Schön, D., 333
Schrank, H. T., 188
Schriesheim, C. A., 365
Schulenberg, J., 98
Schwartz, R. H., 31
Scott, L. R., 329
Seashore, S. E., 222
Seers, A., 288
Seibert, K. W., 333
Seibert, S. E., 39
Seigler, I. C., 187
Seiss, T. F., 35
Seligman, M.F.P., 206
Sennett, R., 290
Settoon, R. P., 130
Severson, S., 258
Shamir, B., 108
Shanley, M., 285
Sharf, R., 4, 93, 94
Sharit, J., 218
Shaver, K. G., 329
Shea, J., 8, 11, 99, 100
Sheehy, G., 191, 192
Shellenbarger, S., 11, 101

Sherman, A., 263
Sherman, K. J., 80
Shiaw, W. T., 221
Shin, Y., 18, 350, 351
Shoemaker, A., 106
Shore, L. M., 228, 229, 359
Shultz, K. S., 228, 232, 234, 361
Shuttleworth, C., 53
Simon, H. A., 105, 106
Simon, S. A., 175
Sklarew, N. D., 197
Skoglind, J. D., 178
Slane, S., 32, 66
Slaney, R. B., 11, 100
Slaughter, S., 359
Slocum, J. W., 326
Smart, J. C., 79
Smart, R., 202
Smith, D. B., 52
Smith, M. B., 113
Smith, P. L., 107, 203, 205
Smith, S., 113, 114
Smither, J. W., 328, 329, 335, 336
Snell, A. F., 74
Snell, S., 263
Snizek, W. E., 223
Snyder, M., 29, 145, 235
Sonnenfeld, J. A., 225
Sparrow, R., 288
Spokane, A. R., 32, 66–68, 73, 77, 82
Spreitzer, G. M., 294
Stark, E., 11, 100
Staudinger, U. M., 189
Staw, B. M., 13, 148
Staw, J., 68
Steinberg, L., 4, 12, 101, 114
Stephens, D. K., 15
Stephens, G. K., 20, 294, 315, 350, 353
Stern, D., 12, 101, 103
Sterns, H. L., 19, 186–189, 193, 196–198, 206, 207, 349, 363
Stockman, K. M., 254
Stokes, G. S., 74
Stone, J. R. III, 80, 101
Strasser, S., 146

Stroh, L. K., 305, 306, 312
Strong, E. K., Jr., 30, 31, 34, 75
Stroupe, K. T., 263
Stumpf, S. A., 3–4, 95, 332
Subich, L. M., 19, 33, 35, 38, 186, 349, 363
Sullivan, S. E., 199, 279, 283, 325, 326
Sunoo, B. P., 265
Super, C. M., 198
Super, D. E., 5, 30, 35, 93, 94, 106, 160, 162, 196, 198–203, 205, 262, 267, 283, 328
Sutton, M. S., 31
Swaney, K., 76
Swanson, J. L., 36, 79, 81
Szymanski, E. M., 98

T

Taber, T. D., 197, 224
Tagalakis, V., 108
Takemoto-Chock, N. K., 40
Takeuchi, H., 326
Talaga, J. A., 228, 229, 232
Tanaka, I., 301
Tang, M., 205
Taylor, M. A., 228, 229
Taylor, M. S., 12, 80, 102, 126, 142, 143, 145, 149
Taylor, S., 52
Teramoto, Y., 302
Terenzini, P. T., 78
Tesluk, P. E., 190
Tett, R. P., 13
Thibodeau, P., 256
Thomas, D. A., 138
Thomas, D. C., 294, 307
Thomas, L. T., 353
Thomas, R. J., 180, 181
Thompson, J. A., 247
Thompson, P., 7, 161, 352
Thompson, P. H., 10
Thomson, L., 223
Thoresen, C. J., 38, 68
Tiedeman, D. V., 97
Tinsley, H.E.A., 15, 16, 31, 43, 46, 48, 64, 65, 68, 82, 107, 113

Todor, W. D., 348, 350
Toerestad, B., 37
Tokar, D. M., 33, 35, 36, 38
Tompson, H. B., 260, 294, 312
Tornow, W. W., 335
Tosi, H., 171
Tracey, T.J.G., 73, 74
Tranberg, M., 32, 33, 49, 66
Triandis, H. C., 146, 147
Tripoli, A., 284
Trusty, J., 72, 106
Tsui, A., 284
Tung, R. L., 294, 307
Tupes, E. C., 27
Turnley, W. H., 12, 102, 112, 116

U

Uggen, C., 267
Updegraff, K. A., 110, 355

V

Valliant, G., 7, 192, 348, 349
Valy-Durbin, S., 312
Van Buren, H. J., III, 264, 277, 287
Van Maanen, J., 114, 115, 139, 142, 143, 152, 166, 170, 172
Van Scotter, J. R., 225
Varma, A., 312
Veblin, T., 99
Vecchio, R. P., 227
Veiga, J. F., 196, 197
Viswesvaran, C., 294
Von Hippel, C., 178
Vondracek, F. W., 98
Voyten, K. K., 4, 12, 94, 97, 104, 106, 205
Vroom, V., 278, 281

W

Wade-Benzoni, K. A., 177
Waggoner, K. M., 76, 77
Wakabayashi, M., 173
Waldman, D. A., 14, 215, 216, 221, 222, 236
Walker, A. G., 335
Walls, R. T., 95, 106

Walsh, J. T., 197
Walsh, W. B., 46
Waltz, P. M., 348, 350
Wanberg, C. R., 13, 38
Wanous, J. P., 143, 149, 171
Waring, J. M., 188
Warr, P., 215, 217, 219, 222, 223
Waterman, J. A., 177
Waterman, R. H., 177
Watson, D., 36, 132, 133
Watt, J. D., 38
Watts, A. G., 245, 250, 251, 260, 262,
    264–266, 268
Wayne, S. J., 225, 288
Webber, R. A., 159, 163
Weber, M., 5
Weckerle, J. R., 228, 234, 361
Weick, K., 298, 309
Weier, A., 256
Weiss, D. J., 41
Weiss, H., 46, 48
Weitz, B. A., 102, 363
Wells, S. J., 259
Werbel, J. D., 67, 78
Werner, J. M., 20, 245, 247, 251, 255,
    259, 260, 267, 352

West, M. A., 131
White, R. W., 146
Whitener, E. M., 348, 350
Whitney, D. R., 32
Whyte, W. H., Jr., 8, 163
Wilk, S. L., 16, 73, 75
Williams, K. J., 353
Williams, S., 221
Willis, R. H., 164
Winogard, T., 298
Wishart, N. A., 327
Wolf, S., 127, 170
Wood, W., 97
Worthington, R. L., 74, 78–81

Y

Young, G., 33, 49
Young, R. A., 246, 261, 266, 337

Z

Zacharatos, A., 100
Zahrly, J., 171
Zanglein, J. E., 258
Zhou, J., 38, 47
Zonderman, A. B., 36

Subject Index

A

Abridged Big Five Dimensional Circumplex taxonomy, 51

Acceleration pools, 331–333. *See also* Career development: programs and processes

Action learning models, 333. *See also* Career development: programs and processes

ADEA. *See* Age Discrimination in Employment Act (ADEA)

Africa, 307

African Americans, 254

Age discrimination, 220–222. *See also* Age-performance relationship; Older workers

Age Discrimination in Employment Act (ADEA), 186, 187, 248, 256, 257

Age, Health, and Employment (Birren, Robinson, and Livingston), 194

Age thirty transition, 174

Age-performance relationship: criticisms of research on, 218–220; moderators of, 216–218. *See also under* Older workers

American Psychologist, 202

Americans with Disabilities Act (1990), 249, 256

America's Career InfoNet, 255

America's Job Bank, 250, 254, 258, 260; Web site, 261

America's Talent Bank (United States Department of Labor Web site), 261

Aptitudes-abilities, relative role of, 72–75

Australia, 305, 306, 347

Authority figures, 173

B

Best Paper Award, 247

Big Five personality traits, 12–13, 29, 42, 51, 192; and career outcomes, 38–41; versus RIASEC variables, 35–37; traits beyond, 45–46

Boundaryless careers, 111–112, 325–326

Buffering, personal and contextual, 96–97. *See also* Early-career development: psychological processes underlying

C

California, 253

California Psychological Inventory (Atwater, Dionne, Avolio, Camobreco, and Lau), 226

Canada, 264

Cap Gemini Ernst & Young, 262, 263

Career anchor, 4, 166–169. *See also under* Establishment years

Career counseling, 337. *See also* Career development: programs and processes

Career development: factors predicting organizational support for and employee involvement in, 338; motivation for, 328–329; organizational trends influencing, 324–327; programs and processes, 330–337; toward a model of organizational support for, 337–341

385

Career development research: and
Big Five and career outcomes,
38–41; current, 35–37; data
sources for, 366–367; and design
and assessment of programs,
367–368; future directions in,
289–290; and identification of
research questions, 367; larger
role for public policy in, 246–250;
linking, with practice, 366–368;
public policy issues in, 247–250;
recurring themes in, 5–10
Career indecision: antecedents of,
106–111; consequences of,
111–115; and delays in formation
of early-career identity, 103–115;
demographic differences and,
107–108; implications of, for
management practice, 115–117;
implications of, for vocational
counseling, 117–119; and normative pressures, 110–111; and
number and types of skills and interests, 109–110; and personality
traits, 108–109
Career process theorists, 30
Career progression, 193; in middle
and later adulthood, 194–195
Career resources: and continuous
learners, 329–330; and individual
expansiveness, 329; individual
trends influencing use of, 327–
330; Internet-based delivery of
self-managed, 334; and motivation for training and development,
328–329
Career-related continuous learning
(CRCL), 329–330
Careers: alternative approaches to,
41–46; challenges in study of,
46–50; current research on, 35–
37; definition of, 5, 28–29; developmental approach to, 10–16;
false dichotomy of objective versus subjective, 315; and fit as psychological construct, 46–50;

limitations to free choice in,
53–54; as repositories of knowledge, 295–297; semantics of,
296–297; syntax of, 296
Careers, organizational context of:
change in, 274–290; and changing nature of employment, 275–
277; and expanding role of external market, 277–282; and future
directions in practice, 288–289;
and future directions in research,
289–290; and organizational
commitment to people, 286–288;
and transfer of risk from organization to individual, 282–285
Carrière, 10
Catalyst, 40
Celerity, 42
Change: versus stability, 349–350;
within-person versus within-
context, 348–349
Charge Statistics, 254, 256
China, 111, 305, 306
Civil Rights Act (1964), 254
Coaching, 334–335. *See also* Career
development: programs and
processes
Cognitive resource theory (CRT), 227
Commission on Family and Medical
Leave, 257, 260
Competency identification and
assessment, 330–331. *See also*
Career development: programs
and processes
Conference Committee, 266
Congruence, 31, 32, 34, 46, 82–83.
See also Fit, person-environment
(P-E); Holland's theory of careers
Continuity: cumulative, 95–96; inter-
actional, 96
Continuous learning, 325, 329–330
Correspondence, 46. *See also* Con-
gruence
Coverdell Education Savings
Accounts, 253
Creative individualism, 171

Cumulative continuity, 95–96. *See also* Early-career development: psychological processes underlying

D

Demographic differences, 107–108
Dependence: as core psychological state of individual in early career, 161; individual responses to issues of, 163–166; psychological, 161–163
Developmental self-concept theory (Super), 198–202
Discontinuous careers, 325–326
Dissonance reduction, 97. *See also* Early-career development: psychological processes underlying
"Drivers of Star Knowledge Workers' Performance: Evidence from a Ranked Analyst Market" (Groysberg), 362
Dustbowl empiricism, 4

E

Early-career development: phases of, 94–95; psychological processes underlying, 95–97; stage models of, 94–97. *See also* Vocational choice
Early-career identity: delays in formation of, 103–106; and frequent switching of career paths and fields of study, 105; and inability to identify early-career goals, 105–106; and procrastination, 104
Earnings, loss of, 112–113
Economic Growth and Tax Relief Reconciliation Act (2001), 249, 253
Empirical research, conducting: and balancing self-report and multisource data, 360–361; and clarification of constructs, 358–360; and creative use of archival data,

361–362; and criteria problem, 363–364; and one-way versus two-way influence, 364–366; and sampling biases, 357–358
Employee Retirement Income Security Act (1974), 248, 250, 257, 263
Equal Employment Opportunity Commission (EEOC), 247, 254, 256
Equal employment opportunity (EEO) legislation, 254, 255
Equal Pay Act (1963), 248
Establishment years: and career anchors, 166–169; dependence perspective on, 159–181; and individual responses to dependence issues, 161–163; mentoring and developmental relationships in, 174–176; and psychological dependence, 161–163; socialization process in, 169–172; tasks of, 160–161; work relationships in, 172–174; and work-family issues, 176–177
Executive Order 11246 (1965), 248
Expansiveness, 329
Expatriation. *See* Careers, international

F

Fair Labor Standards Act (1938), 247, 248
Family and Medical Leave Act (FMLA), 246, 249, 255, 257, 260
Faragher v. *City of Boca Raton* (1998), 267
Fast-track career, 10
Feedback systems, 327, 334–335
Fit: ambiguous status of, as psychological construct, 46–50; antecedents of, 72; dynamic relationships in, 75–76; general framework for, 68–75; model for achieving, during early career, 70–71; and psychological well-being, 113; skill acquisition and, 63–84; skill

development and, 77–82; static versus dynamic, 67–68; theories of, 64–68. *See also* Congruence

Fit, person-environment (P-E): at group level (person-group; P-G), 67; at job level (person-job; P-J), 67; at occupational level (person-occupation; P-OC), 65–66; at organizational level (person-organization; P-O), 66–67; relative role of interests-desires and aptitudes-abilities in, 72–75

Flexibility, versus stability, 3–5

Florida, 253

Fortune magazine, 98

401(k) plans, 258, 277, 278

Free agent nation, 289, 362

Free choice, limitations to, 53–54. *See also under* Personality

G

Gender limitations, 53–54, 72

General Aptitude Test Battery (GATB), 215

Generativity, versus stagnation, 190

Germany, 307

H

Habitat for Humanity, 28

Harvard Women's Law Association, 54

Health Insurance Portability and Accountability Act (1996), 249, 263

Holland hexagonal arrangement of personality types, 32–33

Holland's theory of careers, 31–35, 46, 65; Big Five traits versus, 35–37

I

Identity change process: contextual variables affecting, 147–150; dispositional variables affecting, 145–147; in school-to-work transition, 141–145

Indecision. *See* Career indecision

Individual retirement accounts (IRA's), 253, 258, 265

Information seeking: regulatory focus theory as alternative model for, 133–135; role of, in school-to-work transition, 129–130; uncertainty reduction as motive for, 130–133. *See also* Knowledge, acquiring

Integrating the Individual and the Organization (Argyris), 364–366

Interactional continuity, 96. *See also* Early-career development: psychological processes underlying

Interest inventories, 31, 34

Interests: number and types of, 109–110; and relative role of interests-desires, 72–75; versus skills, 351–352

International assignments: employee transformation in, 308; and enhancing tacit knowledge, 312–313; exploiting knowledge creation potential in, 311–314; and problems in organizational control of knowledge creation, 310–311; problems with sharing tacit knowledge in, 308–310; and sharing tacit knowledge, 313–314; syntactic and semantic issues in, 305–307. *See also* Careers, international; Knowledge creation

International careers: application of knowledge creation to, 305–311; and career paths as spirals of knowledge creation, 301–305; exploiting knowledge potential of, 311–314; implications for future research in, 314–317; and organizations as knowledge creators, 297–301; as repositories of knowledge, 295–297

Intimacy, balancing isolation and, 160–161. *See also under* Establishment years

IRA's. *See* Individual retirement accounts (IRA's)

Isolation, balancing intimacy and, 160–161. *See also under* Establishment years

J

Japan, 301, 306, 308, 309, 312–313, 326–327, 347
Job, definition of, 28
Job performance: and age discrimination, 220–222; age-related changes in, 215–216; and nonperformance outcomes, 222–224
Job Training Partnership Act (1983), 187, 248
Johnson, L. B., 187

K

Kansas, 253
KEOGH plans, 258
Knowing: four types of, 302–303; four types of, over time, 303; types of, in international contexts, 304–305
Knowledge, acquiring: and challenge of knowing what and how to learn, 127–129; and regulatory focus theory, 133–135; and role of information seeking, 129–130; uncertainty reduction as motive for, 129–130, 130–133
Knowledge creation: career paths as spirals of, 301–305; and careers and organizations as knowledge creators, 297–301; and explicit versus tacit knowledge, 298; theory of, process, 299; types of, 298–301
Kuder Preference Record, 30

L

Labor market, early, 101–103
Leader Potential Index (California Psychological Inventory), 226, 227
Learning organizations, 326–327. See also Career development: organizational trends influencing
Legislation: changes in, surrounding career development, 250–251; in United States workplace since 1930, 248–249

Life task approach (Cantor), 29, 43–44
Life-career rainbow, 201
"Life-Span, Life-Space Approach to Career Development, A" (*Journal of Vocational Behavior*), 201

M

Making Vocational Choices, Third Edition (Psychological Assessment Resources, Inc.), 33
Maryland, 256
Massachusetts Institute of Technology (MIT), 166
Matsushita Electric Company, 301
McArthur Foundation, 191
Medicaid, 258
Medicare, 250, 258
Memory distortion, 97. See also Early-career development: psychological processes underlying
Mentoring, 140; and career development programs, 336–337; and developmental relationships, 140; in establishment years, 174–176
Meritor Savings Bank v. *Vinson* (1986), 267
Mexico, 347
Midcareer: career development at, 186–208; crisis and development at, 191–192; and midlife, 189–190; problems in defining, 186–192
Midlife: conceptualizations of, 190; midcareer and, 189–190; models of work at, 206–207; work choices at, 192–198
Midlife Project, 191
Milgram experiments, 165
Mobility: factors influencing, 197–198; models of, 193–196
Moderator variables, 113–115
Monster.com, 261

N

National Academy of Management (2001), 246; Careers Division Program, 246, 247

National Advisory Council for Careers and Educational Guidance, 265

National Center for Education Statistics, 104–108, 110

National Council on Aging, 187

National Defense Education Act (1958), 252

National Longitudinal Survey of Youth, 359, 361

Negative affectivity, 132–133

NEO (neuroticism, extroversion, and openness to experience), 35–37

Network building: individual variation in, 138–141; in school-to-work transition, 135–136; and social networks during school-to-work transition, 136–138

New Hampshire, 253

New York Times, 275

Nigeria, 347

Normative pressures, 110–111

O

Office of Federal Contract Compliance Programs, 247

Old Age Survivors and Disability Insurance (OASDI) program, 252

Older Americans Act, 187

Older workers: abilities and performance of, 214–222; age-related changes in abilities of, 215; age-related changes in job performance of, 215–216; career issues facing, 214–257; and career systems, 225–226; implications of growth in population of, 236–237; job performance and age discrimination in, 220–222; and nonperformance outcomes, 222–224. *See also* Age-performance relationship

Orientation, 116

Osaka International Hotel, 301

Ottawa, Canada, 250

P

Parents, attitudes and values of, 100–101

Pennsylvania, 256

Personal projects, 43–44. *See also* Life task approach (Cantor)

Personal strivings, 43–44. *See also* Life task approach (Cantor)

Personality: alternative approaches to Holland model and Big Five theory, 41–46; and Big Five personality traits, 12–13, 29, 38–41, 192; challenges in study of, 46–54; definitions of, 29; historical perspective of research on, 29–31; and limitations to free choice, 53–54; and occupations at lower levels of specificity, 50–53; traits, 108–109; traits beyond Big Five, 45–46

PLUS loans, 254

Poland, 347

Post-decision dissonance, 97

Proaction, 138

Procrastination, 104

Promotions: career systems and, 225–226; individual factors affecting, 224–225; and leader effectiveness, 226–227; and leader emergence, 226

Protestant work ethic, 223, 224

Psychological Assessment Resources, Inc., 33

Public policy: and changing legal context of career development, 245–268; implications for interface between, and career development, 258–266; integrating, with career development, 251–258; issues related to career preparation, 252–254; issues related to early-career, 255–256; issues related to late career, 257–258; issues related to midcareer, 256–257; issues related to organizational entry, 254–255;

larger role for, in careers research, 246–250; and significant legislation in United States workplace, 248–249

R

Race limitations, 54
Recruitment, 115
Regulatory focus theory, 133–135. *See also* Information seeking
Retention, 116
Retirement: conceptualizing, 227–228; family factors and, 229–230; individual factors and, 228–229; institutional factors and, 230. *See also* Older workers; Retirement, adaption to
Retirement, adaption to: individual factors and, 231; institutional factors and, 232–233; and postretirement leisure activity, 234; and postretirement volunteer activities, 234–235; social factors and, 232; and working in retirement, 233–234. *See also* Older workers
RIASEC (realistic, intellectual/investigative, artistic, social, enterprising, and conventional) typology (Holland), 31–32, 35–37, 42, 48, 65. *See also* Holland's theory of careers
Roth education IRA's, 253, 258
Russia, 303

S

SBA. *See* United States Small Business Administration (SBA)
SCCT. *See* Social cognitive career theory (SCCT)
School-to-Work Opportunities Act (1993), 249, 253
School-to-work transition: and acquiring knowledge, 127–135; challenges of, 126–127; and forging new identity, 141–150; implications of, 151–153; and network building, 135–141; and skill development, 79
Second shift, 177
Selection, 115
Self-concept, occupational, 167
Self-directed learning, 325
Singapore, 347
Skill acquisition: dynamics among, and interests, abilities, and fit, 63–84; and interests versus skills, 351–352; and number and types of skills, 109–110; and person-environment fit, 63–84
Skill development: career counseling and interventions in, 81–82; education and training programs in, 78–80; universal-generalizable, versus specific-technical, 77–82; work experience and internships for, 80–81
Social cognitive career theory (SCCT), 76, 77, 202–206
Social Security Act (1935), 247, 248, 256
Social Security Trust Fund, 258
Social Theory and Social Structure (Merton), 347
Socialization, 116; and anticipatory socialization, 169–170; chains of, 152; change and acquisition phase of, 171–172; and encounter stage, 170–171; in establishment years, 169–172; literature, 126
Stability, flexibility versus, 3–5
Stafford loans, 254
Stagnation, generativity versus, 190
Succession planning, 331–333. *See also* Career development: programs and processes

T

Talent Alliance, 334
Tax Relief Act (1997), 249, 253, 260
Teenage ghettos, 114

Theory, building: and career interests versus work skills, 351–352; and change stages versus life stages, 352–353; and change versus stability, 349–350; developmental perspective on, 347–357; and immediate versus distal influences on career behaviors, 355–357; and middle-range theories, 347–348; and within-person versus within-context change, 348–349; and work life versus family life, 353–354

Theory of circumscription and compromise (Gottfredson), 53–54

Theory of work adjustment (TWA), 29, 41–43, 46, 65

Title VII, Civil Rights Act (1964), 246, 248

Tourism coping strategy, 177. *See also* Establishment years

Training, 116; motivation for, 328–329

Trait-factor career theory, 30

Turnover, 116

TWA. *See* Theory of work adjustment (TWA)

U

Underemployment, 112–113

United Kingdom, 111, 266, 312

United States Bureau of Labor Statistics, 112

United States Department of Labor, 77, 250, 254, 255, 261

United States Internal Revenue Service (IRS), 253

United States Small Business Administration (SBA), 265

United States Social Security Administration, 252

Universities, 152

V

Virginia, 256

Vocation Bureau, 29

Vocational choice: content models of, 97–107; and early labor market experiences, 101–103; and educational experiences, 99–100; macroeconomic conditions and, 99; parental attitudes and values in, 100–101; political and societal trends in, 98. *See also* Early-career development

Vocational counseling: and career indecision, 117–119

Vocational Interest Inventory (Strong), 30

Vocational Psychology: current theories on career development at midcareer, 198–206; personality research in, 29–31

W

Wagner Act (1935), 247, 248

Wall Street Journal, 98

"What Is Beyond the Big Five?" (Saucier and Goldberg), 45

Wisconsin, 253, 265–266

Work attitudes, 116–117

Worker Adjustment and Retraining Notification Act (1988), 248, 264

Work-family issues: in establishment years, 176–177; and work life versus family life, 353–354

Workforce Investment Act (1998), 249, 257, 258